Walls
Come
Tumbling
Down

WALLS COME TUMBLING DOWN:

A History of the
Civil Rights Movement
1940-1970

By

THOMAS R. BROOKS

PRENTICE-HALL, Inc.
Englewood Cliffs, N.J.

Grateful acknowledgment is made to the following
sources for permission to reprint:

The Bobbs-Merrill Company, Inc.: From "Black People"
in *Black Magic Poetry* 1961–1967 by LeRoi Jones
(Imamu Amiri Baraka). Copyright © 1969 by LeRoi Jones.

Dodd, Mead & Company, Inc.: From "A Crust of Bread"
in *The Complete Poems of Paul Laurence Dunbar*, 1972.

Harper & Row, Publishers, Inc.: From *Stride Toward
Freedom* by Martin Luther King, Jr. Copyright © 1958 by
Martin Luther King, Jr.

Harold Ober Associates Incorporated.: From "Tell Me"
in *Montage of a Dream Deferred* by Langston Hughes.
Published by Holt, Rinehart & Winston. Copyright 1951
by Langston Hughes.

Alfred A. Knopf, Inc.: From "The South" and "One-Way
Ticket" in *Selected Poems* by Langston Hughes, 1959.

Pauli Murray: From "Mr. Roosevelt Regrets" in *Dark
Testament & Other Poems*. Published by Silvermine
Publishers, Norwalk, Connecticut, 1972.

Library of Congress Cataloging in Publication Data

Brooks, Thomas R
    Walls come tumbling down.

    Bibliography: p.
    1. Negroes—Civil rights—History.   I. Title.
E185.61.B797   323.1′19′6073
0-13-944330-4   73-22481

*To my wife, Harriet
with gratitude and love*

Contents

Walls
Come
Tumbling
Down

I

We Shall
Overcome....

NE HUNDRED YEARS AND 240
days after Abraham Lincoln proclaimed "all persons held as Slaves within any State, or designated part of a State, the people whereof shall there be in rebellion against the United States, shall be . . . FOREVER FREE," over 210,000 Americans—the majority of them black but many of them white—converged on the nation's capital to proclaim that the time of patient waiting for long overdue rights of citizenship was at an end. By noon, on August 28, 1963, a sea of placards stretching out before the Lincoln Memorial created a living petition. Raised on high, the signs tacked on sticks demanded: "We March for an FEPC Law NOW!" . . . "Voting Rights NOW!" . . . "Decent Housing NOW!" . . . "Jobs for All NOW!" . . . "Integrated Schools NOW!" . . . "Effective Civil Rights Laws NOW!" . . . "First-Class Citizenship NOW!" The crowd moving from the Washington Monument to the Lincoln Memorial was reported the next day in *The New York Times* as "the greatest assembly for a redress of grievances that this capital has ever seen."

The people gathered in Washington on that momentous day had come in response to a call for a "March on Washington for Jobs and Freedom" issued by the "big six" black spokesmen of the time—James Farmer of the Congress of Racial Equality (CORE), Martin Luther King, Jr., of the Southern Christian Leadership Conference (SCLC), John Lewis of the Student Nonviolent Coordinating Committee (SNCC), A. Philip Randolph of the Negro American Labor Council (NALC), Roy Wilkins of the National Association for the Advancement of Colored People (NAACP), and Whitney Young of the National Urban League. The call had been seconded, as it were, by Mathew Ahmann of the National Catholic Conference for Interracial Justice, the Reverend

Dr. Eugene Carson Blake of the United Presbyterian Church in the United States of America, Rabbi Joachim Prinz of the American Jewish Congress, and Walter P. Reuther of the United Automobile Workers and the Industrial Union Department of the AFL-CIO. Together, the people present and those represented by the ten civil rights leaders made up, in A. Philip Randolph's phrase, "a coalition of conscience" that hoped to change America. It was inspired by the upsurge in the struggle for civil rights that, despite violence from racist whites and discouraging setbacks, had opened the decade so promisingly—the Montgomery bus boycott of 1955–56, the student sit-ins of 1960, the Freedom Rides of 1961, and more recently, the dramatic confrontations over integration in Birmingham, in Cambridge, Maryland, and in Mississippi, indeed everywhere blacks were asserting their citizenship.

The 1963 March on Washington climaxed a long journey that had begun with the first slave revolt and would now, hopefully, end with a second reconstruction firmly based on the old promise enacted into federal legislation to guarantee equality and justice for all. Blacks in motion were to be the human catalyst for a new America, and the march was a dramatization of that notion put on for Congress, and above all, for the mass media. Millions around the world would read about the march and see it on television. The coverage was extensive: 2,855 press passes were in use that day in Washington. "When I saw all that gigantic scaffolding erected for the television crews," one of the youthful organizers of the march and a true child of this century of communication has since said, "I knew it would be a success."

Countless viewers saw integration at work. Blacks and whites walked together, ate box lunches together, bathed their feet in the reflecting pool together, raised identical demands, and clasped hands as they sang, "We shall overcome . . . ." Looking out over the vast biracial crowd, singer Josephine Baker exclaimed, "Salt and pepper—just what it should be." Determination and dignity infused the "gentle army"— Russell Baker's felicitous phrase—making the march a celebration of, as well as a claim on, certain inalienable rights. Appropriately, for this is a middle-class country, the marchers were mostly middle-class Americans. The median family income for black marchers was nearly $6,000 a year, and for whites, $9,500. Predominantly Protestant with substantial Catholic and Jewish minorities among the white participants, most of the marchers were white-collar workers or professionals with a substantial sprinkling of trade unionists. Among the vast throng walked the children, grandchildren, and great-, even great-great-grandchildren of slaves and black freedmen. Descendants of the abolitionists marched as did some of slaveholding stock along with innumerable second-generation and immigrant Americans.

Much of our history of social protest was encapsulated in the march. Veteran socialist Norman Thomas—still remembered for his aid to embattled black and white sharecroppers of the 1930s—marched as did fifteen-year-old James Bruce of Danville, Virginia, who had been arrested three times for participating in civil rights demonstrations. He and a group of fellow civil rights activists wore white sweatshirts with crudely cut black mourning bands on their sleeves. "We're mourning injustice in Danville," he explained to inquiring reporters. Walter P. Reuther, bloodied in the great mass CIO organizing drives among auto workers in the 1930s, marched with John Lewis, a 25-year-old former theological student beaten by a white mob when Freedom Riders arrived in Birmingham, Alabama, in spring 1961 and since arrested twenty-four times in civil rights demonstrations. On the platform, Chairman A. Philip Randolph, the grand old man of the march at age 74, could recall leaving a South empty of hope and ladened with terror for the promise that is Harlem. As a young man of twenty-two, he came to the North in 1911, roughly at the beginning of the Great Migration— that flight to freedom that carried millions of blacks out of the South, ultimately resulting in the great congregation now gathered before him. And below in that crowd, fifteen-year-old Charles Macken of Albany, Georgia, who was determined to stay in the South and fight, explained a placard carried by a fellow Georgian, which read: "Milton Wilkerson— 20 stitches. Emmanuel McClendon—3 stitches (age 67). James Williams—broken leg." Said Macken, "That's where the police beat these people up."

Though billed as a March *on* Washington, people came by airplane, automobile, bus, and train. A galaxy of celebrities flew in from Los Angeles, and eighty-seven concerned citizens of that city chartered a plane to be on hand for the march. Six buses came from Birmingham, Alabama, carrying 260 people on a 753-mile, 22-hour trip, and for some it was a first-time visit out of their state. Twenty-year-old Willie Leonard, an upholsterer, perhaps spoke for many: "I guess you could call me a combination Freedom Rider and tourist on this trip." A thirteen-car "Freedom Special" train left Jacksonville, Florida, the night before the march, carrying 650 Riders and adding three more carloads at stops in Georgia, the Carolinas, and Virginia. The Reverend John Adams led two groups of twenty-five—one from Seattle, Washington, the other from Portland, Oregon—while sixty Coloradians came with the Reverend L. S. Odon of Denver. All together, twenty-one special trains and sixteen regular trains carried march participants to Washington, and 1,514 special buses were pressed into service.

Some walked to Washington. Fifteen members of CORE started out on foot from Brooklyn on August 15, and arrived tired and dusty on the evening before the march with five additional members who had joined the group in Philadelphia. Ledger Smith roller-skated 698 miles from Chicago, taking ten days for the trip. "I'm tired," he told the crowd. "Let my legs speak for me." Bruce Marzhan bicycled from Tulare, South Dakota; when he arrived, he fell off his bicycle, cut his head, and was treated at one of the twenty-two first-aid stations set up for such contingencies.

Considering the logistics involved in handling perhaps more than a quarter of a million people, seeing to it that they got in and out of town smoothly, were fed, and had water to drink and toilet facilities, there were remarkably few casualties or, given the potential for counter-demonstrations and violence, few disturbances. Kathleen Johnson of Newark, New Jersey, fell into the reflecting pool at the Lincoln Memorial while taking pictures and was fished out of two and a half feet of water by sympathetic marchers. Sixty-six persons were taken to hospitals by ambulance, but only four were sufficiently ill to be admitted for treatment. Three buses homeward bound for Connecticut were stoned near the Baltimore Harbor Tunnel. No one was hurt. *Newsweek* reported 1,720 casualties. Most were felled by bellyaches, fatigue, the crush of the crowd, and the 83° August heat. Arrests were off sharply, possibly because of a ban imposed on the sale of alcoholic beverages within the District. Only four persons were arrested for offenses having to do with the march. Karl R. Allen, a deputy commander of the American Nazi party, was arrested when he sought to speak to a small band of about eighty sympathizers grouped in a counter-demonstration. One man was seized when the police spotted a shotgun in the front seat of his car; another when he broke into the line of march to tear up a placard. A youth was arrested in Hyattsville, Maryland, for having thrown stones at buses en route to the march.

People continued arriving throughout the day. As the dawn's early light glinted on the eastern horizon, marchers had gathered at the staging area at the foot of the Washington Monument. By 10 A.M., forty thousand people had gathered on the slopes around the monument. An hour later, the crowd had more than doubled and still they kept on pouring in. The stage and screen stars scheduled to entertain the crowd until the march from the Washington Monument to the Lincoln Memorial began were late, so members of the crowd put on a show. Civil rights activists released from jail in Danville, Virginia, sang, "Move on, move on, till all the world is free." Peter Ottley led members of New York Local 144, Hotel and Allied Service Employees Union, in a foot-stomping rendition of "We shall not be moved/ Just like a tree/ Planted by the water/ We shall not be moved."

Joan Baez led the crowd in singing, "We Shall Overcome." Peter, Paul, and Mary sang Bob Dylan's poignant, "Blowin' in the Wind," "How many times must a man look up before he can see the sky?"

Odetta's full-throated voice exalted, "If they ask you who you are, tell them you're a child of God." Notables intermingled with celebrities to the delight of the crowd—Ralph Bunche, Nobel Peace Prize winner and under secretary of the United Nations; playwright Ossie Davis; actors, entertainers, and singers, Ruby Dee, Lena Horne, Marian Anderson, Harry Belafonte, Sidney Poitier, Dick Gregory, Sammy Davis, Jr., Marlon Brando—who was brandishing an electric cattleprod used against civil rights demonstrators—Charlton Heston, Paul Newman, and Burt Lancaster. Author James Baldwin, for once nearly without words, confessed that to explain how he felt, "I'd have to cry, or sing." And Jackie Robinson said, "We cannot be turned back!"

And so it proved to be, at least that day, for the marchers could not be held to the official starting time and spontaneously stepped off for the Lincoln Memorial a good ten minutes early. Over the loudspeakers, a voice pleaded: "We've lost the leaders' delegation. They are hereby instructed to join the march and go to the Lincoln Memorial. Will the leaders' delegation please sound off?" The unflappable Bayard Rustin, deputy director of the march, was overheard crying out, "My God, they're going! We're supposed to be *leading* them!" Imperturbable, Randolph said, "Now, Bayard, it's time for the leadership to follow the followership."

The crowd fanned out before the Lincoln Memorial, thickening into an almost impenetrable mass before the long afternoon was out. To the cries of recognition "Roosevelt," "Humphrey," "Javits," "Powell," and a rising shout that rippled from the front to the back of the crowd, "Pass the bill," some seventy-five senators and representatives filed into a special section reserved for congressmen near the speakers' stand. At around one o'clock, shortly before the ceremonies began, the police handed up a crowd estimate of 200,000, which Chairman Randolph announced and which became the basis of the official count. Yet the crowd continued to grow. A CORE drum and bugle corps circulated Washington's black neighborhoods bringing in even more marchers. Tom Kahn, a Rustin assistant, observed people arriving right up to the end, and so it seems likely that over a half million black and white Americans may have participated in the 1963 March on Washington.

People shucked off their shoes, and dunked hot, aching feet into the reflecting pool; some picnicked on the grass, and others even snoozed. The official program was long and sometimes tedious, though often electric, as when Mahalia Jackson's great voice rent the skies, "I've Been 'Buked and I've Been Scorned." Or, when John Lewis's scarcely constrained passion broke out, "Let us not forget we are involved in a serious social revolution . . . . They're talking about slowdown and stop. We will not stop. If we do not get meaningful legislation out of this Congress, the time will come when we will not confine our marching to Washington. We will march through the South, through the streets of Jackson, through the streets of Danville, through the streets of Cambridge, through the streets of Birmingham."

The Most Reverend Patrick O'Boyle, the Archbishop of Washington, gave the invocation, praying that Christian love might "replace the coldness that springs from prejudice and bitterness." Indicting the churches for failure to put their own houses in order, achieving "neither a nonsegregated church nor a nonsegregated society," the Reverend Dr. Eugene Carson Blake lamented, "We do not, therefore, come . . . in any arrogant spirit of moral or spiritual superiority to set the nation straight or to judge or denounce the American people in whole or in part. Rather we come—late, late we come, in the reconciliating and repentant spirit in which Abraham Lincoln of Illinois once replied to a delegation of morally arrogant churchmen. He said, 'Never say God is on our side, rather pray that we may be found on God's side.' " Drawing on his experience as the rabbi of Berlin's Jewish community at the time of Hitler's rise to power, Rabbi Joachim Prinz declared that the urgent problem was not bigotry and hatred but "silence." From a southern jail, James Farmer sent a message through CORE's national chairman, Floyd McKissick, hailing the march: "Your tramping feet have spoken the message . . . violence is outmoded to the solution of the problems of men." Direct action would continue, he pledged. "We will not stop until the dogs stop biting us in the South and the rats stop biting us in the North." Dry and cool, but nonetheless effective, Roy Wilkins, a frail figure wearing a blue legionnaire-type cap, talked of the necessity of a Fair Employment Practices Committee—"We want employment, and with it we want the pride and responsibility and self-respect that goes with equal access to jobs." Wryly he concluded, "We even salute those from the South who want to vote for it but don't dare to do so. And we say to those people, just give us a little time and one of these days we'll emancipate you." Ever pragmatic, Whitney Young reminded the marchers that the evils of the past "cannot be erased by a one-day pilgrimage, however magnificent." While civil rights in 1963 were "not negotiable," Young pointed out, "we must work together even more closely back home where the job must be done to see that Negro Americans are accepted as first-class citizens."

Randolph, as chairman and originator of the march, placed the day's events into perspective:

> Let the nation and the world know the meaning of our numbers.
> We are not a pressure group, we are not an organization or a group of organizations, we are not a mob. We are the advance guard of a massive moral revolution for

jobs and freedom. . . . But this civil rights revolution is not confined to the Negro, nor is it confined to civil rights, for our white allies know that they cannot be free while we are not, and we know we have no future in a society in which six million black and white people are unemployed and millions live in poverty . . . .

We want a free democratic society dedicated to the political, economic, and social advancement of man along moral lines . . . .

We know that real freedom will require many changes in the nation's political and social philosophies and institutions. For one thing, we must destroy the notion that Mrs. Murphy's property rights include the right to humiliate me because of the color of my skin.° The sanctity of private property takes second place to the sanctity of the human personality. It falls to the Negro to reassert this priority of values, because our ancestors were transformed from human personalities into private property. It falls to us to demand full employment and to put automation at the service of human needs, not at the service of profits . . . .

All who deplore our militance, who exhort patience in the name of false peace, are in fact supporting segregation and exploitation. They would have social peace at the expense of social and racial justice. They are more concerned with easing racial tensions than enforcing racial democracy.

Many have commented on the "holiday" or "revivalist" mood of the crowd. Roy Wilkins, ever wise in these matters, warned, "You got religion here today. Don't backslide tomorrow." Lerone Bennett, Jr., perhaps the most perceptive of the observers of the march, wrote in *The Day They Marched*, "There was about this crowd the wonderful two-tongued ambivalence of the blues. It was neither all one thing nor all another. Many moods competed but two dominated; a mood of quiet anger and a mood of buoyant exuberance. There was also a feeling of power and a certain surprise, as though the people had discovered suddenly who they were and what they had."

Yet, what people carried away from that day, and what has since passed into our history as memorable, was Martin Luther King's incandescent evocation of the dream of freedom.

I have a dream that one day this nation will rise up and live out the true meaning of its creed: "We hold these

---

° The civil rights bill proposed by the Kennedy Administration banning discrimination in public accommodations with a "substantial" effect on interstate commerce excluded the kind of establishments described as "Mrs. Murphy's boardinghouse."

truths to be self-evident; that all men are created equal."

I have a dream that one day on the red hills of Georgia the sons of former slaves and the sons of former slaveowners will be able to sit down together at the table of brotherhood.

I have a dream that one day even the state of Mississippi, a desert state sweltering with the heat of injustice and oppression, will be transformed into an oasis of freedom and justice.

I have a dream that my four little children will one day live in a nation where they will not be judged by the color of their skin but by the content of their character.

I have a dream that one day every valley shall be exalted, every hill and mountain shall be made low, the rough places will be made plains, and the crooked places will be made straight, and the glory of the Lord shall be revealed, and all flesh shall see it together.

I have a dream today . . . .

This is our hope. This is the faith with which I return to the South. With this faith, we will be able to hew out of the mountains of despair a stone of hope . . . .

When we let freedom ring, when we let it ring from every village and hamlet, from every state and every city, we will be able to speed up that day when all of God's children, black men and white men, Jews and Gentiles, Protestants and Catholics, will be able to join hands and sing in the words of that old Negro spiritual: "Free at last! Free at last! Thank God Almighty, we are free at last!"

As the day ended, voices could be heard, plaintive against the Washington backdrop, singing, "We shall overcome—someday."

II

Magnificent Bluff

THE TWILIGHT WAR OF THE 1939–1940 winter that followed Hitler's crushing onslaught against Poland ended on May 10, 1940, when 117 German infantry and 10 armored divisions smashed into Maastricht, Holland, and executed a wide left sweep into neutral Belgium. The British evacuated Dunkirk at the end of the month, and France fell a week later. As Stukas and Spitfires spat in August skies, it seemed as if Great Britain might fall before the Nazi blitzkrieg. But for Americans engaged in a national election contest, the crescendo of war as yet rumbled offstage, across a vast sea. With an eye to reelection for a third term, President Franklin Delano Roosevelt cautiously coaxed a hesitant nation into a posture of defense preparedness. The War Department released surplus or outdated stocks of arms, munitions, and aircraft for shipment to Great Britain. Over $43 million worth was sent in the month of June alone. An expanding defense industry began to absorb the Depression unemployed. In September, an uneasy Congress passed a compulsory military service act as an emergency measure of but one year's duration.

The Selective Service Act reflected accurately enough the existing state of race relations in the country; as usual, intentions were ahead of performance. The act was amended to include a clause forbidding discrimination in the drafting or training of men. Realization of this amendment was something else again. Some draft boards accepted only white men for training on the grounds that there was no housing for Negro recruits. The Marines and the Air Force did not want the Negro, the Navy would only take him as a messboy, and the Army offered him a shovel. In 1940, there were fewer than 5,000 Negroes in an army of 269,023, and about 4,000 in a 160,997-man navy. Black Americans were understandably concerned about what their role would be in the approaching war for democracy. Boxing champion Joe Louis no doubt expressed their patriotic sentiments when he declared, "There may be a whole lot wrong with America, but there's nothing that Hitler can fix." And so did a nameless young black soldier who, on being ordered to the Jim Crow section at the back of a southern bus, yanked off his jacket and said, "Well, I'm fixing to go off and fight for democracy. I might as well start right now."

While Hitler obviously could not fix what was wrong with the United States, a considerable number of black Americans believed that they could. On September 27, 1940, shortly after the passage of the Selective Service Act, Walter White, executive `secretary of the National Association for the Advancement of Colored People, T. Arnold Hill, then acting secretary of the National Urban League, and A. Philip Randolph, president of the Brotherhood of Sleeping Car Porters, arrived in Washington, D.C., to meet with President Franklin D. Roosevelt.

Before going on to the White House, the three black spokesmen met at the NAACP Washington Bureau Office to discuss the points they wished to make to the harassed President. Hill suggested that a memorandum be drafted so that there could be no misunderstanding of their position. The memorandum submitted to the President that afternoon urged that all available reserve officers be used to train recruits; that Negro recruits be given the same training as whites; that existing units in the Army accept officers and men on the basis of ability and not race; that specialized personnel, such as physicians, dentists, and nurses, be integrated; that responsible Negroes be appointed to draft boards; that discrimination be abolished in the Navy and Air Force, and that competent Negroes be appointed as civilian assistants to the Secretaries of War and the Navy. In short, black Americans wanted the armed forces desegregated.

At the meeting, the President was flanked by Secretary of the Navy Frank Knox and Assistant Secretary of War Robert P. Patterson. Knox, who as Robert Sherwood once said, "recognized an enemy when he saw one," was an ardent supporter of President Roosevelt's foreign policy, of aid to Britain, and of military preparedness. A lifelong Republican and publisher of the Chicago *Daily News*, Knox had recently been appointed to the cabinet to give it a bipartisan cast. He was not a New Dealer, and was not known as a friend to the Negro. Patterson, later Secretary of War in President Truman's Cabinet, was much more sympathetic, and indeed would do much during the war to improve the lot of the black soldier.

On this occasion, the President did not indulge his bent for telling stories when confronted with political unpleasantness. As Walter White later recalled in his autobiography, *A Man Called White*, he "listened attentively and apparently sympathetically, and assured us that he would look into possible methods of lessening, if not destroying, discrimination and segregation against Negroes." He did, however, give, as he had on other occasions, a reason for not taking immediate action against discrimination—"the South would rise up in protest." The election was just over a month away, and White may have been reminded of an earlier meeting held in the mid-1930s, when the President explained with disarming frankness why he was unwilling to challenge the southern wing of his party. "I did not choose the tools with which I must work," he told White. "Had I been permitted to choose them, I would have selected quite different ones. But I've got to get legislation by Congress to save America. The Southerners by reason of the seniority rule in Congress are chairmen or occupy strategic places on most of the Senate and House committees. If I come out for the anti-lynching bill now, they will block every bill I ask Congress to pass to keep America from collapsing. I just can't take that risk."

Time had not lessened the political force of that argument in the President's view. He may well have felt he needed the Southerners even more, especially so since they tended to support his defense measures and southern votes were crucial to their passage. Moreover, anti-discrimination forces evidenced little strength in Congress at the time, despite widespread discrimination affecting not only Negroes but other minorities as well. As Dr. Will W. Alexander, the War Production Board's consultant on minority groups, put it, "We have about 13 million Negroes, 5 million aliens, 4,500,000 Jews in the United States, together with nearly 7 million citizens of German origin and 4,500,000 citizens of Italian background. Allow for some overlapping, and you still have more than a quarter of the nation falling into groups widely subjected to employment discrimination." Yet, when Democratic Senators Robert Wagner of New York and Prentiss M. Brown of Michigan along with Republicans Charles L. McNary of Oregon and Arthur Capper of Kansas in March 1941, introduced a resolution calling for an exhaustive investigation of discrimination in defense industries and of segregation in the armed forces, they could not get the resolution out of committee and on to the floor of the Senate. The same fate befell the first Fair Employment Practices measure introduced in the House by Congressman Vito Marcantonio of New York.

Ever politically prudent, President Roosevelt promised his black callers that he would write or talk to them again after conferring with government officials on the problem. What they got, however, was a rebuff. The President had decided to appease the South, perhaps feeling that he could ill-afford the loss of southern votes sure to follow the reversal of traditional segregation practices in the armed forces. His bid for a third term seemed chancy as it was, what with the threat of

European war looming large on an isolationist horizon. On October 9, with the election a month away, White House Press Secretary Stephen Early released a statement, announcing that "the policy of the War Department is not to intermingle colored and white enlisted personnel in the same regimental organizations." Early then strongly hinted that the black spokesmen had acquiesced in the continuation of military Jim Crowism. As the United Press reported, "White House Secretary Early said the segregation policy was approved after Mr. Roosevelt had conferred with Walter White, president of the National Association for the Advancement of Colored People, two other Negroes, and Secretary of the Navy Knox and Assistant Secretary of War Patterson." Furious at what they considered to be Presidential duplicity, White, Randolph, and Hill castigated segregation as "a stab in the back of democracy" and expressed shock that "a President of the United States at a time of national peril should surrender so completely to enemies of democracy who would destroy national unity by advocating segregation."

The President quickly realized that Early's gaffe jeopardized his securing the black vote in such pivotal states as New York and Illinois. Early made a retraction, and Judge William H. Hastie was appointed civilian aide to the Secretary of War. Colonel Campbell Johnson became special aide to the director of Selective Service. And, on October 25, 1940, Colonel Benjamin O. Davis became the first Negro to be promoted to the rank of brigadier general in the United States Army. All in time for the election.

President Roosevelt won reelection, and did indeed garner a substantial proportion of the black vote. The country teetered between "business as usual" and preparation for defense and oncoming war. Vice-president of the United Auto Workers, Walter P. Reuther, gained national prominence at the end of 1940 by proposing that the automobile industry could produce "500 planes a day." In December, the President set up the Office of Production Management to speed defense production and all material aid "short of war" to Britain and her allies. On December 29, the President held a "fireside chat" on national security over a nationwide radio hookup, and called for the immense effort that would make the country "the great arsenal of democracy."

Yet, progress was not anywhere near to what the President wished. Unemployment remained high with over five million out of work even as defense industries began to boom. Strikes doubled in number between December and March 1941. Essential military material remained in dangerously short supply. A private memo to the President on the heavy bomber program noted, "peak production of 500 monthly not expected until middle of 1943 under present schedules." The memo concluded, "COULD BE LATER." There was growing concern about equality of sacrifice. A Treasury official testified before the House Ways and Means Committee that one company with $70 million worth of defense orders was subject to no excess profits tax on 1940 earnings, although its profits had multiplied thirty times over the preceding year. Even the President appeared to vacillate. Columnist and political pundit Walter Lippmann complained, "They [the American people] are not being dealt with seriously, truthfully, responsibly and nobly. They are being dealt with cleverly, indirectly, even condescendingly and nervously."

If indecision can be said to characterize the national mood in 1941—the year of OHIO (Over the Hill in October) among draftees— the mood among black Americans was much more clearly defined, though as yet scarcely known outside black communities and the columns of the Negro press. Outside hiring gates, "No Help Wanted" signs were being replaced by "Help Wanted—White." The president of North American Aviation Company declared, "While we are in complete sympathy with the Negro, it is against company policy to employ them as aircraft workers or mechanics . . . regardless of their training. It is against company policy. There will be some jobs as janitors for Negroes." A Standard Steel Corporation spokesman told the Urban League of Kansas City, "We have never had a Negro worker in twenty-five years and do not intend to start now." Small wonder then that Walter White was later to write of the time, "Discontent and bitterness were growing like wildfire among Negroes all over the country."

Oddly enough, the defense boom appears to have caused a brief halt in the ever-rising migratory flow of black Americans from the rural South into the cities—especially to those of the North, and to a lesser extent, of the West. A 1941 Work Projects Administration study indicates that Negroes were under-represented among later-half 1941 migrants to certain large cities, including some major defense pro- duction centers. The war boom, initially, reversed a long-standing migratory trend whereby the Negro population in urban areas had been increasing faster than the white population. The reasons why are, in retrospect, obvious. Employers not only hired whites preferentially over blacks, but also hired migrant whites over available local black labor. There was, as well, an increased demand for black labor in southern agriculture, encouraging some "to stay down home." And to the extent that blacks were recruited to fill jobs deserted by whites lured to higher paying defense jobs, such work was frequently found without the necessity of moving. Though some work is preferable to no work, such jobs were hardly satisfactory in a nation gearing for a great war, and black morale suffered.

Black America, however, had been—and would continue to be—on the move from the farm to the city, from peonage or sharecropping to wage or salaried work. The civil rights movement is rooted in the black American's condition, but civil rights were only a peripheral matter for most Americans in the 1940s, although a matter of importance to a handful of moralists and radicals. Its rise to a central concern of our time took place against a background shaped by two major developments—first, a worldwide conflict pitting democracy against despotism, and in the Hitler war, against a despotism inflamed by a particularly offensive and virulent racism; and second, the steady migration of American blacks—beginning roughly in 1915 and continuing down to this day, from the rural South to the nation's urban centers. The character of black protest, the strategies, setbacks, and successes of the civil rights movement are all inextricably linked to this phenomena. Different strategies were appropriate to the time when blacks were rooted to the South than were called for when they had become increasingly urban and more widely diffused throughout the nation. During Reconstruction, black freedmen sought to protect their newly won rights to vote and participate in the refashioned state and local governments in the South. Black congressmen and state and local government officials were elected, but there were retaliations and white-hooded Klansmen began to ride. It was a hostile land, and the freed blacks and their Unionist allies relied on federal troops for protection. When federal troops were withdrawn as a consequence of the Compromise of 1877, swift and thorough repression followed. Escape to the North was difficult—if not virtually impossible—largely because jobs in the new factories and mills were being filled by European immigrants then arriving on our shores in increasing numbers. Illiteracy and a lack of skills, too, helped keep many bonded to the land. An archaic agriculture needed their labor, and the terror used to keep blacks "in their place" did so literally, holding hundreds of thousands in virtual peonage. In 1860, only 5.1 percent of all black Americans (4.4 million) lived outside the South; by 1910, that percentage had only increased to 10.4 percent, or 9.8 million. Within the South, however, there was significant movement into the cities over the same period. In 1860, according to Bureau of Census figures, Negroes constituted 19.3 percent of the southern urban population and 24.5 percent by 1910. The urban population of the South, however, was not large as compared to that of the eastern seaboard cities of the North and of the growing industrial heartland in the Midwest. For many black men and women in the South, those years following the betrayal of 1877 are best described by poet Paul Laurence Dunbar:

> A crust of bread and a corner to sleep in,
> A minute to smile and an hour to weep in,
> A pint of joy to a peck of trouble,

And never a laugh but the moans come double.
And that is life.

The new century opened with 214 lynchings within the first two years. Resignation and the tactics of survival appeared only too appropriate. Booker T. Washington advised his people, "Cast down your buckets where you are," appealed to the descendants of northern abolitionists for desperately needed aid to keep schools going, and backed the Republican party. When H. G. Wells, on a visit to the United States, criticized Jim Crow laws, Washington replied, "The only answer to it all is for colored men to be patient, to make themselves competent, to do good work, to give no occasion against us." This was the bitter counsel of survival, and the age of Booker T. Washington trailed off into a reliance on the good offices of the Republican party for patronage. Washington, however, was a complex man—even, of necessity, a devious one—and it says much of the difficulties that Negroes faced in his day to note that while he gave public support to segregation (to be fair, he believed in ultimate integration), he privately and secretively financed some of the earliest court cases against Jim Crow.

Washington's policy reflected the condition of his people; illiteracy was high and education of the utmost importance to their future. But his philosophy also reflected the prevailing wisdom, theories of free competition, and political individualism. So it is not surprising to find his opponents affirming the new philosophies of reform and social democracy. Timothy Thomas Fortune supported the election of Democrat Grover Cleveland in 1884, was influenced by single-taxer and land reformer Henry George, and predicted that the future conflict in the South would be between capital and labor and not between the races. William Edward Burghardt Du Bois, a Massachusetts-born, Fisk and Harvard educated professor at the University of Atlanta, published in 1903 a collection of essays, *The Souls of Black Folk*, in several of which he took Washington's leadership to task. When Du Bois issued a call for an organization of those who believed in "Negro freedom and growth," twenty-nine black intellectuals and professional men responded. They met in Niagara Falls, Canada—hence, the name, the Niagara Movement—in June 1905. The new militancy of Du Bois and his followers developed out of despair—"The work of stealing the black man's ballot has progressed, and the fifty and more representatives of stolen votes still sit in the nation's capital"—and out of rising hopes flowing from the new tides of progressivism and radicalism awash in the country. Even in the South, it appeared as if the time for temporizing was past. Black organizers, for example, were organizing black and white mine workers in Alabama. The integrationist policies of the United Mine Workers became those of the Alabama State Federation of Labor, founded in 1902, with some 235 local unions and roughly 33,000 members. Du Bois, too, was attracted to socialism, and briefly joined the Socialist party of Eugene Victor Debs in 1911 and 1912. The temper of the Niagara Movement, however, was perhaps more poetic than pragmatic. It never developed any real base and was soon absorbed by a new organization that would play a leading civil rights role right down to the present: the National Association for the Advancement of Colored People.

Significantly, the founding of the National Association for the Advancement of Colored People (NAACP) was precipitated by a northern race riot and its early years roughly coincided with the beginnings of the Great Migration of blacks out of the South. Mob actions, contrary to the myth, were not foreign to the North, but the Springfield, Illinois, August 1908 riot shocked the country, largely because of its proximity to Lincoln's long-time home. A white woman claimed that she had been raped by a black man, a charge later retracted but too late. An angry mob destroyed Negro businesses and ransacked Negro homes. A black barber was lynched, and the next night, an 84-year-old black man, who had been married to a white woman for over thirty years, was hanged only a block away from the State House. It took over five thousand militia to suppress this lawless outrage. A socialist journalist, William English Walling, described the Springfield atrocities in *The Independent*, and declared, "Either the spirit of Lincoln and Lovejoy must be revived and we must come to treat the Negro on a plane of absolute political and social equality, or Vardaman and Tillman will soon have transferred the race war to the North . . . . Yet who realizes the seriousness of the situation and what large and powerful body of citizens is ready to come to their aid?"

Some were willing, including Mary White Ovington, a New York social worker and socialist; Dr. Henry Moskowitz, a prominent member of the New York Jewish community; Oswald Garrison Villard, editor of the New York *Evening Post* and grandson of the abolitionist Garrison; Jane Addams of the settlement house movement; novelist William Dean Howells; philosopher John Dewey, Walling, and Du Bois, among others, who formed the NAACP in 1910. Du Bois became the organization's first Negro officer and paid executive as its director of research and publicity. From the first, Du Bois gave the NAACP its tone, especially through its popular journal, *The Crisis*. Originally all white except for Du Bois, the board of directors had thirteen Negro members by 1914, and most were veterans of the Niagara Movement.

While the new organization hoped to widen industrial opportunities for Negroes, it found much of its energies concentrated on its crusade against lynching, for the franchise, for elimination of the poll tax, and a broad-scoped drive against segregation and discrimination in all forms.

In 1911, a group of philanthropists, social workers, and professionals formed an interracial organization, the National Urban League, to open new opportunities to Negroes in industry and to assist newly arrived Negroes in adjusting to urban conditions. Both the NAACP and the National Urban League were to flourish as the Great Migration mounted in number.

The hopes for change in the South that briefly flourished along with the early populist movement and such trade union developments as the integrationist Alabama State Federation of Labor were crushed by the economic recession of 1904 and the rise in redneck racism that followed. Besieged by bad times in the South—a severe recession, an outbreak of the boll weevil, and the 1915 floods—Negroes were ready to take advantage of the opportunities that developed in the North as war in Europe shut off the flow of immigration. The Negro press urged Southern Negroes to flee the South. As the Chicago *Defender* put it, "To die from the bite of frost is far more glorious than at the hands of a mob." Two basic waves flowed North: the first, from 1917 to 1919, brought close to a half million blacks to northern industrial areas to work in munitions and other labor-short factories; the second, from 1921 to 1924, brought another half million to fill jobs left emptied by the legal close-down of mass immigration. In 1910, slightly over one million Negroes lived in the North; by 1940, the number increased to 2.8 million. True, America's 12,866,000 blacks in 1940 constituted less than 10 percent of the total population, and three-quarters of them were still living below the Mason-Dixon line. What counted, however, was the Negro's movement to the cities. By 1940, 37.3 percent of southern blacks lived in cities and 90.1 percent of all Negroes in northern and western states lived in urban areas. In Detroit, the Negro community had grown from 5,700 in 1910 to about 150,000 by 1940; in New York City, which claimed 16.9 percent of all northern Negroes, the Negro population rose from 91,000 in 1910 to 152,000 in 1920, and to 478,000 by 1940. The move from rural areas was more than a simple migration and change in folkways; for blacks, it was a move, almost literally, from no voting to voting. The urban concentration, especially in the North, gave blacks political muscle for the first time since Reconstruction.

In Chicago, black voters had already elected a congressman as they would shortly do in New York City. As the country hovered on the brink of war in 1941, the bulk of American Negroes was still rural, but significant numbers were among the working poor in urban centers and were pressing for greater equality in job opportunities. The urbanization of the Negro, too, created a growing black working class as well as a tiny but important business and professional middle class.

No one as yet had tapped the catalytic possibilities inherent in setting

blacks in motion. The nearest thing to it was the movement inspired by
Marcus Garvey, a messiah from the West Indies, in the 1920s; but that
had been Africa-directed, a kind of myth that set parades marching but
to no visible American purpose. Garvey preached "African for Afri-
cans," an ideological precursor of later anti-colonial and Pan-African
movements, and pushed for the repatriation of Afro-Americans to
ancestral homelands. He also touted black capitalism and promoted
several business ventures, including the spectacular Black Star Line,
which operated several vessels between New York and the West Indies
and ran excursions up the Hudson River. In 1919, Garvey claimed a
membership of two million for his Universal Negro Improvement
Association.

Repatriation, however, was not feasible for the great majority of
black Americans. Garvey's alleged mishandling of Black Star assets
caused a disillusionment among his followers that climaxed over the
revelation of a secret meeting between Garvey and the Imperial Wizard
of the Ku Klux Klan, Edward Young Clarke, during the summer of
1922. "I regard the Klan," Garvey declared in defense of his actions in
seeking Klan support for repatriation, "a better friend of the race than
all other groups of hypocritical whites put together."

By 1940, Garvey was long gone from the streets of Harlem and no
one or no movement had taken his place. The Urban League was
neither a mass nor a protest organization. As a social service institution
with forty-six branches and twenty-six thousand members in 1940
located in most of the major cities around the country, the league
performed invaluable job placement and other welfare tasks. Its surveys
exposed racial discrimination, but as Ralph Bunche put it in a special
study prepared for Gunnar Myrdal's *An American Dilemma*, "As an
interracial, dependent organization it can never develop a program
which will spur the Negro masses and win their confidence. It has not
exerted, nor can it, any great influence upon the thinking of Negroes nor
upon their course of action. It operates strictly on the periphery of the
Negro problem and never comes to grips with the fundamentals in
American racial conflict." While this judgment may seem unduly harsh
in the light of the league's very real accomplishments in easing the entry
of rural blacks into the urban scene, it is not out of line with the league's
own self-conception as "a social service organization attempting to
perform a helpful task in a limited field." Eugene Kinckle Jones, the
league's executive secretary at the time, stated, "Any movement of this
character which advocates understanding through conference and
discussion must necessarily refrain from advocating mass action of one
race calculated to force the other group to make concessions."

The National Association for the Advancement of Colored People, of
course, labored under no similar restraint. But the middle-class

character of its membership imposed a limitation on militancy. As Gunnar Myrdal noted in his great study, the NAACP had "nowhere been able to build up a real mass following among Negroes. The membership is still largely confined to the upper classes." Nonetheless, with some 481 branches and a membership of 85,000 in 1940, the NAACP served as a "watchdog" over Negro rights and as the center for the Negro protest movement. Its objectives were outlined in a 1940 leaflet, "The Acid Test of Democracy":

1. Anti-lynching legislation.
2. Legislation to end peonage and debt slavery among the sharecroppers and tenant farmers of the South.
3. Enfranchisement of the Negro in the South.
4. Abolition of injustices in legal procedure, particularly criminal procedure, based solely upon color or race.
5. Equitable distribution of funds for public education.
6. Abolition of segregation, discrimination, insult, and humiliation based on race or color.
7. Equality of opportunity to work in all fields with equal pay for equal work.
8. Abolition of discrimination against Negroes in the right to collective bargaining through membership in organized labor unions.

President Roosevelt's rebuff of the three black spokesmen, whether intended or not, stirred up the country's black communities. The Negro press, perhaps, best reflected this rising tone of anger among black people. When black and white leaders met at a conference in November 1940, at Hampton Institute, the Negro technical college in Virginia, to discuss "Participation of the Negro in National Defense," George S. Schuyler, the Pittsburgh *Courier's* prominent columnist, snapped, "The masses of Negroes are getting fed up with these frauds [conferences and similar activity]." What was needed, he added, was an organization which "would have worked out some techniques of fighting other than sending letters and telegrams of protest."

While the Negro press can trace its history back before the Civil War, it was World War I, with its contrast between war aims to "make the world safe for democracy" and the treatment of minorities at home, that created the tide of protest upon which the press rose in importance and militancy. It was also the Negro press that made northward migration into a Negro protest movement. The migration, too, made the protest possible by freeing the Negro press, giving it a readership and a place of publication free of southern white-sheeted night-riders. Gunnar Myrdal makes the point that southern Negro newspapers tended to be more cautious and less belligerent, but because of northern competition, managed to give readers "a relatively blunt expression to the Negro protest." According to one study cited in Myrdal, more northern Negro newspapers were read in the Deep South than local ones. The U.S. Bureau of the Census reported, in 1940, that there were 210 Negro newspapers with 155 reporting a circulation of 1.2 million. Myrdal, allowing for the passing of the weekly newspapers from family to family and their presence in barber shops, churches, lodges, and pool parlors, conservatively estimated a weekly readership of at least 1.5 million. The Pittsburgh *Courier*, with the largest circulation, sold 141,500 copies weekly, and the Chicago *Defender*, the second largest, had a weekly circulation of about 83,500. The press, as Myrdal noted, created a sense of solidarity among Negroes, perhaps especially so among the uprooted migrants to the northern cities. For this reason, Myrdal concluded, "The Negro press is far more than a mere expression of the Negro protest. By expressing the protest, the press also magnifies it, acting like a huge sounding board."

In January 1941, however, few white Americans were aware of the reverberations sounding through the black communities of the country. The NAACP designated January 26, 1941, "National Defense Day" and protest meetings were held in twenty-three states. Plans were laid for picketing national defense plants around the country. But as yet all this activity lacked focus or thrust.

Early that winter, A. Philip Randolph, the austere president of the Brotherhood of Sleeping Car Porters, and Milton Webster, its brusque vice-president, were riding south on a train and discussing the impasse over jobs for Negroes in the burgeoning defense industries. As the train rolled through the Virginia hills, the two men fell silent. After a while, Randolph, in his low, deep voice said, "I think we ought to do something about it. I think we ought to get ten thousand Negroes and march down Pennsylvania Avenue asking for jobs in defense plants and integration of the armed forces. It would shake up Washington."

"And where," asked Webster, "are you going to get ten thousand Negroes?"

Randolph was quiet for a few moments, and then explained how he believed they could get them.

At first, few others believed that so many could be mobilized even on behalf of so just a cause. In January 1941, Randolph formally announced his proposal to a group of leading Negro Americans—a distinguished black "Who's Who" that included Walter White of the NAACP; Dr. Channing Tobias, senior secretary of the National Council of the YMCA; Mary McLeod Bethune, president of the National Council of Negro Women; Dr. George E. Haynes, executive secretary of the Federal Council of Churches of Christ; and Lester Granger, newly appointed executive secretary of the National Urban League. But nothing much happened. Even the feisty Negro press was chary. The

February 8, 1941, Chicago *Defender* expressed the prevailing skepticism:

> We would like to share Mr. Randolph's optimism that such a mobilization is possible. It is not possible to get Negroes to march in impressive numbers for denunciation of the miscarriage of justice in the case of the Scottsboro boys; it has not been possible to get them to march in protest against lynching, against peonage and poll tax . . . .
> It would not be necessary to mobilize 10,000. If we could just get 2,000 black folk to march on the Capitol demanding 'the right to work and fight for our country,' that would be an accomplishment of considerable import . . . . To get 10,000 Negroes assembled in one spot, under one banner with justice, democracy and work as their slogan would be the miracle of the century.

Milton Webster later recalled another kind of response. He and Randolph were in Savannah, Georgia, to talk up the proposed March on Washington. "The head colored man in town opened up the meeting," Webster said, "and introduced me, and ran off the platform to take the last seat in the last row."

Randolph's faith in black solidarity and the effectiveness of militancy, however, was unshakeable. He argued, "Such a pilgrimage of 10,000 Negroes would wake up and shock official Washington as it has never been shocked before. Why? The answer is clear. Nobody expects 10,000 Negroes to get together and march anywhere for anything at any time . . . . In common parlance, they are supposed to be just scared and unorganizable. Is this true? I contend it is not."

Later, Lester B. Granger would write, "It was Randolph's immense prestige among all classes of Negroes that made his idea [the March on Washington] something more than a pretentious notion." Randolph, however, never really belonged to the black establishment, and throughout his life would always be something of a loner. As author Roi Ottley put it, writing in *Black Odyssey*, "He was unique among Negro leaders in that he was neither a preacher, educator, nor rabble-rousing politician, but a labor organizer. Tall, dark, and brooding, Randolph impressed Negroes as being all *soul*."

Randolph, in person, appears somewhat above common concerns. Erudite, steeped in Shakespeare and the Bible, his basso voice resonant with broad A's, he would be at home, one thinks, behind ivy-covered walls deep within the groves of academe. In truth, Randolph is something of a paradox: a part of the Great Migration, yet apart from it; an organizer of workers, yet an intellectual. In the Emersonian sense,

Randolph is a representative man; yet, he is also a marginal man in David Riesman's definition of marginality, "left on some margin between belonging and not belonging," which makes for insight and creative noncomformity.

Randolph was born on April 15, 1889, in Crescent City, Florida, where his father was a circuit-riding African Methodist Episcopal minister and his mother, an attractive mulatto daughter of a lumber dealer. The Reverend James W. Randolph tended to the cares of three small rural congregations near Jacksonville, Florida, all of which could not support him. "My father was paid in kind," his son once recalled, "shanks of pigs, potatoes, cabbages, that sort of thing." The family also eked out a living running a laundry. Young Philip and his older brother James delivered bundles of wash to the family's customers.

The elder Randolph was apparently a man of iron will. "My home," his son once told an interviewer, "was almost Calvinistic. It was rigidly moralistic and rigidly supervised. I never saw a bottle of whiskey, nobody used profanity, and there was no playing on Sunday." Many years later, when Randolph, as a result of his participation in Ye Friends of Shakespeare, a Harlem theater group, toyed with the idea of going on the stage, he was dissuaded by the stern admonitions of his father who considered the stage a sin only once removed from drink. Self-educated himself, the elder Randolph began tutoring his two sons early and intensively. They learned the Bible, a love of words, and their pronunciation from their father.

A. Philip Randolph also learned early in life that his people were not helpless.

> Mother and father kept whispering to one another that evening, and there was gloom in the house. Other men came by in twos and threes to talk to my father. I had no idea who was going to be lynched or why or what a lynching was really. But just hearing the rumors and the talk was frightening. Later the men came by for my father. "You get the gun," he told my mother as he left us, "and sit with the boys until I get back." Mother was a good marksman. She took down the shotgun and sat there with it across her lap until daybreak. My brother James and I kept the vigil all night with her. I was only about nine; he was two years older.
>
> Sometime after dawn, my father returned. He was weary, but the gloom was gone. The men of the town—his friends, members of the church where he preached—had gone to the county jail, stood all night like sentries in the street and kept the lynch mob from coming. I'll never forget it. It had a tremendous effect on me.

Randolph was fortunate in attending Cookman Institute in Jacksonville, a Methodist school now called the Bethune-Cookman College in Daytona, where half the teachers were white volunteers from New England. They taught the Randolph youngsters Latin and math, and reinforced the senior Randolph's moral code. Randolph calls Cookman "a glorious chapter in American history." One day, he says, "their story will be told. They suffered isolation and ostracism at the hands of white Southerners who feared education for the Negro as they fear the ballot today." Randolph's brother came north, attended City College, and became a brilliant mathematician, an accomplished medievalist, and a writer of Latin verse. He died suddenly of diphtheria in the early 1930s.

Young Philip, in his early twenties, also came North. A cousin was a janitor in an apartment building at Eighty-ninth Street and Columbus Avenue and he offered young Randolph a summer job as a hallboy at $4.00 a month. (For a number of years, the building bore the scrawl, "P. Randolph swept here.") He started attending City College at night and earned his way at odd jobs.

Restless and intellectually curious, Randolph read widely and deeply, heard Eugene Victor Debs speak, and joined the Socialist party in 1911. He began to organize his fellow workers wherever he went, which was easier than one might expect since his employers kept helping him on his way. He had a job as an elevator operator and got fired for organizing; he became a maintenance man and got fired for organizing; he then found a job as a waiter on a pleasure boat and got fired for organizing.

While at City College, Randolph met a young Columbia law student, Chandler Owen. The two young men decided to open a job bureau in Harlem, but one with social overtones—it provided an improvised job training program on the side for untutored blacks from the rural South. Called "The Brotherhood," the business did not last very long. However, it did reflect one of Randolph's lasting concerns—jobs for black workers as the crux to any civil rights effort. It was a theme he would repeat again in the 1941 and 1963 marches on Washington.

Randolph's wide-ranging interests in the arts, socialism, and life in Harlem secured him invitations to the literary parties of A'Lelia Walker, heiress to the Walker beauty parlor and preparations fortune. There he met the manager of one of the Walker beauty salons, a tall, honey-colored beauty named Lucille Green. Miss Green was a graduate of Howard University with the same interests as Randolph in Shakespeare, socialism, and the world. They were married in 1913. "For our honeymoon," Mrs. Randolph once said, "we took the open streetcar to South Ferry. And back." Mrs. Randolph was a good speaker and once ran for the state legislature on the Socialist ticket. Their relationship was a close one and lasted until her death in 1964. The Randolphs had no children. During the last few years of her life, Mrs. Randolph was ill and her husband would come home each evening, cook supper for the two of them, and spend his evenings reading Shakespeare aloud to her.

The employment bureau indirectly led to Randolph's career as an editor. (He never did finish his studies at City College.) He and Owen met leaders of a new union of Negro headwaiters. "They were real aristocrats," Randolph once said. They wanted a magazine, and Randolph and Owen were hired to put out *The Hotel Messenger*. But they soon discovered that the headwaiters were given to exploiting their underlings, the sidewaiters. "We didn't have any better sense," Randolph recalled later, "than to write about it in the magazine this same group [of headwaiters] was maintaining. We were fired."

Randolph and Owen decided to keep the magazine going by dropping one word from the masthead. In 1915, they started *The Messenger* on a shoestring and played that string out for ten years. It wasn't long before *The Messenger* was called "the most dangerous of all Negro publications." America was drifting toward a "war to save democracy." Yet, President Woodrow Wilson's talk of "The New Freedom" meant for Negroes a stiffening of segregation. Jim Crow, a long-time resident of Washington, D.C., was invited directly into the government under Wilson. Negro employees were shunted off into "separate but equal" rest rooms and eating places within government bureaus.

W. E. B. Du Bois wrote a famous editorial in the NAACP organ, *The Crisis*, calling on Negroes to close ranks and support the war. Randolph, in *The Messenger*, blasted Du Bois and the President. "Lynching, Jim Crow, segregation and discrimination in the armed forces and out, disenfranchisement of millions of black souls in the South—all these things make your cry of making the world safe for democracy a sham, a mockery, a rape of decency and a travesty on common justice."

Randolph's flaming attacks upon the war and the Wilson Administration drew the ire of the federal government. *The Messenger* was banned from the mails. Randolph took to the streets, and in New York, Cleveland, Chicago, Seattle, and Washington, D.C., held rallies and sold copies of the banned publication. "We were selling 4,000 copies in Seattle," Randolph has since recalled. "And nobody knew there were any Negroes out there."

During the war, shortly after the arrest of Eugene Victor Debs, Randolph was arrested for treason. But a paternalistic judge refused to believe *"these boys"*—at twenty-eight, Randolph looked too young for the draft—were anything but victims of some sinister conspiracy. So the judge sent them on their way. Later, though the Justice Department pressed for Randolph's prosecution as "the most dangerous Negro in America," Wilson declined to act because he felt it would not be wise.

Although Randolph was reaching Negroes "out there," patriotic fervor and the postwar hysteria against radicals of all kinds and conditions eroded his influence and readership among the masses of Negroes. When Marcus Garvey came to Harlem and moved the people as no one else ever had with his vision of a black empire across the seas, Randolph won a certain eminence as the only Negro of stature to openly attack Garvey in the pages of his magazine and on the streets. "The United States is our home," Randolph said then as he has repeatedly said since. "Our children are here. We have no other country. We have no other home. If there are wrongs in America, Negroes as Americans must help work and fight to correct them. If the problems of race and color are hard in the United States, so be it. Let us not lose heart and run away from them, but gird to solve them."

It was a lonely eminence in the 1920s as Garveyites paraded through the streets of Harlem. Fewer and fewer people listened to Randolph, but among the attentive were a handful of sleeping car porters. They were trying to organize a union and needed a front man, a leader whom the Pullman Company could not reach. Ashley L. Totten, later the secretary-treasurer of the Brotherhood of Sleeping Car Porters, had just been fired for attending a meeting. Totten, along with Milton Webster —a Chicago Republican ward leader who had been fired in 1918—and four others met with Randolph, urging him to head the drive to organize the ten thousand porters. He agreed, and the union was founded in August 1925.

But it was twelve years before it won recognition from the railroads. Meanwhile, *The Messenger* evolved into the union publication, *The Black Worker.* The union barely survived the bitter, early years of the Depression—years, incidentally, when the black migration out of the rural South dropped. In 1937, the railroads finally did what they said they never would do; they signed a contract with the Brotherhood that quadrupled the income of the porters in a few short years. Randolph had established a link with the black communities of America that few other black leaders enjoyed. On the job, the porter may have been the invisible man who responded to the call "George," but in his community, he was a figure of some importance. He held a steady job—no small thing in a community of the unemployed and under-employed—and often managed to save a little something and to buy his own home. He was ambitious for his children; the porters put more young people through college than any other single group of Negro workers. Yet, he was not part of the black bourgeoisie or the backbone of the NAACP. He was a worker, a trade unionist. When an organizer sets out to unionize workers in a plant, he often seeks out those who are skilled workers, natural leaders, and those whose jobs may offer some freedom of movement within the plant or within a given department.

They can talk to more workers and are more likely to be heeded because of their skills and standing among their fellows. The porters were natural organizers for a black protest movement for the same reasons. Roi Ottley, in *New World A-Coming*, called them, "those efficient couriers"; in 1940, they were some ten thousand strong and ready to tap the Negro masses as never before.

In 1936, Randolph participated in the founding of the National Negro Congress, an attempt to create an umbrella agency embracing all the existing Negro trade unions, religious, fraternal, and civic bodies, and became its president. During the mid-1930s, the Communist party adopted "popular front" tactics, which called for building or participating in alliances of progressive forces. Turning from an attack on liberals and democratic radicals, the communists began joining many liberal organizations, including the National Negro Congress. By the time of the August 1939 Stalin-Hitler Pact, they were influential in, if not in control of, the Congress. Again, the line changed: Where Randolph had been praised, he was damned as a "misleader." At the April 1940 meeting of the Congress, Randolph and the communists fought it out. The communists agitated against "the imperialist war," while Randolph urged the Congress to continue its nonpartisanship. But such a policy, in Randolph's view, did not embrace tolerance of either the Stalin or Hitler dictatorships. Randolph resigned, charging that the Congress was not only a communist front organization but not a Negro one either. To facilitate their take-over, the communists had packed the Congress with white members of the party and white sympathizers. Largely because of this experience, Randolph was determined that the March on Washington Movement should not fall prey to communist machinations. Since the Communist party had had little success within America's black communities and had few black members, Randolph minimized the possibility of communist control by simply declaring the march an all-black affair. Negro communists, too, were hampered by the sudden change in the party line. During the Hitler-Stalin Pact, on May 16, 1941, the *Daily Worker*, the party's newspaper, had declared, "You can't defend Negro rights without fighting against this war"; and in August 1941, after Germany invaded the Soviet Union, *The Communist*, a party monthly, stated, "The Negro people cannot be true to their own best interests without supporting the war."

Randolph's urgings in January 1941, however, did little but stir up some comment in the Negro press. He reiterated his proposal in a stirring call published in the March 1941 *Black Worker* "On to Washington, ten thousand black Americans . . . . We shall not call upon our white friends to march with us. There are some things Negroes must do alone. This is our fight and we must see it through. If it costs money to finance a march on Washington, let Negroes pay for it. If any sacrifices are to be made for Negro rights in national defense, let Negroes make them . . . . Let the Negro masses speak!"

Negro spokesmen, however, concentrated on mounting traditional pressures rather than the march, and the masses had yet to speak. The National Urban League arranged a coast-to-coast broadcast for March 30 dramatizing its plea for greater economic opportunity and an end to discrimination in defense industries. Protests were aimed at the Office of Production Management (OPM), seeking an anti-discrimination order. On April 11, OPM Associate Director-General Sidney Hillman, president of the Amalgamated Clothing Workers of America–CIO, on loan to the government, sent a letter to all holders of defense contracts urging the elimination of bans against the hiring of Negroes. But the letter was not signed by his co-director, William S. Knudsen, who refused to explain why. According to Walter White, Knudsen "refused even to meet or discuss discrimination with any Negro delegation." And Lester Granger charged, "William Knudsen, Hillman's fellow director, was never sympathetic to a program for increasing effective use of Negro labor." Negroes believed Hillman's letter and his subsequent establishment of a Negro Employment and Training Branch and a Minority Group Branch in the OPM Labor Division were too late and much too little. The *Amsterdam News* reflected the new angry mood that would soon set Randolph's proposed march in motion: "Mr. Hillman has spoken boldly, but unless he follows through with something more punitive than a mere plea, his words are going to fall on deaf ears. The policy toward Negro workers in America is well grounded. Nothing short of a major catastrophe will shake it, unless the word to do so comes straight from the top with White House influence behind it. *Mr. Roosevelt must be prevailed upon to speak out.*" (My italics.)

"All roads lead to Washington," Randolph declared again and again. To get black feet marching, he pulled together a March on Washington Committee consisting of himself, Walter White; Lester Granger; Rev. William Lloyd Imes; Frank R. Crosswaith of the Negro Labor Committee; Layle Lane, vice-president of the American Federation of Teachers; Richard Parrish, president of the Negro College Students of New York, and Henry K. Croft.° On May 1, 1941, the committee issued a "Call to Negro America to March on Washington for Jobs and Equal Participation in National Defense" and to rally on July 1 at the Lincoln Memorial:

° Signers of the original "Call." According to the June 28, 1941, issue of the socialist weekly, *The Call*, the march national committee consisted of the above plus Dr. Rayford Logan of Howard University, J. Finley Wilson of the Elks, Noah C. Walters of the Laundry Workers Joint Board, E. E. Williams of the Blasters and Drillers Union, and the Reverend Adam Clayton Powell, Jr.

Dear fellow Negro Americans, be not dismayed in these terrible times. You possess power, great power. Our problem is to hitch it up for action on the broadest, daring and most gigantic scale.

In this period of power politics, nothing counts but pressure, more pressure, and still more pressure, through the tactic and strategy of broad, organized, aggressive mass action behind the vital and important issues of the Negro. To this end we propose that ten thousand Negroes MARCH ON WASHINGTON FOR JOBS IN NATIONAL DEFENSE AND EQUAL INTEGRATION IN THE FIGHTING FORCES OF THE UNITED STATES.

An "all-out" thundering March on Washington, ending in a monster and huge demonstration at Lincoln's Monument will shake up white America.

It will shake up official Washington . . . .

It will gain respect for the Negro people.

It will create a new sense of self-respect among Negroes.

As Herbert Garfinkel points out in his fine study of the march, *When Negroes March*, Randolph had developed a program "simple to grasp by ordinary masses of people and within the official powers of 'a great humanitarian and idealist' [as the call to the march termed President Roosevelt]." The march committee summons put the matter bluntly:

The Negroes' stake in national defense is big. It consists of jobs, thousands of jobs. It may represent millions, yes, hundreds of millions of dollars in wages. It consists of new industrial opportunities and hope. This is worth fighting for.

Most important and vital to all, Negroes by the mobilization and coordination of their mass power, can cause PRESIDENT ROOSEVELT TO ISSUE AN EXECUTIVE ORDER ABOLISHING DISCRIMINATION IN ALL GOVERNMENT DEPARTMENTS, ARMY, NAVY, AIR CORPS AND NATIONAL DEFENSE JOBS.

Once the march was, so to speak, in motion, Randolph and its leaders were caught up in a complex political poker game with a master player, an exceedingly clever but harassed President. The ante was quickly raised by the Negro press and march leaders. Randolph told Roi Ottley, "The administration leaders in Washington will never give the Negro justice until they see masses—ten, twenty, fifty thousand Negroes on the White House lawn." The Chicago *Defender* announced that fifty thousand Negroes were preparing for a "march for jobs and justice"; and the *Amsterdam News* emblazoned "100,000 IN MARCH TO CAPITOL."

The National Council of Negro Women, headed by educator Mary McLeod Bethune, arranged to meet in Washington the day before the march. The Alpha Kappa Alpha, the first Negro sorority, also called its members to a Capitol conference so as to enable them to participate in the march on July 1. "March on Washington" buttons were selling like pigs' feet in a Harlem bar on a hot weekend night. Headquarters were opened in Harlem and Brooklyn and local committees sprang up in eighteen cities, most being key rail terminals. Buses were hired and special trains chartered. In early June, over one hundred Negro ministers urged their congregations to take part in the march. Randolph later recalled roaming Harlem "talking up the march by word of mouth . . . in all the beauty parlors and taverns and barber shops, stores and theater lobbies."

Biographer James MacGregor Burns in *Roosevelt: Soldier of Freedom* sums up the President's attitude toward Negro rights as "a compound of personal compassion, social paternalism, political sensitivity to their increasing articulateness and to racism in Congress, and a practical realization of their importance to the defense effort." Early in the year, he had announced his and the country's commitment to the "Four Freedoms: freedom of speech and expression, freedom of worship, freedom from want, and freedom from fear." The Hitler war was going badly for the Allies. Nazi U-boats prowled the seas in wolf packs, sinking 2,314,000 gross tons between April 1940 and March 1941. Rommel's tank corps overran North Africa in May, and Germany had conquered Yugoslavia, Greece, and Crete by June 1. America was increasingly concerned. In March, the President secured the passage of the Lend-Lease Act which provided arms and other materiel by sale, transfer, or lease to any country whose security the President deemed vital to that of the United States. And, on May 27, he proclaimed an "unlimited national emergency." At the same time, historian Burns reports him as "apprehensive" over the impending March on Washington, which "seemed to offer a rude threat to the image of national unity he was carefully fostering." As Lester B. Granger put it a year later, "It [the march] would have been notice to foreign critics of our domestic disunity at a time when a semblance of unity was most essential to national prestige." Or, as a ranking New Dealer told Randolph, "What will they think in Berlin?"

The first notice the White House took of the march was expressed in a letter to Randolph on June 10 from Mrs. Roosevelt. She reported that she had discussed the situation with the President. "I feel very strongly," she wrote,

> that your group is making a very grave mistake at the
> present time to allow this march to take place. I am

afraid it will set back the progress which is being made, in the Army at least, toward better opportunities and less segregation.

I feel that if any incident occurs from this, it may engender so much bitterness that it will create in Congress even more solid opposition from certain groups than we have had in the past.

I know that crusades are valuable and necessary sometimes, but undertaken when the temper is as tense as it is at present, it seems to me unfortunate, and to run the risk which such a meeting as this carries with it, is unwise. You know that I am deeply concerned about the rights of Negro people, but I think one must face situations as they are and not as one wishes them to be. I think this is a very serious decision for you to take.

Peppery Mayor Fiorello H. La Guardia, another friend of the Negro, invited Randolph and White to City Hall on June 13 to meet with Mrs. Roosevelt, Aubrey Williams, director of the National Youth Administration, and Anna Rosenberg. Mrs. Roosevelt acknowledged the need for definite action against discrimination but firmly opposed the march. Mayor La Guardia added that he thought that penalties ought to be imposed in government contracts against those who failed to provide jobs for Negroes. But he, too, opposed the march. Ever courteous, Mrs. Roosevelt indicated that she also thought the march impractical. "You know where I stand," she reminded her listeners. "But the attitude of the Washington police, most of them Southerners, and the general feeling of Washington itself are such that I fear that there may be trouble if the march occurs." Then she asked where the thousands of Negroes would eat in Washington and where they would stay. Randolph gravely reflected, then answered, "They would go to the hotels and restaurants and register and order dinner."

Mrs. Roosevelt promised, "I will ask the President to call a conference to discuss the matter thoroughly." Aubrey Williams added, "Never before has the administration been so concerned over Negroes. Everybody down there is talking about it." Randolph and White, despite these arguments, remained firm in their resolve to hold the march. "Our aim is jobs, not promises," Randolph said. "The march will do some good. In fact, it has already done some good; for if you were not concerned about it, you wouldn't be here now discussing the question of racial discrimination." In parting, Randolph told the mayor that there would be a march on City Hall on June 27. "What for?" cried the startled mayor. "What have I done?"

The Negroes' war-of-nerves was getting results. Secretary of the Navy Knox sent a telegram that day asking Randolph to Washington to discuss "your project." The President issued a strongly worded endorsement of the Hillman anti-discrimination letter. "Our government," he declared in a memorandum to the OPM, "cannot countenance continued discrimination against American citizens in defense production." But where such a statement would have been greeted with joy by Negroes even a few short weeks earlier, it was characterized by march leaders as "ineffective." In truth, it was a victory of the kind that whets appetites for more. Aubrey Williams telephoned Randolph, informing him that the President requested that the march be called off and that he would meet with march leaders on Wednesday, June 18.

Randolph and White met with the President, who had with him Secretary of the Navy Knox, Assistant Secretary of War Patterson, OPM directors Knudsen and Hillman, Aubrey Williams, Mayor La Guardia, and Anna Rosenberg. For some reason, Layle Lane and Frank Crosswaith of the committee were not allowed to sit in on the conference with the President. In his autobiography, *A Man Called White*, White recalls the meeting opened with some discussion between himself, Patterson, and Knox over segregation in the armed forces. But the meeting soon turned to the major concern at hand, the march and defense industry jobs for Negroes. Already a priority had begun to emerge with the march leaders pressing harder on the defense job issue than on segregation in the armed services.

The President exercised his considerable charm to dissuade Randolph and White from their proposed course of action. The antagonists sparred: They invited him to address the march and he declined. At one point, the President rhetorically asked, "What would happen if Irish and Jewish people were to march on Washington?" He answered, "It would create resentment among the American people because such a march would be considered an effort to coerce the government and make it do certain things." Randolph respectfully begged to differ, pointing out that there was no comparison between the situation of those minorities and that of the Negro. "The public knows that the Negroes have justification for bringing their grievances to the President, and to the American people."

In a test of wills, the President asked White, "Walter, how many people will *really* march?"

As White recounted the event in his autobiography, "I told him no less than one hundred thousand. The President looked me full in the eye for a long time in an obvious effort to find out if I were bluffing or exaggerating. Eventually, he appeared to believe that I meant what I said."

The President then asked, "What do you want me to do?"

Randolph told him—an unequivocal executive order barring discrimination for reasons of race, religion, or creed in defense production industries and the armed services. The President designated a subcommittee of the administration people present under La Guardia's chairmanship to draw up a plan to solve the problem. The subcommittee met immediately afterward with Randolph, White, Lane, and Crosswaith, but soon adjourned. According to White's later recollections, the conferees prepared a draft of an executive order that was apparently satisfactory, at least to White. He returned to New York, and a few days later left for the NAACP's annual conference in Houston, Texas. However, the *Amsterdam News* of June 21 reported, "Definite dissatisfaction with the results of both conferences was indicated on the faces and in the mood of each member of the March Committee." The participants refused to comment publicly on the meetings, but announced: "The march will go on."

On June 24, Randolph and three aides met with Mayor La Guardia and Aubrey Williams. According to journalist Earl Brown, writing in *Harper's* magazine (April 1942), La Guardia greeted them gloomily, "I must tell you, Phil, it looks bad about that executive order. Those Southern congressmen are sore about this thing already and the Negroes will certainly lose many of their 'good white friends' if you go through with the march."

Randolph was not moved; he had heard it all before. The mayor then produced a draft of an executive order for their consideration. According to White, Randolph felt that "there had been steady whittling down of the draft we had made in Washington." White, over the telephone, agreed that they should repudiate "the emasculated version" and "stage the march." What the President apparently offered was an executive order that banned discrimination in defense industries but not one that included bans against discrimination in federal agencies and against segregation in the armed forces. Eventually, the President accepted the extension of the order's scope to include federal agencies. He apparently initialed in the words "or government" himself. A bargain was struck: The President issued Executive Order 8802 banning discrimination in defense industries and in government employment on June 25, 1941, and the march was "postponed."

III

Dream
Deferred

AS IT TURNED OUT, THE MARCH on Washington was to be "postponed" for twenty-two years. Within the space of a few short months, in the spring of 1941, the proposed march had concentrated Negro protest and succeeded in focusing black energies on Washington, D.C. C. Vann Woodward, in his perceptive study, *The Strange Career of Jim Crow*, states: "It is clear at least that the Negro himself played a larger role in the new movement for emancipation [that of this century] than he had in the abolitionist crusade that led to the original emancipation." Until Asa Philip Randolph cried out, "Let the Negro masses speak," however, the Negro did so in uneasy tandem with white liberals and progressives setting the pace. Randolph ushered the Negro masses onto the stage of history, "On to Washington, ten thousand black Americans." The march marked a change in the character of Negro protest; giving impetus, for example, to the growth of the National Association for the Advancement of Colored People, changing it from largely a legal rights agency into a mass membership protest organization. The march, too, is the granddaddy of all the black protest that proliferated through the 1960s. As Bayard Rustin once commented, "Negroes learned we didn't have to beg anymore."

Whether ten, fifty, or a hundred thousand would have marched or not is one of those questions President Franklin D. Roosevelt loved to call "iffy." Herbert Garfinkel, who studied the matter thoroughly in *When Negroes March*, concluded that the "spontaneity of the movement" was its main strength "rather than a highly organized protest." Spontaneity, however, is a ticklish fellow, easily aroused, good for a street corner or a hastily summoned mass rally, but often wanting when it comes to a sustained effort. Randolph commanded an uncertain army with a fine cadre, his ever faithful sleeping car porters. Church congregations, AKA sorority members, Elks, and the National Council of Negro Women were prepared to march. The NAACP cut short its Houston, Texas, convention deliberations to enable delegates to travel to Washington. No one knows how many blacks would have come from the cities of the North or out of the South had the march proved to be necessary. The editor of the Urban League's *Opportunity* was moved to remark after the executive order was issued that had the march been canceled without concrete achievement, "it would have been of little avail since the Negro is so thoroughly aroused by the flagrant abuse of his citizenship rights that hundreds, if not thousands, would have descended upon the capital in spite of anything that the responsible leadership might say or do."

President Roosevelt may or may not have known the strengths and weaknesses behind the march threat. Randolph told Garfinkel that the President had ordered an FBI investigation to determine the extent of Negro preparations to march; it would seem a routine precaution. But white folks, even friendly white folks, have often believed that they knew what black folks thought and would do in this or that circumstance. The march may well have not amounted to much. A large turnout of black Washingtonians—about 30 percent of the capital's 663,000 population—might have been crucial to the success of the march. But Washington was still a southern city in 1941, segregated in countless ways, and its black community apathetic if not fearful. (A straw poll by the Pittsburgh *Courier* taken in October 1942 on the desirability of a March on Washington indicated that 71 percent of the black Washingtonians were against the idea. St. Louis' blacks were much more militant with 65 percent favoring the march.) Even so, surely a march of a few thousand would have been easily contained, dispersed, and dismissed politically. The country was on a military footing, and troops were readily available. The problems of Negroes facing discrimination and in finding employment were of low priority for most Americans. In June 1942, the Hadley Cantril polling organization reported that 62 percent of Americans thought "most Negroes ... pretty well satisfied with things in this country." And, in 1941, neither Walter White nor his organization, the NAACP, which held a convention that year, is cited in *The New York Times Index*. Randolph gets one mention in a brief report on the debate over discrimination in organized labor at the American Federation of Labor convention. The 1940 elections were over, and black political muscle was as yet weak.

Yet, the President bowed before the threat of the march. Clearly, he wanted to defuse Negro protest, more embarrassing to him abroad than at home. And, too, he had the sense to foresee the need for Negro labor in industries geared to a global war. At the same time, however, the

President was extremely sensitive to political pressures from the South. Southern congressmen carried a disproportionate weight on foreign and military affairs committees.* And the South was a region rife with racist rumors tinged with fear and suspicion. "A fact as sure as science," John Temple Graves declared, "is that the white majorities of the South are unwavering and total in the determination not to have race segregation abolished." White Southerners were moving into defense production communities, carrying their mores—and Jim Crow—with the rest of their baggage. The spread of segregation throughout the country was not an unlikely outcome of the vast changes being wrought by the pressing needs of defense and war production. If the President were to act at all, he needed substantial pressures from black Americans. He had to be in a position to say, "Look, I've got to do something—or else." And, given the realities as he saw them, he had to be in a position, after taking action, to say, "Well, I didn't give away so much . . . ."

In the judgment of his biographer, James MacGregor Burns, President Roosevelt issued "a pontifical document with very small teeth." The Fair Employment Practices Committee, set up under Executive Order 8802, lacked subpoena powers, and its implied power to rescind government contracts was never exercised and probably not taken seriously. The committee was understaffed and underfinanced for its entire career. Its scope was limited to defense/war industries, and most important, to the duration of the national emergency. The initial reaction among black Americans, however, was positive. In an editorial, the *Amsterdam News* called Executive Order 8802 "epochal to say the least." And the Chicago *Defender* editorialized in its lead news story, "Faith in democracy, which Negroes had begun to feel had strayed from its course, was renewed throughout the nation when President Franklin D. Roosevelt issued an executive order Wednesday for the correction of abuses practiced against Negroes in the national defense program." There were some dissents. Adam Clayton Powell, Jr., opposed the cancellation of the march, as did the march's youth division by a vote of twenty-three to fourteen, an act that brought a testy retort from Randolph: "It is a grave question in my mind whether the youth

---

* Walter White, speaking at the Madison Square Rally celebrating the success of the march: "I invite you to go down the list of Senate chairmen of important committees: Chairman of the Appropriations Committee is Carter Glass of Virginia. Of Agriculture, 'Cotton Ed' Smith of South Carolina. Of the enormously important Foreign Relations, Tom Connally of Texas, who, *Life* recently said, would be the most influential of Americans at the Peace Conference in troweling out the new world. I invite you to read his bitterly sardonic comments on Negroes during the seven weeks' filibuster which he led against the anti-lynching bill in 1937. Chairman of Finance is George of Georgia. Of Military Affairs, Reynolds of North Carolina. Of Rules, Byrd of Virginia. Of Territories and Indian Affairs—increasingly important because of the global nature of the war and of the postwar world—Tydings of Maryland."

division would have actually mobilized twenty-five youths to go to Washington. There is no tangible evidence to the contrary." The *Defender* reported that "praise of the President's action and of Randolph's decision to postpone the march was not shared universally." Without naming names or providing other specifics, the *Defender* news account continued, saying that Randolph's decision was "characterized as a 'sell-out' in some quarters" and noted in passing that "in many sections of the country, leaders pointed out that there was no penalty for violation of the order." Roi Ottley, in the November 10, 1941, *New Republic*, perhaps came closest to the heart of the matter when he wrote, "the masses of Negroes were bewildered" by the cancellation of the march. He, however, quickly acknowledged, "Randolph and White displayed considerable statesmanship, for the President's proclamation [created] an agency which may well prove to be the opening wedge to the economic equality that Negroes seek." The Pittsburgh *Courier* hailed the first anniversary of the executive order with a banner headline: FEPC CHALKS UP BRILLIANT RECORD DURING YEAR.

For all its real shortcomings, however, Executive Order 8802 was a remarkable piece of social engineering. Sound social policy ought to affect people's lives demonstrably for the better—not necessarily immediately, but certainly over the long run. By this criteria, the order was a smashing success. Resentful whites in the decades that followed would battle embittered blacks over housing, schools, and even in the streets, but they would not do so, by and large, on the job. White workers did strike against the employment and upgrading of black workers, notably in the 1944 wildcat walkout of Philadelphia's transit workers against the employment of eight Negro trolley-car motormen. Federal troops forced the system into operation again. Yet, for all the undeniable hostility between white and black workers, often expressed on the job in racial epithets and off the job as in the violence of the Detroit riot of the summer of 1943, racial strikes constituted only .00054 percent of all wartime work stoppages.

One begins to comprehend the true achievement of Randolph-Roosevelt gamesmanship when comparing the social consequences of Executive Order 8802 with those of the federal housing program. Confronted with the challenge of providing housing to the hundreds of thousands pouring into the country's war production communities, the federal housing authorities decided to abide by prewar "local custom" in coping with race questions. The migration was so massive that local custom was, in fact, meaningless, and in reality, became what the government decided. Instead of using its leverage—as in the field of employment—to end discrimination or at least to reduce its impact, the federal housing authorities imposed the Southern "local custom," Jim

Crow, nearly everywhere.° Such cities as Ann Arbor, Michigan, in which prewar segregation was minimal, if not unknown, received segregated housing, starting a local custom with disastrous reverberations that have plagued the country into the 1970s. By contrast, Western Electric, within the spirit of Executive Order 8802, hired Negroes for the first time in 1941 and put them to work side-by-side with whites in its Kearny, New Jersey, plant. As *Fortune* magazine reported in its June 1942 issue, "The experiment was a success. *No separate cafeterias, no separate washrooms, and no move to get them* [my italics]."

Executive Order 8802 blocked Jim Crow at the factory gate in the North and even within some southern-based defense industries. The first executive order affecting Negroes since the Emancipation Proclamation was a sharp departure from traditions. It was recognized as such by the southern bloc in Congress, which fought it at every opportunity and ultimately succeeded in cutting FEPC purse strings. The order set a precedent for government intervention against discrimination, and for the nineteen state FEPCs established after the war. Fair employment practices became a civil right as a consequence.

The Fair Employment Practices Committee appointed by President Roosevelt on July 8, 1941, was shrewdly composed. Chaired by liberal Southerner Mark Ethridge, publisher of the Louisville, Kentucky, *Courier-Journal*, the committee consisted of David Sarnoff, a leading Jewish citizen and prominent industrialist associated with the powerful Rockefeller interests and president of the Radio Corporation of America; Milton Webster, first vice-president of the Brotherhood of Sleeping Car Porters; Earl B. Dickerson, a black Chicago city councilman and prominent Democrat; William Green and Philip Murray, respectively presidents of the American Federation of Labor and of the Congress of Industrial Organizations.

Gains for black workers were scored almost immediately, though no doubt hastened by the growing critical shortage of labor. In April 1942, *Fortune* magazine reported that by September 1941 "53,000 out of 184,000 additional jobs in both skilled and unskilled categories were declared open to Negro applicants by companies that had never before employed colored labor of any kind." Lester Granger of the Urban League, writing in a November 1942 special issue of *Survey Graphic*, declared, "Today, possibly half our war employers stand committed to the principle of using Negro labor in production jobs according to the workers' training and experience. Some of these employers have made

---

° In 1937, the Federal Housing Administration published a model restrictive covenant, which was dropped in 1949 under pressure from the NAACP.

good in heartening fashion." Granger cited the employment of 6,000 black workers in ordnance plants, 5,000 in aircraft plants where virtually none existed in 1940. In shipbuilding, Negro employment rose from 6,952 in December 1941 to 12,820 by April 1942; and from 6,000 to 14,000 over the same period in navy shipyards. Startling progress, too, was made in federal employment. In 1938, Negroes were 8.4 percent of all federal employees in Washington; in 1944, they constituted 19.2 percent. Much more significant was the change in the character of federal employment of Negroes. In 1938, 90 percent of all Negroes in government service were in custodial jobs; by 1944, 60 percent were working in other job classifications.

The Fair Employment Practices Committee held five major hearings, four—in Los Angeles, Chicago, New York, and Birmingham—within its first year and one on the railroad industry in fall 1943. While gains in Negro employment paralleled a growing labor shortage, the presence of FEPC encouraged Negroes to apply for jobs and employers to hire where they might not have otherwise done so. At its peak, the committee closed an average of 250 cases a month, and of these, 100 were satisfactorily adjusted. As the FEPC *First Report* observed, "Southern shipyards were persuaded to use Negro welders, aircraft plants to upgrade Mexican-Americans, white workers to cooperate with colored workers on the same production lines. Reluctant eastern manufacturers of highly involved war mechanisms through experience discarded their belief that Negro workers could not acquire the requisite skills. Government agencies accepted in new positions qual-ified minority workers referred by Civil Service . . . ."

Two years after the start of the defense effort, in March 1942, Negroes constituted only 2.5 to 3 percent of all workers employed in war production. By November 1944, nonwhites, of whom about 96 percent were Negroes, constituted 8.3 percent of war workers whose industries filed reports with the War Manpower Commission. Negro employment in skilled crafts, as foremen and semiskilled workers, doubled from half a million to one million between April 1940 and April 1944. During the same four years, the most active for FEPC, Negro civilian employment rose by one million persons.

The June 1942 Birmingham fair employment hearings raised a political storm among blacks and whites, among supporters and opponents of the committee. FEPC Chairman Mark Ethridge opened the inquiries by trying to calm the South, and informed a Birmingham audience, "There is no power in the world—not even in all the mechanized armies of the earth, Allied and Axis—which could now force the Southern white people to the abandonment of the principle of social segregation." Negro Americans were furious, but the Southerners had the political muscle. Clearly, the President was not eager to expend his carefully husbanded personal political capital to mobilize public support for FEPC. Congressional elections were coming up. The governors of Alabama and Georgia attacked FEPC, and a week later, in July 1942, the President demoted the agency from a position of executive independence to that of a dependency on the War Manpower Commission, headed by Paul V. McNutt.

McNutt canceled plans for FEPC hearings into the railroad industry while assuring the Negro public that "All of the Manpower Commission is behind it [FEPC]." The committee was reorganized, following the resignation of its chairman and two other members. (The Negro members remained, however.) A. Philip Randolph called a "Save FEPC Conference" in Washington, D.C. on February 15, 1943. In May 1943, well after the elections, a rising black and liberal protest, centering on the conference, caused the President to restore a measure of independence to the FEPC. It was reconstituted as an independent agency within the the Office of Production Management and was later incorporated in the newly created War Production Board. The railroad hearings were rescheduled, but hearings into discrimination against Mexican-Americans, called off by the President at the suggestion of Under Secretary of State Sumner Welles, who feared their effect on Latin America, were never held. When the railroads and the operating unions refused to comply with an FEPC directive ordering them to cease discriminatory practices, FEPC's shaky underpinnings became all too clear. In 1945, Congress, viewing the agency as a wartime executive measure, appropriated $250,000 to enable the committee to "terminate its functions" and the committee went out of existence on June 28, 1946, when it issued its final report.

For a time after winning FEPC, it appeared that Randolph might be the new Garvey or Father Divine, moving the Negro masses as only those two essentially religious figures had. The *Amsterdam News* hailed Randolph as a "courageous champion . . . ranked with the great Frederick Douglass. His name is rapidly becoming a household word." On June 16, 1942, close to twenty thousand Negroes rallied at Madison Square Garden in New York City to honor Randolph, though the meeting was billed as a "mobilization" for jobs, equal rights, and justice. Sixteen thousand turned out in Chicago, and twelve thousand in St. Louis at similar rallies. Edwin R. Embree, in *13 Against the Odds*, wrote, "The power of the new movement is mysterious. It has almost no organization, no big machine for promotion and publicity. Yet it grips the people's imagination and holds their loyalty. Masses of the darker common people are looking to Randolph as the modern messiah."

Randolph, however, was neither a chiliastic figure nor a demagogue. His initial intentions were modest indeed, given the magnitude of the march's achievement and the adulation of his followers. "It's my aim," he declared shortly after the President issued his executive order, "to broaden and strengthen the Negro March on Washington committees all over the United States to serve as watchdogs on the application of the President's executive order to determine how industries are complying with it." Again and again, however, he stressed "the plan of a protest march has not been abandoned." The Negro, he told a group of his followers at a Detroit policy conference at the end of September 1942, "needs mass organization with an action program, aggressive, bold, and challenging in spirit." While he acknowledged the value of "friendly white citizens to give moral support to a fight against the poll tax or white primaries," Randolph insisted that the march must remain an all-Negro movement. "The essential value of an all-Negro movement," he argued, "is that it helps to create faith by Negroes in Negroes. It develops a sense of self-reliance with Negroes depending on Negroes in vital matters. It helps to break down the slave psychology and inferiority complex in Negroes which comes and is nourished with Negroes relying on white people for direction and support."

Randolph clearly was searching for an appropriate vehicle for channeling black discontent into fruitful action. He constantly reiterated the importance of trade unionism, "because well-nigh 99.9 percent of the Negro people are workers of hand and brawn who earn their living in the sweat of their brow by selling their labor in the market for wages." Progress for the Negro, Randolph was convinced, depended "in a large measure upon cleansing the labor unions and personnel manager systems of the sins of race prejudice. This is one fight Negro and white workers must wage which they cannot afford to lose since trade unions are the main bulwark of democracy." Though he urged Negro workers to join the AFL or CIO unions—whichever held jurisdiction where they worked—Randolph was less certain about the character of the needed black protest organization: Was it to have a mass membership, or be an umbrella grouping of all existing Negro institutions? "Our first job," he informed the March on Washington Detroit conference delegates, "is actually to organize millions of Negroes, and build them into block systems with captains so that they may be summoned to action overnight and thrown into physical motion. Without this type of organization, Negroes will never develop mass power which is the most effective weapon a minority people can wield." He drew a comparison with the Gandhian movement in India with its "mass civil disobedience and non-cooperation and the marches to the sea to make salt."

Gandhian civil disobedience, too, allowed for individual protest, satisfying the need to witness in the Quaker sense of the word. Small groups could take what Randolph termed "non-violent good will direct action" against specific acts of discrimination. In his compendium of strategies, "March on Washington Movement Presents a Program for the Negro," Randolph spelled out the direct action technique: "The white friends who precede the Negro patrons to a table in a given restaurant or hotel or place of amusement, upon seeing the Negro citizen denied service, will thereupon join the Negroes in requesting conference with the management to discuss the reason for the anti-Negro policy." If a conference is refused, or fails, successive steps may be taken, including picketing or a sit-down strike in the place "to bring the issue to a head." Before any form of direct action is engaged in, however, all the resources of negotiation must be exhausted. Violence is to be met with nonviolence. "Every individual who participates in such a project is pledged to non-violent action, to the extent of not even using violent language against the management or the employees." The beauty of the Gandhian strategy, in Randolph's view, was that it enabled blacks to protest utilizing a range of possible actions from the individual to the broadest of mass participation. When masses would not follow, leaders could "witness" or act in small groups to score important gains for their people. Using Gandhian strategy, a northern restaurant may be persuaded to serve Negroes as well as whites or Jim Crow in the South boycotted. Randolph acknowledged that "the barriers of racial discrimination in the southern section of the country cannot be abolished overnight and that they must be approached in terms of the conditions of the racial climate of the community. But it [the March on Washington] also insists that a policy of do-nothing is . . . dangerous and provocative." Negroes in the South, Randolph suggested, might refuse to send their children to a Jim Crow school, or avoid the Jim Crow railroad coach "as a leper," or boycott Jim Crow streetcars and buses on specific days chosen for "these forms of social discipline and response, which, of course, can only follow well-planned educational programs." It's only one method of attack, said Randolph, but one that "will have a psychological value of focusing the attention of the South upon this social cancer [Jim Crow]."

At the same time, Randolph stressed political action, urging "the building of a national nonpartisan Negro political bloc." Drawing upon the political lessons of organized labor, Randolph argued that "the technique of setting up such a bloc is simple, and consists in the *federation* [my italics] of religious, fraternal, civic, labor, educational, women, business, and various political groups upon a minimum political program." While Randolph skirted identifying the March on Washington Movement as that bloc, it seems implicit in his argument. Whether an umbrella organization such as the one envisioned in Randolph's "political bloc" strategy is compatible with mass membership, or in a position to mount mass protest at will as envisaged in the march's rhetoric, or can carry on the prolonged education for a sustained program of Gandhian group and/or individual protest, is surely problematical. Randolph was always an educator, but that impulse to spell out all the conceivable strategies of protest warred with the immediacy of his insistence on "the non-violent direct action technique of mass marches."

"Mass social pressure," Randolph believed, "in the form of marches and picketing will not only touch and arrest the attention of the powerful public officials but also the 'little man' in the street. And, before this problem of Jim Crow can be successfully attacked, all of America must be shocked and awakened. This has never been done, except by race riots that are dangerous socio-racial explosions. Moreover, mass efforts are a form of struggle for Negro rights in which all Negroes can participate, including the educated, the rich, and the poor. It is a technique and strategy which the 'little man' in the tavern, poolroom, on the streets, jitterbug, store-front preacher, and sharecropper can use to help free the race."

It is very difficult, however, to sustain the mood for marching without marching. Moreover, the circumstances of spring 1941 were not readily repeated. It is one thing to prepare a march on Washington when the country was not as yet at war, when buses and trains were available, and quite another thing when a nation is at war, gas-rationed, its trains crowded with soldiers on leave or committed to vital troop movements, and when patriotism runs high. Many of the blacks that one might count on to march were working long hours in defense plants, shipyards, or in the armed services. And, in fact, the March on Washington Movement did not grow; it faltered. New units were organized in fall 1942 in Mobile and Montgomery, Alabama, and in Flint, Michigan, where a mass rally of two hundred to three hundred black workers won production jobs for Negro janitors. The New York division reported the success of three block captains in recruiting "more members in September 1942, than in any other month since the Movement came into existence"—590 as against 162 in the preceding month. Nonetheless, the March on Washington Movement soon became another hat worn by various local chapters of the Brotherhood of Sleeping Car Porters.

Randolph's shifting strategies revealed a search for answers to the problems blacks faced in the 1940s and reflected as well the internal weaknesses of the March on Washington Movement. Herbert Garfinkel, in *When Negroes March*, argues that "when Randolph sought to make clear that the march tactic was but one form of mass pressure available to the March as an organization, he was misunderstood and his influence waned." Other factors, too, worked against building the march into a lasting civil rights organization. Randolph was never a good administrator, and perhaps of greater importance, the established leadership of the National Association for the Advancement of Colored People, the National Urban League, the Negro press, and other institutions were not about to allow another into the field if they could help it, especially one with a potential mass appeal. To these, and other factors, one must add the mass of Negroes who were caught up in a civil rights movement of their own in the 1940s, a renewal of the Great Migration out of the cotton patches and tobacco fields into the cities and out of the South into the North.

Countless blacks were asking, as Langston Hughes did:

> Why should it be *my* loneliness,
> Why should it be *my* song,
> Why should it be *my* dream
> deferred
> overlong?

And, they answered, with their feet. In increasing number, they left the land. In 1940, approximately one-half of all Negroes worked on farms; in 1944, less than one-third were so employed. Roughly 300,000 blacks left agricultural pursuits for the factory. Between 1940 and 1950, 1.2 million blacks moved out of the former confederacy. Most migrated to the cities of Illinois, Michigan, New York, Ohio, and Pennsylvania. But others went west. The black population of Los Angeles rose from about 64,000 to roughly 150,000, and similar growths occurred in the industrial communities of San Francisco, Portland, and Seattle.

To the degree that they moved in search of better jobs, the march of the people was a tribute to the March on Washington's success in securing Executive Order 8802. But as Randolph recognized, there was something more here than a simple search for job opportunities. As he put it, "Migration movements of Negroes from the South are instances of Non-Violent Good Will Direct Action." For many headed North, as Richard Wright did at the end of *Black Boy*, "full of a hazy notion that life could be lived with dignity, that the personalities of others should not be violated, that men should be able to confront other men without fear or shame, and that if men were lucky in their living on earth they might win some redeeming meaning for having struggled and suffered here beneath the stars."

For Americans, black or white, leaving agriculture for factory usually has meant a decided improvement in income. While blacks have lagged behind whites, the jump in the nonwhite male median income from $460 a year in 1939 to $1,279 in 1947 was impressive. As a percentage of white male median income, the black rose from 41.5 percent to 54.3 percent over the same period. Home ownership among nonwhites, admittedly lower than among whites, hovering between 24 to 25 percent from 1900 to 1940, advanced sharply to over 30-odd percent by 1950. (The percentages are derived from Bureau of Census figures.)

Such changes for the better were not scorned by the sharecropper deserting his drafty shack for the slums of Atlanta, Chicago, Detroit, Los Angeles, New York, or Philadelphia.

Blacks in motion were engaged in a civil rights act. In the light of the angry outbreaks of Detroit and Harlem in the summer of 1943, one cannot describe the mood of black Americans at the time as euphoric. Slums may be turbulent with vitality, but roach-infested, sleazy tenements also breed despair and disillusionment. Still, a people on the move, with a one-way ticket to "any place that is/ North and West—/ And not South," seeking "The cold-faced North,/ For she, they say,/ Is a kinder mistress,/ And in her house my children/ May escape the spell of the South," may not be in the mood to march on Washington. Poet Langston Hughes, in his poems "One-Way Ticket" and "The South," expressed Randolph's fundamental problem in organizing a new form of black protest; not apathy, but a feeling of movement taking place was perhaps the greatest bar to developing the March on Washington Movement into a mass membership organization. To the extent that blacks joined the NAACP—and they did so in increasing number—it was a conservative choice, and one more in keeping with the mood of the time.

Still, there were undercurrents, sudden swirls of emotion belying the calm acceptance of wartime priorities. The March on Washington Movement and the Pittsburgh *Courier*'s "Double V" campaign—victory at home *and* abroad—were essentially black, racialist, or race proud without nationalistic overtones. As Randolph repeatedly declared, "The fight to annihilate Jim Crow must be led by Negroes with the cooperation and collaboration of white liberals and labor." The NAACP was interracial in its leadership and actively sought white allies in its drives for anti-lynching and anti-poll tax legislation. During the war, however, most white allies held a somewhat different order of priorities than did the leaders of America's black communities. As Walter White observed in his Madison Square Garden speech, "the tragedy of the situation is that only a few intelligent and brave souls like Mrs. Roosevelt, Pearl Buck and one or two writers in the white world are wise enough to see the picture as it is." Mary McLeod Bethune brought cheers from the rally of twenty thousand on June 16, 1942, when she cried out, "We have grown tired of turning the other cheek. Both our cheeks are now so blistered they are too sensitive for further blows."

On June 20, 1943, a hot Sunday in Detroit, a fist fight occurred between a Negro and a white man. Soon there were sporadic fights all over Belle Isle, a recreational park on the Detroit River. That night, an unidentified Negro grabbed the microphone at a dance hall and made an impassioned speech, exhorting his thousand-odd listeners to avenge the "killings" by whites of a Negro mother and her child, who had been thrown in the river and drowned. Hundreds of enraged black men dashed out of the dance hall and headed for Belle Isle but were turned by a police detail. Wild rumors swept Paradise Valley, and soon angry blacks were attacking every white person met in that black neighborhood. Cars were overturned, and looting began. Whites gathered to attack Negroes as they emerged from all-night movies in downtown Detroit. Negro and white bands roved the city, but oddly, as Roi Ottley later reported in *Black Odyssey*, never clashing though finding more than enough victims. At the end of thirty hours, by the time the President proclaimed an emergency and sent six thousand soldiers to patrol the streets, twenty-five Negroes and nine whites were dead, six hundred injured and $2 million in property was either stolen or damaged. Another less bloody riot ensued in Harlem that summer when a white policeman tangled with a black soldier over the arrest of a black woman. Six persons died, five hundred were injured, and there was much burning and looting of stores.

Few paused in the midst of war to consider the significance or import of the Detroit and Harlem riots. Most, no doubt, agreed with President Roosevelt's observation that such race clashes "endanger our national unity and comfort our enemies. I am sure every American regrets this." Pauli Murray, a poet, then a student at Howard Law School and later a visiting professor of American Civilization at Brandeis, fired off an angry bitter poem, *Mr. Roosevelt Regrets*.

> What'd you get, black boy,
> When they knocked you down in the gutter,
> And they kicked your teeth out,
> And they broke your skull with clubs,
> And they bashed your stomach in? . . .
>
> What'd the Top Man say, black boy?
> "Mr. Roosevelt regrets . . . ?

Writing in the Socialist party publication, *The Call*, shortly after the Harlem riot, Miss Murray also raised a question that would haunt black leaders and civil rights spokesmen to this day:

> "What did we accomplish?" For the tragedy of the Harlem riot was mine, the shame was mine, the responsibility was mine just as if I had thrown a whiskey bottle through a window and had reached my own hand inside. I was a "trained Negro," but the bankruptcy of our leadership had been eloquently expressed by the mood of a mob. We also had spun out our word appeals on the race problem. We had not been strong enough or sacrificial enough to reach the masses of Negroes and

organize them into intelligent action, into disciplined and orderly protest, and the mobs had taken matters into their own hands . . . .

What the "hoodlums" had done was what the mass mind had thought.

America, however, paid little attention. Nevertheless, some were moved to protest racial discrimination, even though their actions or words were heard by but a few. Cases of the kind that would catch headlines and loom large on television in the 1960s, rarely, if ever, rated a paragraph or two in the country's major daily newspapers. At Freedman Field, Indiana, more than one hundred Negro officers were arrested for attempting to enter a Jim Crow officers' club. Sergeant Alton Levy, a young socialist and a former International Ladies' Garment Workers' Union organizer, protested the treatment of Negro soldiers stationed at the Lincoln, Nebraska, air base. Three hundred illiterate black soldiers were quartered in segregated barracks some two miles distant from their instructors. They were issued canvas cots instead of the regulation cots with mattresses. As Levy wrote a friend, the black soldiers were "hounded, harassed and yelled at and cursed and insulted." Sergeant Levy did what he could to alleviate conditions, trying to get the black soldiers more liberty passes and a recreation hall. He also spoke up on their behalf at staff meetings and to his officers. In late July 1943, there was a "blow-up," a fight between some Negro soldiers and some Mexican-Americans, and a week or so later, Sergeant Levy was court-martialed for "conduct unbecoming a soldier." He had, so the charges detailed, called the commanding officer "a drunkard," made derogatory remarks about the running of the post, and made statements about the mistreatment of the Negro G.I.s. The affair had all the trappings of a high-class spy thriller: a lovely WAC noncommissioned officer dated Levy and subsequently testified against him. Presumably, she was a plant made by the air base's intelligence officers. Levy denied making derogatory statements, but freely admitted his remarks about the treatment of the Negro soldiers, and indeed amplified them while on the witness stand and under oath. Ironically, the trial judge thought the case against Levy so weak that he predicted acquittal. Nevertheless, the trial court convicted Sergeant Levy on all counts, reduced him in rank to private, and sentenced him to four months at hard labor. His protest, however, did stir up some action. The Army ordered an investigation into the treatment of the black soldiers, and they began getting passes. It was, as Levy wrote, "a bit of a break."

Levy's letters to his friend were published in the Socialist party weekly, *The Call*, and attracted some attention. The Workers' Defense League, a socialist-oriented labor and civil rights defense agency, took his case. Roger Baldwin, James Carey, David Dubinsky, Lester Granger, Reinhold Niebuhr, A. Philip Randolph, Victor Reuther, Norman Thomas, Willard Townsend, Roy Wilkins, and Charles S. Zimmerman were among the labor and liberal figures who spoke up for Sergeant Levy. This public protest finally won Sergeant Levy his freedom after he had served three months of his sentence.

A nation at war paid scant attention to such matters, almost as little as it paid to the plight of its minorities. Over 110,000 citizens of Japanese descent, men, women, and children, charged with no crime, were evacuated from the West Coast into concentration camps by presidential fiat. Liberal Americans, with the notable exception of Norman Thomas, John Dos Passos, Arthur Garfield Hays, Pearl Buck, A. Philip Randolph, and Harry Emerson Fosdick, were silent. The predominantly black United Transport Service Employees spoke up in protest as did the Socialist party, the West Coast Civil Liberties committees, the California Race Relations Commission, and the Fellowship of Reconciliation. The American Civil Liberties Union evaded the issue by accepting the constitutionality of the evacuation and relocation powers exercised by the military under the President's proclamation of February 19, 1942.

The ACLU, however, did attack what it regarded as abuses of discretion in carrying out the order. Liberals presumably fell into line because of their support of the war, but, as Norman Thomas wrote in a pamphlet, "Democracy and Japanese Americans," "it is clear that the American feeling about the treatment of the Japanese is not born exclusively of the fact that we are at war with the country of their origin, but arises mostly from race prejudice."

Negroes moving into the cities and taking new jobs perhaps found the "kind of looseness about this here freedom" that pleased an ex-slave once interviewed by sociologist Robert E. Park,° but they also found Jim Crow dogging their flight to freedom. Recreational facilities were often closed to them, and restaurants refused to serve them. One evening, in the spring of 1942, James Farmer, then a race relations secretary of the Fellowship of Reconciliation (FOR), a religious pacifist group, and James R. Robinson, a student at the University of Chicago, stopped for a cup of coffee at a restaurant called the Jack Sprat, near the university. They were served reluctantly, and only after reminding the manager that he would violate a state law if he refused. At that, he tried to get twenty-five cents out of Farmer for a nickel doughnut.

° Park used to tell a story of an old ex-slave whom he met in Alabama. The old man was poor, and undoubtedly worse off in all material respects than under slavery. In fact, he used to boast about what a good life he had had under his old master. Park asked him whether he was sorry about having been emancipated, and the old man replied that, no, he liked freedom—for, he said, "There's a kind of looseness about this here freedom."

Several days later, an interracial group was served with obvious reluctance, and when they left, the manager raked their money off the counter and threw it after them into the street, shouting, "Take your money and get out."

The rather earnest group of college youth, alas, did not act on someone's proposal that they parade through the Negro community with signs proclaiming, "Jack Sprat Serves Negroes Free." Being neophyte Gandhians, they took counsel with the appropriate texts— Krishnalal Shridharani's *War Without Violence* and the Indian Congress party's manual of tactics. Out of these consultations came a plan of action that would with variations serve as a basic civil rights strategy down through the famous 1961 Freedom Rides. First, gather the facts, then seek negotiations, and failing negotiations, take nonviolent direct action.

"On the eighth day," Farmer later recalled, "we staged what I believe to have been the first civil rights sit-in." An interracial group of about twenty-five entered the restaurant at dinnertime and quietly seated themselves at various places. Several of the whites were served promptly, and the blacks were told they must eat in the basement. The whites did not eat, and when this caught the attention of the manager, they explained that they thought it impolite to eat until their friends had been served. A stalemate soon developed, and the police were summoned. But the group had forewarned the local police station, even reading the unfamiliar state law barring discrimination in public places to the captain. When the police officers called back for instructions, they were told that nothing in the law allowed them to eject the "demonstrators" so long as they remained peaceable. Shortly after that, the manager capitulated and the restaurant service was integrated.

Out of this simple incident, the Congress of Racial Equality (CORE) was born. A. Philip Randolph's quest for appropriate and effective civil rights strategies plus his Gandhian soundings had evoked a response among these young pacifists and radicals. The group in Chicago formed a Committee of Racial Equality, working up a series of projects testing the Illinois law against discrimination in public places. Similar groups sprang up in various cities around the country, some pacifist-inspired after the Chicago group, while others, like the Vanguard Movement in Columbus, Ohio, sprang out of the black community. Interestingly, those that came out of the various black communities tended to stress discrimination problems on the job front while those that were interracial in origin tended to concentrate on discrimination in public places. In Kansas City, the group did not use the name CORE for fear that the term "racial equality" would make their work unnecessarily more difficult.

Independently of this development, Farmer had submitted a memorandum to FOR proposing the establishment of an interracial organization which would apply Gandhian techniques in attacking segregation, "not to make housing in ghettoes more tolerable, but to destroy residential segregation; not to make racial discrimination more bearable, but to wipe it out; . . . to repudiate every form of racism [and to] forge the instrumentalities through which that nationwide repudiation can be effected." Farmer was authorized by FOR to set up a pilot project in Chicago, and as he put it, "we [FOR and the Chicago students] had only to stretch out our hands to one another, and a movement was created."

Some fifteen or so like-minded committees or groups came together in Chicago in June 1943 to form the Congress of Racial Equality. The delegates formulated a statement of purpose and worked out what they called "action discipline." The statement of purpose was to eliminate all racial segregation and discrimination by means of interracial, nonviolent direct action. The action discipline pledged each member to maintain nonviolence of word and deed, regardless of provocation; it demanded humility in the face of one's own inadequacy, and understanding and goodwill before the anger of opponents. It also called for strict group discipline: All members had to obey the designated project leader. No one could withdraw from a project once he had agreed to participate in it unless he felt incapable of remaining nonviolent, in which case, he was to withdraw at once. The group, on the other hand, guaranteed each individual an important voice in all project planning and policy making, and pledged to support him in any difficulty into which CORE activities might lead him.

Though CORE drew on Gandhi's experience and teachings, the organization's philosophy was also rooted in the Quaker notion of witnessing. In the summer of 1942, Bayard Rustin, a former youth organizer for the March on Washington Movement, and a FOR field staff member, took a bus from Louisville, Kentucky, to Nashville, Tennessee. Refusing to sit in the Jim Crow section at the back of the bus, young Rustin informed the angry, frustrated driver, "If I were to sit in back, I would be condoning injustice." Beaten and arrested, he responded with a lesson in nonviolence. It ended, Rustin later recalled, with an assistant district attorney in Nashville, saying, "very kindly, 'You may go, *Mister* Rustin.' "

Writing in *Fellowship*, the monthly journal of the pacifist Fellowship of Reconciliation, Rustin concluded, "I left the courthouse believing all the more strongly in the nonviolent approach. I am certain that I was addressed as 'Mister' (as no Negro is ever addressed in the South), that I was assisted by those three men [who had remonstrated with the police rough-handling Rustin], and that elderly gentleman [a fellow passenger] interested himself in my predicament because I had, without fear, faced the four policemen and said, 'There is no need to beat me. I offer you no resistance.'" It was a lesson Rustin would preach widely in the tumultuous decades that followed, and among his listeners would be a young preacher, Martin Luther King, Jr.

Boycotts, demonstrations, and picketing are tactics refined by the labor movement in decades of struggle for recognition. They have also proved useful in countless battles against discrimination. In 1929, for example, the *Chicago Whip*, a black community weekly, organized a series of boycotts and picket lines to secure jobs and upgrading for Negro workers in South Side business establishments. The butcher's union stepped in and demanded that the owner of a union market pay his Negro butcher the union wage of $45 a week rather than the eight or nine dollars he actually paid. When the owner refused, a union picket line was placed in front of the store, deliveries were stopped, and community leaders joined the picket line. "Don't Spend Your Money Where You Cannot Work," picket signs urged black customers. The owner soon capitulated. Adam Clayton Powell, Jr., Harlem's first congressman (elected in 1944), organized a Coordinating Committee for Employment in 1936, and its skillful use of the boycott and picket lines forced Harlem businesses to employ black workers. At first, the committee did not stipulate any particular percentage, but it soon demanded that 40 percent, and later 60 percent of the people hired by businesses along 125th Street be black. Similar tactics secured jobs for black workers in 1938 in Cleveland's five-and-ten-cent stores, Ohio Bell Telephone Company, dairy companies, bakeries, and other service firms. The March on Washington had its precedents in Coxey's Army of the unemployed which marched on the Capitol in 1894, the Bonus March of one thousand ex-servicemen in 1932, and the July 1917 march of eight thousand blacks down New York City's Fifth Avenue, protesting discrimination "to the beat of muffled drums" as thirty thousand black citizens looked on in "silent approval."

Civil disobedience, hunger-strikes, and sit-ins are Gandhian tactics, or techniques, which, ironically, achieved some of their first successes in this country's federal prisons. The Federal Correctional Institute at Danbury, Connecticut, was established in August 1940 on a segregated basis. It opened with five hundred inmates—among them, one hundred conscientious objectors, ninety Jehovah's Witnesses, and sixty Negroes. When several of the conscientious objectors protested, segregation was partially abolished. In August 1943, twenty-three pacifists went on strike, protesting continued segregation in the mess hall. They were placed in isolation cells where they remained for four and a half months. Letters were censored, and no mention of the strike was permitted. There matters may well have rested but for the help received from the outside. Pacifist organizations naturally publicized the strike as best they could, but it was the Negro press that gave it the widest audience. The NAACP offered help, and finally the warden announced that the mess hall would be integrated.

The two strategies—that of mass action and of nonviolent civil disobedience—would come together in the civil rights movement of the 1960s. This coupling of mass action and Gandhian techniques would prove to be unfeasible until the waking of the South during the Montgomery bus boycott of 1955–56. CORE, in its early years, never developed a mass membership, nor was it ever successful in the Deep South. Its greatest success was with small interracial committees in Chicago and such border cities as Cincinnati, St. Louis, and Washington, D.C. "Attacking race," George Houser, a founder of CORE, has said, "was the clearest issue one could use and provided an area of social action where one could apply nonviolence as a methodology. For a group of young people who wanted to be a part of the struggle for justice in this world, the war issue was one which caught you up and on which you took a certain position but you were not in as good a position for accomplishing something as you were when you were dealing with something right on your own doorstep. CORE was a way that you could make the whole thing come to life and have meaning, and something that you could touch, feel, and see, and possibly win. You weren't trying to change a policy of a government or of the world but you were dealing with a particular barber shop or restaurant or roller-skating rink or whatever."

But CORE had a much wider impact than its small number might signify. It built up a body of experience upon which the Montgomery bus boycotters, the sit-iners and freedom riders, and the marchers on Washington would draw in the decades ahead. By integrating restaurants, roller-skating rinks, barber shops, and swimming pools in northern and border-state cities, CORE's gallant band contributed significantly to the halting of Jim Crow at the Mason-Dixon line. If it had not been for the March on Washington, the President's Executive Order 8802, and CORE, segregation may well have become as deeply ingrained in the North as it was in the South. Civil rights strategies changed as the war developed and came to an end, as black people migrated into the cities and north and west, and as southern blacks took heart and began to fight for their rights. Race relations as truly an American dilemma was a legacy of World War II. As Secretary of the Interior Harold L. Ickes wrote to the President in 1943, "Although [discrimination] can be nibbled at ineffectually locally, it cannot be handled except on a comprehensive national scale. This is not a local question. It is a national one."

IV

To Secure
These Rights

Α T THE END OF WORLD WAR
II, America found itself, in the perceptive phrase of historian Eric P.
Goldman, "in the nagging realm of maybe." Elated by the sudden
release of energies pentup by the exigencies of war, Americans were
also fearful—worried lest "boom" become "bust," and progress,
reaction, and victory be but a prelude to another war. The clouds that
mushroomed over Hiroshima and Nagasaki haunted the postwar mind.
No one was truly exempt from the pervasive euphoric anxiety; few
noticed the shadings within the dominant mood. White defense workers
left quonset huts in Los Angeles, Detroit, and Hartford to head back
home to Alabama, Oklahoma, and the hills of Tennessee; black workers,
however, remained in Watts, west of Woodward Avenue in Detroit,
and in Newark's Central Ward, seeking work wherever they might find
it rather than return to a segregated Southland. Charles G. Bolte,
writing in *Harper's* magazine, cautioned, "in the twelve million veterans
who are disillusioned with the promise of democracy there lies a grave
potential danger" and hinted fearfully at the ex-G.I. potential for
fascism. Walter White wrote of a rising wind, "a wind of determination
by the have-nots of the world to share the benefits of freedom and
prosperity which the haves of the earth have tried to keep exclusively
for themselves." Negro soldiers returning home, White declared in his
report of the postwar mood, *A Rising Wind*, "are determined to work
for freedom as never before."

While no one appeared ready to march on Washington, the nation's
capital was nonetheless a felt presence for most black Americans.
Executive Order 8802 had improved the lot of black workers, and more
federal jobs were opening up for black citizens. Yet, a black soldier
discharged in the North, returning South for a visit, changed to Jim

Crow trains at Pennsylvania Station in Washington, D.C. If the ex-G.I. of color decided to stay overnight, he would find that he could neither eat in a downtown restaurant nor attend a downtown movie or play, nor sleep in a downtown hotel. Should he decide to live in Washington, his children would be condemned to an inferior, segregated education, and if sick, would not be admitted to District hospitals. Segregated slums festered in the shadow of the nation's capital, and black Americans wondered if a Southern-dominated Congress would extend fair employment practices on into the postwar world, abolish the poll tax, and end lynching. Professor Goldman, in *The Crucial Decade—and After*, accurately described the mood of most Americans at the opening of the decade that followed the surrender of Japan in August 1945: "The sense of a scarifying future was accompanied by memories of the last postwar, jabbing, mocking memories. In the America of V-J, the story went around how Franklin Roosevelt had kept a picture of Woodrow Wilson hanging in the meeting room of the War Cabinet, frequently glancing toward it when he discussed the coming years, and everybody got the point of the tale. Woodrow Wilson also had led the United States to victory in a world war. Then came the hard times of 1920–21, less than a decade of prosperity, the brutal depression of the 1930s, and the furies of World War II." For black Americans, such memories were even more disturbing. Woodrow Wilson had segregated federal Washington. Black soldiers had returned from the War to Save Democracy to confront rampant white supremacy in a resurrected Ku Klux Klan. More than seventy Negroes were lynched during the first year of the post-World War I period. Fourteen were burned publicly, eleven of these victims were burned alive. Ten Negro soldiers, several still in uniform, were murdered by mobs in Alabama, Arkansas, Florida, Georgia, and Mississippi. There were twenty-five riots in the summer of 1919. White sailors, soldiers, and marines ran amok through the streets of the nation's capital, killing several Negroes and injuring scores of others. Thirty-eight persons—fifteen whites and twenty-three blacks—were killed in the thirteen-day Chicago race riot. These bitter memories were overlaid by the more recent ones of harsh racial outbreaks in Detroit and Harlem during the summer of 1943.

Writing in *The Crisis* of January 1945, Ernest E. Johnson, veteran journalist and chief of the Washington Bureau of the Associated Negro Press, noted that the NAACP, a leader in the fight for anti-lynching legislation, "has not been unusually vocal on the subject since the outbreak of war." However, he predicted an intensification of anti-lynching efforts "because there is going to be a revival of lynching." An angry August *Crisis* editorial, "Race Hatred First on Agenda of U.S. Congress," blasted the cold shouldering of FEPC by congressmen, and taking note of the racist speeches by Senators James O. Eastland and

Theodore G. Bilbo, declared: "If the performance of both houses of the Congress on the matter of the Fair Employment Practices Committee is a true indication of what the country may expect in the postwar period, then we are in for an era of tension and racial and religious hatred."

Yet the Negro mood, at least at the leadership level, was tempered by a restrained optimism. When Georgia dropped the poll tax, in part as a consequence of the 1944 United States Supreme Court decision, *Smith v. Allwright*, banning the exclusionist "white primary" elections of the South, *Crisis* proclaimed, "One has to rub one's eyes at these developments. 'The sun,' as the old preacher declared, 'do move.' " Negroes registered to vote in increasing numbers: In 1940, Ralph Bunche estimated fewer than 250,000 Negro voters in the southern states. By 1948, after the Supreme Court's knockdown of the Texas white primary, there were 750,000 colored persons registered to vote in twelve southern states, according to an NAACP estimate. These gains were scored despite violence and intimidation, which increased markedly in the congressional elections of 1946. Senator Bilbo urged whites to employ any means to bar Negroes from voting, and several states adopted "qualification" standards under which Negroes could be barred from voting by administrative action. In Alabama, voters had to explain the Constitution; Arkansas merely held separate state and national primary elections, with Negroes barred from the former altogether. Despite adversity, Negroes continued to register, and registration rose from 5 percent of the voting-age southern Negroes in 1940 to 28 percent in 1952. Two Negroes, both Democrats, sat in Congress: Representative William L. Dawson of Chicago (elected in 1942 to replace a black Republican, Arthur W. Mitchell), and Adam Clayton Powell, Jr. (elected in 1944), reflecting the growth of black political power in the North. Northern states and cities began adopting their own FEPC statutes after the expiration of the federal commission. Border-state Governor Simeon S. Willis of Kentucky announced in late 1945 that Negroes would be appointed to state administrative positions for the first time; in November, H. O. Reid became the first Negro appointed as a Massachusetts Supreme Court law clerk, and Jackie Robinson signed with the Brooklyn Dodgers, becoming the first Negro player admitted to major league baseball. School segregation ended, at least for a time, in cities like Trenton, New Jersey, and Gary, Indiana; hospitals in St. Louis and Gary lifted restrictions against Negro physicians. Encouraged by the influx of Negro workers into the ranks of organized labor and similar developments, the first Negro president of Fisk University, sociologist Charles S. Johnson, sat down to write a book, and chose for his title, *Into the Mainstream*.

There was movement into the mainstream of American life, but there were jarring rejections. Six Negroes were lynched in 1946. Not one of the lynchings was the quasi-public spectacle so common scarcely fifteen years earlier when lynchings averaged over fifty victims a year. Brutality and physical disfigurement, however, continued to be an earmark of this barbaric crime. According to a Monroe County, Georgia, coroner's report, over sixty bullets were fired into the barely recognizable bodies of Roger Malcolm, a young Negro accused of stabbing his employer during the course of an argument, and George Dorsey, a Negro overseas veteran, and their wives, who were with them at the time of their release on bail and capture by the mob. Two deputy sheriffs in Minden, Louisiana, and three other persons were indicted and brought to trial in a federal court for their part in a mob-murder of a Negro suspect in a housebreaking case, which was progress as these things were then measured. They were, such were the standards, acquitted. Somewhat more encouraging were police reports that, in 1946, mobs were prevented from lynching twenty-two persons, of whom twenty-one were black and one white.

"All the advances which minorities made during the New Deal and the war seem to be in question," the *Cleveland Plain Dealer* said in 1946. Would there be a revival of the dread Ku Klux Klan? Would mob violence be used to force black Americans back into their "place"? Over sixty hate organizations flooded the country with viciously anti-Semitic, anti-Catholic, anti-labor, and anti-foreign-born literature. Southern cities and towns and a few in the North invested great sums in anti-riot weaponry in fear of armed insurrection from organized labor or returning Negro veterans. The new police commissioner of a mid-western industrial city invited Walter White to drop in for a visit. When the NAACP leader did so, the commissioner showed him enough guns and ammunition to cause White, as he put it in his autobiography, to feel that "I was overseas again in a battle area." "My predecessor bought all this," the commissioner told White, "to take care of any 'bad niggers' who come home with any fancy ideas about occupying a different status from that they knew before they left."

The tactics of legalized violence coupled with mass arrests were tried one tumultuous night in Columbia, Tennessee. With a population of roughly twelve thousand, the boyhood home of President James K. Polk, and the site of the world's largest mule market, Columbia is a prosperous county seat in blue-grass country, forty-two miles south of Nashville on the banks of the Duck River. Columbia's black minority of about two thousand were presumed by whites "to know their place," chiefly a district with the Faulknerian name, Mink Slide.

On Monday morning, February 25, 1946, Gladys Stephenson, a soft-spoken cook for one of Columbia's leading white families, and her nineteen-year-old son, James, entered the Costner-Knott Appliance Store. Mrs. Stephenson was dissatisfied with the repair work done on her radio, for which she had been overcharged. She upbraided the owner, and he and one of his employees struck Mrs. Stephenson. James Stephenson, recently discharged from the Navy after three years service in the Pacific, slugged the repairman, knocking him through a plate-glass window. As a *Crisis* editorial wryly put it: "There it was, an assault case, a police matter."

By evening, however, a mob numbering roughly seventy-five white men gathered in the town square. Columbia had had two lynchings over the past twenty-two years, and when it was reported that a rope had been purchased by a member of the mob, the black community became understandably nervous. The Stephensons were spirited away to Nashville for safety, and the sheriff dispersed the mob before the jail by leveling a tommy gun. Two white men, barely able to stand, were arrested for drunkenness.

Fearful of mob action, black Columbians turned out the lights in Mink Slide and barricaded themselves against the possibility of an invasion by armed whites. When night fell, four of Columbia's eight-man police force entered the darkened Negro district. Nothing indicated that they were law enforcement officers, and they appeared to be the advance guard of a rope-carrying, rifle-toting mob. Someone cried out, "Here they come!" Shots were fired, and all four of the policemen were felled by shotgun pellets. The sheriff requested state aid, and by dawn, Mink Slide was ringed by a force of five hundred highway patrolmen and state guardsmen carrying submachine guns.

Once Mink Slide was secured, the troopers were set loose "to restore order." Homes were searched without warrants, and where residents failed to answer knocks on the door, the troopers fired submachine gun bursts into the building. Black business establishments were looted and wrecked. The office of a Negro dentist was destroyed beyond recovery, and the desks, records, and files of the local office of the Atlanta Life Insurance Company were smashed. Invading the Morton Funeral Home, the troopers destroyed records, broke the chandeliers, floor lamps, and venetian blinds. Caskets were deliberately soiled, and one was marked "KKK" in white powder. Law enforcement officers shot up the big mirror in the barber shop, cut up the four barber chairs, and stole all the electric clippers. After State Safety Commissioner Lynn Bomar announced that the situation was "in hand," he reported the confiscation of "300 automatic rifles, pistols, knives, razors and other weapons . . . as well as much ammunition." What he did not say, however, was that much of the weaponry consisted of shotguns and rifles normally owned for hunting, a popular sport among blacks and whites in Tennessee. Among the hundred or so blacks arrested were the leading black businessmen of Columbia, Saul Blair, a 76-year-old merchant and patriarch, and James Morton, an undertaker for twenty-three years and a black civic figure. Two men were killed in the jail when one allegedly grabbed a rifle.

The official sanction of armed terror in Columbia alarmed black Americans. As a *Crisis* editorial declared, "It fulfilled predictions of many persons that mob violence would be used after the war to force the Negro back into his 'place.'" The outbreak also revealed a new militancy among black Americans, "that Negroes, even in small communities like Columbia where they were outnumbered three to one, do not intend to sit quietly and let a mob form, threaten, and raid their neighborhood." In the face of superior retaliatory forces, however, such defense actions were clearly inadequate. Walter White telegraphed Washington, asking that the Justice Department "act promptly and vigorously to safeguard constitutional rights of Negroes against state violation of those rights." It was a plea that would be central to civil rights throughout the postwar period. As the *Crisis* editorial warned, "Once the idea gets abroad that whites are free to do as they please, that Negroes are fair game for police, and that Negroes may not depend upon any authority, local, state, or federal for equal protection under the law, then we will have terror, riots and bloodshed, and death—and Storm Trooper Fascism in the flesh."

That summer, NAACP attorney Thurgood Marshall shuttled daily from Nashville to Columbia, serving as chief counsel for the twenty-five defendants charged with "attempted murder" in the "riot" case. Maurice Weaver, a young Navy veteran practicing law in Chattanooga who joined the defense team, was warned that his white body might be found at the bottom of Duck River. Alexander Looby, a West Indian-born member of the NAACP's national legal committee, faced danger with a dry wit and insouciance. The defense trio secured a change of venue to Lawrenceburg where over 750 jurors were examined in the five-week joust over jury selection. The trial had its farcical moments; the prosecuting attorney threatened to "wrap a chair around his [Looby's] head" and the judge smiled benignly at the prosecution's foul-mouthed racist tantrums. The all-white jury, however, acquitted twenty-three of the twenty-five defendants. The two found guilty were granted new trials and were subsequently acquitted.

The Lawrenceburg verdict was puzzling, for the circumstances did not allow a reading of the trial's outcome as a fresh wind cleansing the South of its racism. The state's case was exceptionally thin, and the jury may have reacted against the reliance on white supremacy by the prosecution. Vincent Sheean, who covered the trial for the New York *Herald-Tribune* and a number of other papers, stressed the competence of the defense attorneys, noting the success of the religious appeal made by one in his summation before the jury. Looby had varicose veins and had to speak from a seated position with his right leg propped on a cushion. In a West Indian accent that clearly fascinated the jury, Looby spoke forcefully and simply. "His essential argument," Sheean reported, "was of a purely religious nature and it was my impression that it reached home with that jury."

Columbia and its aftermath were a part of the uncertainties that plagued postwar America. Terror then justice: a nagging "maybe" conditioned all action and thought. Two minor riots, one in Athens, Alabama, in which one hundred Negroes were injured, and a second in Philadelphia where several were roughhoused, were promptly quelled by authorities. Isaac Woodard, a black soldier honorably discharged after three years in the Army and with fifteen months service in the jungles of the South Pacific, boarded a bus home to North Carolina, understandably eager to see his wife and family. En route, he was cursed by the bus driver ostensibly for causing a delay at a rest room. Later, in a town in South Carolina, Woodard was arrested, at the insistence of the bus driver, for drunkenness, although he did not drink. The town chief of police beat Woodard with a blackjack, and struck him in the eyes with the end of his nightstick. Kept in jail overnight without food or medical treatment, Woodard was blinded for life. The police chief was subsequently indicted, then acquitted. A NAACP fund-raising effort secured Woodard a modest annuity.

The termination of FEPC, implicit in the war emergency character of Executive Order 8802 (and in subsequent orders), threatened whatever employment gains black workers scored during the wartime economic boom. Naturally enough, the extension of FEPC into peacetime became a major civil rights goal. Again, A. Philip Randolph took the lead in pushing for a permanent Fair Employment Practices Commission. The wartime "Save the FEPC Conference" led to the formation of the interracial National Council for a Permanent FEPC in September 1943. Co-chaired by Randolph and Rev. Allen Knight Chalmers, the council opened a Washington office in early 1944 with Anna Arnold Hedgman, who came to her new job from the March on Washington Movement, serving as executive secretary. The council lobbied for strengthened congressional appropriations for the wartime FEPC and for the enactment of legislation to establish a permanent FEPC. Its strategies were dictated by those exigencies, and as a consequence, were hardly as militant as those envisaged for the March on Washington Movement by Randolph.

The political composition of the postwar Congress was not favorable to the passage of an FEPC act. An FEPC bill succumbed to a southern filibuster that lasted from January 18 to February 7, 1946, despite hastily summoned "Save FEPC" rallies held in Chicago and New York after the filibuster occurred. Plans for a reconstituted March on Washington with white allies were dropped—in part on the insistence of the Congress of Industrial Organizations—in favor of a policy of electoral reprisals against anti-FEPC congressmen up for reelection that fall. The results of the 1946 elections were disappointing, and there would be no major FEPC effort until the Civil Rights Mobilization of 1950. New York, however, adopted a state FEPC Act in 1945, and by 1950, seven others followed suit, including several key northern industrial states. By 1964, twenty-one states had enacted enforceable fair employment practices laws. All were offsprings of President Roosevelt's Executive Order 8802.

The Eightieth Congress elected in the 1946 Republican sweep was led by men, who, as historian Eric Goldman phrased it in *The Crucial Decade—and After*, came "roaring into the capital filled with spleen and plannings. Behind them was a nationwide rancor. It spurted out from all regions of the country and from a dozen different groups, each with its own special resentment. Democratic Georgia crackers hated 'what the niggers are getting away with'; Republican businessmen in any community had their furies at the labor unions; New Dealish secretaries, plumbers, and hairdressers in New York, Toledo, and Seattle spluttered every time they saw the size of the withholding tax in their paychecks. But the most powerful thrust of discontent came from one readily identifiable group, the men and women who had come to be called conservatives and who now emphatically did not want to conserve the existing America." The Eightieth Congress passed the Taft-Hartley Act to curb the alleged "monopoly power" of the trade unions; it adopted a new income tax formula benefiting the rich by reducing the proportion of taxes on high incomes; it refused to do anything about the poll-tax or anty-lynching legislation, and it turned down with scorn fair employment practices legislation.

Anti-Negro violence, the rise in anti-Semitism, and the attacks on organized labor created the civil rights coalition. It first came together to confer with President Harry S Truman on September 6, 1946. Walter White headed a six-man delegation representative of the then emerging coalition: James B. Carey, secretary of the CIO, and Boris Shishkin, AFL education director, represented the labor movement, while the church was represented by the Reverend Dr. Herman Reissig of the Federal Council of the Churches of Christ in America, and education by Dr. Channing H. Tobias, director of the Phelps-Stokes Fund. Leslie Perry, an administrative assistant in the NAACP Washington office, rounded out the delegation.

When Walter White finished his grim presentation of lynchings and racial intimidation, of anti-labor actions and the rising tide of anti-Semitism, President Truman exclaimed, "My God! I had no idea it was as terrible as that. We've got to do something!" As the group grappled with the question, the President, with President Roosevelt's wartime

Executive Order 8802 very much in mind, complained, "Everybody seems to believe that the President by himself can do anything he wishes on matters such as this. But the President is helpless unless he is backed by public opinion." David K. Niles, a presidential aide, suggested the appointment of a committee to investigate the state of civil rights and to recommend corrective programs. Walter White warned that it would be futile to get any such committee out of a Congress dominated by Southerners and conservatives. President Truman agreed, and said he would create an investigative commission by executive order. But he was sure that executive authority alone was not sufficient to insure compliance with fair employment practices in the face of organized opposition. "I saw," the President later wrote in his memoirs, "that legislative authority would be required to put an end to such un-American practices. The Committee on Civil Rights was set up to get the facts and to publicize as widely as possible the need for legislation." Public opinion, in short, needed to be aroused to the need for federal action on behalf of civil rights. In his order creating the committee, the President made the point, "The federal government is hampered by inadequate civil rights statutes." The Department of Justice lacked the tools to do the job of enforcement. "This was a condition that I wanted to see corrected."

"My first reaction," White later wrote in his autobiography, "was skepticism. President Roosevelt had made a somewhat similar suggestion several times to me but I had invariably gained the impression that he had made such proposals as a means of postponing decisions on issues which could bring him into conflict with belligerent anti-Negro Southern congressmen and senators." President Truman appointed a distinguished committee, headed by Charles E. Wilson, president of General Electric Corporation.° In the following year, he became the first President ever to address a convention of black people, at the NAACP Washington, D.C., conclave in 1947. As Americans, he told the delegates, "we believe that every man should be free to live his life as he wishes. He should be limited only by his responsibility to his fellow countrymen. If this freedom is to be more than a dream, each man must be guaranteed equality of opportunity. The only limit to an American's

---

° The President's Committee on Civil Rights consisted of Charles Luckman, president of Lever Brothers soap company; the Most Reverend Francis J. Haas of the Catholic Church; the Right Reverend Henry Knox Sherrill of the Protestant Episcopal Church; Mrs. Sadie T. Alexander, a black lawyer of Philadelphia; James B. Carey of the CIO; Boris Shishkin of the AFL; Rabbi Roland B. Gittelsohn; Presidents Frank P. Graham of the University of North Carolina and John S. Dickey of Dartmouth College; Dr. Channing H. Tobias; Franklin D. Roosevelt, Jr.; Mrs. M. E. Tilly of Atlanta, Georgia, an outstanding figure of the Methodist Episcopal Church South; Morris L. Ernst, famed civil liberties attorney; and Francis P. Matthews of Omaha, Nebraska, a former head of the Knights of Columbus.

achievement should be his ability, his industry, and his character."

If the President's speech left a residue of skepticism among his listeners, the report of his civil rights committee, "To Secure These Rights," did not. Walter White hailed the report as "without doubt the most courageous and specific document of its kind in American history." There were omissions and deficiencies, said White, "but these are so minute in importance and number as to be insignificant when compared to the explicit recommendations of things to be done by the Congress, by administrative bureaus of the federal and state governments, by state legislatures, and by private organizations and individuals. An almost perfect yardstick was thus established by which can be measured the gap between what Americans say they believe and what they do."

On February 2, 1948, President Truman became the first President to request a wide-ranging civil rights program of Congress. His message urged the enactment of legislation embodying the Civil Rights Committee's fundamental recommendations: 1) establishing a permanent Commission on Civil Rights, a joint Congressional Committee on Civil Rights Division in the Department of Justice; 2) strengthening existing civil rights statutes; 3) providing federal protection against lynching; 4) protecting more adequately the right to vote; 5) establishing a Fair Employment Practices Commission to prevent unfair discrimination in employment; 6) the modification of the federal naturalization laws to permit the granting of citizenship without regard to the race, color, or national origin of applicants; 7) providing home rule and suffrage in presidential elections for the residents of the District of Columbia; 8) providing statehood for Hawaii and Alaska and a greater measure of self-government for our island possessions; 9) equalizing the opportunities for residents of the United States to become naturalized citizens; and 10) settling the evacuation claims of Japanese-Americans. The President also urged the abolition of segregation and discrimination in the use of public and private transportation facilities throughout the country. That program, refined and strengthened as the years went on, became the heart of civil rights demands down to the enactment of the legislation of the Kennedy-Johnson era, following the great 1963 March on Washington.

Whatever difficulties black Americans faced during the crucial decade that followed the end of World War II, there were no significant pressures for a resumed March on Washington, or any equivalent mass action. The National Negro Congress secured twenty-one thousand signatures on a petition for anti-lynching laws. A November 1947 anti-lynching rally in Washington, D.C., sponsored by Negro ministers, drew a modest crowd. Protest remained a matter of individual conscience or small group Gandhian actions for most of the period. In

1947, when an integrated group of pacifists and radicals decided to test a Supreme Court decision that banned segregation of interstate passengers on motor carriers, they called their trip into the border states "a journey of reconciliation."

Railroads loom large in black folk imagery of freedom. Trains echo back in the blues of W. C. Handy and Duke Ellington; from the underground railroad of pre-Civil War days down to the "A" train, rails have carried black passengers toward some "mecca of equality." Segregation, however, marred the trip. The first Jim Crow laws enacted in the South were those separating black and white passengers on trains. The United States Supreme Court's first sanction of the pernicious "separate but equal" doctrine occurred in *Plessy v. Ferguson*, when the Court ruled, in 1896, against Homer Adolph Plessy, who contested his prosecution on the charge of refusing to occupy a seat in the colored car of a local Louisiana railroad train. The Jim Crow day coach remained hitched to Southern trains well into the 1950s. And Negro bus passengers were Jim Crowed to the back until Rosa Parks refused to move from her up-front seat in Montgomery in 1955.

With a one-way ticket firmly grasped in hand, the discomfort of Jim Crow was perhaps eased by the knowledge that north of Washington or St. Louis one could ride in any car and sit in any available seat. But when it came to making a visit "back down home," showing off northern-won affluence or the children to their grandparents, Jim Crow travel surely galled, and moving back in the New York to Tampa bus at Washington was simply degrading. Yet, few challenged the Mason-Dixon line changeover, and Irene Morgan, initially, was no exception. On July 15, 1944, Mrs. Morgan boarded a Greyhound bus at Hayes Store in Gloucester County, Virginia, for Baltimore, Maryland. She occupied, without much thought to the matter, one of the five seats at the very back of the bus. As every bus rider knows, these are among the most uncomfortable, stiff-backed, and unyielding. When the bus reached Saluda, Virginia, Mrs. Morgan, and a friend Estelle Fields, moved to newly vacated seats just ahead of the Jim Crow back row. Later, when a white couple boarded the bus, the driver asked Mrs. Morgan and her companion to give up their seats to the white passengers, a normal, everyday occurrence at the time. Mrs. Morgan allowed that she would be willing to give up her seat if the driver would give her another, but since she did not see any empty seats on the bus, she would stay where she was. Later, the driver contended that there was a vacancy on the long rear row of seats and that Mrs. Morgan refused to move when asked to do so. No matter, a start had been made on a long journey from a lowly county court up to the United States Supreme Court, a journey in search of justice. The bus driver procured a warrant from a Middlesex County justice of the peace, charging that

"Irene Morgan . . . unlawfully refus[ed] to move back on the Grey-hound bus in the section for colored people." Mrs. Morgan was arrested and then released on a $500 bond.

Mrs. Morgan was tried on October 18, 1944, before a circuit court judge and found guilty. The Middlesex County judge fined her $10.00 and costs—$15.25 in all. Her case was appealed, and her conviction upheld by the Virginia Supreme Court of Appeals. On November 19, 1945, the first case to challenge the constitutionality of interstate Jim Crow travel since 1877 came before the United States Supreme Court in a petition for appeal and assignment of errors, with a prayer for reversal, filed by NAACP attorneys acting on behalf of Mrs. Morgan. On June 3, 1946, the Court, in a six-to-one decision, declared segregation on interstate buses by race unconstitutional. Segregation, said the Court, "imposes undue burdens on interstate commerce."

Morgan v. Virginia became the legal precursor of a series of court actions that ultimately made an end of Jim Crow on the statute books. It encouraged the NAACP in its belief that black Americans could secure relief from segregation and its attendant evils through the courts. Yet, court decisions against segregation are likely to remain meaningless unless integration does, in fact, take place. In the months that followed the high court's decision in the *Morgan* case, nothing much changed on the buses and trains that rolled through the South. A June 4 Associated Press dispatch began, "Interstate bus travel segregation has been banned by a Supreme Court decision, but Negroes in the South continued to file to the rear seats." L. C. Major, vice-president of the Greyhound Lines at Richmond, Virginia, said that "of course, we'll comply," but company officials throughout the South reported that Negro passengers were still taking the back seats. Governor Thomas Bailey of Mississippi asserted, "Segregation will continue down here. Neither the whites nor the Negroes want it any other way. I don't believe there will be any friction. There never has been in this matter."

Grappling with the ingrained practices of a caste system is no easy matter. How do you get people to put into practice rights won in a court of law? In the months that followed the *Morgan* decision, that question worried Bayard Rustin, then race relations secretary of the Fellowship of Reconciliation, and George Houser, FOR field secretary in Cleveland and national secretary of the Congress of Racial Equality. They raised the issue that winter at a Cleveland meeting of CORE's continuation committee, the group that ran the organization between conventions. Out of that discussion, as Houser recalls it, came the idea of a trip to challenge the practice of Jim Crow travel. If an interracial group set an example, perhaps others would follow—or, so Houser and Rustin hoped. They thought it would be useful to determine to how great an extent bus and train companies were ready to comply with the

Morgan decision. "We wanted to learn," Houser and Rustin later reported, "the reaction of bus drivers, passengers, and police to those who nonviolently and persistently challenged Jim Crow in interstate travel."

"We talked to AJ [A. J. Muste, noted pacifist and FOR's executive secretary]," Houser reminisced many years later. "He was for anything of that sort." Houser and Rustin were given time by FOR to organize what became the 1947 Journey of Reconciliation. They were an odd couple, preparing a risky challenge to Jim Crow; a lanky, chain-smoking, talkative black Quaker and a stocky, soft-spoken, white divinity-school graduate, but canny strategists committed to integration. "We put in a good many months of work," Houser recalled. "We took one trip into the South together, visited each spot on the line of travel, and arranged for lawyers, fund raising, places to stay, that sort of thing." They were thorough; Houser took a second trip to doublecheck all the arrangements. One weekend in April, sixteen Negro and white activists met in a co-op house in Washington, D.C., for training sessions in preparation for the trip to test the *Morgan* decision. James Peck, a Harvard graduate, ex-seaman, pacifist, and then editor of the Workers' Defense League *News Bulletin*, describes that weekend in his book, *Freedom Ride*: "The training session taught not only the principles but the practices of non-violence . . . . What if the bus driver insulted you? What if you were actually assaulted? What if the police threatened you? These and many other questions were resolved through socio-dramas in which participants would act the roles of bus drivers, hysterical segregationists, police—and 'you.' Whether the roles had been acted correctly and whether you had done the right thing was then discussed. Socio-dramas of other bus situations followed. In all of them, you were supposed to remain non-violent, but stand firm."

For two days, eight blacks—Rustin; Wallace Nelson, free-lance lecturer; Conrad Lynn, New York attorney; Andrew Johnson, Cincinnati student; Dennis Banks, Chicago musician; William Worthy, journalist; Eugene Stanley of A. and T. College, Greensboro, North Carolina; and Nathan Wright, a Cincinnati church social worker—and eight whites—Houser; Peck; Ernest Bromley, a Methodist minister from North Carolina; Igal Roodenko, New York horticulturalist; Worth Randle, Cincinnati biologist; Joseph Felmet of the Southern Workers' Defense League; Homer Jack, executive secretary of the Chicago Council Against Racial and Religious Discrimination; and Louis Adams, a North Carolinian Methodist minister—scrapped through a series of mock encounters. "After two days of training," writes Peck, "we felt better prepared."

The journey was a model for CORE actions down to the Freedom Rides of 1961, and for such mass protests as the Montgomery bus boycott of 1955–56 and the student sit-ins of the early 1960s. Peck describes the lessons learned at the Washington weekend retreat, "If a driver or a policeman should order you to move to the segregated section of the bus, refuse in a polite manner. Tell him simply and briefly that you are within your rights under the Supreme Court decision. In the case of a policeman, do not leave your seat and accompany him unless you actually are placed under arrest. In other words, do not let the police violate your legal rights by sheer intimidation."

Just how the segregated pattern on a particular bus or train was to be broken was determined at meetings of the group held each eve of departure. Since it was vital that all sixteen not be arrested at once, thus halting the trip, some would ride Jim Crow during various stages of the journey. Observers were necessary, and someone had to be ready at all times to handle bail in the event of arrests. The roles were shifted daily.

Traveling almost constantly from April 9 to April 23, 1947, the interracial group visited fifteen cities in Virginia, North Carolina, Tennessee, and Kentucky. The *Morgan* decision and the purpose of the journey were explained at more than thirty speaking engagements before church, NAACP, and college groups. The audiences were mostly black. Half of the group traveled by Greyhound, and half by Trailways. Several short trips by train were undertaken, since a Court of Appeals for the District of Columbia had held that the *Morgan* decision applied to interstate train travel as well as bus travel. The group, however, deliberately traveled only through the upper South. As Peck wryly put it, "To penetrate the Deep South at that time would simply have meant immediate arrest of all participants, an end to the trip—and possibly of us." An interracial test of court bans on segregated travel in the Deep South would wait until the Freedom Rides of 1961. The 1947 Journey of Reconciliation received little or no coverage in the white press. Television coverage was nonexistent, and there was little public support except within various black communities and in the black press. NAACP attorneys in the various cities visited by the interracial group were prepared to defend arrested members, and they were taken into the homes of NAACP members during stopovers. The journey was not without danger. As a black passenger told Houser and Roodenko on the first lap from Richmond to Petersburg, Virginia, "A Negro might be able to get away with riding up front here, but some bus drivers are crazy, and the further south you go, the crazier they get." A white South Carolinian, speaking about Wallace Nelson seated up front in the Greensboro to Winston-Salem bus, told Reverend Ernest Bromley, "In my state, he would either move or be killed."

Much to the journey group's surprise, the only violence on the trip occurred at Chapel Hill, North Carolina, home of the highly regarded University of North Carolina, presided over by the noted southern liberal Dr. Frank P. Graham. As it happened, their visit was but one in a series of acts against Jim Crow that had taken place recently in and around the university. Eleanor Roosevelt had refused to eat at a segregated university function, preferring Coke and sandwiches on the university steps. Dorothy Maynor, the noted Negro singer, gave an on-campus concert before an integrated audience. Dr. Graham was serving on the President's Committee on Civil Rights, and the Reverend Charles Jones, a white Presbyterian minister who acted as Chapel Hill host for the weary members of the Journey of Reconciliation, had permitted interracial CIO union meetings in his church. As Peck writes, "It just happened to be our action which exploded the growing hatred among the poor whites, many of whom tenaciously clung to their only privilege in southern society—that of being recognized as superior to Negroes."

When the group boarded a Trailways bus, leaving Chapel Hill for Greensboro, Andrew Johnson and Joseph Felmet were arrested, and roughly handled by the police. Rustin and Igal Roodenko moved up to take their places at the front of the bus, and were arrested in turn. It was a gray Sunday afternoon in April, and the white cab drivers hanging around the Chapel Hill bus terminal did not have much to do. The arrests delayed the Greensboro bus for over two hours and caught the attention of assorted hangers-on, lending excitement to their frustration and boredom. Two vociferous whites harangued the idle crowd, gesturing at the bus. When Peck got off to put up bail for those arrested, five white men crowded around him and a husky one—with cold steel-gray eyes, as Peck recalls him—slugged Peck on the side of the head. "Coming down here to stir up the niggers?" he snarled. Peck asked in soft tones, "What's the matter?" The burly attacker was clearly taken aback, and he edged away. A passenger standing by shouted, "What's wrong with you? That man didn't do anything to you."

When the four arrested men had been bailed out, they were taken home by Rev. Charles Jones. Two cabs filled with angry whites followed, emptying at the Jones home. Two men waved heavy sticks while the others picked up rocks from the roadside. They started for the house, but were called back by one of their number. Shortly after they drove away, the Jones telephone rang and an unidentified caller told the minister, "Get those damn niggers out of town or we'll burn your house down. We'll be around to see that they go!" Though the police were summoned, it was decided that the interracial travelers would leave for Greensboro in the interests of safety for the Jones family. Several university students drove the group on to a Greensboro black church, where they joined the others at a capacity-crowd meeting.

There were other arrests, though none so dramatic. Peck and Dennis Banks were arrested in Asheville, Tennessee, which gave rise to the first appearance of a Negro attorney, Curtiss Todd from Winston-Salem, in the local courts. (The trials took place several months after the arrests in all cases.) It was also the first time a white and a Negro sat side by side at the defendant's table. But little else changed. The court Bibles were Jim Crowed. A court clerk held the "white Bible" when a white witness was sworn in, but a black witness had to hold the "black Bible" himself as he raised his right hand and swore "to tell the truth, and nothing but the truth." Peck and Banks were sentenced to thirty days "under the supervision of the State Highway Commission"—a polite way of saying, "to the chain gang, boys." Their case was dropped by the state on appeal. Rustin, Roodenko, and Felmet, however, served thirty days on Carolina road gangs as a consequence of their arrests at Chapel Hill.

The Journey of Reconciliation worked no miracles, although it demonstrated what firmness of purpose could accomplish. Over the years, interstate travel was desegregated—in part because others took courage from the sixteen Reconciliation pilgrims. Significantly, the reactions to the journey accurately reflected the times. As Rustin and Houser reported, "The one word which most universally describes the attitude of police, of passengers, and of the Negro and white bus riders is 'confusion.' " When the Reverend J. W. Routte donned a turban and sported a Swedish accent while on a trip to Mobile, Alabama, where, he said, he was "treated like a dignitary," many enjoyed a good laugh at the expense of southern bigotry, but others were simply bewildered. At the core of "the nagging realm of maybe" was considerable bewilderment, puzzling dilemmas. The country emerged from World War II as a rather reluctant world power. A nation in the mood to let go and relax in the unfolding of an unprecedented boom was asked instead to shoulder new burdens. President Truman ordered a rapid demobilization, reducing the armed forces from roughly eleven million men to barely a million. It was an exceedingly popular move. Yet, within a very short span, the President called for universal military training, a proposal in keeping with the country's new responsibilities on the world scene. "Our policy," Secretary of State George Marshall declared at the Harvard Commemoriam in 1947, is "directed not against any country or doctrine, but against hunger, poverty, desperation, and chaos. Its purpose should be the revival of a working economy . . . so as to permit the emergence of political and social conditions in which free institutions can exist." The open hand proffered to Russia—"Any government that is willing to assist in the task of recovery will find full cooperation, I am sure, on the part of the United States Government"—was slapped aside by Stalin. The Cominform was organized to counter the Marshall Plan. The Soviet Union blithely ignored Yalta agreement provisions for free elections in the liberated countries of Eastern Europe. Czechoslovakian patriot and Foreign Minister Jan Masaryk was defenestered in

Prague, and democracy was doomed behind the Iron Curtain that stretched from the Baltic to the Adriatic. Engaged in a cold war with a former ally, an adversary who mouthed democratic and revolutionary phrases, the country faced anew the problem of definition. A new word crept into public usage—un-American. Liberal and civil rights organizations, the trade unions, and other groups found it necessary to confront the communist question: How do you cope with a well-disciplined cadre whose tactics, strategies, and politics were prompted, to put it mildly, by a totalitarian foreign regime and party? Communism was never an internal threat to the country as a whole, despite the ravings of Senator Joseph McCarthy. The Stalinists, however, posed a real problem for a number of democratic, voluntary institutions, movements, and organizations. The resolution of that problem, complicated by the necessity of fending off McCarthyist attacks, consumed a considerable amount of liberal energies in the decade that followed Yalta.

Though the Communist party of the United States had wooed American Negroes from its beginnings in 1917, the party actually made few converts. Those who were possibly interested were put off by solutions to problems imposed by the Comintern that had little or no relevance to American conditions and by sudden, disconcerting changes in the party line. During the days of the famed "Scottsboro boys"—nine itinerant Negroes who were sentenced to death for allegedly raping two white women aboard a Chattanooga freight train—the communists used a good portion of the monies raised in defense of the Negro youths to discredit the NAACP. As a means of raising funds, the mothers of the Scottsboro defendants were introduced at meetings all over the country. There were only five living mothers, but the Communist party had no difficulty producing "mothers" on demand. In one instance, Walter White reports, the woman presented as a Scottsboro "mother" had lived for more than twenty years in the northern city in which she spoke. Ultimately, the communists gave up on the Scottsboro case. A group of liberals led by the Reverend Allen Knight Chalmers, Morris Ernst, Walter White, and Grover Hall of Montgomery, Alabama, came to their rescue, and the defendants were freed. "I think," Chalmers wrote, "that the Communists would have been content to lose the case if only they could publicize their part in it and point out the weaknesses of American legal practice." This willingness to sacrifice victims in the greater interest of communist propaganda did not sit well with most black Americans. The party, however, did score some small successes, capturing the American Negro Congress in 1939, as an instance. They quietly dumped the Congress for a policy of infiltration of the NAACP, following the end of World War II, largely in the hopes of securing the NAACP's endorsement of the Progressive party presidential candidate, Henry A. Wallace, and in this, as in much else, they failed.

For many Americans, however, the cold war presented an overriding question: How can one combat totalitarianism abroad with racism rampant at home? "There is an argument in progress between black men and white men as to the true nature of American reality," novelist Ralph Ellison wrote in 1948. The argument broke out before a nationwide audience during the debate over universal military training. Segregation in the armed forces galled black Americans for generations, and especially so during World War II when political considerations and the gains to be secured by federal anti-discrimination action in defense and government jobs forced a grudging acceptance of continued segregation in the armed forces. A determined government *might* have ended segregation in the armed forces during World War II, but the Commander in Chief himself was uncertain as to what best might be done. Negro soldiers were given combat assignments, but only reluctantly and under great pressures generated by the war and the Negro protest.

By mid-winter 1944, Negro discontent over the treatment of black servicemen sufficiently disturbed the White House to prompt the President to talk frankly before a meeting of the Negro Publishers' Association. What he had to say is revealing, and serves as a background for the 1948 struggle to integrate the armed forces. "It is perfectly true," the President told his audience, "there is definite discrimination in the actual treatment of the colored engineer troops, and others. And you are up against it, as you know perfectly well. I have talked about it—I had the Secretary of War and the Assistant—everybody in on it. The trouble lies fundamentally in the attitude of certain white people—officers down the line who haven't much more education, many of them, than the colored troops and the Seabees and the engineers, for example. And well, you know the kind of person it is. We all do. We don't have to do more than think of a great many people that we know. And it has become not a question of orders—they are repeated fairly often, I think, in all the camps of colored troops—it's a question of the personality of the individual.

"And we are up against it, absolutely up against it."

If the President sounded distraught, he was. Desegregation of the armed forces was that kind of issue, morally inescapable but loaded with political dynamite for a President dependent upon southern support in Congress. The end of the war and demobilization diluted pressures for desegregation, at least for a brief time. Nearly everyone's attention was directed elsewhere to job problems and the like. When the Truman Administration proposed universal military training, however, a NAACP *Crisis* editorial crackled a warning: "Before official Washington can expect any kind of support from a goodly segment of the Negro population on this proposal, it must announce the abolition of Jim Crow as part of this plan."

The desegregation issue, however, tended to become lost in the welter of argument over universal military training. The northern Baptists, for example, opposed universal military training on traditional anti-military grounds, pointing out that Negro enlistments were "too rigidly limited" by Jim Crow to give the policy of voluntary service a fair trial. Speaking for the National Fraternal Council of Negro Churches of America, Dr. W. H. Jernagin, director of the council's Washington office, opposed the revival of selective service, saying, "the very sincerity of our Government's claim regarding universal military training as a means of defending democracy and our national security is open to serious question when we understand that Jim Crow is the official policy of our Government with respect to the armed services." The NAACP opposed peacetime military conscription as "unsound in principle" and because "present legislation would permit the continuation of the present racial segregation and discrimination in the armed forces." Liberals, churchmen, trade unions, opposed both conscription and a Jim Crow armed forces. The CIO flatly opposed both while the AFL favored "the application of selective service on a limited basis" and urged "the elimination of the caste system." But it remained for A. Philip Randolph to cut the racist Gordian knot.

In mid-March 1948, Randolph headed a delegation calling on President Harry S Truman to urge an end to Jim Crow in the armed services. "Negroes," Randolph told the President, "are in no mood to shoulder another gun for democracy abroad while they are denied democracy here at home." The peppery President spluttered, "I don't like that kind of talk at all. I wish you hadn't said that." Ever cordial but firm, Randolph asked, "You want to know how Negroes feel, don't you?" President Truman simmered, but conceded, "I am interested in the facts."

Three weeks later, on March 31, Randolph appeared before the Senate Committee on the Armed Services, chaired by Senator Chan Gurney, Republican of South Dakota. Randolph had some harsh truths for the good senators. "Whatever may pass in the way of conscription legislation will become permanent," Randolph said, "since the world trend is toward militarism." In that light, he argued, "how could any permanent Fair Employment Practices Commission dare to criticize job discrimination in private industry if the Federal Government itself were simultaneously discriminating against Negro youth in military establishments all over the world?" He assured his listeners that "Negroes do put civil rights above the high cost of living and above every other major issue of the day . . . . Even more significant is the bitter angry mood of the Negro in his determination to win those rights in a country that subjects him daily to so many insults and indignities." Randolph repeated the warning he had made earlier to the President, adding that "passage of a Jim Crow draft may only result in a mass civil disobedience movement along the lines of the magnificent struggles of the people of India against British imperialism."

Hitler's racism, Randolph said, "posed a sufficient threat for [the Negro] to submit to the Jim Crow army abuses." But, he pointed out to the Senate committee, "this factor of minority group persecution in Russia is not present, as a popular issue, in the power struggle between Stalin and the United States. I can only repeat that this time Negroes will not take a Jim Crow draft lying down." Then, before a hushed Senate chamber, Randolph announced, "I personally will advise Negroes to refuse to fight as slaves for a democracy they cannot possess and cannot enjoy." To ensure that he was clearly understood, Randolph spelled out his intentions: "I personally pledge myself to openly counsel, aid, and abet youth, both white and Negro, to quarantine any Jim Crow conscription system, whether it bear the label of universal military training or selective service."

Randolph's basso profundo deepened, rolling out broad A's in a nonviolent credo that would characterize Negro protest for over a decade. "I feel morally obligated to disturb and keep disturbed the conscience of Jim Crow America. In resisting the insult of Jim Crowism to the soul of black America, we are helping to save the soul of America. And let me add that I am opposed to Russian totalitarian communism and all its works. I consider it a menace to freedom. I stand by democracy as expressing the Judeo-Christian ethic. But democracy and Christianity must be boldly and courageously applied for all men regardless of race, color, or country.

"We shall wage a relentless warfare against Jim Crow without hate or revenge for the moral and spiritual progress and safety of our country, world peace, and freedom.

"Finally, let me say that Negroes are just sick and tired of being pushed around and we just do not propose to take it, and we do not care what happens."

Worried and a little shocked, the liberal senator from Oregon, Wayne Morse, leaned over the podium to caution Randolph, warning "that the doctrine of treason would be applied to those people participating in that disobedience." Randolph answered that he recognized the risk and anticipated "terrorism against Negroes who refuse to participate in the armed forces," but, he added, "we would be willing to absorb the violence, to absorb the terrorism, to face the music, and to take whatever comes . . . . I believe that that is the price we have to pay for the democracy that we want."

Grant Reynolds, a black minister, a former army chaplain, a

Republican, a member of the New York State Commission of Corrections, and national chairman of the Committee Against Jim Crow in Military Service and Training, joined Randolph at the Senate hearings "in everything he shall propose, including civil disobedience." The two created a League for Nonviolent Civil Disobedience Against Military Segregation. Randolph took the campaign of noncompliance with the draft to the streets, urging draft-eligibles not to register and to refuse induction. On one hot July day, he cried out, "I am prepared to oppose a Jim Crow army until I rot in jail."

The established Negro leadership was somewhat more cautious, though supportive of Randolph's effort to desegregate the armed forces. Lester Granger of the Urban League headed a delegation of prominent Negroes to confer with Secretary of Defense James W. Forrestal. The Granger group announced afterward, "The group agreed that no one wanted to continue in an advisory capacity on the basis of continued segregation in the armed services." The NAACP expressed itself as "dubious about the method" but desiring the end result. *Crisis* prominently reprinted a *PM* editorial by Max Lerner in praise of the Randolph-Reynolds action. Lerner hailed their stand before the Senate committee as "the most impressive and courageous that has ever been made before a Congressional committee by any man, white or black." Lerner said it opened "a new chapter not only in the history of the American Negroes, and of American military measures, but also in the history of the deadly serious struggle for American democracy." Morally, the liberal columnist wrote, "Randolph and Reynolds are right, and they have gone far deeper into the relations of democracy and national security than any of the military men or congressmen have done. What they are saying is that you cannot shunt aside the struggle for democracy on the plea of a national security emergency. For it is not the armed forces which can protect our democracy. It is the moral strength of democracy which alone can give any meaning to the efforts at military security." Lerner reported that many other Negro leaders felt that Randolph and Reynolds went too far. Yet, he added, "I think there can be no question but that Randolph and Reynolds come closer to the true feeling of the masses of American Negroes, in the North as in the South, than their more cautious and circumspect colleagues." It was an impression amply borne out in an NAACP poll of draft-eligible Negro students that found that 71 percent were sympathetic with the Randolph-Reynolds civil disobedience campaign.

For all that, however, no great number refused to register or refused induction. In part, this was so because events moved too swiftly for a proper, full-scale civil disobedience campaign to take effect. President Truman's special civil rights message in February 1948 set southern Democrats simmering. A. Philip Randolph joined a picket line outside the Philadelphia Democratic party convention in July, and inside, a young maverick from the West, Hubert Humphrey, then mayor of Minneapolis, insisted that the party endorse item by item the civil rights program advanced by the President in February. When the Young Turks won, 651½ to 582½, J. Strom Thurmond, governor of South Carolina, staged a Dixiecrat walkout into the pouring rain outside the convention hall. When a reporter pointed out to Governor Thurmond that "President Truman is only following the platform that Roosevelt advocated," Thurmond replied, "I agree, but Truman really means it."

After his nomination as the Democratic party candidate, President Truman summoned Congress for a special session on July 26, "Turnip Day" in Missouri, according to Truman, "to ask them [the Republican dominated Congress] to pass all of these laws they say they are asking for in their platform." While Congress wrangled, spending six days of the twelve-day session in a filibuster precipitated by Southerners to block Senate consideration of an anti-poll tax bill, the President, on July 26, issued two executive orders aimed at bias in federal employment and in the armed services. His orders, commented an editorial in *Crisis*, "represent a spirit and a courage on these issues as refreshing as they are rare."

Executive Order 9981 set in motion the integration of the United States armed services, a move that took two to three years and the Korean War to accomplish. Because the order banning discrimination in the armed forces did not mention segregation, there was some confusion—and skepticism—about its intent among black leaders. When questioned about this at a White House press conference, the President assured doubters that he expected all segregation of the races in the armed services to be abolished eventually, and that his order had that in mind. What the order did, actually, was to set a policy—"there shall be equality of treatment and opportunity"—and created a committee, later known as "the Fahey Committee" after its chairman, former Solicitor General of the United States, Charles Fahey, to carry it out. Subsequently, Randolph and Reynolds met with Senator J. Howard McGrath, chairman of the Democratic National Committee, and he convinced them that President Truman meant what he said. Randolph and Reynolds, thereupon, announced the end of their civil disobedience campaign.

Some of the young people involved in the campaign, including Bayard Rustin, disagreed, holding that civil disobedience ought to continue until the last vestige of discrimination had been wiped out and until protestors who had been jailed were released from prison. They were unable, however, to continue the campaign. There was little or no response from other young people on its behalf, and hardly any support from the black communities of the country. This is not to say that there was no discontent. As a young, slight-bodied black writer, James Baldwin reported to readers of *Commentary*, "All over Harlem now there is felt the same bitter expectancy with which, in my childhood, we awaited winter; it is coming and it will be hard; there is nothing anyone can do about it." The "fire next time" would not break out until the late 1960s. Meanwhile, the closest black Americans would come to a mass action during the period from 1945 to 1955 would be to vote for Harry S Truman in the 1948 election.

That summer, Clare Boothe Luce declared, "Truman is a gone goose." And most people agreed. The Republicans had a strong candidate in Thomas E. Dewey, popular with his party and appealing in his stance as a crusader against corruption. The Democrats were divided—Dixiecrats defecting to the right, and Progressives to the left. Truman's advocacy of civil rights seemingly did him little good; as a *Crisis* editorial put it, such a course "is dynamite—and death—to political ambitions in this country." Yet, the peppery Missourian kept hitting away at the "do-nothing Eightieth Congress," stressing his fights with the conservatives in control over civil rights, housing, minimum wages, and his veto of the Taft-Hartley Act (which was passed over that veto). The campaign of 1948 was the last time that both candidates toured the country extensively by train, and Truman's fiery attacks gained him whistling, foot-stomping, "give 'em hell, Harry" audiences across the country. Truman became the first major-party candidate to campaign in Harlem, a gesture that was not lost on black voters. Their turnout helped create Truman majorities in the country's thirteen largest industrial cities, and though not sufficient to offset "upstate" Republican votes and Democratic defections to Wallace in New York, Pennsylvania, and Michigan, it was ample to put Ohio, Illinois, and California electoral votes in the Truman column, decisively winning the Presidency for the man from Missouri. Labor, Negroes, and the farm vote came through to do the job. Blacks in motion once again had marched on Washington.

V

"Separate but Equal" *No More*

FREDERICK DOUGLASS ONCE wrote, "Under a harsh master, a slave could but think of survival; under a good master, he began to think of freedom." The 1930s were a harsh master: the black migration north to freedom receded; sharecroppers clung tenaciously to the eroding earth; anti-lynching laws hadn't a prayer of passage; the "dark, dishonest decade" dimmed all hopes, even that of survival. The war years were those of reviving hope, of passage to as yet unknown ports. The years that followed were of a good master: rising incomes aroused expectations of more; the flight from the land became a flood; thinking of freedom, people once again marched on Washington. They came seeking guarantees of fair employment and an end to discrimination as promised under the Fourteenth Amendment to the Constitution.

Civil rights forces grouped and regrouped in Washington in the 1950s much as battered G.I.s grouped and regrouped on the war-torn Korean peninsula before the Chinese onslaught. Southern reactionaries retained power in Congress, and in concert with northern Republicans were able to defeat all progressive, labor, and civil rights legislation. At the 1949 inaugural of President Truman, prominent black Americans were invited to the top social events for the first time. The Fair Deal, the jaunty President insisted, encompassed a far-ranging civil rights program. The inaugural, declared Walter White, "had about it a special tone of recognizing the new place of all ordinary Americans." Yet, 1949 slipped by without congressional action, a year-long "ho-hum" through the most dramatized issues of the day—civil rights, Taft-Hartley, aid to education, and health insurance.

Overseas, the brilliance of the Marshall Plan was dimmed by the failure of containment, especially in the Far East. China fell to

Chairman Mao's forces, and on August 5, 1949, a Department of State white paper confirmed what most Americans by then knew or feared. China had fallen to communist armies despite American expenditures in the billions aimed at shoring up the tottering government of Chiang Kai-shek. On September 23, 1949, the President announced, "We have evidence that within recent weeks an atomic explosion occurred in the U.S.S.R." On the heels of that shock came further revelations that well-placed Americans had betrayed their country, passing on knowledge "of the highest value to a potential enemy," and, indeed, by so doing had speeded up the production of the Soviet bomb by "at least a year." Senator Homer Capehart, Republican of Indiana, fulminated in the Senate: "How much more are we going to have to take? Fuchs and Acheson and Hiss and hydrogen bombs threatening outside and New Dealism eating away the vitals of the nation. In the name of Heaven, is this the best Americans can do?" On February 9, 1950, in Wheeling, West Virginia, an obscure Republican, the junior senator from Wisconsin, Joseph McCarthy waved a piece of paper, saying in a flat, Midwest drone, "I have here. . . ." His exact words remain in dispute, but his allegation that communists shaped American foreign policy continued to fester in the body politic.

Alarmed and/or bemused, Americans in 1950 were scarcely in the mood to consider dispassionately civil rights or any other major reforms. The old ways appeared to be dissolving, and the new had as yet to come to fruition. The moment belonged to those sociologist Theodore W. Adorno dubbed pseudo-conservatives, "who, in the name of upholding traditional American values and institutions and defending them against more or less fictitious dangers, consciously or unconsciously aim at their abolition." Fundamentalist Protestants and fundamentalist Catholics, uncertain Texas oil millionaires, resentful automobile dealers and real estate manipulators, small-town folk, and cankered ex-communists clustered about Senator McCarthy as bees swarm, forming a volatile, noisy cluster on the radical right.

For all the buzzing, little that lasted was produced by the political swarming of the uneasy in status. To be sure, there was much to be uneasy about. Totalitarian communism was—and is—a problem, both internationally and ideologically. The American economy was something of a patchwork, a quilt of free-enterprise scraps, corporate backing, welfare threads, and even snippets of socialism. Blacks, Chicanos, Catholics, Jews, Puerto Ricans, and the children of immigrants jostled WASPs for jobs and status. It was all very disturbing. Yet, out of this urban welter emerged a coalition for social change.

It was not, however, the competition for jobs that created the coalition as much as the opening up of opportunities. The performance of the economy exceeded all expectations. Remember, many people expected a repeat of the Depression. The total civilian labor force rose from 53.8 million in 1945 to 59.9 million in 1950. Despite an unemployment rate of roughly 4.5 percent over 1954 and 1955, the labor force continued climbing to 63.1 million in 1955. The country's gross national product rose sharply from $213.6 billion in 1945 to $284.6 billion in 1950 and on up to $397.5 billion in 1955. Personal consumption expenditures reflected economic well-being, mounting steadily from $121.7 million in 1945 to $195.0 million in 1950 to $256.9 million in 1955. The general expansion afforded growth in opportunities with the number of professional and technical workers rising over 1950 to 1955 from 4.4 million to 5.7 million, and the number of craftsmen and foremen from 7.6 million to 8.3 million. Catholics, Jews, blacks, Japanese-Americans, and various other ethnic groups were traditionally excluded, or not found, in a wide variety of careers and occupations, and so discrimination created a coalition for change.

The economic, political, and social conditions of the late 1940s and early 1950s called for a reordering of strategies, if not priorities. A choice of tactics depends on the resources available in money, people, and political clout. The two strategies Randolph used to notable effect—mass action or its threat in the 1941 March on Washington and civil disobedience in the desegregation of the armed forces—were simply not applicable to the 1950s fight for fair employment practices or for an end to segregated schooling. The freedom riders of 1947 had made their point in the Journey of Reconciliation, and CORE groups effectively continued chipping away at discrimination in public accommodations in northern and border states. Jim Peck and Bayard Rustin bought a few shares of Greyhound stock and startled Wilmington, Delaware, with its first interracial picket line at the 1950 Greyhound stockholders' meeting. The stockholders were considerate, but the corporation was not appreciably moved by the two determined protestors' demand that it abolish Jim Crow riding in the Deep South. President Truman was convinced that he had done all that a President could do; executive orders have limitations, and if anything were to be done, Congress had to act. To get Congress to act, one must lobby and engage in political action.

FEPC, was, in a sense, old business, a leftover from the New Deal that had overlooked black minority interests. But it was also new business, a Fair Deal issue gaining impetus from the newly felt presence of the black masses. With the support given Truman by black voters in key cities and states, the 1948 election was viewed by many as a mandate for the civil rights program that President Truman again proposed in 1949 and 1950. And so it came about that in 1949 civil rights strategists considered how best to harvest the political sowings of 1948.

There had been debate over the House-first or Senate-first approach for FEPC legislation, and A. Philip Randolph carried the day for the latter in 1946. He had done so, in part, out of a fear of the possible complications that would ensue from involvement with Congressman Vito Marcantonio, a left-leaning, Communist party traveler from Manhattan, who, indeed, had a bill in hand to offer his colleagues. But getting it on the floor of the House was another matter, and Randolph succeeded in securing in the Senate what he could not in the House. The 1946 defeat by filibuster, however, cost the National Council for a Permanent FEPC dearly in money and morale. Walter White, prestigious head of the NAACP, differed with Randolph over the council's concentration on FEPC. In 1948, White, a member of the council's strategy committee, wrote Randolph and Rev. Allen Knight Chalmers, co-chairmen of the council, to "disassociate myself" from a council telegram to Senator Taft requesting priority for FEPC over anti-lynching and anti-poll tax bills. "Despite its record of more than a quarter of a century in support of anti-lynching legislation," White wrote, "the NAACP has abstemiously refrained from asking priority for that legislation."

Sometime after the 1948 election, in a White House strategy session, Clark Clifford convinced civil rights leaders of the necessity of securing the broadest public backing for the President's civil rights program. Aside from questions of morale and indebtedness, the Council for a Permanent FEPC was too narrowly conceived, or so it was argued. Fresh funds, too, would be forthcoming for a new effort. The NAACP, therefore, launched a nationwide mobilization for civil rights, a mini-march on Washington of activists from the sixty national church, civic, labor, fraternal, and minority group organizations secured as sponsors. Cooperation between the temporary National Emergency Civil Rights Mobilization and the National Council for a Permanent FEPC was assured, however, despite Randolph's displeasure. He saw "no need for another co-ordinating organization working principally for a federal FEPC" but was "willing to give his wholehearted cooperation . . . if such an effort will hasten the federal anti-discrimination law," noted the *Black Worker* in February 1950. But Roy Wilkins, assistant director of the NAACP and chief organizer and chairman of the *ad hoc* mobilization also served as the chairman of the council's executive committee. Arnold Aronson of the National Jewish Community Relations Advisory Council served as secretary to both the council and the mobilization. Their cooperation helped to knit the two groups together.

"The Mobilization was Roy's [Wilkins'] show," according to Arnold Aronson. Walter White, who had served as the NAACP's one-man lobby in Washington as well as its secretary, had been given a year's leave of absence. When the 1949 NAACP convention called for an

Emergency Mobilization for Civil Rights, it fell to the acting secretary, Roy Wilkins, to carry out the task. It was, as *The Crisis* put it, "a herculean effort," pulling together the support of Elks and Masons, Catholics and Jews, fraternities and the labor movement. Ever since his youth in St. Paul, Minnesota, Wilkins had impressed people with his diligence. His grandparents had been sharecroppers in the Mississippi delta country, and the family had migrated north, up river, seeking a better life. His father was a foreman in a St. Louis brick kiln when Roy was born on August 30, 1901. The elder Wilkins became a Methodist minister, moving from congregation to congregation in the Midwest. It was an itinerant life, and the young boy was sent to live with his uncle and aunt in St. Paul, who subsequently adopted him. His uncle was "a private car man," a waiter on the Pullman car reserved for the president of the Northern Pacific Railroad. St. Paul's black community was small, about 2,500 at the time, and Roy Wilkins grew up in an integrated neighborhood, "60 percent white and 40 percent black," according to Wilkins, where houses were kept neat and lawns mowed. "The neighborhood had a middle-class outlook," Wilkins likes to say, "but a poor man's income."

Young Roy attended Whittier Grade School and St. Paul's Mechanical Arts High School where he became editor of the school's monthly magazine in his junior year and president of the Literary Society in his senior year. "You were automatically named," he once told an interviewer, "if you were picked as the best English student of the year." He took pre-engineering courses in high school and worked his way through the University of Minnesota as a red cap and dining car waiter during summer vacations. In his senior year, Wilkins ran a small Negro weekly newspaper in St. Paul. He was also active in the local NAACP chapter, becoming its secretary and a delegate to the national convention in 1923, the year he graduated.

As it happened, the editor of the *Kansas City Call*, a four-year-old black weekly newspaper, was looking for a reporter and mentioned this to Wilkins' father, who recommended his son as having a journalistic bent. At the time, Kansas City had a black population of some forty thousand and the *Call* was widely read, so young Roy grabbed at the chance to work on a big city paper. Moving to Kansas City was an eye-opener for the young newspaper man. "I remember," he told an interviewer in 1962, "the shock of Kansas City, and its segregation, and its attitude toward colored people, in contrast to the atmosphere in which I had grown up in St. Paul."

Always a journalist, Wilkins nonetheless had a talent for organization that few in his profession are fortunate enough to possess. He became active in the Kansas City NAACP chapter and eventually was elected its secretary. In those years, he met Walter White, James Weldon

Johnson, Dr. W. E. B. Du Bois, and other NAACP luminaries. In 1930, Wilkins was active in Kansas and western Missouri on behalf of the NAACP campaign against the Senate confirmation of Judge John J. Parker, considered anti-black, to the United States Supreme Court. (He was defeated by one vote.) Wilkins also helped organize the subsequent defeat of Senator Henry J. Allen of Kansas, who had voted for Parker's confirmation. Wilkins' contribution to the drive against Parker caught the attention of the NAACP's national office, and in 1931, Walter White asked him if he would come to New York and serve as assistant secretary.

Walter White had a penchant for on-the-spot investigations, and he expected his staff to go and do likewise. In December 1931, Wilkins and George Schuyler, the Pittsburgh *Courier* columnist, went off to investigate the conditions of black workers employed on the Mississippi levees south of Memphis, following the great floods of that year. As expected, they were deplorable. Because of their accents, Schuyler and Wilkins passed themselves off as being from Alexandria, Virginia, looking for work. When an observant boardinghouse keeper remarked on the softness of their hands, Wilkins quickly allowed as to how they had been employed as elevator operators. Schuyler was arrested by mistake for a robber, and kept in jail overnight. This caused the two investigators to decide that it was time to leave with their findings. Men were working ten to twelve hours a day, they reported, for ten cents an hour. The highest wage was that paid the "cat man," the operator of a caterpillar tractor, who earned $2.50 a day. Their report caused a mild stir, and in the depths of the Depression, resulted in wages on the levees being upped 50 percent, a rise from ten to fifteen cents an hour.

The journey to the Mississippi levee was only the first of many Roy Wilkins would make to keep in touch with his constituency. No matter how small the NAACP chapter or remote the community, NAACP members could count on Wilkins for a response to their requests. And, somehow, there was always time for his first calling, journalism—the editorship of *The Crisis*, taken on after Dr. Du Bois departed to teach at Atlanta, and more recently, a weekly newspaper column. As Walter White's stature grew and his role in the broader community expanded —becoming almost global during World War II and after—Wilkins tended the organizational home fires. He ran the NAACP during White's leave of absence, and assumed many of its burdens during White's last years. When White died in 1955, Wilkins was his natural successor. The dedicated organization man followed the one-man crusader as secretary of the NAACP.

Wilkins' organizational ability was clearly evident in Washington, D.C. over the three-day, January 15 to 17, Emergency Civil Rights Mobilization. Over four thousand delegates from thirty-three states converged on the Capitol to listen to speeches and spread out through the halls of Congress buttonholing legislators on behalf of civil rights. Over half of the grassroots lobbyists came from NAACP chapters. The breakdown of the mobilization delegates indicates the breadth of the existing civil rights coalition. In addition to the NAACP's 2,891, there were: CIO, 383; American Jewish Congress, 185; B'nai B'rith, 350; National Baptist Convention, 53; AFL, 119; the African Methodist Episcopal and other church organizations, 41; National Alliance of Postal Employees, 23; Committee for a Permanent FEPC, 11; Greek Letter Fraternities, 12; Americans for Democratic Action and Students for Democratic Action, 60; Elks, Masons, and other fraternal organizations, 17; Catholic Interracial Council, 5.

While the mobilization had been summoned to create pressure for President Truman's entire civil rights program, the delegates pretty much limited themselves to a pitch for FEPC. AFL, CIO, NAACP, and National Jewish Community Relations Council (NJCRC) spokesmen had already urged that FEPC be given "top priority." In January 1950, Wilkins wrote to members of the Senate, "Major religious, labor, civic, veterans, racial, and ethnic organizations have declared FEPC to be 'the most fundamental' of all pending civil rights bills."

The decision to concentrate on FEPC reflected strategic considerations and objective realities for minority Americans. All things considered, it would be easier to lobby for one bill than several. And of the various civil rights proposals, FEPC was the most vital, insuring increased job opportunities for a host of minority Americans. Important as they were, anti-lynching and anti-poll tax bills were less pressing. The number of lynchings had declined, and the postwar rise in incomes made the poll tax less onerous to white and black poor.

The House-first route was chosen this time, largely because the congressman from Harlem, Adam Clayton Powell, Jr., had by then achieved a position from which he could provide invaluable help. He had a good working relationship with Representative John Lesinski, a Democrat from Michigan who chaired the House Committee on Education and Labor. Powell introduced the FEPC bill—Senator J. Howard McGrath, Democrat of Rhode Island, did so in the Senate—and chaired the subcommittee hearings. The preliminaries went well, but FEPC was blocked at nearly every turn by its opponents' skillful use of House and Senate rules. The problem in the House appeared simple enough—get the Powell bill on the floor. The buttonholing of congressmen by mobilization delegates paid off when the House thumbed down an effort by Congressman Eugene E. Cox, Democrat of Georgia, to restore the power of the House Rules Committee to hold up legislation indefinitely. The Rules Committee is responsible for the ordering of business in the House, and under a 1949 rule pushed through by House liberals, the committee could keep a bill from the floor only twenty-one days; hitherto it could have done so forever. At the end of twenty-one days, a committee chairman whose bill had been refused "a rule," or a place on the House agenda, could bring a measure before the House on the second or fourth Monday of the month, provided he was recognized by the Speaker of the House. Speaker Sam Rayburn, however, failed to recognize Representative Lesinski, and FEPC was immobilized. Representatives Powell and Franklin D. Roosevelt then sought a "discharge petition" ordering FEPC to the floor, but they were unable to secure the required number of signatures. As a last resort, Representative Lesinski relied on "Calendar Wednesday"—when the roll call of House committees is called alphabetically and chairmen may present any measure approved by their committees, to get FEPC before the House.

The House opened its session on Washington's birthday, February 22, 1950, at noon. After the usual daily prayer, a Southerner rose to call a quorum, a run-through of the members to see if enough are on hand to conduct business. That exhausted a half hour, and before the afternoon was over, southern congressmen had called for seven more quorums and made other calls. Finally, the put-off came to a close, and the FEPC debate began at 5:40 P.M.

The House spectators' galleries were crowded, mostly with FEPC supporters. In the chamber, representatives shouted at one another across the packed floor. Two members came in drunk and were escorted out by worried conferees. Dixiecrat members yippied Confederate battle cries, and offered amendment after amendment. As one Southerner said, "We've got hundreds." As the ninth hour of debate approached, it became clear that the most important amendment was one put forward by Representative Samuel J. McConnell, Jr., Republican of Pennsylvania. It called for the substitution of a "voluntary FEPC," one without enforcement provisions, for the Powell bill. Southerners voted with Republicans to put the Powell bill aside in favor of the McConnell measure. The vote was 221 to 178, and the House adjourned at 3:14 A.M. That afternoon, the McConnell substitute was passed, 240 to 177. House friends of FEPC were divided, most refusing to vote for the McConnell bill since it was "an outright sham," while others supported the measure on the grounds that it was necessary to keep the issue alive for Senate consideration.

The Senate began its deliberations on May 5, when Senator Scott Lucas, Republican of Illinois and majority leader, introduced a motion calling for consideration of the McGrath bill. Senator Lucas had assured FEPC supporters, "A determined fight will be waged—and I mean 'determined.'" Washington expected a tough, grueling filibuster from the Dixiecrats. Congressional buffs, however, were disappointed. As *The*

New York Times reported on May 16, 1950: "Developments have not borne out this prediction. Instead of all-night sessions with hoarse and weary southern Senators drawing crowded galleries, the Senate quit before dinner time." A desultory debate and a lackluster filibuster followed the introduction of the McGrath FEPC bill. Senator Lucas moved to close debate on the motion to consider FEPC, but the cloture motion, which required a two-thirds vote of the entire Senate, or sixty-five votes, lost fifty-two to thirty-two. The Senate then proceeded to other business. Another attempt was made in July when the fifty-five votes were cast for cloture. The 1950 movement for federal FEPC lost momentum, and the only bill to leave committee in either House down to 1957 was one reported out on July 3, 1952, in the Senate just three days before adjournment.

In his explanation of "the murky maneuvers" that enveloped the FEPC fight in Congress, *New York Times* columnist Arthur Krock wrote, "most of the principals in the parliamentary farce now going on want to keep the FEPC issue alive for campaign purposes in the congressional elections of 1950." President Truman's failure to mention FEPC to Speaker Rayburn just a few hours before the Speaker had to decide whether or not to recognize Representative Lesinski stemmed from political considerations, Krock said. "The President," he wrote, "will not be displeased if it is unfinished business when the voters go to the polls in 1950." Even the southern Democrats, Krock claimed, gained from keeping the issue alive, "not only because on a showdown it would probably pass both the House and the Senate, but because as unfinished business their opposition to it will serve to head off aspirants for their seats in the oncoming primaries." In discussing the Senate vote, *Crisis* concluded, "So neither the Republicans nor the northern Democrats can blame the Dixiecrats. Cloture on FEPC was blocked by northern and western senators of both parties, nine Republicans and twelve Democrats." °

In addition to its potential as a hot 1950 election issue, there were other factors that entered the admittedly murky calculations that contributed to the defeat of FEPC. President Truman was eager to secure passage of a crucial European Recovery Program appropriations bill, and he needed some southern as well as Republican support. The Democratic Senate Policy Committee, therefore, gave priority in April to the appropriations measure, a question of timing that adversely affected the FEPC outcome in the Senate. The President told reporters that if action were not taken on the appropriations bill right away, the money for European recovery would not be included. Every attention would be given to FEPC, the President said, but there was no use in

---

° See footnote at bottom of next page.

starting a filibuster which would delay an international matter of vital importance.

What counts in Congress is political clout, and there seems to be no question but that the civil rights forces in the country that year did not have the strength to force cloture on recalcitrant, irascible southern senators, nor to make FEPC a matter of top priority for Congress. In analyzing the Senate cloture vote for the joint executive committee of the Emergency Mobilization and the National Council for a Permanent FEPC, Arnold Aronson pointed out that six Republicans and six non-southern Democrats had voted against cloture on both tests. "Only four of these men," Aronson said, "are up for reelection this year [1950] and all come from the states which are removed from centers of minority group population and pressures. Even assuming that every other member of the Senate could be prevailed upon to be present and to vote favorably, the thirty-three recorded negative votes supplemented by the vote of Senator-elect Smathers, would be more than sufficient to prevent cloture." Accordingly, Aronson concluded, "Prospects for civil rights legislation in the 82nd Congress appeared dim under the existing cloture rule."

The Emergency Mobilization and the National Council for a Permanent FEPC merged in the Leadership Conference on Civil Rights, which has remained the chief lobbying instrumentality of civil rights forces in Washington down to this day. The civil rights coalition

* Two Senate Votes on Cloture, Eighty-First Congress							
			May 19, 1950			July 12, 1950	
	Total	Yea	Nay	Not Voting	Yea	Nay	Not Voting
Total	96	52	32	12	55	33	8
Republicans	42	33	6	3	33	6	3
All Democrats	54	19	26	9	22	27	5
Northern Democrats	32	19	6	7	22	6	4
Southern Democrats	22	—	20	2	—	21	1

"Northern" includes all non-southern senators.

"Southern" includes Alabama, Arkansas, Florida, Georgia, Louisiana, Mississippi, North Carolina, South Carolina, Tennessee, Texas, and Virginia.

The twelve Democrats mentioned by *Crisis* were the six "nay" northern Democrats plus the seven absentees.

(Roll calls in Congressional Record, Vol. 96, Part 6, 7299–7300; and Vol. 96, Part 8, 9981–9982. Cited in Herbert Garfinkel, *When Negroes March*, New York: Atheneum, 1969, p. 167.)

went to the country in the 1952 presidential election crying, "ABOL-ISH RULE 22 IN '52," a zinger of a slogan aimed at Senate filibustering but one with little apparent effect.

With the advent of the Korean War, FEPC once again became a matter of presidential province. President Truman had already established, in 1948, a Fair Employment Board in the Civil Service Commission. In 1951, after pressure from civil rights forces including a commemorative ceremony on the tenth anniversary of the first FEPC order at President Roosevelt's Hyde Park grave with Mrs. Roosevelt participating, President Truman created the President's Committee on Government Contract Compliance to oversee the enforcement of anti-discrimination clauses in government contracts. President Eisenhower reconstituted the agency in 1953, placing it under the chairmanship of the Vice President, who, to everyone's surprise (Nixon opposed FEPC in Congress), did a commendable job.

Despite the defeat of federal FEPC, civil rights forces did not despair of social justice. On looking back from this side of the turbulent 1960s, the presidency of Dwight David Eisenhower appears positively euphoric. It was not, entirely. Secretary of State John Foster Dulles rushed to the brink of one international catastrophe after another. Business appeared to be in the White House, if not in the saddle. "Eight millionaires and a plumber," TRB of *The New Republic* sardonically characterized the President's cabinet. Charles Wilson, former president of General Motors and Secretary of Defense, told the Armed Services Committee that for years he had assumed that "what was good for our country was good for General Motors, and vice versa." Adlai Stevenson remarked, "While the New Dealers have all left Washington to make way for the car dealers, I hasten to say that I, for one, do not believe the story that the general welfare has become a subsidiary of General Motors." Somewhere between Wilson's assumption and Stevenson's witticism, the mood of the country emerged. President Eisenhower did go to Korea, and the war came to a close. Senator McCarthy got his comeuppance at the hands of the chief Army counsel, Joseph Welch, in the televised Army hearings of 1954, and McCarthyism faded into history. Unemployment fell from 5.0 percent in 1950 to 3.0 percent in 1951, to 2.7 percent in 1952, and down to 2.5 percent in 1953. Blacks continued to move off southern farms into the urban areas of the South, and from the South to the big cities of the North, Midwest, and Pacific Coast. Between 1940 and 1950, the South lost through migration over one million blacks, and 1.5 million more in the following decade. The black migration to California jumped from slightly over 4,000 a year in the 1930s, to roughly 25,890 a year in the 1940s, and about 35,400 a year during the 1950s. As the table shows, the bulk of the migrants moved to New York, Illinois, Michigan, Ohio, and California—all states with FEPC laws.° The strains attendant on so great a movement of peoples, many of them young, were easily overlooked in periods of full employment. Indeed, few during the 1950s worried about the social consequences of this great youthful influx into overcrowded urban slums.

White supremacy appeared to be on the run, if not fully overcome by economic and social gains. "The year 1950 is past," declared a January 1951 editorial in *The Crisis*. "It is not easy to draw up a balance sheet in race relations. Yet we feel that Negroes reaped more wheat than tares." The awarding of the Nobel Peace Prize to Dr. Ralph J. Bunche, *Crisis* declared, "is a personal achievement which redounds to our credit and which racial barriers would have denied Negroes fifteen years ago." Advances, said the NAACP journal, "have been tucked away in small news items buried in fillers on the inside pages of the daily papers." The editorial cited the employment of Fred Cooper on a white professional football team in Richmond, Virginia; the awarding of the *Prix de Rome* to Ulysses Kay; the appointment of Dr. Howard McNeil to the Michigan State Board of Registration in Medicine; the installation of the Reverend Maurice Dawkins as a member of the ministerial staff of the Community Church in New York City; the appointment of Dr. Kenneth McClaine at the Columbia University College of Physicians and Surgeons. "Some," said *Crisis*, "might call these mere straws in the wind, but they do indicate the direction in which the wind is blowing."

Blacks, as *Crisis* phrased it, "reaped some tares, too,"—straws tossed about in more disturbing winds. There was the shocking attempt to burn the house of distinguished scientist Dr. Percy Julian, because he had bought in a white neighborhood. Restrictive covenant suits were brought by some whites in the Firestone-Florence area of Los Angeles against those who sold homes to Negroes. When Henry E. Clark, Jr., a Negro veteran, sought to move his family into a new home, a $60-a-month apartment, in all-white Cicero, Illinois, on July 11, 1951, a

° Estimated Net Intercensal Migration of Negroes for Selected States:

State	1950–60	1940–50
New York°°	282,000	243,600
Illinois	189,000	179,800
Michigan	127,000	163,300
Ohio	133,000	106,700
California	354,000	258,900

°° 1952 had FEPC with enforcement powers.
New Jersey, Connecticut, Massachusetts, New Mexico, Oregon, Rhode Island, Washington, Indiana, and Wisconsin had laws relying on persuasion.
Illinois, Indiana, Michigan, Minnesota, Montana, Ohio, Pennsylvania, Colorado, and California bills introduced, but not passed (1952).
(*The American Negro Reference Book*, John P. Davis, ed., Englewood Cliffs, N.J.: Prentice-Hall Inc., 1970, p. 110.)

mob, aided by the local police, started fires in the building and forced Clark to flee at gunpoint. "Get out of Cicero," the police chief told him, "and don't come back to town or you'll get a bullet through you." A year later, an investigating grand jury, with "a passion for irrelevancy," as Charles Abrams once put it, indicted an NAACP attorney defending Clark as well as the owner of the apartment house, her lawyer, and her rental agent, charging them with conspiracy to injure property by causing "depreciation in the market selling price." The indictments were later dropped, but then no blacks live in Cicero even though many work in its manufacturing plants. Even more disturbing was the murder of H. T. Moore, NAACP coordinator for Florida. He was killed and his wife injured by a bomb placed under his home in Mims, Florida, on Christmas night, 1951. An organizer of voter registration drives, Moore was a special target for Florida racists.

Alarming as such events were, most black leaders believed that they were offset, at least partially, by court victories over segregation and gains in black voting. In a 1944 decision, *Smith v. Allwright*, the so-called "Texas case," the United States Supreme Court abolished "white primary" laws and rules that had excluded Negroes from participation in Democratic party primaries. Voter registration in the South, chiefly in the cities, rose from 5 percent of the southern voting-age black population in 1940 to 28 percent in 1952, roughly a million new voters. By the 1950s, the great migration to the North created a new massive source of black voting strength, causing, according to Walter White, "such distribution of the Negro vote that it holds the potential balance of power in seventeen states with 281 votes in the electoral college—fifteen more than the 266 necessary to elect a President."

Economically, there was some cause to rejoice, too. According to a 1952 study prepared for a Senate subcommittee on Labor and Management Relations by the Bureau of Labor Statistics, 1950 census figures showed that the Negro wage and salary worker earned an average of about $1,300, or 52 percent of the average for white workers that year. The 1939 average had been about $400, or less than 40 percent than that of white workers. Death rates remained higher among blacks than among whites, but the difference had narrowed. In 1935, the death rate among Negroes was 17.3 per 1,000, and among whites, 11.1. By 1949, the respective figures were 12.6 and 8.4. Life expectancy rose, largely because of the control of infectious disease. Back in 1920, the life expectancy of a Negro male at birth was forty-seven years, or nine years less than that of a white male, fifty-six. In 1950, the comparable figures were fifty-nine and sixty-six years of age. In 1950, blacks over twenty-five had completed an average of seven years in school, nearly three years less than the average for whites. School enrollment, however, had increased appreciably between 1940 and 1950, with approximately 15 percent of all blacks eighteen to twenty-four enrolled in schools in 1950, as against 9 percent in 1940.

This growth in educational enrollment gave added weight to what NAACP's *Crisis* termed the "most far-reaching achievement" of 1950—the successful arguing by NAACP attorneys and lawyers for the Negro fraternity, Alpha Phi Alpha, of three key segregation cases before the Supreme Court. The Court acted unanimously in all three, striking down Jim Crow on railway dining cars in the South (*Henderson v. United States*), abolishing segregation at the University of Oklahoma (*McLaurin v. Oklahoma State Regents*), and ordering the admission of Herman Marion Sweatt to the University of Texas Law School (*Sweatt v. Painter*). "Although these rulings do not bring the millennium," declared *Crisis*, "they do remove major barriers to our fight on segregation."

They did more than that. By encouraging the NAACP to undertake a direct assault on *Plessy v. Ferguson*—the "separate but equal" doctrine as applied to public schools—the above cases set the stage for the final knockout of *de jure* segregation in the United States. Back in 1934, a young, lanky black lawyer in Baltimore, Maryland, Thurgood Marshall, met a black student, Donald Murray, who wanted to enroll at the University of Maryland Law School. He was denied admission, and Marshall, who had commuted to Howard Law School to earn his degree, brought suit against the state of Maryland. Since the state had failed to provide a separate law school for its black citizens, Marshall argued, Murray was entitled to admission. The Maryland courts agreed, ruling that under the "separate but equal" doctrine, the university law school had to admit Murray. The *Murray* case did not go to the United States Supreme Court—in part, because Marshall had done so well in his argument—but, in 1938, the Court held that an out-of-state scholarship to Lloyd Gaines, a black student wishing to study law in Missouri, was a denial of equal protection of the laws as guaranteed under the United States Constitution. The Court said that the state could only guarantee equal protection within its borders. In *Sipuel v. Board of Regents*, a 1948 decision, the Court ruled that Negroes were not required to first demand of the state—in this instance, Oklahoma— the erection of separate facilities for them before they could claim a denial of equal protection. When Herman Marion Sweatt sought admission to the University of Texas Law School, the university, in an attempt to meet Court criteria, hastily set up a law school for Negroes in a basement. Sweatt claimed it was impossible to secure an equal education under those conditions, and the Supreme Court agreed. As yet, however, the Court had not set aside *Plessy v. Ferguson*, holding that it was not necessary to reexamine the doctrine to grant relief to the Negro plaintiffs.

In *Missouri ex rel. Gaines v. Canada*, Chief Justice Charles E. Hughes had ruled that "equal" came first, and that laws separating the races were only admissible where both groups start off with equal privileges. The NAACP, in the late 1940s, launched a series of "equalization" suits in Virginia and elsewhere, taking advantage of the Hughes interpretation in an effort to improve education for black pupils. Facilities and opportunities in separate schools were unequal and discriminatory. Injunctions were sought requiring school officials to cease discriminating against black pupils, without, however, as Spottswood W. Robinson III, an NAACP counsel, put it, "either admitting the validity of separate school laws or directly attacking them at this stage." Courts began ordering immediate equalization, notably in the King George County, Virginia, *Smith* case. As a result, the Virginia legislature voted a grant of $45 million for emergency construction in the years following the 1951 *Smith* decision and 69 percent went to black schools. Harry S. Ashmore estimated in 1954 that white-black equalization would require $1.3 billion in new facilities and another $1.7 billion to eliminate substandard schools.

"Separate but equal" threatened to become a financial burden that the South could ill-afford. Desegregation on the face of it would prove less costly, and the NAACP hoped the South would see the financial light if forced to desegregate. Encouraged by the *McLaurin* and *Sweatt* rulings, Thurgood Marshall called a conference of NAACP attorneys in New York City from June 26 to 27, 1951, and there it was decided to take on segregated education directly as discriminatory *per se*, no matter how equal the facilities and opportunities. As Marshall, then director of NAACP's Legal Department, put it, "We are going to insist on non-segregation in American public education from top to bottom—from law school to kindergarten." Black leadership had traveled a long way from the time, only two short decades before, when leading black educators would meet, as they did at Howard University in 1931, to discuss ways and means of improving Negro schools under the "separate but equal" doctrine. A similar gathering at Howard in 1952 aptly described its deliberations as "The Courts and Racial *Integration* in Education [my italics]." By then, a series of court cases challenging segregated education were well on their journey to the Supreme Court.

Behind the NAACP's frontal attack on segregated schools was the growing despair of Negro parents, who realized that Jim Crow education was not preparing their children for the opportunities of the second half of the century. An FEPC law may open up hitherto closed doors, but it could not make up for an inadequate education. The young people leaving the land in droves simply were not prepared for the life they found in the big city. Harry S. Ashmore notes in *The Negro and the Schools* that in the early days of segregated education "most school officials gave little attention to their Negro charges. They reflected the attitude of the great majority of whites who believed that Negroes needed no more than the bare essentials of grade school education to assume their proper place in the social order, and no matter what the statutes might show for the record, this became the settled policy in the region."

Since World War II, according to Ashmore, "the South has made its greatest effort on behalf of public education, and it has given Negro children the largest share of the total outlay they have ever known." During 1951 and 1952, the thirteen southern states spent more than $1.2 billion for school operations—nearly four times the expenditures for the 1939–40 school year. Of this, some $220 million went toward Negro schools. The then current expenditure per pupil was $164.83 for whites and $115.08 for black students. Negro children accounted for one-fourth of the South's public school population in 1952, making up nearly one-half of Mississippi's total, 42 percent of South Carolina's, and nearly one-third of Georgia's, and smaller percentages in each of the remaining states. (School attendance and expenditure figures are from data gathered by the staff of the Southern States Cooperative Program in Educational Administration for Harry S. Ashmore's Fund for the Advancement of Education Study, *The Negro and the Schools*.) The disparity in expenditures per pupil between white and black in metropolitan and rural districts reveals the discrepancy in treatment afforded black students. In Mississippi, for example, metropolitan expenditures in 1952 were $152.60 per white pupil, $78.11 for blacks, as against an expenditure for rural white youngsters of $82.73, and $27.05 for rural black students. Alabama spent $147.20 per white pupil in metropolitan areas, and $105.40 for blacks; in rural schools, the state spent $122.14 for whites, and $96.41 for blacks. Florida spent the most, with $204.58 going to white metropolitan students, $179.54 to black; $189.51 to white rural students, and $119.22 to black youngsters. North Carolina's expenditures were the most equitable of all the seven Deep South states, spending $169.64 for metropolitan whites, $161.14 for blacks, as compared with $148.98 for rural whites, and $117.23 for rural black students. Perhaps more telling are the figures giving the number of books per student in the libraries of white and Negro schools in the South—better than four books per pupil in white schools to one in those for blacks.

Mary E. Mebane [Liza], professor of English at South Carolina State College, writing in *The New York Times*, has given a graphic account of what it means to be a child in a segregated school system. "What is a segregated school?" she asks. "It's when you're in the second grade and your eye reads the name 'Bragtown High School,' and you also see in front of the book 'discard' and even though you're only 7 years old, you know, as you turn the pages that have tears patched with a thick yellowing tape, that you're using a book that a white girl used last year and tore up, and your mother is paying book rent just like her mother paid book rent. You get the secondhand book. And it gives you a thing about secondhand books that does not go away until you are teaching yourself and are able to buy all the new ones you want."

Segregation, she continues "is when you leave your teaching job on Friday after lunch and ride west across eastern North Carolina—Martin, Edgecombe, and Nash counties—and the orange school buses are in the yards of the white schools—they are in session, but bending over green fields are black children—they are on a short day or no session at all until the crop is in." The purpose of total segregation, Ms. Mebane points out, "was to insure that from one-third to three-fourths of its population, that part which was black, would never get the education which would make them economically competitive. It worked."

Whatever rationale there may have been for a short school year and only the rudiments of reading and writing in a predominantly agricultural society or area or time, there was none for such educational policies in the 1940s and 1950s. For southern agriculture was undergoing a much delayed revolution, one that would drive more people off the land than the burgeoning cities could comfortably absorb.

Cotton was king, and the character of its production reinforced the caste system of the South. Cotton is labor intensive, requiring an abundance of cheap, manual labor. Since, as one historian puts it, it cannot be pilfered and is worth little until ginned, it lends itself to absentee ownership and sharecropping. Two-thirds of the farming South's cash income, in pre-World War II years, came from cotton and tobacco—over half of the South's farmers depended on cotton alone. As a report on the economic conditions of the South, prepared for the President in 1938, noted, "They are one-crop farmers, subject year after year to risks which would appall the average businessman. All their eggs are in one basket which can be upset, and often is, by the weather, the boll weevil, or the cotton market." A world glut in cotton, the farm policies of the New Deal which paid farmers to reduce acreage, the growth of industrialization in the South, postwar competition with synthetics—all have contributed, each in its own fashion, to a major agricultural revolution in the South. In the years 1909 to 1913, when the first heavy infestation of boll weevil occurred east of the Mississippi and when the black migration North began, nine southern states planted 32,218,000 acres of cotton from which 12,640,000 bales were harvested. Over the decades, acreage planted decreased while the yield per acre has increased so that much less land, 12,640,000 acres in 1960, produces nearly as much cotton, 9,561,000 bales.

In 1947, an official of a large manufacturing company announced that his firm hoped to "build more than 1,000 mechanical [cotton] pickers for the 1948 crop season." He sounded the end of the old ways. The yield per acre in cotton rose from 226 pounds in 1939 to 485 in 1965. Manhours per acre fell from 99 in 1939 to 83 in 1945, 66 in 1955 and to 30 by 1965. Manhours used in producing a bale of cotton fell even more sharply, from 209 in 1939 to 146 in 1945, to 74 in 1955, and to 30 in 1965.

"Cotton," writes historian Thomas D. Clark, "was still the South's chief single cash crop in 1964, but . . . corn, grass, and livestock became the foundation on which [the modern South] stands." Hay became one of the Southland's five leading crops in cash value. In many areas of the South, cover cropping (hay and grain) replaced row cropping (cotton and tobacco), further reducing the need for agricultural labor.

"It is the plantations," a southern economist wrote, "with their croppers that can most easily be recast into large-scale, mechanized agriculture that offers efficiency in the economic sense . . . ." And that is what has happened, with disastrous consequences for sharecroppers and tenant farmers. In 1925, there were 2,891,423 farms of an average size of 57.7 acres in the South; by 1959, the number of farms had shrunk to 1,440,934, a 15 percent reduction, while the size of the average farm had more than tripled to 192.7 acres. The reduction is even greater in tenant holdings: 1,790,783 farms in the depths of the Depression in 1930, down to 381,000 farms in 1959. Negro tenants in 1930 numbered 698,839, but only 138,000 in 1959. Mechanization, crop diversification, and the growth of what are, in Carey McWilliams' descriptive phrase, "factories in the field," changed the character of agriculture in the South. "Thus," writes historian Clark, "both tedious row crops and an army of unskilled and largely illiterate laborers have been forced off the southern farms." It was, as he put it, "a social displacement of staggering proportions."

The urbanization of the Negro changed the nature of the Negro problem. As Professor Emmett E. Dorsey, head of the Department of Government at Howard University, observed in a 1955 paper on the "Political Ideologies of the New Negro," urbanization "gives a new urgency to the civil rights issue. Discrimination irks Negroes more forcibly in the new economic and social relationship of the urban economy. Urban Negroes must seek aid from trade unions and above all from government. A Fair Employment Practices Commission becomes a basic security measure—indeed, an aspect of civil rights. Government must afford better housing, more and better health services and recreational facilities. The importance and effectiveness of the traditional leadership is declining. Bargaining with and appealing to the sympathies of the leading white people are no longer adequate techniques, nor, indeed, are they very relevant ones for the pressing institutional needs of the new urban population."

Black awareness of the potential inherent in the new condition of the black populace gave urgency to the five cases then before the United States Supreme Court. As the NAACP summed up its position, "At ultimate stake is the future of the anachronistic system of segregation not only in education but also in all other phases of public life in the nation. We of the NAACP have long maintained that segregation is a divisive and anti-democratic device designed to perpetuate an obsolete caste system which flatly contravenes the basic ethical concepts of our Judeo-Christian traditions. We have held that segregation *per se* is unconstitutional. Should the Court uphold this point of view, it could mean that all laws requiring or permitting racial segregation in schools, transportation, recreation, shelter, and public accommodations generally would ultimately be invalid.

"When Thurgood Marshall and the other NAACP lawyers associated with him address the nine justices of the country's highest tribunal . . . they will contend, at least by implication, that integration cannot be a halfway measure. Our nation cannot remain half-integrated and half-segregated today any more than it could continue half-free and half-slave a century ago."

Aptly enough, it was the Topeka, Kansas, case that gave its name *Brown v. Board of Education of Topeka*° to the consolidated opinion of the United States Supreme Court on segregated schooling. Topeka had segregated black pupils in the first six grades, and their parents charged that this denied their children "equal protection of the laws." The plaintiffs conceded that school facilities, in this instance, were substantially equal for the two races. NAACP attorneys brought in a battery of expert witnesses to testify that segregation imposed serious social and psychological handicaps upon Negro children. Unlike the southern courts, the three-judge Kansas court accepted the NAACP thesis, "segregation with the sanction of the law . . . has a tendency to retard the educational and mental development of Negro children." But, said the court, it could not declare segregation unconstitutional, feeling itself bound by United States Supreme Court precedents to uphold "separate but equal" in the absence of any demonstrable inequalities in a dual school system. Ironically, the Topeka Board of Education terminated segregation on its own before the United States Supreme Court handed down its historic decision.

° The other cases were: *Briggs v. Elliot*, Clarendon County, South Carolina; *Davis v. County School Board*, Prince Edward County, Virginia; *Belton v. Gebhart*, Wilmington, Delaware; and *Bolling v. Sharpe*, Washington, D.C.

Three years earlier, Judge J. Waties Waring, the dissenting judge in the South Carolina case in which the state court upheld segregation, wrote with discerning clarity, "Segregation is *per se* inequality . . . . The whole thing is unreasonable, unscientific, and based upon unadulterated prejudice." His dissent earned him some stones thrown through the windows of his house and a social ostracism that, ultimately, drove him in his retirement to live in the North. Unhappily, the whole unsavory business of segregation could not be dismissed with such disarming simplicity, though it ought to have been.

Dr. Kenneth B. Clark, then an assistant professor of psychology at the College of the City of New York, marshaled the testimony of social scientists and psychologists for the "Brandeis-type" brief NAACP attorneys presented before the Supreme Court. Dr. Clark reported tests that he and others had administered showing that discrimination and segregation caused black children to be disturbed and confused in their own self-esteem and gave them feelings of inferiority and hostility toward themselves. Dr. Clark reported that the injuries were enduring and prevented wholesome development. Before the high court, NAACP attorneys also cogently argued: In a democracy, citizens from every group, no matter what their social or economic status or their religious or ethnic origins, are expected to participate widely in the making of important decisions. The public school, even more than the family, the church, business, political, and social groups, and other institutions, has become an effective agency for giving to all people that broad background of attitudes and skills required to function effectively as participants in a democracy. Thus, said the attorneys and witnesses, education comprehends the entire process of developing and training the mental, physical, and moral powers and capacities of human beings, and these capacities cannot be developed properly, even in the finest of school buildings, if the students are segregated by law. As Thurgood Marshall put it on one occasion, "The Negro child is branded in his own mind as inferior; he thus acquires a roadblock in his mind which prevents his ever feeling that he is equal. You can teach him the Constitution, anthropology, citizenship, but he knows it is not true."

After much delay—the earliest cases reached the Court for the first time in 1951—the Court, on May 17, 1954, "Decision Monday," in a unanimous opinion read by Chief Justice Earl Warren, declared: "We conclude that in the field of public education the doctrine of 'separate but equal' has no place. Separate educational facilities are inherently unequal . . . ."

That evening, at a party of friends, many of whom were deeply involved in civil rights, Walter White said, "We together have created a miracle . . . . This is a day of jubilation."

VI

Montgomery: "New Negro... New Times"

ROSA PARKS, A COMELY, soft-spoken, brown-skinned seamstress, had had a hard day, sewing white folks' clothes at Montgomery Fair, a leading department store in Alabama's capital city. When she boarded the Cleveland Avenue bus for home, she found a seat to the front of the Jim Crow section, just behind that reserved for white passengers. Thursday evening, December 1, 1955, was a busy time; early Christmas shoppers crowded the streets and traffic was heavy. At the next stop, more whites thrust their way onto the bus, and Mrs. Parks was asked to move to the back. She refused. "Just having paid for a seat and then only ride a couple of blocks without being disturbed and then I would have to stand, was too much."

Martin Luther King would write later, in his account of the Montgomery bus boycott, *Stride Toward Freedom*, "She was anchored to that seat by the accumulated indignities of days gone by and the boundless aspirations of generations yet unborn." Mrs. Parks puts it more modestly, and succinctly, "I was just plain tired, and my feet hurt." Her calm, dogged determination forestalled the customary arrest for disorderly conduct or drunkenness. Driver J. P. Blake, empowered to enforce segregation under a city ordinance, placed Mrs. Parks under arrest, and summoned the police. She was booked explicitly for violating the municipal code segregating the races on Montgomery buses.

Mrs. Parks called E. D. Nixon, a Pullman porter, who was long respected in the Negro community for his raw courage and fight for civil rights. He had been head of the Alabama NAACP and Mrs. Parks had served as his secretary. Nixon posted the bail bond, and drove Mrs. Parks to her home. Meanwhile, telephones rang in black homes throughout the city. Members of the Women's Council, created in 1951 when the local League of Women Voters refused to integrate, discussed the arrest and what to do. The council's two hundred or so members were in a feisty mood. Hadn't they just pressured white merchants to eliminate separate white/black drinking fountains and to drop the custom of not supplying the courtesy titles of Mrs. and Miss when billing black customers? Hadn't they secured, in 1954, the employment of four black policemen? The council's energetic president, Jo Ann Robinson, couldn't have agreed more when Nixon boomed over the telephone, "This is what we've been waiting for!"

The idea of a boycott was in the air. Historian L. D. Reddick, in his biography of Martin Luther King, *Crusader Without Violence*, reports, "Credit [for the idea of a boycott] must go to an unidentified professional man and a teacher." As a long-time activist in the Brotherhood of Pullman Car Porters, Nixon was familiar with strikes and boycotts, and through A. Philip Randolph, he knew something of Gandhian philosophy and tactics. As Bayard Rustin would say years later of Nixon, "He, too, had been touched by Randolph." The Women's Council had considered a protest action earlier when a young woman had been arrested for refusing to yield her seat to a white passenger. The discovery that she was an unwed mother put an end to that project, however. Mrs. Parks was just what was wanted. As Nixon later told Ted Poston of the New York *Post*, "She was perfect for what was needed. There was nothing they could point the finger at. Her character was untouchable. And she was a grown-up, no kid."

Mrs. Robinson urged Nixon to take the lead in organizing a protest. Later that night, Nixon sat on the edge of his bed, and said to his wife, "You know, I think every Negro in town should stay off the buses for one day in protest for Mrs. Parks' arrest. What do you think?"

"I think you ought to stop daydreaming," Mrs. Nixon replied. "Turn out that light and get some sleep."

Nixon rose early the next morning, and called Ralph David Abernathy, pastor of Montgomery's First Baptist Church. Born and raised in Marengo County, the heart of Alabama's rigidly segregated black belt, Abernathy served as an Army sergeant in World War II. His father owned a 500-acre plantation, and the younger Abernathy liked to say he had "never worked for a white man." Stocky, earthy in language, pragmatic, Abernathy, a graduate of Alabama State College and Atlanta University, was a hearty preacher, at twenty-nine closer to the old-style, rollicking, spirited "hell-fire" preaching than his youthful colleague, Martin Luther King, Jr., at the "fashionable" Dexter Avenue Baptist Church. Not surprisingly, Abernathy readily accepted Nixon's suggestion that a protest be organized.

When Nixon called the new preacher at the Dexter Avenue Baptist

Church, he plunged straight into the story of Mrs. Parks' arrest. "We have taken this type of thing too long already," he told King. "I feel the time has come to boycott the buses. Only through a boycott can we make it clear to the white folks that we will not accept this type of treatment any longer." King agreed that protest was the order of business for Montgomery's Negro community. So, for the next half hour, the three men called back-and-forth discussing plans and strategy. Nixon suggested a meeting that evening of all ministers and civic leaders, King offered the use of his church, and, along with Abernathy, they settled down to the day's roundup of community leaders.

Meanwhile, the Women's Council promoted the boycott idea. Mimeographed leaflets were distributed, saying, ". . . This has to be stopped . . . if Negroes did not ride the buses, they could not operate . . . every Negro stay off the buses Monday [the day set for Mrs. Parks' trial] in protest . . . ."

On Friday evening, some forty people, representing every segment of Negro life in Montgomery, turned up at the meeting held at the Dexter Avenue Baptist Church, "I saw physicians, schoolteachers, lawyers, businessmen, postal workers, union leaders, and clergymen," King later recalled, though the larger number were of the clergy, reflecting the importance of the churches in southern Negro life. Abernathy, King, and Mrs. Robinson were pleased at the turnout, an unusual display of solidarity. There had been, as King noted in Stride Toward Freedom, "an appalling lack of unity among the leaders [of the Negro community]." E. D. Nixon headed the Progressive Democrats, and Professor Rufus Lewis, the Citizens' Committee; both organizations dedicated to voter registration and black participation in politics. The Women's Council and the NAACP competed for civil rights leadership, and, as King put it, "smaller groups further divided the Negro community. While the heads of each of these organizations were able, dedicated leaders with common aims, their separate allegiances made it difficult for them to come together on the basis of a higher unity." King also complained about complacency, indifference, and apathy.

E. D. Nixon had to work that evening, and in his absence the Reverend L. Roy Bennett, president of the Interdenominational Ministerial Alliance, chaired the meeting. "Now is the time to move," he told the audience. "This is no time to talk; it is time to act." The chafing audience, however, did want to talk and participate in the planning, and Bennett's high-handedness created an uproar that threatened to end the boycott movement before it began. Soon, however, the meeting developed a consensus. Negro taxicab companies were to be asked to transport people at bus-fare cost; a citywide mass meeting was to be called to cap the Monday demonstration and make further plans. A leaflet was drafted for distribution urging "Don't ride the bus to work, to town, to school, or anyplace Monday, December 5. Another Negro woman has been arrested and put in jail because she refused to give up her bus seat . . . . Come to a mass meeting, Monday at 7 P.M., at the Holt Street Baptist Church for further instruction."

Over the weekend, preparations went ahead with growing enthusiasm. Leaflets were passed out on street corners, in poolrooms, and at home. L. D. Reddick, however, reported in the spring 1956 issue of *Dissent*, that only a fraction of Negro bus riders saw the boycott appeals. News of the boycott, nonetheless, gained widespread circulation through an unexpected break. According to King, a semiliterate maid gave a copy of the boycott leaflet to her white employer, who then turned it over to the *Montgomery Advertiser*. Nixon, however, claims he gave a copy to reporter Joe Azbell, saying, "If you promise you'll play it up strong in your paper Sunday, I'll give you a hot tip." King's biographer, David L. Lewis, points to the objectivity of Azbell's subsequent reporting of the boycott as giving credence to Nixon's claim. In any event, on Sunday, a front-page story alerted Montgomery, black and white, of the impending boycott. "Negroes laugh when they tell about this," Reddick reported in *Dissent* mid-boycott. "They say that the newspaper was mostly interested in letting the white folks know what the Negroes were up to." But Montgomery blacks got the message, too, as preachers hammered it home in Sunday sermons throughout the city.

Sunday evening, the Kings hoped to get to bed early. But their infant daughter, Yolanda, cried, and the telephone kept ringing. The young minister and his wife discussed the projected boycott, plagued by doubts. "Another striking fact about Montgomery's Negro community," King wrote in *Stride Toward Freedom*, "was the apparent passivity of the majority of the uneducated. While there were always some who struck out against segregation, the largest number accepted it without apparent protest." The Kings finally agreed that if the boycott was 60 percent effective, it would be a success. Shortly before midnight, "with a strange mixture of hope and anxiety," the young couple fell asleep.

They woke early the next morning, and after toast and coffee in the kitchen, Mrs. King went into the living room to watch for the first bus, due at 6 A.M. at the bus stop just outside the house. With headlights blazing in the December morning darkness, the bus rolled by. Mrs. King shouted, "Martin, Martin, come quickly!" The first bus, normally loaded with domestics off to their jobs, was empty, and so was the next, and the next, and so would they all be for a year and fifteen days.

Mrs. Parks was convicted and fined $10 plus $4 costs. On the courthouse steps, Abernathy, King, Nixon, and the Reverend E. N. French, minister of the Hilliard Chapel A. M. E. Zion Church, discussed the need for an *ad hoc* organization to carry on with the boycott. They decided to raise the question at a 3 P.M. meeting called by Bennett to prepare for the evening's mass meeting. The elated boycott leaders, "a well-balanced group" according to King, "including ministers of all denominations, schoolteachers, businessmen, and two lawyers," readily accepted the proposal. Abernathy came up with a name: the Montgomery Improvement Association (MIA). Professor Rufus Lewis nominated King for president, and the motion was carried by acclamation. "The action caught me unawares," King later recalled. "It had happened so quickly that I did not even have time to think it through. It is possible that if I had, I would have declined the nomination."

King recently had declined the presidency of the local NAACP chapter, pleading the press of his pastoral duties. He had broadened the auxiliary program of his church, establishing committees to revitalize religious education, to reinvigorate services to the sick and needy, and to develop social and political action, among others. His week was taken up by five to ten such meetings, fifteen hours of sermon preparation, not to mention marriages, funerals, visiting the sick, and personal conferences. There was a new baby to consider, and the Kings were reluctant about taking on additional community responsibilities. But E. D. Nixon had informally canvassed the leaders of the boycott, and they were favorable to the suggestion of King's presidency. Nixon was fully aware of the potential for jealousy that existed among the established leaders of Montgomery's Negro community. He himself was a logical choice to head the MIA, but he felt his lack of education to be inhibiting, and knowing that his job required that he be out of town a good deal of the time, decided against undertaking the task. According to an anecdote told by Bayard Rustin, when Nixon broached the idea of King's taking over, saying, "I'm too old, too tired, I want you to lead the boycott," King replied, "I can't. I've only been here a few months." Nixon said, "Exactly! You haven't had time to earn any enemies."

It was a wise choice. The boycott movement was a spontaneous uprising of the Negroes of Montgomery. As L. D. Reddick put it in his *Dissent* account, "everything was *ad hoc* and tentative . . . . No leader was calling the shots . . . . The indignation and demands for action by the 'common people' swept everyone along like a flood." There was, however, an able, collective leadership coming together in the Montgomery Improvement Association—Abernathy; King; Nixon; Mrs. Robinson; Professor Lewis; Professor James E. Pierce, economist and political scientist, who briefed King, the newcomer, on the intricacies of Alabama politics; Fred D. Gray, Montgomery-born, a year out of law school, who guided MIA and the court cases through southern legal booby traps; the Reverend Robert S. Graetz, white pastor of Montgomery's Lutheran congregation, who was the only white member of MIA and who interpreted the boycott to the white community and arranged the all-too-few interracial meetings held in secret; P. M. Blair, "the bronze mayor of Montgomery"; S. W. Lee, mortician, whose accounting skills were such a great asset to the MIA; Dr. Moses Jones, and the many ministers. "Together and separately," Reddick wrote in *Crusader Without Violence,* "they helped him [King] lighten up Montgomery heavens and remove the darkness from the path of walking feet."

King became the voice of the boycott. In his rich natural baritone, he established a unique rapport with his audiences. People were deeply moved; one woman said that when she heard King speak she felt that God himself was near. "In some instinctive way," Louis E. Lomax wrote in *The Negro Revolt,* "he helps Negroes understand how they themselves feel and why they feel as they do; and he is the first Negro minister I have ever heard who can reduce the Negro problem to a spiritual matter and yet inspire the people to seek a solution on this side of the Jordan, not in the life beyond death."

On the evening of the first day, the Holt Street Baptist Church was packed with people by five o'clock and close to four thousand others were standing patiently outside waiting for the eight o'clock mass meeting to begin. It opened, a half hour late, with the singing of "Onward Christian Soldiers," with the assembled voices sounding as "a mighty ring like the glad echo of heaven itself" to the man who gave voice to their aspirations.

Standing at the rostrum without notes, seeming taller than his five feet seven and with his light brown face glistening beneath the glare of kleig lights, Martin Luther King briefly reviewed the arrest of Mrs. Parks, the history of abuses suffered by black bus passengers, and then hit his stride, "But there comes a time when people get tired.

"We are here this evening to say to those who have mistreated us for so long that we are tired; tired of being segregated and humiliated; tired of being kicked about by the brutal feet of oppression. We had no alternative but to protest. For many years, we have shown amazing patience. We have sometimes given our white brothers the feeling that we liked the way we are being treated. But we come here tonight to be saved from the patience that makes us patient with anything less than freedom and justice."

King emerged as if by chance, but as biographer David L. Lewis noted, he was chosen for certain very pragmatic reasons. "Whoever headed the MIA, to be effective, must not have resided in Montgomery's querulous black community long enough to have acquired a great many enemies," Lewis comments. "Such a person would ideally be able to pack up for another job elsewhere in the likely event of failure of the movement and retribution from the white community. He should also be sufficiently naive, or brave, to accept designation as the exclusive leader of the boycott."

King possessed all these qualities in abundance, including a charisma that would attract a growing following. Born in Atlanta, Georgia, on January 15, 1929, King had roots deep in the black South. His father, Martin Luther, Sr., the prestigious pastor of Atlanta's Ebenezer Baptist Church, was the son of a hard-working, hard-drinking sharecropper of mixed Irish and African ancestry. He left home at fifteen with a scant four years of education, worked in an Atlanta garage, went to school evenings, and ultimately earned his degree at Morehouse. The senior King had the call early in his teens, and soon served as pastor to two small Baptist congregations. In 1926, he married Alberta Williams, daughter of the Reverend A. D. Williams, the patriarch of Ebenezer Baptist Church.

A. D. Williams, born the year of the Emancipation Proclamation, was a "hard" preacher with a redeeming sense of humor. Once, after a proper parishioner had upbraided him for his ungrammatical English, Williams announced, while reporting on the state of the church's finances, "I done give a hundred dollars, but the gentleman who corrected me has given nothing." Martin's maternal grandfather was a charter member of the NAACP. He led a successful fight against a school-bond issue that did not provide for the construction of black schools. His son-in-law continued this active tradition by taking over the Ebenezer Baptist Church after A. D. William's death in 1931. Presiding over a congregation of four thousand, he led the fight in Atlanta to equalize black teachers' salaries with those of white teachers, and was instrumental in the elimination of Jim Crow elevators in the courthouse.

Martin Luther, Jr., grew up in a relatively protected atmosphere. Black enterprises flourished in Atlanta along with varied professions producing a substantial black bourgeoisie. Barber Alonzo F. Herndon founded the Atlanta Life Insurance Company in 1905, and by 1948, its assets exceeded $19 million. The Citizens' Trust Bank, America's third largest black financial institution and sole black member of the Federal Reserve System, thrived on Auburn Avenue along with the Atlanta *Daily World*, the only black radio station, WERD, and other successful black businesses. The King residence on upper Auburn Avenue was surrounded by the comfortable homes of prosperous black Atlantans, comprising a community of college professors, contractors, real estate agents, insurance executives and bankers, physicians, dentists, and morticians. The boisterous, mischievous boy tussling with his friends was scarcely conscious of this, much of which he took for granted as the young do. He was isolated from southern bigotry in its crudest and harshest form, yet neither the solid comforts of home nor the prosperous neighborhood could shield him from the outrageous stings of a rampant racism. Among his playmates as a child were two white boys, sons of a neighborhood grocer. When Martin entered elementary school, they went to another. Whenever Martin ran over to visit, their mother sent him away, telling him finally that they were not to play together any longer. Heartbroken, young Martin sought comfort from his mother, who told him as countless black mothers have told their children, "Don't let this thing impress you. Don't let it make you feel you are not as good as anyone else, and don't you forget it."

The second of three children, young Martin enjoyed a thoroughly normal boyhood, the sweet thrill of crack of bat against ball, the roughhouse of football, the responsibility of a paper route. He was a good student with an active and inquiring mind, skipping the ninth and twelfth grades at Booker T. Washington High School to enroll at Morehouse College as a freshman at the age of fifteen. The lessons that stuck, however, were not all learned at school. Once, when his father accidentally drove past a stop sign, a policeman came alongside, saying, "All right, boy, pull over and let me see your license," and the elder King retorted, pointing to Martin, "This is a 'boy.' I'm a man, and until you call me one, I will not listen to you." It was a nervous policeman, Martin observed, who hastily wrote up a ticket and fled the scene. Martin Luther King, Sr., never rode buses because of segregation. After a brush with a shoe salesman who insisted that the Kings move to the back of the store, the elder King stalked out with his son, muttering angrily, "I don't care how long I live with this system, I will never accept it."

"As far back as I could remember," King said, "I had resented segregation." As a Morehouse undergraduate, however, he took little part in civil rights activities. His studies and an active social life occupied much of his time. He majored in sociology and in adolescent rebellion toyed with the idea of becoming a lawyer. One summer, Martin worked as a laborer in Connecticut tobacco fields, enjoying the free access to Hartford movies and restaurants denied blacks back home. When he entered the dining car below the Mason-Dixon line on the journey home and the waiter pulled a curtain down in front of him, young King felt "as though that curtain had dropped on my selfhood." As a member of the Intercollegiate Council, he met white students as equals. "The wholesome relations we had in this group," he later recalled, "convinced me that we have many white persons as allies, particularly among the younger generation. I had been ready to resent the whole white race, but as I got to see more of white people my resentment was softened and a spirit of cooperation took its place."

The call to the ministry proved irresistible, and young Martin was ordained in 1947. He graduated from Morehouse a year later, and entered Crozier Theological Seminary in Chester, Pennsylvania, earning his doctorate at Boston University's graduate school of theology. King developed his interest in philosophy, reading widely in works ranging from the Old Testament prophets down to Karl Marx, Jaspers, Heidegger, and Sartre. King was strongly influenced by the social gospel of Walter Rauschenbusch, the hard-headed pragmatism of Reinhold Niebuhr's Christianity, and the existentialism of Paul Tillich. He was drawn to the personalism of Edgar Sheffield Brightman, and Brightman's associate L. Harold De Wolf profoundly affected King's belief in a personal God.

Martin Luther King was not an original philosopher. His homegrown, ingrained Baptist theology was overlaid by an encyclopedic knowledge of the principal ideas of Western philosophy from Thales of Miletus to Camus. He did, however, perceive the kinship between the Greek notion of *agape*, "love seeking to preserve and create community," and Gandhi's *satyagraha*, a like moral striving. He had read Thoreau's "Civil Disobedience" in college, heard the noted pacifist A. J. Muste speak at Crozier, and was deeply affected by Dr. Mordecai Johnson's account, given at Fellowship House in Philadelphia, of the Mahatma's life and beliefs. "His message," King later wrote of the talk given by the president of Howard University, "was so profound and electrifying that I left the meeting and bought a half-dozen books on Gandhi's life and works." But King would make the connection between his own religious roots and the discovery of the appropriateness of Thoreauvian-Gandhian tactics and philosophy to the civil rights struggle after the Montgomery bus boycott was well underway.

While in Boston, King met and wooed lovely Coretta Scott. Her father was a prosperous farmer and store owner in Perry County, some sixty miles west of Montgomery. She attended Lincoln School, a missionary institution in Marion, Alabama, staffed by black and white teachers, where she first heard Bayard Rustin speak. After graduating from Antioch College, she went to Massachusetts to study voice at the Boston Conservatory. Married at the Scott's home by Martin's father, the couple returned to Boston to complete their respective studies. The following spring, the youthful theological graduate had several choices of pastorates. Coretta King favored the North; she had had her fill of the South, and wanted to pursue a musical career. The Kings talked, thought, and prayed; Martin's sense of duty finally prevailed. For a young would-be minister, anxious to serve his people, the South may have been particularly attractive because churches there remained strong, enjoyed steadier, more committed congregations than those of the urban North. The South, too, was their home. Both had strong family ties, and for them, the South did not solely represent, as it did for so many black migrants to the North, nothing but deprivation and degradation. "Finally we agreed," King wrote in *Stride Toward Freedom*, "that, in spite of the disadvantages and inevitable sacrifices, our greatest service could be rendered in our native South. We came to the conclusion that we had something of a moral obligation to return—at least for a few years."

The Kings chose Montgomery over another offer, largely because it was conveniently located, roughly midway between their respective families. And, too, the Dexter Avenue Baptist Church was an attractive one, standing at one corner of a handsome square diagonally across from the state capitol. Coretta Scott King describes it as "definitely *affluent*." The congregation, she adds, consisted of physicians, teachers, college professors, and prosperous business people. "Poor people in Montgomery referred to it as 'the big people's church.' " The congregation was comparatively small—about three hundred people—but a select group of influential and respected citizens, many of whom taught at Alabama State College, provided an intellectual climate that could not but attract their 25-year-old pastor. Altogether, it was a fortuitous choice. As King later wrote, "we had a feeling that something remarkable was unfolding in the South, and we wanted to be on hand to witness it." Hindsight, of course, but no young black, aware and sensitive, could help but feel that change was in the offing. The Korean War had ended the year before, and black and white veterans were returning with tales of the success of integration in the armed forces. The very month that Martin Luther King and his wife came to the Dexter Avenue Baptist Church, the United States Supreme Court handed down its momentous decision barring school segregation. As writer Louis E. Lomax put it, "That was the day we won; the day we took the white man's laws and won our case before an all-white Supreme Court with a Negro lawyer, Thurgood Marshall, as our chief counsel. And we were proud."

Black expectations ran high. Mary McLeod Bethune, in a response that reflected the feelings of countless black Americans, declared, "Let all the people praise the Lord." The initial jubilation, however, was tempered by certain realities and past experience. Marvin Griffin was nominated for governor of Georgia on the pledge, "Come hell or high water, races will not be mixed in Georgia schools." Significantly for future developments, Virginia's Governor Thomas B. Stanley, who had promised, initially, to work for a plan "in keeping with the edict of the court," reversed himself, announcing, "I shall use every legal means at my command to continue segregated schools . . . ." The NAACP convened a meeting of Negro leaders from seventeen southern and border states over the May 22–23, 1954, weekend to formulate a program to bring about the implementation of the school desegregation decision. As Henry Lee Moon reported in *The Nation*, "the leaders of the association's southern units were neither fearful nor gloating. They were assured but not vaunting; reasonable but not compromising."

The Atlanta conferees instructed all NAACP branches in the affected states "to petition their local school boards to abolish segregation without delay . . . ." Clearly, however, the group was prepared for a struggle—"we will resist the use of any tactics contrived for the sole purpose of delaying desegregation." Moon reported that the conference ended on "a note of hope and anticipation. New impetus has been given to the NAACP drive to complete emancipation by the 100th anniversary of Lincoln's Proclamation of January 1, 1863."

There was cause for encouragement as well as for doubt. In October 1954, *The Crisis* declared, "The general pattern of desegregation as we go to press is good in the border and non-southern states . . . . States in the Deep South have adopted a wait-and-see policy and seven states have asked to appear as friends of the court when the Supreme Court hears arguments on December 6 on the kind of decrees it should issue to enforce its May 17 decision—they are Arkansas, Florida, Maryland, North Carolina, Oklahoma, Texas, and Tennessee." Georgia, Mississippi, and South Carolina were openly defiant, even to the point of threatening to abolish their public schools.

While there were sporadic outbreaks of violence during the year following *Brown, et al.* (notably in small border state cities or towns, Milford, Delaware; White Sulphur Springs, West Virginia; and later in Sturgis and Clay, Kentucky) desegregation of the Wilmington; Baltimore; Washington, D.C.; Kansas City; St. Louis, and Louisville school systems demonstrated that the court decision might be carried out peaceably. Cautiously, the NAACP drew the lesson for the fall of 1954 in the December issue of *The Crisis*, "immediate desegregation, when it is undertaken forthrightly and intelligently, works."

The Supreme Court on May 31, 1955, issued its implementation order, disappointing to some, calling for "a prompt and reasonable start toward full compliance." While opposition continued to build in the Deep South, local boards, chiefly in the border states, proceeded to comply. In Hoxie, Arkansas, a town of two thousand, a determined school board carried out desegregation in the fall of 1955, integrating twenty-six black youngsters into a school system of about eight hundred, despite a white supremacy boycott and intimidation. Such victories were hopeful signs. Negroes pressed for the integration of schools throughout the South. In August 1955, Negroes in seven Alabama counties, including Montgomery, petitioned educational authorities to begin immediate steps toward desegregation of the public schools. The cruel murder of fourteen-year-old Emmett Till in August 1955, because he allegedly "wolf-whistled" at a white woman in Sumner, Mississippi, appeared to be a reversal to the worst days of a lynch-ridden South, doubly shocking because it occurred at a time of rising hopes. The Supreme Court, after all, was pointing the way, extending its May 17, 1954, *Brown* ruling against segregation to public housing, publicly supported colleges and universities, and to tax-supported recreational facilities. Six days before Mrs. Parks' fateful bus ride, the Interstate Commerce Commission, following the lead of the high court, banned segregation on all vehicles and in all facilities engaged in travel between the states.

If Montgomery, the cradle of the Confederacy, seemed an unlikely birthplace for the civil rights movement of the following decade, it was no more unlikely than the boycott itself. The "passive majority," deplored by King during his moments of doubt about the efficacy of the proposed protest, pushed their leaders into an extended boycott, thrusting from a limited demand for courtesy to a full-fledged fight for desegregation of the buses. Writing in *Portrait of a Decade*, Anthony Lewis makes the point, "The [boycott] experience demonstrated that the Negro could fight for his own rights with courage and dignity. Montgomery was the genesis of 'direct action' as a technique in the movement for social justice, and it was a great demonstration of the effectiveness of social protest." With the rise of Dr. King as a major new Negro spokesman, young and indigenous to the South, the phrase "New Negro," first used by philosopher Alain Locke in the title of an anthology celebrating the Negro Renaissance of the 1920s, came again into vogue. As Abernathy liked to put it, "The Negro no longer grins when he isn't tickled nor scratches where he isn't itching." Yet, black history is no more a series of discontinuities than white, or any other, history. If it is sometimes difficult to discern the threads running back through the past beneath highly publicized current events, that does not mean that the threads are not present. As Joseph A. Schumpeter once observed, "Human protagonists have always been shaped by past situations." Montgomery's black community, itself, was a human thread running back into the bloody soil of the segregated, often terrorized, black belt as well as forward into a more hopeful urban future. There was E. D. Nixon, "touched by Randolph," in Rustin's phrase, in whom the 1941 March on Washington Movement remained a living memory; Professor Rufus Lewis, with whom voter registration was a passion fueled by favorable court decisions; Jo Ann Robinson, agitating for civil rights for heartbreaking untold years; the local NAACP chapter, expending its funds and energies in a vain battle to save the life of Jeremiah Reeves, a drummer arrested at sixteen, accused of raping a white woman; the Reverend Vernon Johns, King's predecessor at the Dexter Avenue Baptist Church, who waged a fierce if erratic one-man war against segregation and organized a successful black cooperative supermarket, Farm and City Enterprises; Lieutenant Nora Green, an Army nurse stationed at Tuskegee Army Air Force Training School, who refused to get off a "white bus" after a shopping trip in Montgomery during World War II and was badly beaten and jailed; a

Mr. Brooks, shot and killed because he insisted on the return of his fare when ordered by a driver to get off and reboard an already jammed bus by the back door; fifteen-year-old Claudette Colvin, handcuffed and jailed because she refused to give up her seat to a white passenger; Aurelia S. Browder and Mary Louise Smith, and two other (unnamed) women who also refused to budge when Jim Crowed and sued to have Alabama's and Montgomery's segregation laws declared unconstitutional.

If, as Schumpeter noted, "both the attainment and the practice of leadership is aided by a tradition of leadership," then Montgomery's black community was amply provided with the necessary tradition. As a quizzical black mail carrier responded to a *New York Times* correspondent, "It's not the 'New Negro—it's just us old Negroes, the same old folks. It's not the 'New Negro'—it's the 'new times.' Only we know it, that's all, and the white folks here haven't caught on to it yet."

The cradle of the Confederacy was being rocked by the winds of change. For all its quiet gentility, Montgomery was a rapidly growing city, rising from about 78,000 in 1940 to well over 124,000 in population by 1956. Roughly 40 percent, or some 50,000 of this number, were black. Located in one of the most fertile agricultural sections of the country, Montgomery is a major market for cotton, livestock, yellow pine, and hardwood lumber. It is a center for the manufacture of commercial fertilizer, and although there is a dearth of heavy industry, 1955 investments in new industrial installations amounted to $5.5 million and the manufacturing payroll came to $21.7 million for the year. *Forbes Magazine* ranked Montgomery the fifth city in the nation in the increase of business activity over 1955. Retail sales climbed from $159 million to over $175 million, and bank deposits totaled $144,413,166. The Maxwell and Gunter Air Force bases contributed much to the economic life of the city, channeling $58 million, according to the Montgomery Chamber of Commerce, into city businesses during 1955 alone. The military bases, by then, were integrated, so one in every fourteen employed Montgomerians spent their working days outside the segregated South. Cotton, long the staple support of stately mansions in Montgomery, had faded and was replaced by cattle, making Montgomery the largest cattle market east of Texas and south of the Ohio River, marketing roughly $30 million of cattle annually. Appropriately, for the new, progressive South, Montgomery's Coliseum, a striking example of modern architecture, "a flat turtle on a flat plain," built to house livestock fairs and business and civic conventions, did not have, as most public buildings in the South, built-in provisions for Jim Crow seating, entrances, exits, or rest rooms.

Black Montgomery also shared in the general economic growth and prosperity, but to a lesser extent. After a visit in the summer of the boycott, New York *Post* reporter Ted Poston informed his readers,

"Negro employment is widespread and stable." Many black workers were domestics—63 percent of the women and 48 percent of the men were either domestics or laborers. Black workers, however, dominated the bricklayers, plasterers, cement finishers, and several other crafts in the flourishing construction industry. They were the laboring backbone of the light industries, wholesale houses, trucking firms, and commercial establishments of Montgomery. Not only were blacks employed in shirt factories, lumber mills, cotton gin mills, and the like, but some were foremen and strawbosses. But there were few opportunities for white-collar or managerial jobs, except in a handful of black businesses; Montgomery employed five hundred black teachers and administrators in the segregated school system and at Alabama State College, but there were only two black lawyers in the city. Earnings were low. Alabama ranked forty-sixth among the forty-eight states in per capita income, which led a fervent Alabaman to remark, "Thank God for Mississippi. It keeps Alabama from being on the bottom." ° Per capita income for the state in 1950 was $880 a year, and for 1955, $1,232. Median income for whites in Montgomery, in 1950, was higher at $1,730; for blacks, $970 a year. Maids earned $10 to $15 a week; factory workers, roughly $20 to $40. Teachers were among the privileged, earning $2,950 a year with a bachelor's degree, and $3,300 with a master's. According to Jaquelyne Johnson Clarke's study, "These Rights They Seek," 44.7 percent of the membership of the Montgomery Improvement Association were in unskilled or semiskilled occupations, and the mean annual family income for the group was $3,094.

As was often the case in the South, blacks and whites lived side by side in the upper low-income sections of the city. Yet, unpaved streets were often black streets, and, increasingly, the worst slums were all-black. Ted Poston of the New York *Post* caught a new disturbing trend on his trip: "Montgomery is developing the same pattern of most major cities in the North; that of rapidly expanding all-white suburbs while the Negro population is being confined to the central city." As of 1955–56, however, the troubles that would stem from this concentration were still on the far horizon. Of 1,637 low-rent housing units built by the Montgomery Housing Authority, 956 were occupied by black families, and more were scheduled for construction and occupancy. Despite formidable barriers, 2,150 black citizens registered to vote, and Rufus Lewis talked optimistically of a goal of 10,000. There were approximately 30,000 blacks of voting age in Montgomery, and only 27,500 black and white voters registered in the whole city. In the 1956 presidential election, roughly eight thousand voted Republican; seven

---

° As did also Arkansas, whose rank was forty-seven.

thousand, Democrat; and three thousand, Independent. Almost any increase in the black vote would enlarge its importance. Indeed, black Montgomerians gleefully told Poston of white politicians coming to solicit their vote, saying, "they don't mean what the [White] Citizens' Council makes them say." The year 1956 was an election year, and as the Eisenhower equilibrium teetered uneasily on its outcome, black Americans, perhaps more than most, felt the need for change and sensed the opportunities ahead.

Before the boycott, race relations in Montgomery were what white Southerners liked to describe as "good." As Grover C. Hall, Jr., told Ted Poston, "Montgomery was one of the finest cities in the South where race relations were concerned. The people were—and are—easygoing and not given to sharp divisions and tensions. Everybody got along with everybody else and there were no major complaints on either side." L. D. Reddick, writing in *Dissent*, wryly agreed, adding that race relations had been " 'good' in the sense that Negroes seldom challenged their state of subordination." And he explained why: "The structure of society was more or less set. Opposition seemed futile. Personal difficulties might be adjusted through some prominent Negro who would speak with an influential white person. This was the established pattern of paternalism; and it did not disturb the status quo."

Even though the best of southern whites were not conscious of it, there was much that was irksome in the daily life of their black compatriots—the piling on of petty slights, unrelenting reminders of a supposed inferiority. Perhaps none was as irritating as the daily discourtesies experienced by the seventeen thousand black bus riders of Montgomery. One was not compelled to shop every day and submit oneself to Jim Crow service in the stores, but most blacks in Montgomery had to take the bus to work and back home again, and thus were twice daily reminded of the indignity of being black in the Deep South. The first four rows of seats, holding roughly ten persons, were reserved for whites; in theory, the last three rows, with about the same number of seats, were reserved for black passengers. But this wasn't always observed. During rush hours, black passengers had to get on in front, pay their fares, disembark, and reboard at the back door. If the white reserved seats were filled, the bus driver would ask black passengers already seated in the mid-bus unreserved section to get up and "move back." Sometimes this was done courteously; in whatever manner, it was demeaning.

Whether Montgomery's bus service had become more rude or not is difficult to ascertain, but there is no question that segregated service had become intolerable for its black customers. A black passenger who did not have the correct fare was driven off the bus by a gun-wielding driver. A blind man, his leg caught in the door, was dragged several blocks; his wife reported the incident, but the company did not even apologize. A matron was called "an ugly black ape." And so it went, each affront fueling a righteous anger. To be sure, segregation in the South was pervasive; the difficulty was to find ways to destroy it. Federal courts had just begun to offer a remedy at law by applying constitutional guarantees of equality. But remedies at law take time, and there was a deeply felt need on the part of a repressed minority to assert themselves. Court victories were important; let no one diminish the value of eliminating restrictive and unjust laws. Reliance on the rules of law, too, made practical sense. Schools, for example, could not be desegregated other than through court decisions effectively enforced by the federal government. Black parents simply did not have the economic leverage or political or social clout to compel school desegregation through either direct or political action—at least not in the South of the mid-1950s. But the bus service was vulnerable. Roughly 70 to 75 percent of all the customers of the Montgomery City Lines—owned by the Chicago-based National City Lines—were black. Not only did the company stand to lose approximately $3,000 a day in revenues, but the city of Montgomery would lose a portion of its $20,000 a year in taxes on the bus lines, and merchants, it was later estimated, would lose upward of $1 million in sales.

Men, however, often do not react rationally to objective conditions, even those affecting their pocketbooks, howsoever they may bend with them over the long run. The emergence of a new industrialized and urbanized South, replacing the old King Cotton plantation system, made segregation as obsolete as chopping cotton by black hands. But, as Schumpeter reminds us, "in explaining any historical course or situation, account must be taken of the fact that much in it can be explained only by the survival of elements that are actually alien to its own trends"—and so it would be with the South over the next two decades. Reporting on the boycott in *Dissent*, L. D. Reddick notes that many whites, who feel that Negro demands are reasonable, fear that giving in on this or that point means "all" is lost. "An absurd goblin hovers over every white household," Reddick wrote, "sincere apprehensions that desegregation at any one point will lead to general racial integration— and that means intermarriage!" Paradoxically, nonsegregation already existed in many areas of southern life—at the supermarket, for example. (The supermarket, one might note in passing, is modern, sharing with the Montgomery Coliseum a functional up-to-dateness that has no room for the anachronisms of racial segregation.) Reddick makes the sensible observation—one that might have saved so many so much grief had it been kept in mind—that both blacks and whites were wrong about desegregation. It would neither work miracles or precipitate disaster. As Reddick correctly put it, "a non-segregated society is merely a crude, basic precondition for creating a social order in which the higher sensibilities can flourish." But a racism rooted in the old agricultural South blocked the rational acceptance of change.

The Montgomery bus boycott was the first of many nonviolent direct actions to be carried out by southern blacks over the next decade. It was also a paradigm of much that would follow—peaceful resistance, escalating violence. Montgomery, however, was unique in the steadfast support given the movement by its participants. Where other marches or demonstrations would last but a few weeks, or at most, over some months, the Montgomery boycott stretched out successfully for more than a year. The initial enthusiasm for other demonstrations might wax or wane, but black Montgomerians kept on walking.

As Congressman Adam Clayton Powell described it, "The movement in Montgomery is religious not political, politicians come and go, but faith and God march forward." Mass meetings—"the soul of the boycott," in Professor Reddick's apt phrase—were held each Monday and Thursday as long as the boycott lasted. Rotated from church to church, these meetings served a practical purpose in a Negro community without its own newspaper or radio and where communication was frequently by word of mouth. But the twice-a-week coming together at church also served to reinforce the religious character of the Montgomery movement. "It was their religious duty now," Norman W. Walton wrote in his *Negro History Bulletin* account of the boycott, "The Walking City," "not only to go to church, visit the sick and to pray, but they must attend the mass meetings." To the Negro of Montgomery, Christianity and boycott went hand in hand. Poet Eve Merriam caught the religious spirit of the boycott in her line, "Walk, walk, *walk* with the Lord." Carl Rowan, then a reporter for the Minneapolis *Star*, remarked in *Go South to Sorrow*, "The Negro ministers . . . had achieved the most unbelievable by pulling the hoodlums out of the crap games and honky-tonks into the churches, where they sang hymns, gave money, shouted amen and wept over the powerful speeches." The walkers were sustained by faith. As one elderly woman responded when asked if she were tired, "It used to be my soul was tired and my feets rested; now my feets tired, but my soul is rested." This religious faith was not without its vein of humor or its touch of practicality, as illustrated in a story told by Ted Poston in a New York *Post* series on Montgomery: A Negro janitor driven each day by a volunteer to his job some fifteen miles from Montgomery insisted on being left off about a half mile from his place of work. He then jogged the rest of the way, working up a good sweat. When his boss questioned his walking "that far," the janitor retorted, "Now we never did rightly know from the Bible just how far it was that Christ walked from Bethlehem to Jerusalem, did we?"

The boycott strategy developed naturally out of the situation; the

Gandhian gloss came later as a protective response to white intimidation and violence. The first mention of the venerable Hindu in connection with the boycott came in a letter written by an elderly white librarian, Juliette Morgan, that was published in the *Montgomery Advertiser* on December 12, 1955, a week after the boycott began. "Not since the first battle of the Marne," Miss Morgan said, "has the taxi been put to as good a use as it has this last week in Montgomery. However, the spirit animating our Negro citizens as they ride these taxis or walk from the heart of Cloverdale to Mobile Road has been more like that of Gandhi than of the 'taxicab army' that saved Paris." King's predilection toward some sort of nonviolent resistance to evil was reinforced by the support the boycott received from the pacifist movement in the United States. The Fellowship of Reconciliation (FOR) helped to publicize the boycott in the North, producing a widely viewed seventeen-minute film short, *Walk to Freedom*. The Reverend Glenn E. Smiley, a white Texan Methodist and an FOR field secretary, and Bayard Rustin, a former FOR staff member and at that time executive secretary of the War Resisters' League, arrived in Montgomery during the first months of the boycott to offer whatever assistance they could muster. Both men were influential in shaping King's nonviolent philosophy, and Rustin soon became King's secretary as well as a tactical advisor. Deeply committed to an active though nonviolent resistance to evil, Rustin was a superb strategist with over two decades of experience behind him. A founder of the Congress of Racial Equality, Rustin had been active in rallying youth support for A. Philip Randolph's 1941 March on Washington and in his 1946 "refuse to register" campaign against segregation in the armed forces. Although no longer on the FOR staff, Rustin kept in close touch with his mentor, A. J. Muste, the noted pacifist and FOR executive secretary. As Rustin told writer Nat Hentoff, "During all my work with Martin King, I never made a difficult decision without talking the problem over with A. J. first." King's conversion, if it can be called that, to nonviolent resistance began during the Montgomery boycott. "I became convinced," he wrote in *Stride Toward Freedom*, "that what we were preparing to do in Montgomery was related to what Thoreau had expressed [in his essay "Civil Disobedience"]. We were simply saying to the white community, 'We can no longer lend our cooperation to an evil system.'"

The stress on nonviolence, no matter what its precise philosophic origin, stemmed from a pragmatic recognition of white power. King realized that if blacks, especially at that time in Montgomery, responded to white provocation with violence, they would be the losers. Desperately needed white support from the North—the boycott cost $5,000 a week to maintain—would dry up and the movement would die. "Nonviolent resistance," "noncooperation," and "passive resistance" were attractive notions in a nation already uneasy at the prospect of white violence in the South as blacks pressed for an end to segregation. King also knew his people, how close they were to the fundamentalist church of the black belt, and how they could be moved to act in "Christian love" and be restrained, when necessary, by appeals to the example of Jesus.

When the King home was bombed the night of January 30, an angry crowd gathered, thirsting for vengeance. As he made his way to the house, having been elsewhere at the time of the explosion, King overheard one bitter black man tell a pushing policeman, "You white folks is always pushin' us around. Now you got your .38 and I got mine; so let's battle it out." After assuring himself that his wife and baby were safe, King walked out on the porch, and said, "Don't get panicky! Don't do anything panicky at all! If you have weapons, take them home; if you do not have them, please do not seek to get them. We cannot solve this problem through retaliatory violence . . . . Remember the words of Jesus: 'He who lives by the sword will perish by the sword.'

"We must love our white brothers no matter what they do to us. We must make them know that we love them. Jesus still cries out in words that echo across the centuries: 'Love your enemies; bless them that curse you; pray for them that despitefully use you.' This is what we must live by. We must meet hate with love. . . . I did not start this boycott. I was asked by you to serve as your spokesman. I want it to be known the length and breadth of the land that if I am stopped, this movement will not stop. What we are doing is just, and God is with us."

The crowd dispersed to cries of "Amen." As King perceptively noted in *Stride Toward Freedom*, "It was Jesus of Nazareth that stirred the Negroes to protest with the creative weapon of love." Fundamentalist Christianity, however, acquired a Gandhian patina under King's tutelage. When the boycott coordinators rejected a proposal for a one-day work stoppage, Bayard Rustin was impressed by the adherence "to the Gandhian principle of consideration for one's opponents." As King said at the time, "We do not want to place too much of a burden upon white housewives nor to give them the impression that we are pushing them against the wall." When it became time to prepare for integration of the bus service, the MIA ran sessions to school people in nonviolent techniques. As King later wrote, "I had come to see early that the Christian doctrine of love operating through the Gandhian method of nonviolence was one of the most potent weapons available to the Negro in his struggle for freedom. . . . Nonviolent resistance had emerged as the technique of the movement, while love stood as the regulating ideal. In other words, Christ furnished the spirit and motivation, while Gandhi furnished the method."

King's commitment to *satyagraha* deepened over the years. It was firmly rooted in his Baptist background and fed by the pragmatic recognition that the black minority in the United States cannot afford violence on an enlarged or protracted scale. While occasional outbreaks might be tolerated, as were the riots of the 1960s in a sense, extensive violence, given the odds of twelve white Americans to one black American, would be self-destructive. But there was more to King's philosophical *cum* tactical posture than a mere recognition of hard realities. "Nonviolence," King believed, "can take men where the law cannot reach them. . . . It is the method which seeks to implement the just law by appealing to the consciences of the great decent majority who through blindness, fear, pride, or irrationality have allowed their consciences to sleep." It is well, however, to recognize, as King biographer David Lewis reminds us, that King's *satyagraha* was "home-grown." Even Thoreau's civil disobedience doctrine was, so to speak, an ideological graft on black belt fundamentalism. The noted sociologist E. Franklin Frazier viewed the southern black resistance to segregation as a "falling back upon his religious heritage in time of crisis." Gandhianism, he added, "as a philosophy and a way of life is completely alien to the Negro and has nothing in common with the social heritage of the Negro." This may overstate the case. The fervor of the movement in Montgomery, however, was sustained by faith, a revitalized faith. One cannot understand it truly unless one recognizes the truth in Frazier's observation: "For the Negro masses, in their social and moral isolation in American society, the Negro church community has been a nation within a nation."

For the duration of the boycott, the blacks of Montgomery became as one congregation. As Reddick observed, "The automobile-owning folk, who never rode the buses, and the maids and day-laborers, who depended upon the buses, have come to know each other." As is often the case, this solidarity was reinforced by the opposition. During the days of the boycott, those who needed a ride to work relied on the black taxi companies, who ferried passengers for the cost of a bus fare. When the city enforced an ordinance requiring minimum taxicab fares, MIA responded by organizing a car pool augmented by the purchase of a station wagon for each of Montgomery's black churches. "Negotiations," such as they were, quickly broke down. Jack Crenshaw, the attorney representing the bus line, insisted that the company could not accede to the modest boycott proposals within the then present law. Later he asserted, "If we grant the Negroes these demands, they would go about boasting of a victory that they have won over the white people; and this we will not stand for." As incredible as it may now sound, the MIA negotiators did what they could to assure Crenshaw that this was not, nor would be, the case.

As late as February 1, 1956, MIA sought no more than a "first-come, first-served" arrangement with black riders seating themselves from the rear to the front, and whites in reverse. A city commissioner timidly differed from Crenshaw, saying, "I don't see why we can't arrange to accept this seating proposal. We can work it within our segregation laws."

Crenshaw's adamancy hardened white opposition and strengthened black determination to see the boycott through. King described the process well; what happened to him following the negotiations happened to others as well. "Feeling that our demands were moderate, I had assumed that they would be granted with little question. . . . I came to see that no one gives up his privileges without strong resistance. I saw further that the underlying purpose of segregation was to oppress and exploit the segregated, not simply to keep them apart. Even when we asked for justice *within* the segregation laws, the 'powers that be' were not willing to grant it. Justice and equality, I saw, would never come while segregation remained, because the basic purpose of segregation was to perpetuate injustice and inequality." This insight was, in a sense, fostered by the adamancy of the Crenshaws, and so white opposition assisted the movement of blacks forward, from seeking justice *within* segregation to striking a blow against segregation itself.

Attempts were made to divide the black community. White employers told their black workers that their leaders "were only in it for the money"; that the Kings had purchased fancy cars for themselves. A phony settlement was floated but quickly punctured after Carl Rowan called King to check if it was true that MIA had settled for a "half loaf." Mayor W. A. Gayle took to television, threatening that the city commission was going to "stop pussy-footing around with the boycott." He called upon white employers to stop driving black employees to and from work. Black boycotters were harassed by the strict enforcement of traffic laws; arrests were made for petty offenses normally ignored by the police. Car-pool drivers were stopped and questioned; people waiting to be picked up were told that there was a law against hitchhiking, or threatened with arrest for vagrancy. Morale wavered, but the arrest of King for speeding at thirty miles an hour in a twenty-five mile an hour zone perked it up again.

The harassment, however, increased, building toward an acceptance of violence. Threatening telephone calls kept awakening boycott leaders throughout the night; hate mail mounted. It was as if the opponents of the boycott were working themselves up to some momentous act. The city's three commissioners joined the White Citizens' Council, a group once described by the editor of the *Montgomery Advertiser* as "manicured Ku Klux Klansmen" but now elevated to a strange sort of respectability. Born in Mississippi, the councils were beginning to flourish elsewhere in the South as die-hard white opposition to school desegregation mounted. In Montgomery, the bus boycott apparently stimulated whites into joining the racist group. "The bus boycott made us," State Senator Sam Englehardt, executive director of the Association of White Citizens' Councils in Alabama, boasted to *Post* reporter Ted Poston in the summer of 1956. "Before the niggers stopped riding the buses, we had only 800 members. Now we have 13,000 to 14,000 in Montgomery alone. We've got 75,000 members in 80 chapters all over the state. They made us."

Violence escalated; abusive words led to abusive deeds, culminating in the bombing of the King home on the evening of January 30, and the exploding of a dynamite stick tossed on E. D. Nixon's lawn two nights later. Bayard Rustin reported in his "Montgomery Diary," published in the April 1956 issue of *Liberation*, "I learned this morning from reliable sources that there is some indication that the bombings of the King and Nixon homes were not the work of irresponsible youth or cranks, but had the support of powerful vested interests in the community. There is some evidence that even the dynamite used passed through the hands of some people in the community who should be responsible for the maintenance of order." If so, nothing was ever done about it.

On February 10, 1956, twelve thousand people attended a mass rally sponsored by the Citizens' Council at the Coliseum. Senator James Eastland of Mississippi was the chief speaker. A leaflet was passed out at the rally that illustrates the kind of hate literature that was being circulated in the South at the time. It was unsigned and not circulated with the approval of the meeting's sponsors; however, not one of the speakers denounced its virulent racism:

> When in the course of human events it becomes necessary to abolish the Negro race, proper methods should be used. Among these are guns, bow and arrows, sling shots and knives.
>
> We hold these truths to be self-evident: that all whites are created equal with certain rights; among these are life, liberty and the pursuit of dead niggers.
>
> In every stage of the bus boycott we have been oppressed and degraded because of black, slimy, juicy, unbearably stinking niggers. Their conduct should not be dwelt upon because behind them they have an ancestral background of Pygmies, head hunters and snot suckers.
>
> My friends it is time we wised up to these black devils. I tell you they are a group of two legged agitators who persists in walking up and down our streets protruding their black lips. If we don't stop helping these African flesh eaters, we will soon wake up and find Reverend King in the White House.
>
> LET'S GET ON THE BALL WHITE CITIZENS.

One is tempted at this distance of time and place to treat such malodorous stuff as a gross parody of race hatred. But distribution of the leaflet was palpably threatening. When Rustin arrived in Montgomery on February 21, 1956, he found the situation so tense "that it is important that I have the bolts tightly drawn on the windows in my hotel." A hotel employee advised him not to go out into the streets after dark. "If you find it necessary to do so," Rustin was warned, "by all means leave in the hotel everything that identifies you as an outsider. They are trying to make out that communist agitators and New Yorkers are running our protest."

A week earlier, King and more than one hundred others had been indicted under an old Alabama law against boycotts; eighty-nine were later to stand trial. King returned from a lecture tour to join the others who had walked to the police station and surrendered. The first, E. D. Nixon, walked in saying to the flustered police, "You are looking for me? Here I am." Television cameramen were on hand when King arrived to be booked the following day. Expressions of support mounted from all over the country: Chicago pickets ringed the home office of the bus company. Over five hundred clergymen declared their backing in response to an appeal sent out by the Fellowship of Reconciliation, and over three hundred volunteered to fill Montgomery pulpits if black preachers were jailed.

The trial was set for March 19, and the courtroom was dramatically filled with black people wearing cloth crosses bearing the message, "Father, forgive them." On March 22, when Judge Eugene Carter found Martin Luther King guilty of violating the state's boycott ban, King was fined $500 and court costs, or 386 days at hard labor in the county of Montgomery. (The other cases were deferred pending an appeal of King's conviction.) King was convicted in Montgomery, but in the national court of public opinion he was not only acquitted but vindicated. With Mrs. King at his side, he came out of the the courtroom to be greeted by hundreds of people, black and white, shouting, "Long live the King," and "God bless you"; then the crowd sang, "We ain't gonna ride the buses no more."

The boycotters, as it were, marched on Washington; they sought national attention and support. The boycott was widely covered in the press and on television. Support from the North was strong, and perhaps not unrelated to the growing popularity of television. While only 53 percent of all households in the South had television sets in 1955, 80 percent of homes in the Northeast had sets, where coverage was perforce liberal in interpretation. Donations from private persons poured in from all over the world—Singapore, Tokyo, New Delhi, Paris, and from northern and western states. "Labor, civic, and social groups were our staunchest supporters," King later reported. NAACP chapters responded generously to a fund appeal sent out by Roy Wilkins; the United Auto Workers contributed $35,000; and when Bayard Rustin came to Montgomery, he brought a check for $5,000. According to King, these varied contributions added up to $250,000.

Inexorably, the fate of the boycott came to rest in the courts. A suit was filed in the United States Federal District Court, asking for an end to bus segregation on the grounds that it was contrary to the Fourteenth Amendment assurance of equal rights to all. In April, before the Montgomery case could be heard, the United States Supreme Court handed down a decision that *The New York Times*, among others, headlined as holding bus and streetcar segregation unconstitutional. A dozen cities in the South integrated their transit facilities without incident. In Montgomery, the bus company announced it would comply, but city officials declared that they would continue to enforce segregation. As it turned out, the Court did not do what the newspapers had reported. Sarah Mae Flemming of Columbia, South Carolina, had brought a damage suit against the bus company there, claiming that her civil rights were infringed on by segregation. Her complaint was dismissed in a lower court, but a federal appeals court held that she was entitled to a trial of her suit. The bus company appealed to the Supreme Court, which dismissed the case, an act the press interpreted as agreeing with Miss Flemming's contention that segregation infringed on her rights as a citizen. But all the Court had done was to declare that it would not review non-final judgments, so Miss Flemming's case had to be tried.

Meanwhile, the Montgomery case was heard in a federal district court where three judges must sit whenever a constitutional question is involved. Two of the three ruled bus segregation unconstitutional, and the court enjoined Montgomery city officials from enforcing racial laws. The city commissioners appealed the decision, and at long last, the United States Supreme Court faced up to the fundamental question as to whether or not bus segregation, and by extension, all segregation, was unconstitutional.

The boycott continued, and Martin Luther King carried his people's case to an overflow crowd at the Cathedral of St. John the Divine in New York City, to the NAACP national convention in San Francisco, and before the platform committee of the Democratic party. Civil rights, he told the latter, is "one of the supreme moral issues of our time," urging the Democrats to call for "strong federal action." Insurance agents notified the MIA that they were canceling policies as of September 15; the risks were too high for car-pool drivers, they said. Lloyds of London stepped into the breach, and another crisis was surmounted. In late October, the city moved to halt the operation of the car pools, seeking an injunction on the grounds that car-pool operation had cost the city an estimated $15,000 in lost revenue from the blocked bus lines. It also claimed that the car pool was "a public nuisance" and a private enterprise operating without license fee or franchise. While King, E. D. Nixon, and Abernathy sat through the first day's proceedings on November 13, 1956, Rex Thomas, a reporter for the Associated Press, approached King during a brief recess, saying, "Here's the decision you have been waiting for." The United States Supreme Court had affirmed the decision of the district court in the Montgomery case declaring Alabama's state and local laws requiring segregation on buses unconstitutional.

The boycott, however, lasted for another month while everyone waited for the Supreme Court order to reach Montgomery. At 5:55 Friday morning, December 21, 1956, with television cameras grinding and reporters questioning, Martin Luther King, Glenn Smiley, E. D. Nixon, and Ralph Abernathy boarded the first integrated bus in Montgomery's history. The driver greeted his passengers, "We're glad to have you this morning." King had cautioned restraint, and only one minor incident marred the new day—a black woman was slapped by a white youth as she stepped off a bus. *New York Times* reporter George Barrett told of one exchange that apparently set the tone for the changeover. One of two white men seated behind a black passenger said, "I see this sure isn't going to be a white Christmas." The black man turned, smiled, and said with good humor and firmness, "Yes sir, that's right." Everybody in the bus smiled, reported Barrett, "and all rancor seemed to evaporate."

Then came the inevitable reaction. Buses were fired upon by white snipers; a teen-age girl was beaten by four or five white rowdies as she got off a bus. Four Negro churches were bombed at an estimated damage of $70,000, the homes of Ralph Abernathy and Robert Graetz were dynamited on January 10, 1957, and someone fired a shotgun blast into the front door of the Kings' home. This time, however, respectable white Montgomery spoke up against the terror. On January 31, much to everyone's surprise, seven white men were arrested in connection with the bombings and five were indicted. While justice miscarried and the defendants were freed by a jury despite signed confessions of guilt, the bombings ceased. And, as King later wrote, "The skies did not fall when integrated buses finally traveled the streets of Montgomery."

VII

Second Civil War

WHEN WORD OF THE SUPREME Court's decision declaring Alabama's state and local bus segregation laws unconstitutional circulated the Montgomery courtroom where Martin Luther King and his codefendants were on trial for operating an unlicensed transit system, the boycott car pool, an exultant spectator cried out, "God Almighty has spoken from Washington, D.C." The boycotters had persisted in the faith that the Supreme Court, or the federal government, would act sooner or later on the side of righteousness. Washington, indeed, loomed as large as Mount Sinai in the minds of many who pressed for an end to segregation and battled for social justice. Every hope for civil rights rested ultimately on the Constitution, and given the shelter afforded segregation in states rights doctrine and practice, on its enforcement by the federal government. Nearly every act or gesture, whether calculated or spontaneous, from A. Philip Randolph's "magnificent bluff" in 1941 down to the March on Washington in 1963 (and beyond for that matter), occurred with participants eyeing Washington either in the hopes of a favorable court decree, or presidential action, or a strengthening of the law, or federal enforcement of equal rights statutes and constitutional provisions.

This reliance on Washington was rooted in experience going back to the Civil War. Washington, in the persona of Lincoln, freed the slaves; Washington, through the Freedmen's Bureau, guaranteed slaves' rights throughout Reconstruction. Washington, too, offered whatever refuge there was during the long bitter years that followed the betrayal of the Compromise of 1877. The Great Migration, urbanization, and the industrialization of the South, however, added a new dimension—the power of the ballot. Once safely ensconced in the North, blacks began to vote in ever larger numbers, underwriting vital northern political machines, especially in Chicago and New York. By the 1940s, black support was crucial to an increasing number of northern politicians, notably in New York, Pennsylvania, Illinois, Michigan, and California, where elected officials disregarded blacks at their peril. In 1944 and 1948, as Henry Lee Moon reminds us, a reversal of the black vote would have assured the election of Republican Thomas E. Dewey over his winning rivals, Franklin D. Roosevelt and Harry S Truman. If, for example, in 1944, President Roosevelt had received no larger proportion of the black vote than his Democratic predecessors, the sixty-eight electoral votes of New York, New Jersey, Michigan, Illinois, Pennsylvania, Maryland, and Missouri would have been toted in the Republican column. Black votes may not have been absolutely essential to the Roosevelt/Truman victories. Had blacks voted otherwise, there may have been other shifts sufficient to assure the same result. Nonetheless, such political gamesmanship is the stuff of politics, and ultimately, of public policy. The ballot was not the only force for change, but it was among the most powerful. After World War II, politicians had to take into account the black vote in the North, and as blacks moved into southern cities, the demand for the vote—if not the vote itself—below the Mason-Dixon line. Thus, black voting power became leverage moving the nation in the 1950s and 1960s to resume the implementation of promises made a century before in the Fourteenth and Fifteenth Amendments to the Constitution. By arming themselves with the ballot, as Pat Watters and Reese Cleghorn put it in their perceptive analysis of the growing black participation in southern politics, *Climbing Jacob's Ladder*, "Negroes propelled *themselves* into the mainstream of American politics (if not into the mainstream of American society)."

Truman's decision to stand on the Democratic party's civil rights platform of 1948 rested on principle and a shrewd calculation that the loss of the South would be more than offset by gains, shored up by the black vote, scored in the industrial North. The conversion of blacks to the Democratic standard, underway since the New Deal, was almost completed by the commitment to civil rights pushed through the 1948 Democratic convention by the youthful senator from Minnesota, Hubert H. Humphrey. In the South, however, the emerging black vote, largely found in the cities, was not as tied to the Democratic cause as that of the North. Local southern Democrats were off-putting, to phrase it mildly, and ardent segregationists were in the ascendancy by the mid-1950s. With the end of the "white primary," progressive Democrats hoped to build in the South a liberal coalition similar to that of labor, liberal, and black voters in the North that had sustained the New and Fair Deals of Presidents Roosevelt and Truman. Black registration in the eleven southern states had quadrupled, rising to over a million

(1,238,000) registrants by 1952.° But union efforts to organize workers in the new plants sprouting throughout the South failed, and one leg of the prospective coalition buckled. Moreover, as political prognosticator Samuel Lubell observed, the first effects of the increase in black voters was an intensification of the anti-Negro vote. Moderate gubernatorial incumbents in Alabama and Mississippi were replaced by intransigent racists. At the same time, the South's new middle class identified with the rise of industrialization and a locus of a new liberalism, headed the drive that swept four southern states—Florida, Missouri, Tennessee, and Virginia—as well as Texas for Dwight D. Eisenhower in 1952.

All of this, of course, was not lost on Republican strategists, some of whom began to hope that they might woo blacks back to their traditional allegiance to the party of Lincoln. The President's heart attack in the fall of 1955 raised some doubts about his reelection even though he had fully recovered. His strategists recognized a need to broaden the base of his support. During his first administration, Eisenhower had moved, however cautiously, from a conservative to a progressive Republicanism. As a consequence of the Senate hearings on the clash between the United States Army and Senator McCarthy over alleged communists, televised during June 1954, McCarthyism was no longer a serious threat on the President's right. No longer inhibited, his administration coped with the mild recession of 1953 and 1954 by applying, as Elliot V. Bell, publisher of *Business Week*, said, "compensatory fiscal and monetary policies that some of its leaders would probably have denounced as downright New Deal heresy." *The New York Times* correctly characterized his domestic proposals as the "limited extension of measures along the lines of the New Deal." The administration, Eisenhower said in 1954, "must be liberal when it was talking about the relationship between the Government and the individual, conservative when talking about the national economy and the individual pocketbook." At that, Eisenhower's programs of the mid-1950s would raise federal spending for highways, schools, slum clearance, medical insurance, and improved Social Security to an annual level $4 billion higher than had been spent by the Truman Administration.

After his election in 1952, President Eisenhower pressed the desegregation of the armed forces, a program launched by President Truman, and by 1955 virtually eliminated racial quotas and all black units as well as discrimination in housing, schools, hospitals, transportation, and recreation at all Army, Navy, and Air Force bases and installations. He

---

° Twenty-five percent of voting-age blacks were registered as compared to 60 percent of eligible whites, still a substantial increase in black political power when compared with the previous decade.

told his chief of staff, Sherman Adams, that he wanted qualified Negroes to be considered for key positions in his administration, and several notable "firsts" were scored. Lois Lippman, a member of the campaign secretarial staff, became the first black to work in the White House office and E. Frederic Morrow, the first black administrative officer to serve on a presidential staff. Scovel Richardson was appointed chairman of the United States Parole Board; Archibald Carey, chairman of the President's Employment Policy Committee and an alternate delegate to the United Nations; Cora M. Brown, associate general counsel in the Post Office Department; and J. Ernest Wilkins, appointed Assistant Secretary of Labor in 1953, became the first black to sit in at cabinet meetings, representing his department whenever Secretary James Mitchell was absent. Such appointments were perhaps well within a long-standing Republican practice of awarding patronage to blacks, but the rising level of appointments reflected an awareness of the growing importance of civil rights concerns and of the black vote. This awareness was intensified by the *Brown* decision and its aftermath. When the President's 1956 message to Congress was discussed before-hand in the cabinet, Attorney General Herbert Brownell, Jr., remarked that the proposal for a civil rights commission would be inflammatory because it would be interpreted in the South as counteraction to the White Citizens' Councils then springing up. He added that desegrega-tion was the greatest issue in the social field ever faced by the nation. Max Rabb, the President's troubleshooter on minority problems, broke in to say, "This is not just the biggest issue in the social field. It is the biggest issue of any kind in the United States today."

Eisenhower, in truth, handled the issue gingerly enough. By compari-son, however, with the waffling of Democratic party candidate Adlai Stevenson, Eisenhower's posture seemed to be one of commitment. Stevenson thought it imperative to soothe southern sensibilities if he were to win in 1956. Fences were mended to a degree, but at the expense of the party's forthright 1948 civil rights stand. Stevenson took up the Southerner's plea for gradualism. As he told a black audience in Los Angeles, "We must proceed gradually, not upsetting habits or traditions that are older than the Republic." It was a sentiment that went down more easily before southern audiences than before his immediate listeners. Stevenson also wrote, "In the *long run,* segregation will yield *quickly* to the general advance of education." As literary critic Irving Howe, who supplied the italics, quipped, "This is on par with Governor Dewey's famous prediction that 'the future lies before us.' "

Civil rights, therefore, appeared to offer the Republicans a chance to separate blacks—and some liberals—from the Democrats. It was astute politics, for it seemed likely that a properly managed southern strategy might bring to the South a viable two-party system with segregationists enrolled in either Strom Thurmond's States' Rights party or in the Democratic party, and moderates—black men and white—enlisted in the Republican cause. Eisenhower's appointment of Earl Warren as Chief Justice won him some reflected glory for the desegregation decisions. Sherman Adams reported in his account of the Eisenhower Administration, "In the South, Eisenhower himself has been denounced as the author of the school desegregation law and in the North he has been praised for it." During 1956, the Eisenhower strategists were reasonably careful not to disabuse voters, particularly black voters, of this notion. In his 1956 State of the Union message, Eisenhower asked Congress to establish a civil rights commission to examine charges "that in some localities Negro citizens are being deprived of their right to vote and are likewise being subjected to unwarranted economic pressure." The Eisenhower civil rights image was given another boost when one hundred and one senators and representatives from eleven southern states presented to Congress in March 1956, their "Declaration of Constitutional Principles." Much to their credit, Senators Lyndon Johnson of Texas and Estes Kefauver and Albert Gore of Tennessee refused to sign the so-called "Southern Manifesto." The manifesto termed the *Brown* decision of the Supreme Court a "clear abuse of judicial power" exploited by "outside agitators" and pledged the signers "to use all lawful means to bring about a reversal of this decision which is contrary to the Constitution."

Black Montgomerians, striding toward freedom, were not alone in looking to Washington and the White House for succor. The Eisenhower Administration introduced a civil rights bill in April 1956, raising black hopes. The bill would create a civil rights commission, empowered to subpoena witnesses in investigations of interference in voting or the use of economic pressure because of race, color, or creed; a civil rights division in the Department of Justice; authority for the Department to initiate a petition to prevent any individual from being deprived of his civil rights; federal prosecution of any person charged with intimidating a voter in a federal election; access to the federal courts for anybody with a civil rights complaint; federal authority to bring civil suit against conspirators attempting to repress anybody's civil rights. The proposed legislation hadn't a prayer of passage, but it did contribute to making civil rights an issue in the presidential election.

The issue embarrassed the Democrats, then attempting to make up to the South in the hopes of winning the election. Dissatisfied blacks defected in large numbers from Democratic ranks in 1956, nearly reversing the black commitment to the party of Roosevelt and Truman. From 1940 through 1952, blacks gave each successive Democratic presidential candidate an ever-increasing percentage of their vote.

An estimated 79 percent of all black voters cast their vote in 1952 for Adlai Stevenson, but in 1956 only 61 percent did so. While the black vote in the urban North and West remained reasonably steadfast, reflecting the hold of big city machines, the labor movement, and the Democratic economic appeal, black voters in the South defected in greater number. James Q. Wilson, writing in *The American Negro Reference Book*, notes, "The defection to Eisenhower of some Negroes in 1956 was greater among middle-class than among lower-class Negroes." In key predominantly black districts in Chicago, Detroit, and Philadelphia, for example, the break in percentage points was, respectively, 9, 6, and 4, while the all-black Fifth Ward in Greensboro, North Carolina, which had given Eisenhower only 5 percent of its vote in 1952, gave him 66 percent in 1956. The percentage of the black vote for Eisenhower rose sharply throughout the South, 20.2 percent to 55.1 percent in New Orleans; from 15.7 percent to 40.9 percent in Jacksonville, Florida; from 10.5 percent to 34.8 percent in Houston, Texas; and from 30.9 percent to 85.3 percent in Atlanta, Georgia. Eisenhower won handily, and did not need the black vote to do so; still, the defection served warnings to the Democrats and had its impact on the 1957 Congress.

Eisenhower had a personal decency that was appealing to Americans, but though his popularity carried him into a second term with a comfortable margin of over 9.5 million votes, he did not bring with him a Republican majority for Congress. In the Senate, the parties were almost equally divided with forty-nine Democrats, of whom eighteen were from the Deep South, and forty-seven Republicans, of whom only a handful were relatively liberal. It was a division that made the passage of the Civil Rights Act of 1957 all the more remarkable—and significant.

The black vote for Eisenhower revealed more than restlessness. In the South, at least, it was an assertion of independence in keeping with the spirit of Montgomery—blacks were serving notice. As journalist James L. Hicks wrote in the New York *Amsterdam News*, "One of the great surprises of 1956 to the Negro leaders themselves has been the fact that they suddenly found that the Negro masses were far ahead of them in their willingness to demand their freedom and to back up their demands with sacrifice." When the White Citizens' Council of Orangeburg, South Carolina, sought to intimidate black petitioners seeking school desegregation by evicting black tenants, firings, recalling mortgages, and the refusal of credit and goods to black merchants, Orangeburg's black citizens retaliated by circulating their own boycott list of twenty-three businesses known to be owned by White Citizens' Council members or close sympathizers. Students at the all-black South

Carolina State College joined in refusing to patronize these establishments and the boycott was successful in terminating the white refusal to
do business with blacks of Orangeburg.

The Reverend Charles K. Steele visited his friend Martin Luther King
in the winter of 1956 and returned home to Tallahassee, Florida, to
organize a bus boycott. "When a Negro pays the same fare as a white,
he wants the same privileges," declared the determined reverend. The
boycott began on May 28, 1956, cutting bus revenues by 60 percent;
and services were terminated on June 30, 1956. Steele formed an
Inter-Civic Council modeled on the Montgomery Improvement Association. Out of that, the Nonpartisan Voters' League later evolved, which
increased black voter registration in Tallahassee from 1,200 to more
than 5,000 in 1959 and 1960. While the Supreme Court's Montgomery
decision banning segregated bus services made boycotts moot, blacks
continued to test the decision, notably in demonstrations organized in
Atlanta, Birmingham, and Chattanooga among other southern cities
during 1957.

Blacks took heart from acts of affirmation and resistance. An Atlanta
minister on his way to jail in a patrol wagon for testing bus laws, said,
"There's no segregation on this bus." Gus Courts, a sixty-year-old grocer
in Belzoni, Mississippi, who headed the local NAACP and a voter
registration drive, told tormentors, "Damn the Citizens' Council." He
was evicted from his store premises, moved to another location, and
persisted, personally leading a group of twenty-two black voters to the
poll. Their ballots were invalidated, but only after being critically
wounded by a shotgun blast did Courts flee to Chicago where, he said,
he was an "American refugee from Mississippi terror." When a gang
told Rev. H. H. Hubbard of Alabama that they ought to beat him and
throw him into the river, he calmly replied, "I wouldn't advise you to do
that." They let him go. When a seven-year-old boy begged to go to a
nearby all-white school, his mother said, "If you got the guts to go, I've
got the guts to send you."

Whites in the South spoke ominously of impending conflict. When
political pollster Samuel Lubell sounded Southern opinion during the
1956 presidential campaign, he was told, "A war between the whites
and blacks is coming sure as you are standing here." The phrase he
heard most often was, "Why is the North trying to cram the nigger
down our throats?" For all the inherent viciousness of racism, there is a
plaintive note, a whining defensiveness about that question that would
be the dominant mood of white extremists on into the 1960s. The whites
who jeered and spat at black youngsters entering integrated schools
present no pretty picture, make no heroic stand. By no stretch of the
imagination, even their own, could they be clothed in gallant gray.
Clearly, the rebel yell was badly cracked.

While blacks were increasingly assertive of their rights, they were not, by any definition, overly aggressive. The NAACP, with its 300,000 members in 1,100 branches, more than one half in border and southern states, was decidedly cautious. When bus boycotts were proposed during June 1956 in Miami and St. Petersburg, Florida, an NAACP statement advised "all citizens to comply with existing city and state laws governing seating on buses." When Martin Luther King suggested black children might study-in at white high schools as an example of nonviolent tactics that might hasten compliance with the Supreme Court's *Brown* decision, Thurgood Marshall scathingly retorted, it was "neither wise nor heroic to send children to do the work of men."

In truth, blacks, particularly in the South, were caught in a cruel dilemma. On one hand, there were the decisions of the Supreme Court against segregation and the encouraging—indeed exhilarating—victory of the Montgomery bus boycott; on the other hand, there was a growing—and partially successful—white reaction and repression, especially against school desegregation. The NAACP was virtually driven underground in many areas of the Deep South and black resources were severely taxed by the struggle for school desegregation that had to be carried on school district by school district. (Court cases cost money and eat up time, not to mention the wear and tear on the individuals involved.) The 1956 Southern Manifesto had set a seal of respectability on the tactics, if not directly on the White Citizens' Councils then flourishing in the South. Founded in July 1954 by Robert P. Patterson, the manager of a 1,585-acre Leflore County, Mississippi, plantation, the council movement organized the respectable middle class—bankers, mayors, sheriffs, planters, small businessmen—in defense of segregation. Though infected at the fringe by anti-Semitism and a native proto-fascism, the council leaders condemned night-riding violence and the Ku Klux Klan because, as Judge Thomas Pickens Brady, the movement's resident philosopher, put it, "They hide their faces, because they did things that you and I wouldn't approve of." In reality, as historian Neil R. McMillen writes in his authoritative history, *The Citizens' Councils*, "The Council demonstrated a marked preference for the subtler forms of intimidation. Disdaining exotic rituals, secret oaths, and paraphernalia of disguise, just as it eschewed the rope, faggot, and whip, it forswore lawlessness and pledged itself to strictly legal means of defiance. Whatever may have been the theoretical relationship between the explosive atmosphere it so often created and the actual outbreak of violence, there is no tangible evidence which suggests that it engaged in, or even overtly encouraged, criminal acts. From time to time, individual council members were implicated in acts of vigilantism, including homicide and bombing, but the organization itself was never directly linked with these things."

In all likelihood, open advocacy of violence, illegality, or armed resistance to desegregation would have scared off the very people that the councils sought to recruit. Community pressure was to be brought against recalcitrant blacks and community pressure could no longer be embodied in night-riding Klansmen. Blacks were not so easily intimidated by flapping white sheets; other weapons were more effective, or so the councils' leaders believed. Typically, the individual councils, which were highly autonomous units, sought to "squeeze" the more militant blacks into quiescence. As attorney Alton Keith, chairman of the Dallas County, Alabama, council, declared, "We must make it difficult, if not impossible, for any Negro who advocates desegregation to find and hold a job, get credit, or renew a mortgage." Staid bankers, who would not personally don the white hoods of the Klan, could apply economic pressure, for surely an "uppity Nigra" or a moderate white was a bad risk. The Columbus, Mississippi, Bank of Commerce told dentist Emmett Stringer, ex-president of the state NAACP, that he would not be lent any money. Strangers then called his mother, saying, "Dr. Stringer has been killed." One added, "Do you have his body yet?" T. B. Johnson, a black undertaker in Belzoni, Mississippi, belonged to an integrationist group. He was warned that he had better drop the leadership of a black Boy Scout troop or he would receive no more credit and might be run out of town. Dr. Clinton Battle was the first black to register to vote in Indianola, Mississippi, home of the White Citizens' Council, and his patients were warned that if they consulted him they would lose their jobs. At the next election, no blacks registered, not even Dr. Battle.

White Citizens' Council membership fluctuated wildly for, as Professor McMillen noted, it was "a fever chart" of the second civil war then raging in the South. In Mississippi, for example, council membership rose precipitously immediately following the *Brown* decision in May 1954, but waned considerably during the period of waiting for the implementation decree of May 31, 1955. It waxed as the NAACP pressed school desegregation cases in the law courts throughout the South. Within two weeks of February 3, 1956, when Autherine Lucy won a three-year-old court battle to enter the University of Alabama, the Alabama Association of Citizens' Councils was formed and council officials claimed that twenty-six councils in seventeen counties had enlisted forty thousand members. Students and outsiders harassed Miss Lucy and the university officials who escorted her to class, and, finally, the university acceded to the pressure, suspending Miss Lucy indefinitely for her own safety. When she charged university officials of conspiring to keep her out, the trustees summarily expelled her. As for the Citizens' Councils, flushed with success, they flourished. As of November 1955, the councils had an estimated membership of sixty to sixty-five thousand, rising to three hundred thousand by March 1956.

Intimidation intensified, not only against individual blacks but against black organizations. According to Roy Wilkins, some 260 to 300 special laws were passed in southern states with respect to halting school desegregation and "several score" of these were directed specifically against the NAACP. "Georgia wants us to pay an income tax," Wilkins said, "although we are a non-profit membership corporation, and Arkansas tried to get us into court under their law disclosing names of our members and filing certain information every two months. Louisiana got out an injunction [against the NAACP]. Virginia is trying to enforce a barratry statute, saying that the NAACP as an organization has no right to bring test cases in the courts. Laws have been passed in South Carolina and Mississippi requiring teachers and other employees on the public payroll, Negroes, to disclose what organizations they belong to. This was an effort to frighten the teachers away from joining the NAACP." The NAACP was fined $100,000 in one state and outlawed in five more in the mid-1950s. As Wilkins wryly put it, "We have had our hands full."

Violence escalated. Crosses flared; churches, homes, and schools were bombed; and, during the period from January 1, 1955 to January 1, 1959, forty-four persons were beaten, twenty-nine individuals, eleven of them white, were shot and wounded in racial incidents, and six blacks were killed. The Southern Regional Council, the southeastern office of the American Friends Service Committee and the Department of Racial and Cultural Relations of the Churches of Christ in the U.S.A. compiled and published in *Intimidation, Reprisal and Violence* two hundred and twenty-five acts over the same period against private liberties and public peace. Benjamin Muse wisely reminds us that "this blunt tabulation of outrages could give an impression of a kind of anarchy which did not exist." These incidents occurred in a region of forty million people over a four-year period. Nevertheless, as Muse added, "they reflect a degree of malignancy and lawlessness more serious and more pregnant with crisis than many realized." Such was the nature of the second civil war.

It was an uneasy time. As North Carolina's governor, Luther H. Hodges, later told a Harvard Law School Forum, "I frankly confess to you today that there were many times during that period when it seemed that not only were the pillars of education to fall, but also the pillars of stable and responsible government. . . . There were times when it seemed almost our state, our region, and indeed the whole nation must suffer an orgy of great internal discord, and that we must pass through a period of neighbor against neighbor, citizen against citizen, state against state, and in truth a nation divided against itself . . . ."

What next? This was a hard, perplexing question for the new black leadership then emerging in the South. Martin Luther King's answer was an attempt to pull together the black leadership of the South, capitalizing on the success of the Montgomery boycott to do so. King, the Reverend Fred Lee Shuttlesworth of Birmingham, Alabama, and the Reverend Charles K. Steele of Tallahassee, Florida, issued a call for a conference at Atlanta, Georgia, on January 10, 1957. The response was favorable, and sixty persons—mostly clergymen, several state and local NAACP officials, three businessmen, two labor leaders, two college professors, and one farmer—from twenty-nine communities met for two days to "share thinking, discuss common problems, plan common strategy, and explore mutual economic assistance."

As it happened, the power of prayer and of nonviolence as expressed at the conference was apposite to an outbreak of violence in Montgomery early that morning. King and Abernathy were roused from their beds at 5:30 with the news that four churches and two ministers' homes, one Abernathy's, had been bombed. They left for Montgomery, and Coretta King presided over the first day's sessions in the absence of her husband. Outside Ebenezer Baptist Church, Atlanta police kept an uneasy watch. Detective Clarence N. Nelms told Bayard Rustin, "Be careful. We got word that a carload of white men has started up from Florida to break up your meeting and raise hell in general. If you see anybody suspicious, call this number and be damn quick about it." Inside the church, the first conferee to speak was a man who had been shot because he dared to vote. King returned to Atlanta the next day, and after reporting on the bombing, he said, "Let this be a sign unto you. God is truly our protector. He permits men the freedom to do evil. He also has His way to protect His children."

"For a time there was a great silence," Rustin wrote in the following month's issue of *Liberation*. "Then a minister began to pray. At the end of the prayer, King spoke movingly on the power of nonviolence. After this, the session broke up in silence."

A religious pacifism infused the movement. "True pacifism," King would write in *Stride Toward Freedom*, "is not unrealistic submission to evil power, as Niebuhr contends. It is rather a courageous confrontation of evil by the power of love, in the faith that it is better to be the recipient of violence than the inflictor of it, since the latter only multiplies the existence of violence and bitterness in the universe, while the former may develop a sense of shame in the opponent, and thereby bring about a transformation, and change of heart."

Moved by this spirit and reinforced by the Christianity of the ministers present, the conference called upon "all Negroes . . . to assert their human dignity," and "to seek justice and reject all injustice, *especially that in themselves*." The Negro people were urged to adhere to nonviolence "in word, thought, and deed," and "to accept Christian love in full knowledge of its power to defy evil." Nonviolence, the conferees insisted, "is not a symbol of weakness or cowardice, but, as Jesus and Gandhi demonstrated, nonviolent resistance transforms weakness into strength and breeds courage in the face of danger." The conference adopted as its motto: "Not one hair of one head of one white person shall be harmed."

The first act of the newly formed group, calling itself the Southern Leadership Conference on Transportation and Nonviolent Integration, was to fire off two telegrams—one to President Eisenhower asking him to "come South immediately to make a major speech in a major southern city urging all Southerners to accept and to abide by the Supreme Court's decisions as the law of the land" and another to Vice President Nixon urging him "to make a tour of the South similar to the one he made on behalf of Hungarian refugees."

At a press conference called to release the text of the telegrams to President Eisenhower and Vice President Nixon, a *New York Times* correspondent asked about the motto: "Do you mean it, *even if others start the violence?*"

"Individuals had better speak for themselves on that," King answered. "But I mean it."

The correspondent queried the others. One by one, all sixty said, "yes," or nodded their heads in assent.

All things considered, it was a remarkable moment.

Washington rejected the conference's pleas for a major civil rights address from the President, for a vice-presidential tour of the South, and for a meeting with the Justice Department.° The southern black leaders met again in New Orleans on February 14. Attendance swelled to ninety-seven persons from thirty-five communities in ten states. Once again, the focus was on Washington, or rather, on the desirability of positive action from Washington. The President was urged to call a White House Conference on Civil Rights patterned after recent meetings on education and juvenile delinquency. Vice President Nixon was reminded that he would be "better able to represent America's defense of justice and freedom" at the Gold Coast Independence Celebration on March 16 if, prior to leaving for Africa, he arranged a "fact-finding trip" into the South. The Attorney General was urged to invite all southern district attorneys to a meeting with the conference

---

° "I showed the invitation to Brownell and we both agreed that such an expedition could not possibly bring any constructive results. I wrote a reply to the Negro clergyman declining his invitation, and when the President was asked about the reply at a press conference, he said, 'I have expressed myself so often wherever I have been about this thing that I don't know what good another speech will do right now.'" (Sherman Adams, *First-Hand Report*, New York: Harper & Brothers, 1961, pp. 339–340.)

spokesmen. Reflecting perhaps an inner uncertainty, the conference changed names—becoming the Southern Negro Leaders Conference and then the Southern Negro Leadership Conference. King was elected president, and Abernathy, treasurer. And President Eisenhower was warned, "If some effective remedial steps are not taken, we will be compelled to initiate a mighty Prayer Pilgrimage to Washington . . . we will ask our friends, Negro and white, in the North, East, and West, to join us in this moral crusade for human dignity and freedom."

The Montgomery boycott made Martin Luther King, Jr., a black spokesman, but the Prayer Pilgrimage confirmed his position. Up until then, the national Negro leadership came from the North. Randolph was born in the South, as was Walter White, but both operated from the North with their bases respectively in the black urban mass and the black elite of northern cities. Wilkins, though born in a border state, came out of the Midwest. He broadened the NAACP base beyond that of the elitist 10 percent of an earlier day to include support from the urban and Southern black middle class. Nonetheless, his style and administrative ability were very much of the North. King was not only born in the South, but was of the South as was much of his following. The Prayer Pilgrimage was important, too, for as L. D. Reddick pointed out, when King, Randolph, and Wilkins sat down together to plan the pilgrimage, "three fairly distinct lines of Negro leadership were joined."

Set to commemorate the third anniversary date of the *Brown* decision, on May 17, 1956, the Prayer Pilgrimage was in the direct line of march from Randolph's projected gathering of 1941 down to the momentous coming together of 1963. The call to the pilgrimage stated five objectives, modest goals in the light of future developments: 1) a demonstration of Negro unity; 2) provision for northern aid to southern "freedom fighters," a phrase made popular by the recent gallant uprising in Hungary; 3) defense against "the crippling of the NAACP" in key southern states; 4) mobilizing support for pending civil rights legislation; and 5) protest against the rising tide of violence. A conference of seventy-odd concerned civil rights leaders met in Washington on April 5 to set the pilgrimage in motion. The Reverend Thomas Kilgore, Jr., was asked to direct the effort with Ralph Abernathy in charge of rousing the South. Behind the traditional distinguished letterhead with its fifty "sponsors" and half-dozen honorary chairmen, "special organizers" Bayard Rustin and Ella Baker toiled feverishly to make concrete the "rousements" of the agitators and preachers. The mayors of New York City and Los Angeles and the governors of California, Maryland, Iowa, and Missouri proclaimed May 17 "Pilgrimage Day." The NAACP underwrote most of the promotional costs, with the Southern Negro Leadership Conference and the Pullman Porters chipping in. Roy Wilkins worked out the details of the program.

Garment, transport, automobile, steel, millinery and bartender local unions in New York City came through with delegations and transportation and financial aid. District 65, then of the Retail, Wholesale, and Department Store Union, rallied 1,200 of its members, who sacrificed a day's pay and ponied up their own expenses for the pilgrimage to Washington. The notables flew in; other pilgrims came by automobile, bus, and train; and the Reverend Milton Perry walked over 180 miles from Jersey City.

Shortly before noon, the crowd gathered before the Lincoln Memorial. There were exclamations as people spotted celebrities—Ruby Dee, Harry Belafonte, Sydney Poitier, Sammy Davis, Jr., and Jackie Robinson. Novelist John O. Killens was there, and a host of speakers—Mordecai Johnson, president of Howard University, bursting the fifteen-minute limit imposed on each speaker; Rev. William H. Borders of Atlanta, Rev. Charles K. Steele of Tallahassee, Rev. Fred Shuttlesworth of Birmingham, and Rev. A. L. Davis of New Orleans, each told a dramatic tale of the fight for freedom; Roy Wilkins counseled the crowd, quoting Paul's epistle to the Ephesians, "Put on the whole armor of God . . . . For we wrestle not against flesh and blood, but against principalities;" and Adam Clayton Powell, Jr., cried out for a "third force—nonpartisan but political" on behalf of civil rights. A. Philip Randolph presided; Mahalia Jackson sang, "I've Been 'Buked and I've Been Scorned."

It was, as L. D. Reddick later reported, a representative crowd of the civil rights forces of the day. Thirty-seven thousand people came from thirty-three states, according to the pilgrimage's sponsors. (The Washington *Post* estimated 25,000; the Washington police, 15,000.) "By and large," Reddick noted, "it was a liberal-conservative crowd of church-going Negro Americans," well-dressed and looking reasonably prosperous. Only about 10 percent were white; possibly a rough reflection of the amount of interest in civil rights that existed among even concerned white Americans in 1957. As Reddick remarked, "In many ways, it was a great big Montgomery mass meeting." And when Martin Luther King rose to climax the afternoon-long pilgrimage, it was clear that the bulk of the crowd had come to hear him, breaking out in a spontaneous ovation as he stood before them.

As King's rich baritone rang out over the assembly, a hush descended that lasted until the pejoration: "Give us the ballot . . . and we will no longer plead to the Federal government for passage of an anti-lynching law . . . .

"Give us the ballot . . . and we will transform the salient misdeeds of bloodthirsty mobs into abiding good deeds of orderly citizens.

"Give us the ballot . . . and we will fill our legislative halls with men of good will . . . ."

"Give us the ballot . . ." the crowd chanted in unison, with King adding, "and we will place judges on the benches of the South who will do 'justly and love mercy.' "

"Give us the ballot," chimed the pilgrimage congregation, "and we will quietly and nonviolently, without rancor or bitterness, implement the Supreme Court's decision of May 17, 1954 . . . ."

King assailed the Eisenhower Administration as "too silent and apathetic" and Congress as "too stagnant and hypocritical." He exhorted his audience to return home and work for civil rights in the spirit of Montgomery. "We must never be bitter. If we indulge in hate, the new order will only be the old order . . . . We must meet hate with love, physical force with soul force."

"Amen . . ." chorused the crowd, and the speech was over. King was truly a national figure at last. James L. Hicks of the *Amsterdam News* bestowed the encomium "the number one leader of sixteen million Negroes in the United States . . . . At this point in his career, the people will follow him anywhere."

There were skeptics. New York City Councilman Earl Brown said, "You can't exorcise the devil with prayer alone!" And, in truth, it would prove difficult to turn the pieties of the pilgrimage into action and achievement. The pilgrimage suffered from a lack of focus, of concrete goals. For example, despite Wilkins' programmatic bent, neither did the pilgrims spend time lobbying nor were they guided in any practical way into working "back home" for pending civil rights legislation. True, the pilgrimage did dramatize the issue, and its success may have been a factor in Vice President Richard Nixon's willingness to follow through on an invitation he had extended the Kings while at the Ghana independence celebration to visit him in Washington. The timing of the meeting certainly helped in keeping public attention on Eisenhower's civil rights bill as it made its way through committee hearings, committee sessions, and finally to the floor of the House.

Back in March, Congressman Adam Clayton Powell, Jr., wrote to Sherman Adams saying that Eisenhower's refusal to speak out in response to King's—and the Southern Negro Leadership Conference's —invitation was widely criticized by blacks and suggesting that the President's reply to a letter be enclosed. As Sherman Adams later recounted, the President did not reply, presumably on Adams' advice, "but an alternative to the speech that Dr. King had requested, an expression from the administration of support for desegregation was arranged at a meeting between Dr. King, Nixon, Senator Ives, and Secretary of Labor Mitchell."

Six days after the Prayer Pilgrimage, Vice President Nixon arranged a meeting with King and Ralph Abernathy for Thursday afternoon, June 13. King and Abernathy were briefed by civil rights colleagues and warned against Nixon's charm. Bayard Rustin prepared an extensive memorandum, reviewing the necessary background and urging that the two black spokesmen concentrate on putting across six specific points—1) the idea that *neither* party had done enough for civil rights; 2) that the South could not solve its problems without positive federal action; 3) that the great majority of *white* Southerners were ready for changes, but needed prodding; 4) that President Eisenhower ought to take the civil rights issue to the country as he did foreign aid; 5) that Nixon ought to speak out *in the South* on civil rights and express to Republican legislators the importance of passing the civil rights bill; and 6) "indicate to Vice President Nixon and Secretary Mitchell that something beyond logic and mind is needed at this point."

Though the meeting was scheduled for only an hour, the Vice President insisted that the conferees "take plenty of time," and the four men talked for two hours and ten minutes. The conference was inconclusive, although it did lead to a meeting with the President a year later. Vice President Nixon was interested, polite, and noncommittal. Secretary Mitchell detailed the work of the Committee on Government Contract Compliance, effectively chaired by the Vice President. Abernathy apparently felt that King did not press the Vice President hard enough, and there was some feeling that an opportunity was missed. Louis Lautier of the National Negro Newspaper Publishers Association complained that King answered specific political questions with generalities where Secretary Mitchell had come to the point in post-meeting press conferences. King, wrote Lautier, "showed that he has more homework to do if he is to become a political as well as a spiritual leader." Nonetheless, the meeting received a good press. The Eisenhower civil rights bill was being debated that week in the House and by helping to keep civil rights in the news the meeting contributed to the overwhelming passage of the bill five days later.

There the matter may have rested, except for Senator Lyndon Baines Johnson, Democrat of Texas. Defeat in the Senate appeared foreordained even though the southern bloc's habitual Republican conservative allies were under great pressure from the Eisenhower Administration to vote for the bill. And had the administration succeeded in mustering the country against the South, a filibuster may well have wrecked chances of passage. A *New York Times* dispatch from Washington, in January, reported as a matter of course that Senate Majority Leader Johnson, "will oppose" the Eisenhower civil rights package. But ambition, a parent of virtue in this instance, determined otherwise. As journalists Rowland Evans and Robert Novak note in their able account of the "Miracle of '57," in *Lyndon B. Johnson: The Exercise of Power*, passage of the act was indispensable to Johnson's national aspirations. He hadn't a prayer for the presidential nomination of his party in 1960 unless he emancipated himself from the Confederacy and entered the mainstream of national politics. This Johnson did with undisputed political brilliance.

What Johnson did, in short, was to convince Southerners that it was to their interest to permit a bill to be passed, without filibuster, in order to preserve the two-thirds cloture, a rule that made it virtually impossible for the Senate to close debate to end marathon "talk-it-to-deaths." However, no matter how strong their interests in the cloture rule, the Southerners would not tolerate a bill that empowered the Attorney General of the United States to seek injunctions against those who deprived others of their civil rights. Embodied in "Part III" of the proposed legislation, this ensured not only the right to vote but would have speeded the desegregation of schools. Senator Richard Russell of Georgia, speaking for the white South, termed Part III a "cunning device to integrate the races." Eliminating Part III, Johnson shrewdly realized, would sidestep the explosive issue of school desegregation while the adoption of an amendment requiring a jury trial in contempt-of-court cases arising from violations of the proposed trimmed-down act would de-fang Southern opposition altogether.

Word went out to civil rights forces that it was no bill or a compromise bill. President Eisenhower had, unexpectedly, cut the ground from under Republican support for Part III, saying at a crucial presidential press conference, "I personally believe if you try to go too far too fast in laws in this delicate field that has involved the emotions of so many Americans, you are making a mistake." Later, in his memoirs, the President would describe the defeat of Part III as "a blow," indicating that Evans and Novak are right in describing the President as "confused and ambivalent" on this issue. The jury trial amendment, permitting trial by jury for criminal contempt of court only if a judge's sentence exceeded a $300 fine or forty-five days in jail, won the backing of organized labor, which reacted in support of the amendment out of its own bitter experience with the injunction.

Johnson wheeled and dealed; black, liberal, and labor leaders caucused together and decided to accept the emasculated bill "now and come back for more next year." Vice President Nixon indicated that the Republicans might block final passage, dividing the Democrats and creating an issue for the 1958 and 1960 elections. Civil rights leaders, however, believed, and rightly so, that a bill in 1957 was far better than a campaign issue in 1958. By August 1957, the bill was no longer Eisenhower's but Lyndon Johnson's. After a 24-hour filibuster mounted by Senator Strom Thurmond, the bill passed on August 29 by a vote of sixty to fifteen.

In retrospect, it was a weak bill, doing nothing much about its main purpose—the protection of voting rights. It created the Commission on

Civil Rights, a civil rights division within the Justice Department, and authorized injunction relief in cases of proven voting irregularities. Aside from Johnson, now a national figure rather than a regional one, the immediate beneficiary of the adoption of the civil rights measure was the Democratic party. As Richard Rovere observed in the *New Yorker,* "The party that seemed about torn in two by the controversy achieved greater unity than it had had in two decades." The stage was set for the Democratic success in 1958 and the electoral victory of 1960. Many of the more militant in the black and liberal communities considered the 1957 act a "sell-out." Senator Wayne Morse of Oregon termed it "a sham." Its impact on voter registration appears to have been minimal. According to the 1961 report of the United States Commission on Civil Rights, there were roughly one hundred counties in eight southern states in which there was "reason to believe that Negro citizens are prevented—by outright discrimination or fear of physical violence, or economic reprisal—from exercising the right to vote." In 1956, about 5 percent of voting-age blacks in these counties registered to vote; by 1963, black registration in these counties had increased only to 8.3 percent of the eligible adult black population. Abject poverty, however, also operated in these areas to keep voter registration and turnout low. The spurt in black voting that followed the abolition by the Supreme Court in 1944 of the "white primary" laws and rules took place in the cities of the South, and notably among the more prosperous and middle-class black citizens. A stronger civil rights act *and* a more actively intervening administration as well as the intensive voter registration drives—many sparked by the remarkably energetic Voter Education Project of the Southern Regional Conference—accounted for the second great rise in black registered voters in the South between 1963 and 1964.

Despite its weaknesses, the Civil Rights Act of 1957 was of great importance. It was, after all, the first civil rights legislation that Congress had passed in eighty-two years, and, as such, laid the legislative groundwork for subsequent legislation. Strom Thurmond's filibuster may not have been the last, but it did mark, in its own way, the end of an era when overt racism was openly fashionable, even in high places. However slowly, the Bilbos, Rankins, and Talmadges were passing from the scene. The federal government's responsibility in the area of civil rights was acknowledged in 1957 not only by the executive and judicial branches but also by Congress. And, as historian John Hope Franklin points out, black citizens of Tuskegee and elsewhere now had a national agency to which they could complain of gerrymandering and the denial of the vote. Acts of violence and intimidation against blacks seeking to vote could be aired before a national body. The reports of the Commission on Civil Rights would build an irrefutable case for the much needed civil rights legislation of the 1960s. Astute as always, Roy Wilkins offered the best defense of the compromised legislation: "If you are digging a ditch with a teaspoon and a man comes along and offers you a spade, there is something wrong with your head if you don't take it because he didn't offer you a bulldozer."

While the Senate deliberated over the 1957 Civil Rights Act, Martin Luther King called another meeting of southern black leaders, this time in Montgomery on August 7 and 8. The idea that clergymen in various southern communities were the natural civil rights leaders of the region—an idea tested in Montgomery, Birmingham, and Tallahassee—took organizational shape. Coretta Scott King stresses the point in her autobiography, *My Life with Martin Luther King, Jr.*: "Most of the delegates were activist leaders of their southern black communities but more importantly to us, they were also ministers. Our organization was, from the first, church-oriented, both in its leadership and membership and in the ideal of non-violence—a spiritual concept in deep accord with the American Negro's Christian beliefs." The Southern Negro Leadership Conference changed its name to the Southern Christian Leadership Conference, becoming a somewhat amorphous grouping of some sixty-five affiliate organizations in various southern cities. Charismatically, King dominated SCLC, serving as its president with Charles K. Steele acting as first vice-president, Fred Shuttlesworth, secretary, and Ralph Abernathy, treasurer. SCLC offices were set up in Atlanta, with Ella Baker—who, as Howard Zinn aptly described her, "moved silently through all the protest movements in the South, doing the things that the famous men don't have time to do"—serving as its first executive secretary.

Originally, King hoped to fill the vacuum created by the attempted suppression of the NAACP in several southern states. But that organization was not so easily put down, and the SCLC avoided a possible conflict with the NAACP by not becoming a membership organization. That SCLC was chiefly an alliance of Baptist ministers, each zealous for his congregation, also contributed to the amorphousness of SCLC. The rumors of conflict between SCLC and the NAACP may have been exaggerated. Reddick reports that King and Wilkins "always got on famously together." If there was some competition over voter registration drives and differences over tactics, SCLC did nonetheless stay away from direct involvement in the one pressing area of concern to the NAACP—the school desegregation fight. There were often expressions of mutual support, but the NAACP remained the chief strategist of, and carried the bulk of the burden in the struggle against school segregation.

When schools opened in the fall of 1957, Arkansas Governor Orval Faubus, then considered a liberal, posted two hundred and seventy

National Guardsmen outside Little Rock's Central High School to block the enrollment of a handful of black students. On the advice of the school board, the children did not appear. Federal District Judge Ronald N. Davies ordered desegregation "forthwith." On the morning of Wednesday, September 4, fifteen-year-old Elizabeth Ann Eckford was the first of nine black children to appear in an effort to exercise their legal right to attend Central High along with nearly two thousand white students. With a quiet dignity, she walked to the school entrance where a guardsman barred her way. Then she walked a jeering 100-yard gauntlet back; reaching a bench at a bus stop, she sat down. A white woman went over to comfort her. Someone shouted, "What are you doing, you nigger-lover?" The woman replied, "She's scared! She's just a little girl!" The two left on a bus.

After an investigation by the FBI of the blocking of the school desegregation order, the United States Government asked Judge Davies to enjoin Governor Faubus from interfering with the integration of Little Rock's schools. President Eisenhower missed a great opportunity to rally moderate opinion in the South by forthright, moral action—for example, by taking a child by the hand to lead the black children into Central High. Instead, the mob gained a free hand when the National Guardsmen were removed by Governor Faubus in response to the injunction. A *Times* dispatch by Benjamin Fine from Little Rock on September 23, 1957, described what happened, "A mob of belligerent, shrieking, and hysterical demonstrators forced the withdrawal today of nine Negro students from Central High School here." Bowing before the fury of about one thousand white supremacists, city authorities ordered the Negro students to leave the school. Backed by state and local police, the integration attempt, Fine reported, "lasted three hours thirteen minutes."

President Eisenhower immediately decried the "disgraceful occurrence," saying, too, that a federal court's orders "cannot be flouted with impunity by any individual or mob of extremists." He issued a proclamation directing the obstructionists "to cease and desist therefrom and to disperse forthwith." When the mob did not do so, the President ordered one thousand paratroopers to Little Rock and placed ten thousand members of the Arkansas National Guard on federal service to quell the mob. For the first time since Reconstruction, federal troops were in the South to protect the rights of blacks. They remained in reduced force after November for the balance of the school term. Little Rock high schools closed for the 1958–59 school terms, opening on August 12, 1959, as Little Rock police enforced the desegregation order.

L. D. Reddick, writing in *Crusader Without Violence*, draws an illuminating distinction between Little Rock and Montgomery. Little

Rock, he says, poses the constitutional question: What will the federal authority do when its judicial order is defied, even by a governor? The Montgomery story, Reddick adds, "was not so much what the government would do as what the people would do. Specifically, what are the Negro people of the South prepared to do about their condition?" Of course, Daisy Bates, president of the Arkansas NAACP, who sustained and guided the black high-school youngsters throughout their travail, exemplifies one answer. Her heroism—and that of the children—is a part of the Montgomery story, individual increments to the massive, substantial, nonviolent character that Reddick correctly describes as the distinguishing feature of the Montgomery movement. Yet, while people are occupied with the former, there is little time or energy left for the development of the latter, which explains in part why the Montgomery movement did not spread throughout the South as expected by some whose imaginations were fired by that magnificent stride toward freedom. The drawn out fight for school desegregation, especially during the first five years following the *Brown* decision, drained energies that might have been channeled into a massive, nonviolent movement for civil rights in the South.

Martin Luther King was personally busy, making two hundred speeches in 1957, writing *Stride Toward Freedom*, and, after being stabbed by a demented woman in a Harlem department store while autographing copies of his work, recuperating from a near-fatal wound. The Montgomery Improvement Association's second Institute on Nonviolence, held in December 1957, was poorly attended and considered a flop. In an effort to create "a sustained mass movement on the part of Negroes," King launched a Crusade for Citizenship. For 1958, as Mrs. King writes in her autobiography, *My Life with Martin Luther King, Jr.*, it was "our main emphasis." SCLC held twenty-one simultaneous mass meetings in key southern cities—all on Lincoln's birthday. It was appropriately symbolic, and as Reddick reports, "the general morale effect was good but actually the names of few voters would get on the books during the next month or so." Representative Charles Diggs from Michigan rendered a harsher judgment, telegraphing King, "Rallies and speeches are fine for inspirational purposes, but a successful registration campaign demands skillful follow-up in the field." The emphasis SCLC placed on voter registration was underscored in the appointment of a new executive director, the Reverend John L. Tilley, who scored a success registering voters in Baltimore, Maryland. SCLC held a "down-to-earth" conference on May 29 in Clarksdale, Mississippi, a kind of rejoinder to the 1956 warning, "stay away," from the governor of the Magnolia State to King.

The conference wrote President Eisenhower requesting an audience, which he readily granted. On June 23, King, Roy Wilkins, A. Philip

Randolph, and Lester B. Granger met with the President. In its lack of consequences, the meeting was appropriately symbolic. The black spokesmen urged nine points on the President, including a national pronouncement that the law would be vigorously upheld; a White House conference on school desegregation; that federal resources be made available to all officials and community groups "seeking to work out a program of education and action"; the enactment of Part III, originally in the 1957 act, "so that constitutional rights other than voting rights may be enforced by the United States Attorney General; that the President should "direct" the Department of Justice "to act now" to protect the right to register and vote and act against the wave of bombings of churches, synagogues, homes, and community centers; that the life of the Civil Rights Commission be extended; and that federal money not be used to underwrite segregation in education, hospitals, housing, and so on. The President listened intently and politely and answered in broad terms, citing the administration's record on behalf of all Americans. As the meeting broke up, the President murmured to King, "Reverend, there are so many problems . . . . Lebanon, Algeria . . . ."

The presidential murmur accurately reflected the American mood. The previous October, the Russians had launched the first man-made satellite, Sputnik, creating great public agitation over the state of education. As America ambled down the middle road, the world resounded with alarms, missile-rattling, and intimations of nuclear doomsday. Marines were ordered into Lebanon in the summer of 1958; the Chinese threatened Quemoy and Matsu, islands off Formosa; and Khrushchev announced that Berlin must be "free" or become communist in Soviet parlance. John Kenneth Galbraith tartly condemned Americans' compulsive concern over material goods, arguing that our idea of a good society was an obsolescent carry-over from times of depression. The "social balance" wobbled because current "affluence favored private pursuits as against the public good." What was needed, said Galbraith with his customary brilliance, was a redistribution of income to end poverty in public services. Published and widely acclaimed in 1958, Galbraith's *The Affluent Society* made no mention of civil rights and made light of poverty.

Ironically, as Galbraith's readers debated affluence and its consequences, the economy slid into a recession. Unemployment rose from a low of 3 million in January 1956 to a new high of 5.2 million in July 1958. In an economy where workers in some industrial plants had to possess twenty years or more seniority to retain their jobs, blacks, as the newest entrants, were bound to be badly hit by layoffs. The economy, moreover, was undergoing a structural change that boded ill for the unskilled and semiskilled. In 1956, the country tipped toward what sociologist Daniel Bell has termed the "post industrial society." For the first time, the number of workers producing goods was less than the number offering services. By 1958, automation, or more correctly, technological change, was eliminating the very jobs immigrants and migrants traditionally filled on their arrival on the industrial scene. Growth in plant and equipment investment per employee is one indication of the growth of job-displacing technology. According to the First National City Bank of New York, this investment just about doubled over the 1950s, rising from $5,400 per employee to $10,000. Automation struck at service industries as well as manufacturing, virtually eliminating such traditional jobs for the young as bowling alley pinsetters as well as such semiskilled jobs as elevator operators. The 1958–59 recession eroded economic gains scored by blacks following World War II, even though at the close of his presidency Dwight David Eisenhower could cite solid economic gains—output of goods and services up 25 percent, average family income up 15 percent, and real wages up 20 percent. The unemployment gap between blacks and whites increased. By the mid-1950s, Negroes constituted between 20 and 30 percent of all long-term unemployment covering more than fifteen weeks.

Despite these grim statistics, blacks continued to move into the cities, to the north and west. Economically, blacks were better off in the cities than in the rural regions of the South. The character of the migration, however, had changed. When the Great Migration began shortly before World War I, all sorts of obstacles were placed in the way of Negroes moving north. The South needed black labor badly. In Montgomery, Alabama, for example, jail sentences were meted out to persons found guilty of enticing Negroes to the North. Trains were sidetracked and outward-bound blacks were arrested for vagrancy. Toward the end of the 1950s, the White Citizens' Councils were offering to pay the fare for blacks wanting to leave the South. The mockery, however, was scarcely needed. By 1960, the country's twelve largest metropolitan areas contained 31 percent of all blacks in the United States. There were 1.1 million blacks in New York City, 813,000 in Chicago, 529,000 in Philadelphia, 500,000 in Detroit, and 464,000 in Los Angeles. Roughly 52 percent of all black Americans lived in the North and West, and the overwhelming majority dwelt in the cities, despite growth in the black population of the South, which rose from nearly 4 million in 1940 to over 9 million in 1960. Of these, more and more were daily moving into such cities as Atlanta, Birmingham, Houston, and Dallas. As historian John Hope Franklin observed, "The northern Negro was already a city dweller, and the southern Negro was rapidly becoming one."

There was a good deal of movement—over 1.5 million blacks moved out of the South between 1950 and 1960. To this must be added an untold number moving around in the South, notably from rural to urban areas. For perspective, one must keep in mind that—black or white— we are a mobile people. About one in every five American families shifts residences every year. What complicated the black migration were the problems of poverty, a lack of education and skills appropriate to the city, and the shock of being uprooted. Little noted during the so-called affluent, contented, or "fat fifties," the migration, concentrating an ever greater number of black citizens in the center cities of the country, produced a crisis that would erupt in the riots of the 1960s. "In the city environment," sociologist E. Franklin Frazier wrote in his study, *The Negro Church in America*, "the family of the masses of Negroes from rural areas, which lacked an institutional basis and was held together only by cooperation in making a living or by sympathies and sentiments generated by living together in the same household, was unable to stand the shock of the disintegrating forces in urban life." The hold of the church, formerly the center of black social life and a refuge from a hostile white world, loosened. The social dislocation of the crowded slums, however, intensified the need for faith while eroding past forms, creating, in St. Clair Drake's and Horace R. Cayton's perceptive phrase, "New Gods of the City." Escapism characterized the cults and sects lodged in storefronts, Father Devine's "Heaven," and various brown-stone temples. Yet, there was among the proliferating oracles and prophets a quest for identity, perhaps most clearly visible in the astronomical rise of the Black Muslims, an outcropping of black assertiveness that would have a profound effect on the civil rights movement. This impact is something of a paradox, for the Muslims were nationalists, non-Christians, racists, anti-assimilationists, and anti-integrationists, while the majority of blacks were presumably Christian, pro-integration, and not seeking a black nation.

The Muslims were founded by Wallace D. Fard, or F. Mohammed Ali, who appeared in Detroit mid-summer 1930, drawing upon the Bible to teach the religion of the Black Men of Asia and Africa, only to disappear under somewhat mysterious circumstances some four years later. The Prophet of Islam left his newly founded nation in the exceedingly capable hands of Elijah Muhammad, born Elijah Poole and a 1920s migrant to Detroit from Georgia. Under Fard, the nation scarcely numbered eight thousand, many of whom were former followers of Marcus Garvey. Elijah Muhammad, the "Spiritual Head of the Muslims in the West," tapped the discontent of the newly urbanized black masses of the post-World War II period, and by 1960, the Muslims claimed a membership of 100,000 in sixty-nine temples or missions in twenty-seven states. As the black-suited, bold, young males with the red ties and distinctively military bearing graced the Muslim temples and missions, a visible appeal to black pride was reinforced by the virulence of the Muslim's verbal attack on the hostile "white nation." It was heady stuff for the young slouching on street corners in the black slums of Chicago, Detroit, New York. The Muslims, C. Eric Lincoln correctly points out in *The Black Muslims in America*, were neither pacifists nor aggressors. They engaged in neither sit-ins nor marches on Washington, but did "believe in keeping the scores even, and they have warned all America that 'an eye for an eye and a tooth for a tooth' is the only effective way to settle racial differences." It proved to be a popular appeal in the 1960s. Meanwhile, the success of the Muslims among the so-called "street Negroes" exerted an unacknowledged pressure for increased militancy. As C. Eric Lincoln observed, the Muslim's "lashing indictment of the white man . . . strikes a responsive, if reluctant, chord in many Negro hearts." It was a chord that would reverberate throughout the 1960s.

While anger, frustration, and rootlessness seethed in northern cities, the South, too, was changing in unexpected ways. Braving the taunts of hate-filled whites to enter previously all-white schools, black children testified to a moral strength and self-discipline that has few parallels in our history. Their courage inspired others to go and do likewise. In October 1958, the Reverend Fred L. Shuttlesworth and twenty other black Birminghamites were arrested for protesting bus segregation, and the Reverend William Holmes Borders launched a boycott in Atlanta that ended segregated busing. "We aren't mad at anyone," said Borders. "We believe in Christian love."

Others, however, thought that Christian love might have limits when it came to convincing white supremacists to give ground to demands for justice. In Monroe, North Carolina, an ex-Marine and head of the county NAACP, Robert Williams, organized a gun club. When Klansmen came night-riding in cars to threaten the home of an NAACP member, Williams' armed young men drove them off with gunfire. Some southern blacks, at least, had served notice that if shot at, they would shoot back.°

There were other stirrings as the decade drew to a close. With King's blessing, Bayard Rustin organized a Youth March for Integrated Schools, which sparked local sit-ins in Oklahoma City, Oklahoma, and Wichita, Kansas, and brought ten thousand youths to Washington,

---

° "The Montgomery bus boycott," Williams later wrote for *Liberation* (September 1959, p. 5), "was a great victory for American democracy," but not a prescription for every situation. "If Mack Parker [recently lynched in Mississippi] had an automatic shotgun, he could have served as a great deterrent against lynching." Williams incurred the wrath of NAACP officialdom for his unpolitic avowal of self-defense. His dismissal as a branch officer was a *cause célèbre* at the 1959 NAACP convention. Later, Williams was charged with the alleged kidnapping of a white during a racial outbreak in 1961 in Monroe. He fled to Cuba, then to China. Subsequently, he returned to the United States, becoming involved for a time in a black nationalist movement in Detroit.

D.C., in 1958 and twenty-five thousand on April 18, 1959. A Pilgrimage of Prayer for Public Schools, under CORE auspices, attracted two thousand persons to Richmond, Virginia, to protest Virginia's "massive resistance" to school desegregation. CORE moved into the Deep South for the first time, boycotting to integrate an ice-cream stand in Marion, South Carolina. CORE members also sat-in at a Grant's lunch counter on April 29, 1959, in Miami, Florida, to open a drive to integrate dime-store lunch counters. Interracial groups, sponsored by CORE, tested Miami's famed beaches without incident. As Jim Peck noted, these events "would have been unthinkable a few years before." In July 1959, SCLC, CORE, and the Fellowship of Reconciliation sponsored the first nonviolent institute held on the Spelman College campus in Atlanta. Randolph, Reddick, Rustin, Lawson, and Richard Gregg, author of *The Power of Nonviolence*, were among the speakers. Workshops were devoted to training in nonviolent techniques. FOR, among other activities, published a "comic book," *Martin Luther King and the Montgomery Story*, prepared by its staff and executed by the Al Capp Organization with the aid of a $5,000 grant from the Fund for the Republic. By 1960, some 200,000 copies had been circulated.

VIII

Sit-ins . . .
Freedom Rides

IT WAS A ROUTINE OCCURRENCE in the South: A black youth wanted a bite to eat, and when seeking service at the lunch counter in the Greensboro, North Carolina, bus station, he was told, "We don't serve Negroes." Back in the North Carolina Agricultural and Technical College dormitory, eighteen-year-old Joseph McNeil reported the incident to three fellow freshmen— Ezell Blair, Jr., Franklin McCain, and David Richmond. While leafing through *Martin Luther King and the Montgomery Story*, McNeil asked the question that agitated more and more minds as the 1960s began: "What can *we* do?" Pausing a moment, he answered his own question: "Let's have a boycott!"

Acting on McNeil's suggestion, the four students went downtown the next afternoon and at about 4:30 P.M. on Monday, February 1, 1960, entered the local Woolworth's "five-and-dime" store to make what they called a "passive demand for service." They purchased several small articles without difficulty for, as Harry Golden once wryly remarked, "no one in the South pays the slightest attention to a 'VERTICAL NEGRO.'" They then took seats at the lunch counter and ordered coffee. When the waitress said, "We don't serve colored in here," Blair answered, "I beg to disagree with you. You just finished serving me at a counter only two feet from here." Flustered, the waitress flounced off and the four young men were ignored. "I told the waitress we'd sit there until we were served," McNeil later told a student reporter. "She said nothing. Policemen came in and stared at us and walked up and down the aisle, but said nothing to us. We figured it was an effort on their part to frighten us away, but we stayed until 5:30, when the store closed." And so began the sit-in that set off a wave of nonviolent and direct action protests throughout the South against segregation at lunch counters, in public parks, swimming pools, theaters, restaurants, churches, interstate transportation, libraries, museums, art galleries, laundromats, employment agencies, beaches, and courtrooms.

The next day twenty-odd students joined McNeil, Blair, Richmond, and McCain, enough to occupy most of the seats at the counter, and there they remained for the day. By the third day, the students had organized shifts to carry on the sit-ins. By the following week, sit-ins were underway in a half-dozen North Carolina towns. (A. & T. College played five basketball games in two weeks and students at the rival schools shortly thereafter engaged in sit-ins.) Before the month was out, sit-ins had spread to more than twelve cities in four states—Virginia, Tennessee, and the two Carolinas. By August, sit-ins succeeded in ending lunch-counter segregation in twenty-seven southern cities. In September 1961, the Southern Regional Council reported: "Since February 1, 1960, each southern and border state, as well as Nevada, Illinois, and Ohio—20 in all—has been affected by protest demonstrations.

"Over 100 cities in the South and in the border states have had sit-ins or other forms of direct action.

"An estimated 3,600 students and supporters—in southern and border states—have been arrested.

"At least 70,000 Negroes and whites in those states actively participated in some way; this figure counts persons who sat-in, picketed, marched and attended mass meetings (sometimes in the face of intimidation). It does not account for thousands of others who supported the movement by letters to the editor, financial contributions and expressions of moral support."

It would take six months of sitting-in and negotiations to open the Greensboro Woolworth's lunch counter to all seeking service. In retrospect, the sit-ins with their limited goals—"We don't want brotherhood," a black student told Michael Walzer reporting on the sit-ins for *Dissent*, "we just want a cup of coffee, sitting down"—may not seem so much when compared with the heady slogans of the late 1960s—"Freedom Now," "Black Power," or "Power to the People." Yet, the four A. & T. freshmen did precipitate a revolution, if only of a limited kind. The Greensboro sit-in set off a wave of nonviolent actions that toppled segregation in public accommodations.

The soft-spoken, neatly dressed, polite but firm young men and women who so bravely asserted their rights in so simple a fashion also struck at the mystique of racism. "Every normal human being," declared a manifesto drafted by Atlanta college students, "wants to walk the earth with dignity and abhors any and all proscriptions placed upon him because of race or color. In essence, this is the meaning of the sit-down protests that are sweeping the nation today." In keeping with the new faith articulated by Martin Luther King, Jr., a compound of the teachings of the Prophets, Christ, and of the secular Thoreau and Gandhi, the sit-in students exhibited, in the face of considerable provocation, a remarkable consideration for their opponents. Their courage and demeanor won respect even from enemies, as an editorial in the rightwing, segregationist Richmond *New Leader* attests: "Many a Virginian must have felt a tinge of wry regret at the state of things as they are, in reading of Saturday's 'sit-downs' by Negro students in Richmond stores. Here were the colored students, in coats, white shirts, ties, and one of them was reading Goethe and one was taking notes from a biology text. And here, on the sidewalk outside, was a gang of white boys come to heckle, a ragtail rabble, slack-jawed, black-jacketed, grinning fit to kill, and some of them, God save the mark, were waving the proud and honored flag of the Southern States in the last war fought by gentlemen. *Eheu!* It gives one pause."

Segregation in the South of 1960 was a ludicrous patchwork, laughable but for its serious intent—the degradation of a people. Harry Golden once persuaded the manager of a department store to shut-off the water to the store's "white's only" fountain and put up a sign, "Out of Order." Little by little, as Golden reported in *Only in America*, whites began drinking out of the "coloreds" fountain and soon everybody was drinking "segregated" water with no complaints. Throughout the South, blacks and whites shopped at the same grocery, deposited money at the same bank teller's window, paid telephone and light bills to the same clerk, and shopped at the same counters in five-and-dime and department stores. The money that was good enough to buy, say, a student's notebook was, however, in black hands, not good enough for a hamburger or soda at the store's lunch counter.

Some radicals now scoff at the sit-ins as being "middle class," not truly revolutionary in intent or consequence. Economic gains and/or political power are rated above mere equality of treatment in public accommodations. Getting a room in a Holiday Inn, so the argument runs, is of no importance to a poor black. Forty-three percent of black families owned automobiles in 1960 as against 73 percent of white families, and therefore, only a minority of blacks could possibly benefit from desegregation of highway eating places, motels, and the like. But this is a misreading of economics, history, and the dynamics of social change. Black expenditures on automobiles had doubled between 1950 and 1960 and were increasing. More blacks than ever were driving, passing hot dog stands, Howard Johnsons, motels, public recreation facilities, out of fear that they would not be served, or if served, insulted. And for every middle-class black family en route to Mexico for a vacation, driving all night through Texas because they could not find a place that would take blacks, there were hundreds riding Greyhounds and Trailway buses in and out of the South, daily facing the insult of Jim Crow. "Nothing," writes John A. Williams in *The King God Didn't Save*, "is quite as humiliating, so murderously angering, as to know that because you are black you may have to walk a half mile farther than whites just to urinate; that because you are black you have to receive your food through a window in the back of a restaurant or sit in a garbage-littered yard to eat."

The students, though undeniably middle-class or upwardly mobile, had hit upon an issue that affected and moved the black masses profoundly.° The sit-ins would convince more people that direct action was a more effective route to the goal of desegregation than any other. Direct action joined the strike, the recall, and the referendum in the repertoire of political last resorts. As for the South, there was a special significance. As Pat Watters and Reese Cleghorn put it in *Climbing Jacob's Ladder*, "Never again after the 1960 sit-ins was a large portion of the South's white liberals or moderates or Negroes to be completely trapped in that most real fear of enraging the beast of racial violence lurking in all the picturesque farm lands, lethargic cities, and pleasant little towns, threatening to howl through every warm mystical night . . . . [The beast] could still evoke fear, and inflict defeat. But he could no longer paralyze action over the whole South as he did when everyone conspired to keep him hidden."

That black college students should be the catalysts exposing the conspiracy is all the more remarkable when one considers the accepted role of the black colleges. Seeking to adapt the educated black to the dominant institutions of American life, the black colleges encouraged deference to the mores of the South. What had been, or still was, a tactic for survival had deleterious effects. Ralph Ellison catches this brilliantly in the first section of his novel, *Invisible Man*. "How all of us at the college hated the black-belt people," his hero declares, "the 'peasants,' during those days! We were trying to lift them up and they, like Trueblood, did everything it seemed to pull us down." Sociologist E. Franklin Frazier is as harsh in condemnation as novelist Ellison is in revelation: "The second and third generation of college students," he wrote in *Black Bourgeoisie*, "are as listless as the children of peasants. The former are interested primarily in the activities of Greek letter societies and 'social life,' while the latter are concerned with gaining

---

° When *Tuesday* reporter Gene Grove interviewed the four freshmen who started it all ("Where Are They Now? The 4 Original Sit-ins," *Tuesday Magazine*, February 1966) six years later, he found that Joseph McNeil had become a first lieutenant in the Air Force; Franklin McCain, a research chemist for Celanese Corporation, in Charlotte, North Carolina; Ezell Blair, Jr., an instructor at a Job Corps Center in New Bedford, Massachusetts; and David Richmond, a student again at North Carolina A. & T., majoring in accounting after dropping out to support a wife and family by working at the Cone Mills in Greensboro.

social acceptance by the former. Both are less concerned with the history or the understanding of the world about them than with their appearances at the next social affair . . . money and conspicuous consumption are more important than knowledge or the enjoyment of books and art and music."

Yet, for all of that, these institutions (107 in all) housed teachers who did survive and educate down through all those years when night-riding racists spread terror across a hot and humid land. For over one hundred years, black colleges in the South and several in the North—Lincoln and Cheyney in Pennsylvania, Wilberforce in Ohio, and Howard in Washington, D.C.—produced the black community's doctors, lawyers, preachers, teachers, pharmacists, and morticians. As recently as 1947, between 80 and 90 percent of all blacks who had graduated from college received their education in black institutions in southern states. Out of these educational havens came A. Philip Randolph, Martin Luther King, Angie Brooks, John Hope Franklin, Asa Spaulding, Ralph Ellison, Thurgood Marshall, and thousands of others not as well known but who have each contributed to the quality of black life in America.

For generations, the black colleges reached out into the cotton fields of the Mississippi Delta, the tobacco fields of North Carolina, the red clay fields of Georgia, the piney woods and ramshackle edges of cities and into towns where the raw youth were to be found, brought them out and educated them. Black colleges are closer to the mass of black people than are white institutions to white folk. This relationship may have even been intensified during the late 1950s and early 1960s as the children of prosperous blacks increasingly enrolled in predominately white colleges in the North. The number of students enrolled in black institutions rose sharply during the period, up from 76,561 in 1950 to 88,859 in 1960 and to 105,561 only four years later. Michael Walzer, who visited several black colleges in North Carolina for *Dissent* shortly after the sit-ins began, reported that in the schools he visited one-third to one-half the students were from the North, mostly from Pennsylvania, New Jersey, and New York. This suggests that though the majority of the student population in the black colleges are from the South (a 1968 survey found that 58.5 percent of male freshmen and 64.3 percent female freshmen were from the South), the students were not isolated from migratory developments among the blacks. Their fathers were unskilled or semiskilled workers and their families more often than not poor (the 1968 survey found that 62.3 percent of black freshmen had parents with less than a $6,000 yearly income). Many, too, had been in the army (integrated) or spent time in the North, working or on vacation.

Walzer found that it was the southern students who kept the sit-in movement going. The Northerners were too blasé or too cynical. "The

A. Philip Randolph, Eleanor Roosevelt, and Fiorello La Guardia
at a rally to save the Fair Employment Practices Commission
right after World War II.

Lined up for first Freedom Ride, April 1947, are Worth Randle,
Wally Nelson, Ernest Bromley, Jim Peck, Igal Roodenko,
Bayard Rustin, Joe Felmet, George Houser, and Andy Johnson.

A. Philip Randolph leads line of protestors outside
1948 Democratic National Convention.

Grant Reynolds and A. Philip Randolph testify against
segregation before a Senate Armed Services Committee in 1948.

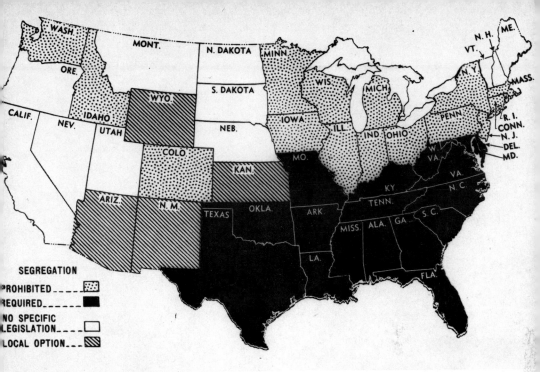

SEGREGATION

PROHIBITED _ _ _ _ _ ⬚

REQUIRED _ _ _ _ _ _ ■

NO SPECIFIC
LEGISLATION _ _ _ _ ☐

LOCAL OPTION _ _ _ ▨

UNITED PRESS INTERNATIONAL

Segregated America. The map shows the variations in state law
before the Supreme Court decision banning segregation in 1954.

Separate is no longer equal. Thurgood Marshall flanked by
George E. C. Hayes and James M. Nabrit after the
decision was rendered.

UNITED PRESS INTERNATIONAL

Rosa Parks, flanked by her attorney and a deputy, on her way to the jail.

Martin Luther King, Jr., and the Reverend Glenn Smiley on the first integrated bus ride in Montgomery, Alabama.

Autherine Lucy and attorney Arthur Shores fire a round in the legal battle to gain her admission to the University of Alabama.

Federal troops escort nine black children into previously all-white Central High School in Little Rock.

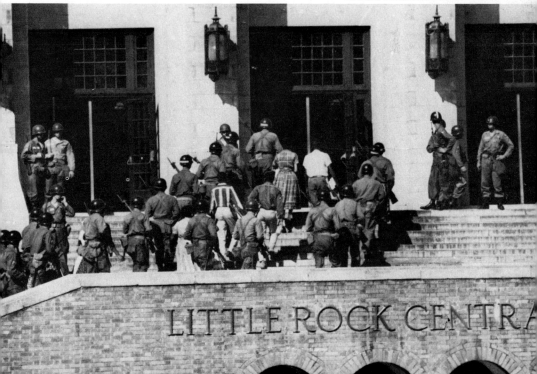

LITTLE ROCK CENTRA

UNITED PRESS INTERNATIONAL

Sit-in at a Greensboro, North Carolina, Woolworth's.

Police Chief Laurie Pritchett of Albany, Georgia, placing
Martin Luther King, Jr., and Dr. W. G. Anderson under arrest.

UNITED PRESS INTERNATIONAL

Waiting for the paddy wagon, Birmingham demonstrators—
some praying, some singing.

Blind singer Al Hibbler gets the word from "Bull" Connor.

James Meredith gets his degree.

Roy Wilkins and Jackie Robinson
at a civil rights benefit.

Civic and business leader
A. G. Gaston examining his just
fire-bombed house in Birmingham
Alabama.

The leaders of the March on Washington meet President
Kennedy: (in front) Whitney Young, Martin Luther King, Jr.,
Rabbi Joachim Prinz, A. Philip Randolph, the President,
Walter Reuther, and Roy Wilkins. Note the then Vice
President Lyndon Johnson behind Walter Reuther.

Alabama Governor George Wallace defies the federal
government in the person of Nicholas Katzenbach over the
admission of two Negroes to the University of Alabama.

Some of the thousands at the historic march.

Martin Luther King, Jr., and Ralph Abernathy defy injunction
in Birmingham.

Little Rock after integration.

The era of militancy begins—garbage on the Triborough Bridge in New York City.

Civil rights leaders meet in 1964; clockwise from Bayard
Rustin are Jack Greenberg, Whitney Young, James Farmer,
Roy Wilkins, Martin Luther King, Jr., John Lewis, and
A. Philip Randolph.

Malcolm X addressing a church meeting in Selma, Alabama.

Murdered martyrs of Mississippi freedom summer—Andrew Goodman, James Chaney, and Michael Schwerner.

Aaron Henry, leader of the Mississippi Freedom Democratic Party, barred from admission to the Democratic National Convention in 1964.

The President of the United States listens, as does Whitney
Young, to A. Philip Randolph.

Sit-down over voter registration in Birmingham.

Fannie Lou Hamer speaks out about poverty in Mississippi.
Rev. Killingsworth backs her up.

Stokely Carmichael gets steamed up about "black power."

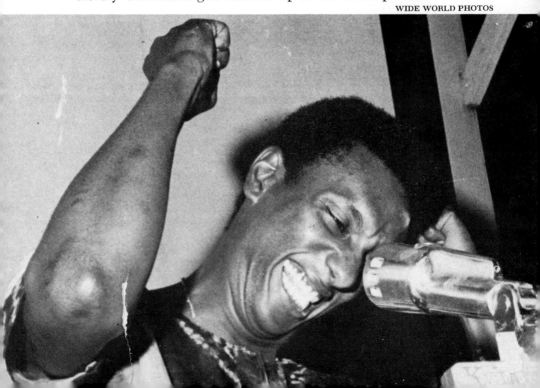

Barbara Jordan, first black congresswoman from Texas.

Andrew Young, Jr., first black congressman of the South
since Reconstruction.

Southerners," he wrote, "were more militant (and religious), committed to a long and grueling struggle." Howard Zinn reported that of fourteen Spelman College girls arrested the first day of the Atlanta sit-ins, thirteen were from "the Deep South . . . the Faulknerian towns of traditional Negro submissiveness." The sit-in generation was inspired by the Montgomery boycott and Martin Luther King, Jr. But above all, it was the generation whose friends and relations had braved white mobs to desegregate the public schools. What terrors remained after that experience? After their own fashion, the students also looked to Washington for the Supreme Court decisions that would—and did— come their way, and more. When President Eisenhower sent troops to Little Rock, was he not saying to white supremacists, "Thus far you may go but no farther?" And surely the students were aware that 1960 was an election year, possibly more significant than most. Vice President Richard M. Nixon, the likely Republican candidate, had established a good record as the working chairman of the President's Committee on Government Contract Compliance, established by President Eisenhower in 1951. And within Democratic folds pressures were mounting for a strong civil rights posture, pressure that would gain impetus from the student sit-ins.

"It was a state of mind," Joseph McNeil recalled in an interview with *Tuesday* reporter Gene Grove some six years after the first sit-ins. "It was something, a feeling of urgency, a feeling that something had to be done.

"I was from North Carolina," McNeil added, "but I had lived in New York and when I went back down there to school I realized the transition, the difference in public accommodations. It seemed to be that people in Alabama, where they had the Montgomery bus boycott, were at least trying to do something about it. The people in Little Rock, with the trouble at Central High School, were trying to do something. And we weren't."

When they did act, the students tapped wellsprings of resistance that lay deep within the black community. "In a way," a student told Michael Walzer, "we have been planning it all our lives." There had been other sit-ins, but Greensboro not only caught the public eye but did so as the public mood was about to change; the sit-ins were the first intimation that the acquiescent fifties were about to make way for the activist sixties. "It is with a desire to do *something*," Ted Dienstfrey, a University of Chicago student, wrote in the June 1960 issue of *Commentary*, "that many northern white college students look at the sit-in movement of their southern Negro counterparts."

While sit-ins proliferated, few among the students gave thought as to where passive resistance/direct action might lead, except, of course, to jail, an eventuality that a growing number of students would embrace with joy, producing, among many other "ins" of 1960, the "jail-in." Adults, however, while no more prescient than the activist youngsters, were anxious, concerned, even worried about direction and possible consequences. CORE and the NAACP sent out their youth and field secretaries to give counsel. Martin Luther King, Jr., gave his support, and SCLC leaders, as did the Reverend C. K. Steele in Tallahasee, acted as mentors for student sit-ins in their respective communities. Ella Baker, who sensed the volatility inherent in student protests, suggested that SCLC call a conference of sit-in leaders, which was held over Easter weekend, April 15 to 17, 1960, at Mrs. Baker's alma mater, Shaw University in Raleigh, North Carolina. SCLC put up $800 to finance the affair, and some 212 participants deliberated the goals and tactics of the sit-ins and how to best coordinate student efforts.

Martin Luther King, Jr., apparently hoped to father a youth wing for SCLC at the conference. But Mrs. Baker and the Reverend James Lawson, who had been expelled from Vanderbilt School of Theology for leading sit-ins in Nashville, advised against it. The presence of CORE, friendly but with its own organizational interests, may have further inhibited King's plans. Be it as it may, King limited himself to suggesting "some type of continuing organization." He urged a nationwide campaign of "selective buying" to reward progressive firms and punish those practicing segregation and called for "volunteers who will willingly go to jail rather than pay bail or fines." Many, if not most of the students present, tended to view nonviolence as a tactic and not a matter of principle, which perhaps accurately reflected the predilections of their fellows. King pressed the students to delve deeper into the philosophy of nonviolence. Resistance and nonviolence, he warned, are not in themselves good. "There is another element in our struggle that makes our resistance and nonviolence truly meaningful. That element is reconciliation. Our ultimate end must be the creation of the beloved community. The tactics of nonviolence without the spirit of nonviolence may become a new kind of violence."

The discussion of philosophy and goals left some of the students cold. Dienstfrey reported that some simply left the meetings to go and picket. One black youth from Virginia rose to declare, "I don't dig all this," and urged consideration of money, jobs, and scholarships for poor blacks. According to Dienstfrey, the most heated discussion of the conference was over an organizational question: Should Northerners be represented on the temporary planning committee for the proposed new organization? Lawson feared a dissipation of southern intent by a northern influx but many of the students were offended by the notion of a "second-class membership." The compromise was in its way typical of what was to become "the movement." An all-southern planning committee was set up; Northerners could *earn* the right to join by participation in nonviolent demonstrations against segregation in the North.°

The fifteen-member planning committee met the following month in Atlanta with King, Lawson, and Ella Baker on hand to advise. The group decided not to operate as an affiliate of SCLC and to call themselves the Student Nonviolent Coordinating Committee (SNCC, or as student vernacular soon had it, SNICK). Marion Barry, a graduate student at Fisk, was named chairman. SNCC's statement of purpose was a gratifying tribute to King's influence: "We affirm the philosophical or religious ideal of nonviolence as the foundation of our purpose, the presupposition of our faith and the manner of our action . . . ."

A "plenary" conference in October 1960 put SNCC on a permanent footing, though still loosely organized. In 1961, the youth organization had a budget of $14,000 and a staff of sixteen. There was no formal membership—in effect, one became a member by going on staff—and a minimum of structure with a maximum of spontaneity and fluidity. Operationally and politically, SNCC would, in time, tighten up, becoming a more disciplined and rigid group. In the beginning, however, there was a great distrust of organization and great virtue was placed on "staying loose." Robert Moses, a SNCC mentor, once seriously proposed that SNCC members abolish all committees and offices, walk out the door, and "go where the spirit say go and do what the spirit say do." °°

As is often the case with student affairs, the sit-ins peaked in the spring of 1960 and dropped in number over the summer. Political considerations were now of increasing importance to civil rights forces. There was some concern that some untoward demonstration would tip over any one of several political applecarts. There was also an increasing awareness of direct action as a means of mounting pressure for civil rights in the political arena. The black vote had become increasingly vital, and in 1960, for the first time, both parties seemed equally aware of that political fact. Illinois, Pennsylvania, New York, and Michigan total 132 electoral votes, almost half the number needed to win the presidency. In each of these states, the black vote in a major city might make the difference in a close contest. The tactical question for black leaders was how to best use this leverage to compel equality for fellow blacks in the South.

Bayard Rustin proposed to Martin Luther King, Jr., that he should

---

° The North-South question was ultimately resolved by the formation of the Northern Student Movement (NSM), an organization of students on off-southern campuses dedicated to the support of the movement in the South. For a time, NSM was SNCC's chief financial backer.

°° Moses, an enigmatic and charismatic figure, later did just that. He changed his name and simply "disappeared." On August 29, 1973, Paul Delaney reported in *The New York Times*, in one of a series of articles on civil rights ten years after the 1963 March on Washington that Moses was teaching school in Tanzania.

present to the Democratic and Republican parties' platform committees seven major demands:

1. Both parties should repudiate segregationists within their own ranks and make a forthright declaration that any form of discrimination is unconstitutional, un-American, and immoral.
2. Both parties should endorse the spirit and tactics of the sit-ins as "having the same validity as labor strikes."
3. In accordance with the Fourteenth Amendment, congressional representation ought to be reduced in those areas where Negroes are denied the right to vote.
4. Both parties should explicitly endorse the 1954 Supreme Court decision as morally right and the law of the land.
5. That Section III of the proposed civil rights legislation, empowering the federal government to bring suits on behalf of Negroes denied their civil rights, be enacted into law.
6. That Congress pass the "federal registrar" plan of the President's Civil Rights Commission and that the responsibility for the protection of voting rights be placed squarely with the President and not with Southern courts.
7. That the two parties and their candidates take a clear moral stand against colonialism and racism in all its forms, especially in Africa.

To draw attention to these demands, Rustin also proposed to picket the conventions. Michael Harrington, in Los Angeles to help organize such a demonstration, found the going rough. The student sit-ins had won admiration but had not as yet stirred an equivalent militancy throughout America's black communities. The prospects were bleak, so Harrington reported over the telephone to Rustin in New York City. "My friend," Rustin replied, "there will be a march, and there will be at least one person in it—you." As it turned out, five thousand picketed with Randolph, King, and Wilkins leading the way. The contenders for the Democratic crown were asked to speak at a civil rights gathering at the Shrine auditorium. Senator John Kennedy was booed on his arrival, despite pleas for courtesy by Chairman Clarence Mitchell. Most of those present were committed to Senator Hubert H. Humphrey, whose civil rights record was unmatched by that of any other candidate.

When Senator Kennedy won the nomination, it seemed a reasonable gamble for Vice President Richard M. Nixon, the likely Republican candidate, to woo crucial black votes in the North. At the Republican convention, he threw his weight behind the progressive civil rights campaign plank drafted by New York Governor Nelson Rockefeller, thereby defeating a "moderate" proposal. The conservative Republican senator from Arizona, Barry Goldwater, later claimed that this decision cost Nixon the election. By it, he failed to clearly reorient the Republican party on a conservative North/South axis. Nonetheless, as the campaign progressed, it appeared that Nixon's gamble might well pay off, winning key northern states for the Republicans.

On October 19, Martin Luther King and seventy-five black students walked into Rich's Department Store in Atlanta and sought service at the lunch counter. King and thirty-six others were arrested and charged with trespassing. When they declared that they would "rather be jailed than bailed," Mayor William B. Hartsfield intervened and arranged a two-month truce. Charges were dropped, and the students released. But a judge in an adjoining county revoked King's probation on a trivial traffic offense committed in the spring. On moving to Atlanta, King neglected to obtain a Georgia driver's license within the statutory time, and had been hooked by a state trooper while driving on his "expired" Alabama license. De Kalb County Judge Oscar Mitchell held that King's participation in an "illegal" sit-in violated his probation, and so on October 26 King languished in solitary confinement in Reidsville State Prison, sentenced to four months at hard labor. Many believed the judge's action a pretext for "getting King," for it was certainly unusual and certain to be overturned on appeal. Beatings, even shootings of "escaped" prisoners were not unheard of, especially in the handling of unrecalcitrant blacks; there were grounds for believing that King's life was endangered even within the brief time it would take to arrange bail and to lodge an appeal.

When the news of King's arrest broke, the White House was inundated with demands for federal intervention on behalf of the imprisoned civil rights leader. With the election only eight days away, King's incarceration posed a moral and political challenge for the presidential candidates. At the suggestion of Deputy Attorney General Lawrence E. Walsh, the Justice Department drafted a statement for President Eisenhower. It proposed that the President say: "It seems to me fundamentally unjust that a man who has peacefully attempted to establish his right to equal treatment free from racial discrimination should be imprisoned on an unrelated charge, in itself insignificant." The Attorney General was asked by the President "to take all proper steps" with King's attorneys for his release. Eisenhower, however, waffled; the statement was never issued, and candidate Nixon declined to comment. Why he did not is perplexing in view of his earlier commitment to a strong civil rights plank in the Republican party platform. Moreover, he had much to gain in winning black votes in the industrial states of the North, normally Democratic strongholds. However, with the election only a few days off and the states of Texas,

South Carolina, and Louisiana precariously tipped in his favor, Nixon apparently felt he could not afford to offend the white voters in those states. Instead, he opted for cautious silence.

Within the Kennedy camp, the opposite reaction carried. Harris Wofford, Jr., a Notre Dame law professor, an admirer of Gandhi and FOR member who was serving candidate Kennedy as an adviser on minority affairs, suggested that Senator Kennedy call Mrs. King and express his sympathy. Wofford's suggestion was relayed with enthusiasm to the candidate by Sargent Shriver, a Kennedy brother-in-law and head of the campaign's civil rights section. According to Anthony Lewis of *The New York Times*, some members of the Kennedy entourage were skeptical, but Shriver prevailed, getting the candidate alone in a room and dialing the King number in Atlanta.°

As Mrs. King recalls the ensuing telephone conversation in her autobiography, after exchanging greetings, Senator Kennedy said: "I want to express to you my concern about your husband. I know this must be very hard for you. I understand you are expecting a baby, and I just wanted you to know that I was thinking about you and Dr. King. If there is anything I can do to help, please feel free to call on me." The next morning, the Senator's brother and campaign manager, Robert Kennedy, called the judge involved and persuaded him to release King on bail. Although King himself was personally grateful, he made no political endorsement. His father's enthusiasm, however, carried him from a previous endorsement of Nixon to one for Kennedy. From his pulpit that Sunday, the senior King cried out, "Because this man was willing to wipe the tears from my daughter [in-law]'s eyes, I've got a suitcase of votes, and I'm going to take them to Mr. Kennedy and dump them in his lap." To ensure that the black voters got the message, Wofford drafted a pamphlet: " 'No Comment'—Nixon versus a Candidate with a Heart, Senator Kennedy." White reports that a million copies were printed; Anthony Lewis, two million; both agree that a half million copies were distributed in Chicago alone. Rarely does a single leaflet or pamphlet or issue decide a campaign; last-minute conversions, too, are rarely decisive. Yet, as Theodore H. White observes in *The Making of a President 1960*, Illinois, the state that carried Kennedy into office, was won by barely 9,000 votes. Michigan was won for Kennedy by 67,000 votes. In each of these states, an estimated quarter-million black votes were cast for Senator Kennedy. In South Carolina, where 40,000 black votes were tallied in the Democratic column, the Senator won by 10,000 votes. In Nashville, Tennessee, where President

---

° According to Theodore H. White in *The Making of a President 1960*, Senator Kennedy's reaction was "impulsive, direct and immediate," and "without consulting anyone," he placed the long-distance call to Mrs. King.

Eisenhower carried three black wards in 1956, 3,258 to 2,861, Kennedy pulled 5,710 to 2,529. When the count was in, Kennedy had more black votes in Texas, North and South Carolina, Illinois, New Jersey, and Michigan than his margin of victory in those states. It may be, then, that, as President Eisenhower somewhat sourly observed, "a couple of calls" not only swung the black vote to Kennedy but had won him the Presidency.*

John F. Kennedy's thousand days were amply filled with crises, both domestic and international. Though the President described his administration as the "New Frontier," a phrase with a decidedly domestic ring, foreign affairs remained his chief preoccupation, from an initial fiasco, the abortive Bay of Pigs invasion of Castro's Cuba, through the Berlin and Cuban missile crises, to the successful encouragement of the European Common Market and the negotiation of the nuclear test-ban treaty. Of all the administration's figures, Robert Kennedy had the greatest interest in civil rights. Yet even he could not avoid placing civil rights within an international framework. After the integration of the University of Georgia in 1961, the youthful Attorney General declared: "In the worldwide struggle, the graduation at this university of Charlayne Hunter and Hamilton Holmes will without question aid and assist the fight against communist political infiltration and guerrilla warfare." Tactically, in the interests of America abroad, the Kennedy Administration sought to cool black protests with the balm of black appointments. Andrew Hatcher was named associate White House press secretary, and later Robert Weaver as administrator of the Housing and Home Finance Agency, Carl Rowan as ambassador to Finland, Thurgood Marshall to the United States Circuit Court and, in recognition of the nation's capital becoming in 1960 the first major city in the country with a black majority (54 percent), John B. Duncan as a member of the District of Columbia's board of commissioners. The number of black attorneys within the Justice Department rose from ten to seventy. Arthur M. Schlesinger, Jr., reports in *A Thousand Days* that

---

* Other factors, however, must be kept in mind. Black Americans were more adversely affected by the recession, which hit its low point in October 1960, than white Americans. Overall unemployment rose to 3.8 million in 1960, or to a rate of 5.5 percent. White males experienced an unemployment rate of 5.4 percent while that of black males was nearly double at 10.7 percent. The black migration to the North continued at a high pace as automation and technological change knocked out jobs traditionally filled by unskilled and semiskilled migrants. Greater Cleveland, for example, lost eighty-thousand blue-collar jobs during the period 1952–1963 when eighteen thousand black males entered the Cleveland labor force. Ironically, as blacks fled the South to the North, factories fled South. The number of non-agricultural jobs in the South rose by 32 percent between 1950 and 1960. Economic adversity, as we know, tends to build the Democratic vote, but in weighing the factors that went into the Kennedy victory of 1960, one must conclude with historian William L. O'Neil, writing in his informal history of the 1960s, *Coming Apart* that "since his [Kennedy's] margin was so slight, everything contributed to it."

the number of Negroes holding jobs in the middle grades of the civil service increased 36.6 percent from June 1961 to June 1963; in the top grades, 88.2 percent.

Black Americans were no doubt as moved by the Kennedy inaugural as white Americans: "We observe today not a victory of party but a celebration of freedom." Was not that what the Montgomery boycott, school desegregation, and the sit-ins were all about? And were not civil rights activists already responding to the Kennedy pejoration: "Ask not what your country can do for you; ask what you can do for your country"? John Kennedy promised an activist presidency. As a candidate, he declared that such a President "could integrate all federally assisted housing with a strike of a Presidential pen." After a year and a half, some of those who asked what they could do for the country opened a "Pens for Jack" campaign, and inundated by pens, the President finally signed a watered-down order.

Others who asked crucial questions about their country, however, did not wait upon presidential action. Student sit-ins continued unabated, and CORE mounted an integrationist thrust into the heart of the Deep South. When the Greensboro freshmen sat-in, they called on Dr. George Simpkins, president of the local NAACP branch, for aid—and he became the first of many to call on CORE for assistance. "I had just finished reading a pamphlet CORE prepared on nonviolent protests," Dr. Simpkins later told Louis E. Lomax, "and I called CORE because I was certain they were ready and able to give aid to the students." As a result of many such calls, CORE expanded almost overnight from a tiny, little-known organization into a major civil rights force.

James Farmer, then forty-one and program director of the NAACP, was a natural choice to head the invigorated CORE as national director. Handsome, round of face, a large, coffee-colored man, outgoing and at ease with himself, Farmer helped found CORE in the early 1940s. He came of the class that until recently provided most of the country's black leadership. "I grew up in the South," Farmer wrote in *Freedom When?*, "living in the sheltered atmosphere of several Negro colleges. . . . It was an *Alice in Wonderland* world, located at best on the fringes of Negro life." His father, J. Leonard Farmer, taught classics, and his mother was a schoolteacher. The elder Farmer was no ordinary man. Born of former slaves in South Carolina and raised in the turpentine, piney woods country of Georgia, he walked to the Bethune-Cookman Institute in Daytona Beach, Florida, where he won a scholarship. Later, he hiked to Boston with all his worldly possessions in a knapsack to continue his studies in theology at Boston University. "My father," his son later recalled, "seemed to know ancient tongues [Aramic and Greek, among others] and folkways more intimately than those of his own time and place."

Born on January 12, 1920, in Marshall, Texas, where his father taught at Wiley Cottage, James Farmer grew up, as he likes to say, in his father's library. He graduated from Wiley in 1938 and went to Howard University to study for the ministry. Though his childhood may have been a sheltered one, Farmer developed his commitment to social justice early in life. He received his divinity degree in 1941 but refused ordination. "I did not see how I could honestly preach the gospel of Christ in a Church that practiced discrimination." He then worked in pacifist and socialist groups, studying Gandhi, Shridharani, Tolstoi, Marx, Thoreau, and Veblen with friends. "We thought and talked and dreamed with each other long into the night." They also took action, striking out at discrimination and injustice whenever possible. As race relations secretary of the Fellowship of Reconciliation from 1941 to 1945, Farmer helped found CORE and to develop the sit-in and other nonviolent tactics. He met his wife, the former Lula Peterson, at a Chicago CORE meeting in 1945. A year later, he was organizing for the Upholsterers' International Union in the South. From 1950 to 1954, he served as the youth secretary to the League for Industrial Democracy, a socialist-oriented educational group. After another stint as a union organizer, he became program director for the NAACP. All the while, he continued his interest in CORE, though participating only intermittently in its activities.

The student sit-ins were more or less spontaneous popular direct action aimed at discrimination in public accommodations. Under Farmer's direction, CORE introduced a new element, the sustained and conscious use of direct action, or of the crowd in motion, as an instrument of pressure for change. "Our function," Marvin Rich, CORE's community relations director, once said, "is to translate law and morality into practice." If blacks and whites, out of apathy, fear, or hatred, continue to segregate themselves despite court decisions banning segregation, then the law remains as so much paper. In the spirit of Frederick Douglass, CORE believed that without struggle there can be no progress. Laws had to be tested to give them life and meaning. As Douglass put it in a letter to philanthropist Gerrit Smith, "Those who profess to favor freedom, and yet depreciate agitation, are men who want rain without thunder and lightning. They want the ocean without the roar of its many waters." Power, added Douglass, "concedes nothing without a demand. It never did, and it never will."

The immediate occasion for CORE's first major effort after Farmer's appointment as national director on February 1, 1961, was a Supreme Court decision. In the Bruce Boynton case, handed down in December 1960, the Court extended the *Morgan* ruling banning segregation in interstate travel to cover facilities as well as the vehicles used. The idea of testing the decision occurred to CORE field secretaries Gordon

Carey and Thomas Gaither as they rode a bus one winter day en route from one sit-in to another. They proposed a "Freedom Ride" to the next national CORE council meeting, which enthusiastically accepted the idea. On March 13, Farmer announced that CORE was seeking volunteers to test the Supreme Court decision in the *Boynton* case. "Our intention," he said later, "was to provoke the southern authorities into arresting us and thereby prod the Justice Department into enforcing the law of the land."

The 1947 Journey of Reconciliation had, so to speak, skimmed the South with the integrated group riding buses through Virginia, Tennessee, and Kentucky. This time, after three days of training in nonviolent techniques, thirteen volunteers would plunge directly into the Deep South, crossing Georgia and Alabama into Mississippi and riding down to New Orleans. Thomas Gaither acted as advance man, as Houser and Rustin had in 1947, traveling the entire route beforehand to set up meetings and arrange housing for overnight stops. Roy Wilkins secured the aid of various NAACP branches along the way. On April 28, 1961, Farmer wrote President Kennedy to advise him of the proposed trip. He included a map outlining the journey, and requested that the law be enforced. On May 4, the thirteen volunteers—seven blacks and six whites—boarded buses in Washington, D.C., heading South to New Orleans.

James Peck, the only rider on the 1947 journey who was part of the 1961 group, was heartened by his discovery that aboard the buses "desegregation had become a reality." The first ominous "white–colored" signs appeared over rest-room doors at the Greyhound stop in Fredericksburg, just fifty miles south of Washington. In Danville, Virginia, several white riders were served at the colored lunch counter after a brief discussion with the manager. Black passengers were directed to a colored waiting room in Greensboro, North Carolina, but the colored lunch room had just been closed the week before and service was integrated in the formerly white restaurant. The first arrest occurred in Charlotte, North Carolina, when a black rider decided he wanted a shoeshine. Denied service, he was arrested for trespassing. Acquitted the next day, the young man, Joseph Perkins, rejoined the group at the next stopover. It was, as one Freedom Rider put it, the nation's first "shoe-in."

Violence erupted in Rock Hill, South Carolina, when hoodlums assaulted stocky John Lewis, a black divinity student and a leader of the Nashville Student Movement, and Albert Bigelow, a lanky former navy commander turned pacifist, as they approached the entrance to the white waiting room. In the melee, Genevieve Hughes, a white CORE member, was knocked to the ground. At this point, the police intervened. Lewis and Bigelow refused to press charges against their assailants, and the CORE group entered the white waiting room unmolested. Henry Thomas, a black student, and Peck, the scion of Peck & Peck (women's clothiers), were arrested in Winnsboro, South Carolina, for sitting-in at the terminal's "white's only" lunch counter. Thomas was released in the dead of the night; Peck, at dawn; neither was informed that the other had been freed. Crossing through Georgia, where the Freedom Riders were served "without question," as Peck later recalled in *Freedom Ride*, was a welcome relief as well as "clear proof of how desegregation can come peacefully in a Deep South state, providing there is no deliberate incitement to hatred and violence by local or state political leaders." °

Mother's Day, Sunday, May 14, 1961, dawned bright and clear with a promise of warmth. The riders had been forewarned by the Reverend Fred Shuttlesworth to expect a mob on their arrival in Birmingham.°° When the Greyhound bus carrying the first contingent of Freedom Riders pulled into Anniston, Alabama, a rest stop on the route to Birmingham from Atlanta, it was surrounded by a mob armed with iron bars. The arrival of the police enabled the bus to depart, but with the mob in pursuit. About six miles from Anniston, a slashed tire gave out and the bus was forced over into a gas station. The mob resumed its attack, smashing a window and throwing an incendiary device inside. However, the passengers, including the Freedom Riders, managed to escape before the bus burst into flames. Henry Thomas, who pushed the door open for his fellow passengers, had his head bashed by a waiting white citizen. The police dispersed the crowd, and twelve passengers were taken to the hospital, most of them for smoke inhalation.† When the second bus arrived at Anniston, eight citizens clambered aboard and forced the riders to the rear. Walter Bergman, a retired professor, was badly beaten, and when he had his appendix taken out some time later, he nearly died of a stroke which the doctors attributed to a pre-existing condition of brain damage. Others were pushed, punched, and kicked. "Upon our arrival in Birmingham," Peck wrote in his account, *Freedom*

° In Augusta, for example, where only a few months before a black serviceman had been arrested for trying to eat at the terminal restaurant, the Freedom Riders used all facilities without incident. According to Peck, it was the first time, too. In Athens, where a mob rioted against the admission of Charlayne Hunter and Hamilton Holmes the previous fall, the riders were served without difficulty.
°° CORE Director Farmer had to leave the group in Atlanta because of the death of his father. John Lewis, who held a scholarship at the American Baptist Seminary in Nashville, left earlier to take his final examinations.
† A week later, federal agents arrested four men on the charge of firing the bus. Such exemplary promptness was something new in such offenses, and no doubt is related to the involvement of Attorney General Robert Kennedy in subsequent developments.

Ride, "I could see a mob lined up on the sidewalk only a few feet from the loading platform. Most of them were young—in their twenties. Some were carrying ill-concealed iron bars. A few were older men. All had hate showing on their faces." When Birmingham Police Chief T. Eugene "Bull" Connor was asked why there were no policemen at the bus terminal to prevent violence, he explained that since it was Mother's Day, most of his men were off duty visiting their mothers.

Charles Person, a slim young black Atlantan, and Peck had been designated by the group to test the lunch counter that day. Standing on the landing platform, the two looked at one another, and Person said, "Let's go." They were grabbed by a gang of white toughs and shoved into an alley where five men worked over Person and six slugged Peck with pipes and their fists. Both were beaten unconscious. Person came through with a gash on the back of his head and a swollen face. Peck was hospitalized; his lacerated face required fifty-three stitches. When the Riders attempted to resume their journey, the bus drivers refused to drive. Finally, the group decided to fly to New Orleans so that they might attend a mass rally called to mark the end of the Freedom Ride and to commemorate May 17, the anniversary of the Supreme Court's school desegregation decision.

On the same day, the Nashville Student Movement decided to continue the Freedom Ride from Birmingham to New Orleans. The group—eight black, two white students—was taken into "protective custody" by the police along with five sympathizers on their arrival in Birmingham. Alarmed by the possibilities for further violence, Attorney General Robert Kennedy tried in vain to telephone Alabama Governor John Patterson. Frustrated in his efforts to secure protection for the riders, Kennedy managed to reach the Greyhound bus dispatcher: "I think you should—had better be getting in touch with Mr. Greyhound or whoever Greyhound is and somebody better give us an answer to this question. I am—the government is—going to be very much upset if this group does not get to continue their trip. In fact I suggest that you make arrangements to get a driver immediately and get these people on the way to Montgomery. . . ."

John Siegenthaler, an administrative assistant to the Attorney General, managed to track down Governor Patterson and exacted a promise of protection for the riders. In a public statement, however, the governor declared: "We are going to do all we can to enforce the laws of the state on the highways and everywhere else, but we are not going to escort these agitators. We stand firm on that position." Governor Patterson's statement notwithstanding, the bus from Birmingham to Montgomery carrying the youthful Freedom Riders was accompanied that morning, May 20, 1961, by sixteen highway patrol cars and one airplane. The Federal Bureau of Investigation advised the Montgomery authorities of probable violence, and were assured that all was well. When the bus drew up at the Montgomery station, a surly mob of about three hundred greeted the arrivals. William Orrick, head of the Justice Department's Civil Division and an eyewitness to the events that followed, reported that the mob, though armed with pipes, sticks, and clubs, "could have been readily controlled by proper police work." James Zwerg, a white student from Wisconsin, was the first passenger off the bus. Women shrieked, "Kill the nigger-lovin' son-of-a-bitch," and some sixteen white toughs did their best to comply. Before they left him for dead, one kicked in his front teeth. Zwerg lay stunned for over an hour before being taken to the hospital. William Barbee, a black student, was so badly beaten by baseball bats that he remained hospitalized for a week. John Lewis, who had rejoined the ride, was knocked down. Orrick observed, "People with no apparent connection to the trip were beaten, a boy's leg was broken and another boy had inflammable liquid poured over him and set on fire." Time-Life News Bureau Chief Norman Ritter was among the four reporters and photographers roughed up by the irate crowd. While trying to help Diane Nash, a black Freedom Rider, escape into a car, Siegenthaler was knocked unconscious. He laid upon the sidewalk for twenty-five minutes before the police picked him up and took him to the hospital.

When Police Commissioner Sullivan was asked why an ambulance was not called for Siegenthaler, he retorted, "Every white ambulance in town reported their vehicles had broken down." The police, according to a chronology of the Freedom Rides drawn up by the Southern Regional Council, arrived about ten minutes after the riot began but were unable to cope with the crowd. Orrick noted, "A sheriff's posse of deputies assigned to control riots did not arrive on the scene until an hour and 15 minutes after the first wave of violence, thereafter ten or more police cars arrived to restore order." By then, the mob numbered over a thousand. Observers, however, reported that the violence was the work of some two dozen men. The police finally resorted to tear gas to disperse the rioters.

President Kennedy appealed to state and local officials for order. The Justice Department secured an unprecedented court order enjoining the Ku Klux Klan, the National States' Rights party, and the Birmingham and Montgomery police from interfering with "peaceful interstate travel by bus." Deputy Attorney General (now Supreme Court Justice) Byron White headed a contingent of U. S. marshals dispatched to Montgomery; 400 arrived the evening of the riot and 266 more the next morning. Governor Patterson protested, and Attorney General Kennedy was overheard on the telephone, saying, "John, John, what do you mean you're being invaded? Who's invading you, John? You know better than that."

Martin Luther King, Jr., interrupted a speaking tour in Chicago and flew to Montgomery to address a mass rally for the Freedom Riders held the evening following the day of the bus station riot. As over 1,500 blacks and a handful of whites gathered at Ralph Abernathy's First Baptist Church, carloads of hate-filled whites converged on Montgomery from surrounding towns and countryside. King castigated the governor for his failure to keep the peace and to enforce the law. "The law may not be able to make a man love me," King cried out, "but it can keep him from lynching me." Outside the church, federal marshals were doing their best to prevent such an eventuality. Several thousand whites hemmed the church, hurling bottles and stones, smashing windows, and otherwise working themselves up to an all-out attack. The Freedom Riders led the congregation in song, and as the marshals lobbed tear gas where it would do the most to discourage the mob, voices in the church were raised, singing, "We shall overcome, someday."

Washington put the heat on Alabama to declare martial law. When Governor Patterson reluctantly agreed, he told Attorney General Robert Kennedy that Major General Henry Graham, the commander of the National Guard, could not guarantee the safety of Martin Luther King. Kennedy replied, "Have the General call me. I want him to say it to me. I want to hear a General of the United States Army say he can't protect Martin Luther King, Jr." Martial law was declared, and eight hundred National Guardsmen were ordered to Montgomery. Meanwhile, the federal marshals and state patrolmen, with some help from the local police, managed to disperse the mob outside Abernathy's church. A weary rally audience left at dawn, safe.

While the Freedom Riders prepared to resume their journey on into Mississippi, Justice Department officials sought to avoid further violence. Attorney General Kennedy secured a promise from powerful Mississippi Senator James Eastland guaranteeing the physical safety of the riders in Mississippi. Governor Ross Barnett placed the Mississippi National Guard on a stand-by alert, and on the morning of May 24, heavily protected by National Guardsmen, the first busload of Freedom Riders left for Mississippi. They were escorted to the state line where Mississippi state patrolmen took over. On their arrival in Jackson, all twelve on the first bus were arrested as they attempted to use "white's only" rest-room facilities. The second group of fifteen, including James Farmer, was arrested while seeking service at the lunch counter. The arrests, trials, and sentencing were all cut and dried—and peaceful. The initial twenty-seven were given sixty-day suspended sentences and two hundred dollar fines. Having decided beforehand to refuse payment, they were sent to Parchman Penitentiary.

In keeping with the administration's peace-keeping, crisis-managing approach to potentially explosive problems and, in particular, civil rights, Attorney General Robert Kennedy called for a "cooling off period," a recommendation heartily seconded by such opinion makers as *The New York Times* and the influential Washington *Post*. Martin Luther King, Jr., at first rejected the proposal, but then qualified it by announcing that there would be a "temporary lull but no cooling off" in the rides. His reaction puzzled many, but King was subjected to more than ordinary pressures at the time. The financial needs of SCLC obligated an intensive speaking tour and he may have felt constrained by his recently acquired mantle as a national black spokesman. His biographer David L. Lewis hit upon the most likely reason: ". . . for the time being, Martin probably wished to maintain a posture of judicial respectability in order to be more effective in his dealings with the timid new Administration." He did so, however, at some cost, a lessening of his influence over the growing militancy of the young, in particular, the SNCC youngsters.

Roy Wilkins rejected the idea of a cooling-off period, as did James Farmer, who retorted, "We have been cooling off for one hundred years. If we get any cooler, we'll be in a deep freeze." Riders continued to pour into the South. CORE, SNCC, the Nashville Student Movement, and SCLC set up a coordinating committee. Organized labor gave moral and financial support; the AFL-CIO's Industrial Union Department gave CORE $5,000 for the Freedom Rides. Riders were jailed in Montgomery, Tallahassee, and Jackson, the focal point of the Freedom Rides. More than three hundred were arrested there over the summer and in the fall. The Reverend T. C. Vivian, a SCLC leader from Chattanooga, was the first to have his head bloodied for refusing to say, "sir," to Parchman prison guards.

The upward spiral of arrests placed the Kennedy Administration, as it were, under the gun. It owed its presence in Washington to the black vote; yet, as Robert Kennedy later confessed, "I did not lay awake at night worrying about the problems of Negroes." Though the Justice Department, in contrast to previous administrations, did intervene on behalf of civil rights protestors, the Department, under Robert Kennedy, had no civil rights program in the sense that it did an organized crime program. As Victor S. Navasky points out in his brilliant account, *Kennedy Justice,* the Attorney General approached each crisis "on the assumption that it was a temporary eruption which he and his remarkable team could cool . . . The trick was to encourage the inevitable integration but never at the cost of disturbing the social equilibrium." In this instance, that of the Freedom Rides, the Attorney General worked out an imaginative solution that avoided costly court battles over the integration of interstate travel facilities. It was an extraordinary proceeding, one department of the government petitioning an autonomous agency, the Interstate Commerce Commission, to ban segregation by regulation. Working with William Tucker, a Massachusetts Democrat who had been appointed a commissioner by President Kennedy, the Justice Department anticipated legal objections on the part of the ICC and the order was issued on September 22, effective for November 1, 1961. Interstate terminal segregation soon became a thing of the past; not, however, without further testing—but the major drives were over.

"Our philosophy was simple," James Farmer explained in *Freedom— When?* "We put on pressure and create a crisis and then they react. I am absolutely convinced that the ICC order wouldn't have been issued were it not for the Freedom Rides." A good many other people agreed, and CORE was credited, rightly so, for the success of the rides. By the time the ICC order took effect, there had been a dozen or more rides, involving over a thousand persons. The rides cost an estimated $20,000, and the legal fees mounted to over $300,000.° In 1962, CORE launched the Freedom Highways campaign, seeking to desegregate motels and highway restaurants across the country. The highway Freedom Riders concentrated on the national chains, particularly Howard Johnson's and Holiday Inn. By the end of 1962, Farmer was able to report, "a Negro could drive along the national highways and know that when he was hungry or tired, there would be a place where he would be welcome to stop and rest."

CORE flourished: Its budget rose from $233,000 in fiscal 1961 to $750,000 for fiscal 1962. The staff jumped over the five years following 1959 from 7 to 137. According to CORE's Community Relations Director Marvin Rich, CORE had 145 chapters and a mailing list of 70,000 or more contributors and supporters in 1964. Before the rides, CORE was predominantly white, roughly a quarter of its membership was black; after the rides, CORE became one-half black and one-half white. SCLC remained a leadership organization as did SNCC. Both were black, rooted in the South, and the former was largely confined to the Baptist ministry. The National Urban League, properly speaking, was not a civil rights organization, even though its new executive secretary, forty-year-old Whitney Young, soon won a place of prominence in the black leadership establishment. The NAACP, with roughly 400,000 members, was the major black mass membership organization despite a loss of about 15,000 members between 1960 and 1961. The loss was attributed to the recession, but Louis Lomax also believed that it reflected disillusionment over the NAACP's lack of militancy. Though

---

° A debt assumed shortly after the successful conclusion of the rides by the NAACP Legal Defense and Education Fund, a tax-exempt fund that ought not be confused with the NAACP, a membership group.

the NAACP leadership denied that this was the case, they could not dispel the widespread feeling that the organization was too cautious. CORE, second only to the NAACP in membership strength, benefited. And for the first half of the 1960s, CORE would be *the* militant, activist, integrationist civil rights organization.

IX

Quest for a More Perfect America

LL SORTS OF EXPECTA-
tions rose rapidly with the election of John F. Kennedy as President of
the United States. "I knew that if he became President," novelist
Norman Mailer wrote for *Esquire*, "it would be an existential event: he
would touch depths in American life which were uncharted . . . . and
we as a nation would finally be loose again in the historic seas of a
national psyche which was willy-nilly and at last, again adventurous."
Wit and charm, glamor and beauty replaced the pedestrian Eisenhow-
ers in the White House, and on the banks of the Potomac rose a new
Camelot. Knights of the Round Table jousted for political favor and
power, renewing the quest for a more perfect America, an existential
chalice if ever there was one.

What counted in the political tournaments of the Kennedy reign was
style. Or so it seemed to America's eggheads, tread-spotters, fashion-
makers, and would-be Norman Mailers. But style for the Kennedys
always possessed a cutting edge, and sometimes carried clout, a favorite
phrase among New Frontiersmen. Civil rights leaders and others
engaged in trying to secure specific gains were often skeptical, but just
as frequently they were immobilized by the Kennedy appeal. The
highly publicized telephone call to Coretta Scott King, the sending of
federal marshals to protect Freedom Riders, and later to enroll James
Meredith at the University of Mississippi, created a nearly inexhaustible
fund of goodwill for the Kennedys among black Americans. If
Eisenhower could send troops to Little Rock, could the Kennedys do
less? Even the President's patent unwillingness to demand civil rights
legislation of Congress, or to act executively against discrimination
within a wide range of federal programs despite persuasive argument

that he could do so, or the appointment of racist judges in the South, could not erode black confidence in the President.° It was a constraint on black leadership. As late as January 1963, when civil rights leaders considered issuing a statement condemning the President, they were brought up short by Roy Wilkins. He had recently spoken to a black group in North Carolina and the response was typical. "I attacked John Kennedy for ten minutes," Wilkins said, "and everyone sat on their hands. Then I said a few favorable words about the things he had done and they clapped and clapped."

Ever aware of the razor-edge margin of victory in 1960, the Kennedys sought to contain and manipulate civil rights agitation.°° At the outset of his administration, John F. Kennedy evidenced, in Arthur Schlesinger's words, "terrible ambivalence about civic rights. While he did not doubt the depths of the injustice or the need for remedy, he had read the arithmetic of the new Congress and concluded that there was no possible chance of passing a civil rights bill." He feared, too, according to Schlesinger, "that the inevitable defeat of a civil rights bill after debate and filibuster would heighten Negro resentment, drive the civil rights revolution to more drastic resorts and place a perhaps intolerable strain on the already fragile social fabric." He opted for executive action, but was evasive. He did, on his inaugural, launch an inquiry as to why there were no blacks in the Coast Guard (and ordered a corrective recruiting program), and he extended the federal surplus food program to victims of economic reprisals in black voter registration drives in Fayette and Haywood counties, Tennessee. Nevertheless, as Roy Wilkins, as chairman, and Arnold Aronson, as secretary, of the Leadership Conference on Civil Rights, both observed in a memorandum drafted for the President and his advisers, "the sum total of these

---

° According to Victor Navasky in *Kennedy Justice*, "The Kennedys named no fewer than 25 percent non-law-of-the-land followers (five out of twenty-five appointments) to lifetime judgeships in the Fifth Circuit, the district which encompasses Florida, Texas, Georgia, Alabama, Louisiana, and Mississippi, the heart of the Deep South." These judges, incidentally, were instrumental in developing the South's "legal" resistance to desegregation. It was a Kennedy appointee, Judge W. Harold Cox of Jackson, Mississippi, who enjoined CORE from "encouraging" Negroes to use the McComb, Mississippi, bus terminal *after* the ICC declared all such facilities desegregated. Cox, in this and a host of like cases, was reversed on appeal, but the delay was fatal for immediate desegregation efforts.

°° While the President owed his victory to the black vote, he also owed it to others—the Jewish, labor, and Catholic vote, and if he is to be believed, Norman Mailer. As James Q. Wilson observed, "With so many apparently marginal votes cast, a President might be forgiven if he allowed himself to be paralyzed by the competing demands of their spokesmen." Moreover, the Kennedys had not given up on the South, either for support on foreign policy issues or for the 1964 elections. Most first-term Presidents want to be reelected, and the narrow margin of 1960 made President Kennedy nervous about his prospects and, therefore, cautious on controversial matters. Despite the myth, his was not an adventurous administration.

[and other] actions is dwarfed, and in fact nullified, by the massive involvement of the federal government in programs and activities that make it a silent, but nonetheless full partner in the perpetuation of discriminatory practices." The President, they urged, should promulgate by executive order a general Federal Civil Rights Code governing "the *whole executive branch* of government." This would assure non-discrimination in personnel appointments, in all institutions, facilities, and services of the federal government, and in all state or local operations receiving federal assistance. Federal grants in excess of $1.1 billion to eleven southern states, Wilkins and Aronson pointed out, continued to "require, support or condone discrimination." This expenditure constituted 10 to 22 percent of all funds expended by state and local governments in these states, and as such a fraction, constituted a powerful force for desegregation or segregation. Which, depended on the federal government.*

The President, however, was reluctant to confront the South with federally-backed and enforced desegregation by the cut-off of funds. He postponed until November 20, 1962, a long-promised executive order banning discrimination in federally sponsored housing for much the same reasons he remained chary about undertaking a wide-ranging executive attack on segregation. He needed southern support for education, minimum wage, and trade expansion bills as well as for a Department of Urban Affairs with a black, Robert Weaver, as secretary. That he did not get all that he wanted, or got some without southern backing, was moot, for the need nonetheless entered his political calculations. Immobilized, as it were, on the executive and legislative fronts, the Kennedys cast about for alternatives. They wanted to minimize or contain civil rights agitation, especially that of a direct action or confrontationist character, *and* to encourage black progress. Political to the bone, they believed, and correctly so, that blacks could not enter the mainsteam unless they could vote. All rights follow the ballot. The Kennedys could not have agreed more when, in November 1961, Martin Luther King, Jr., declared: "The central front . . . we feel is that of suffrage. If we in the South can win the right to vote it will place in our hands more than an abstract right. It will give us the concrete tool with which we ourselves can correct injustice."

For their part, the Kennedys were willing to push voter rights suits.

---

* When Howard B. Pickard of the Department of the Agriculture's General Counsel's office, in February 1961, asked if the Justice Department wanted to withhold Louisiana's $2,224,607 in school lunch programs money and $508,418 in school milk program money for the year, since Louisiana was not passing on funds to Orleans Parish schools, which were attempting to desegregate, Burke Marshall said Justice would rely on "the legal course of action presently sought through the civil contempt proceeding of compelling the payment of those funds to the Orleans Parish School Board, and that we did not wish, at present, to pursue the possible alternative of withholding funds from the entire state."

The 1957 and 1960 civil rights acts empowered the Justice Department to bring suit against a state to enforce the right to vote. The Eisenhower Administration brought six such suits; by May 1963, the Kennedy Justice Department filed thirty-seven suits—eleven in Mississippi and the rest in Georgia, Louisiana, Alabama, and Tennessee. White supremacy, however, was not easily overcome; the Kennedys would persist well into 1963 in overlooking or failing to recognize the need for a greatly strengthened voting rights act. The 1961 report of the United States Commission on Civil Rights estimated that there were about one hundred counties in eight southern states in which "there is reason to believe that Negro citizens are prevented—by outright discrimination or by fear of physical violence or economic reprisal—from exercising the right to vote." In 1956, about 5 percent of voting age blacks in those counties could vote; by 1963, only 8.3 percent could, despite some 140 voter registration drives "in progress or in prospect."

When the Reverend June Dowdy, pastor of two churches in Fayette County, Tennessee, decided he wanted to vote, he went to register in Somerville where he was given a runaround. "Finally," he recalled later, "I asked one white man where the registration office was and he directed me to go down to Hatchie Bottom. That's the swamp along the Hatchie River, where a Negro was lynched back about 1940 after he tried to vote." At the time, 1961, Fayette County was 68.5 percent black, and neighboring Haywood County, in southwestern Tennessee, was 61.3 percent black. Yet, no black had ever voted in Haywood since Reconstruction, and only seventeen had voted between 1952 and 1959 in Fayette. Blacks, however, were voting in nearby Memphis, and J. F. Estey, a Memphis lawyer who was encouraged by this evidence of a second reconstruction, organized the Fayette County Civic and Welfare League and a similar Haywood County group in the spring and summer of 1959. By that winter, black landowners who had registered to vote were refused crop loans, and black tenants, who had registered, were being evicted. Black merchants were refused credit and the deliveries of goods were delayed, or not shipped at all. The evicted, some one thousand at peak, were housed in "Tent City," and CORE began a national campaign for food and relief. The Kennedy Administration assured the flow of surplus food. Between 1959 and the end of 1960, some one thousand blacks registered and voted in Fayette County.

Even so small a gain was encouraging in the light of the denial of suffrage in the South's black belt countries. Voter registration drives were viewed as an answer to the administration's double problem—how best to achieve a cooling off in civil rights agitation and how best to strengthen the black position within the American mainstream. Channel civil rights energies into voter registration, so the argument went, and one would accomplish both objectives. The name of the game was politics, at which the Kennedys excelled as they did at touch football. But the playing fields were not on the banks of the Charles, nor the teams, Houses of Harvard. There was considerable suspicion of Kennedy motives among putative players. Martin Luther King, Jr., and his followers were committed to nonviolent resistance as a way of life and as a tactic. Voter registration was bound to be a long, drawn-out affair; desegregation of bus service or interstate travel facilities, with federal backing, amounted, by contrast, to instant integration. And for a people struggling to assert themselves, immediate victories were of great importance, especially for morale. Burke Marshall, the administration's civil rights chief and Assistant Attorney General, has said, "It was as if they [the President and his brother] were asking Negro leaders to divert their energies, and those of their organizations, into channels which would require as little change and movement as possible."

Working behind the scenes, as Schlesinger phrased it, in "an effort reminiscent of the campaign to save the Bay of Pigs prisoners," the administration built up pressure for voting registration drives. Civil rights goals, administration spokesmen reminded activists, would be either unattainable or forever jeopardized unless blacks obtained the vote. The argument had merit, and when finally backed by large grants of money from the foundations, proved irresistible. Burke Marshall attended a series of spring 1961 meetings, ostensibly sponsored by the Taconic Foundation, to sound out civil rights organizations and spokesmen on voter registration. CORE, SNCC, SCLC, and the NAACP, all expressed interest and agreed to cooperate. Ultimately, the Taconic Foundation contributed $339,000, the Edgar Stern Family Fund, $219,000, and the Field Foundation, $225,000, to what became the Voter Education Project.

If, as Pat Watters later claimed in *Down to Now*, there was "promise of even more than the ordinary protection that never came" implicit in the inducements to undertake voter registration and a "failure of the foundations ever to deliver as much money as they seemed to promise for the drives," the beginnings were auspicious enough to satisfy even the wary Kennedys. SNCC went out into the black belt to begin voter registration drives. Andrew Young and Wyatt Walker of SCLC opened a school, teaching how-to-do-it civics, voter registration techniques, something about state politics and candidates. Their graduates went out to set up miniature voter education schools in their own home towns and cities. By February 1962, fifty-one such schools had been opened in Mississippi, Georgia, Alabama, Virginia, and South Carolina. The Kennedy effort at diverting the energies of the civil rights movement, however, was doomed. The movement could neither be contained nor directed into convenient channels. Even the leaders of the movement experienced difficulties; followers would not follow—at least, not always. As Andrew Young later told Pat Watters, "We tried to warn SNCC. We were all Southerners and we knew the depth of depravity of southern racism. We knew better than to try to take on Mississippi. We saw Birmingham as having realistic possibilities, as the reality." But the movement was seized by a religious fervor, beyond the understanding of cool administrators in Washington, D.C. Individually or in concert, blacks were determined to do something about their condition. What, where, and when were not always predictable.

Mississippi galled the young. If one wanted to take on racism head-on, here was the place where one could test one's manhood as well as do battle in a noble cause. Once a majority, blacks were, in 1960, roughly 42 percent of the Magnolia State's predominantly rural, poor population of 2,178,141 souls. Few blacks dared to vote; over 95 percent of the whites, but less than two percent of the blacks over twenty years of age, were registered. Confederate flags, sported on automobiles and displayed in front of homes, shops, and local government offices, intimated a willingness to resort to violence if necessary to preserve southern ways. Ross Barnett, who defeated a relative moderate, J. P. Coleman, in 1959 for the governorship, liked to say: "The good Lord was the original segregationist. He put the Negro in Africa—separated him from all other races." Sporadic terror reinforced the submission of intimidated black Mississippians. In August 1955, Lamar Smith, who reportedly urged his fellow blacks to vote, was shot to death on the courthouse lawn in Brookhaven. There were three lynchings in Mississippi that year, including that of Emmett Till, a fourteen-year-old schoolboy who purportedly whistled at a white woman. Four years later, Charles Mack Parker, identified as her rapist by a pregnant white woman—"the picture in the paper looked exactly like the man"—was dragged from the Poplarville jail by a masked mob and murdered. And in September 1961, Herbert Lee, a black farmer active in a voter registration drive, was shot dead by a member of the state legislature—a "justifiable homicide."

When SNCC leaders got out of Parchman, where they served time as Freedom Riders, they went on to McComb to give a hand with voter registration and with desegregation efforts. They were beaten and jailed. As Tom Hayden, then a field representative of the Students for a Democratic Society, laconically reported in the October 27, 1961, issue of *New America*, the Socialist party weekly, "Most of SNCC's leadership is now in jail in McComb." ° Charles McDew, then chairman of SNCC, Robert Zellner, a white SNCC field secretary from

---

° SDS was then affiliated with the League for Industrial Democracy, a socialist educational group, and, as yet, not in its radical-extremist phase.

Montgomery, Charles Sherrod of Richmond, and Robert Moses of New York, were arrested with some 150 black high-school students for participating in a protest march, "a breach of peace." The march was called to protest the dismissal of two students for their participation in a voter registration school and in nonviolent sit-ins.

Mississippi was a hard case. After two months of voter registration activity, only six blacks registered in Pike, Amite, and Walthall counties. "There have been intimidations, reprisals and beatings," Hayden's eyewitness account continues. "There has been the continued refusal by local registrars to discharge their duty and, at times, direct assault on the students running the program." A white man attempted to run his car into a group of demonstrators. A man who had registered to vote was shot in "an unrelated incident." Voter registration schools were closed because people were afraid to attend. Significantly, in the light of subsequent events elsewhere in the South, a spokesman for the Justice Department, when queried about the mass arrests and the intimidation and violence in McComb, said it would be extremely difficult to tie what happened in McComb to voter registration (over which the Department presumably had some jurisdiction). Mississippi blended, with some success, violence and legal reprisal against civil rights activists. SNCC's leadership was under constraint, either by jail or warrant. CORE was enjoined from encouraging blacks to use McComb bus facilities.° Bail bonds—set at $400 each for the demonstrating high-school students—tied up much needed money. Activists, perforce, had to move on elsewhere—at least for a time.

Over 1961 and 1962, civil rights hopes and fears were centered in Albany, Georgia, an average-size city of 56,000, roughly 40 percent black, just four hours drive due south of Atlanta. The fifth largest and fastest growing city in the state, Albany was a thriving commercial center on the banks of the Flint River deep in the heart of the new agricultural South. Corn, peanuts and pecans, and cattle flourished on the rich black soil that once nurtured vast fields of cotton in the surrounding black belt counties, "Terrible" Terrell and "Bad" Baker. Expanding textile, candy, farm-implement, and furniture industries added to the overall prosperity of the region. Though most of Albany's blacks were poor, there was a comfortable middle class of professionals and some wealthy black families. The Clennon W. King family had amassed a considerable fortune through extensive real estate holdings and numerous commercial establishments. A cluster of black associations provided leadership, the Ministerial Alliance, the Federation of Colored Women's Clubs, the local NAACP branch and youth council, and the Criterian Club, a group of black professional men. A nearby Air

---

° Issued by Judge W. Harold Cox of Jackson, Mississippi, a Kennedy appointee.

Force base and a Marine Corps camp introduced a touch of integration into an otherwise unrelievedly segregated society.

SNCC was attracted to Albany by stirrings of a home-grown militancy, an active NAACP Youth Council on the 650-student campus of Albany State College, and the city's proximity to the black belt. In January 1961, a group of local black clergymen wrote to James Grey, white supremacist editor of the daily Albany *Herald*, requesting that the paper stop defaming blacks. The next month, Albany's black leaders petitioned the city fathers to desegregate public facilities. These mild gestures provoked nighttime rock throwings through ministerial windows, irate editorials in the *Herald*, and white marauders in automobiles who threw eggs, fired shots, and tried to run down students on the Albany State College campus. Younger blacks began pressuring their elders for more action, less talk and letter writing. As A. C. Searles, editor of the black weekly *Southwestern Georgian* later recalled, "In 1961 the talk became 'Let's integrate.' It had never occurred to me before that much could be done about it [segregation]." SNCC arrived in the persons of 22-year-old Charles Sherrod, a casually dressed ex-theology student, and 18-year-old Cordell Reagan, another veteran of McComb and Parchman. They arrived with twelve dollars between them, managed to open a voter registration campaign office a few short blocks from the Shiloh Baptist Church, and captivated the NAACP youth council. "We planned to work on voter registration in Albany," Reagan recalled several years later, "but not extensively, but to work out of Albany into the surrounding counties. We also felt that whatever affected Albany would have some bearing on the surrounding communities. And I think it proved to be true—after we got kids involved in direct action and after we went to jail."

Ever willing to try conclusions with the segregationist maelstrom, SNCC quickly demonstrated the futility of trying to confine civil rights energies to voter registration. The evils of segregation were not so easily compartmentalized. Even so simple an act as entering Albany confronted "the SNCC kids" with choices they, at least, were determined no longer to make. Even *after* the ICC ruling banning the segregation of interstate travel facilities, a black traveler arrived in Albany, having ridden in the colored section of the bus, entered a colored waiting room, drank from a colored water fountain, used a colored rest room, walked eight blocks to find a colored restaurant, and had to go six miles to find a good black motel. Sherrod and Reagan decided to test the ICC ruling on November 1, the date it went into effect. Nine Albany State students slipped into the "whites only" waiting room where they were shortly told to leave or face arrest. It was a clear-cut violation of the ICC ruling, but when Salynn McCollum, a Memphis white student who observed the event for SNCC, reported the incident to the Justice Department, she was politely thanked—and that was that.

The test of Albany's bus facilities precipitated the formation of the Albany Movement on November 17 when various local black organizations came together to present a united front in the attack on discrimination. Students were the catalysts as they proved so often to be in this period. As a leader of the movement later told its historian Howard Zinn, "The kids were going to do it anyway . . . they were holding their own mass meetings and making plans . . . we didn't want them to have to do it alone." If the seeds of future conflict were present at the founding of the Albany Movement, they were well-covered.° The elected leaders reflected the importance of the role played by the professional class, the talented tenth of Albany's black community.°° Dr. William G. Anderson, an osteopath, was elected president; Slater King, a real estate agent, vice-president; Mrs. Emanuel (Goldie) Jackson, secretary; and Marion Page, a retired railroader, executive secretary. (Page would later replace Anderson as head of the Albany Movement.) Chevene (C. B.) King served as the movement's attorney.

The crucial first phase of the Albany Movement coincided with local city elections and the interim between a new and old city administration. Elections were held on December 4, with a large white turnout sparked by fears of a black one, which, however, did not materialize. Asa Kelley was elected mayor, but the new administration was not due to take office until January 11, 1962. This, in effect, strengthened the hand of Chief of Police Laurie Pritchett, whose cool professionalism would so fatally shape the course of the Albany Movement. On November 22, just two weeks before the city elections, three members of the NAACP Youth Council and two Albany State students (the first of forty to be expelled for participation in the movement) were arrested when they sought service in the bus station restaurant. Charged with disorderly conduct, failure to obey a police officer, and behavior tending

---

° A running conflict between the adult NAACP members and those on campus was exacerbated when the latter were won over by SNCC's advocacy of direct action and by the personal and political attractiveness of Sherrod and Reagan. Significantly, given the preponderance of pastoral leadership in the struggle for civil rights in the South and the participation of the Ministerial Alliance, particularly as exemplified by the pastor of the Bethel A. M. E. Church, the Reverend Benjamin Gay, and the pastor of the Shiloh Baptist Church, the Reverend Benjamin Welles, in the Albany Movement; none of the movement's top leadership came from ministerial ranks. Benjamin Welles, incidentally, had been active in sustaining voter registration since the 1940s and backed SNCC's efforts wholeheartedly. As Sherrod put it in a 1962 report on the drive to register voters in "Terrible" Terrell and "Bad" Baker counties: "Our faithful friend the Reverend Samuel B. Welles of East Albany never fails to drive out [to meetings in the counties], which helps us provide transportation for those citizens of Albany who wish to accompany us . . . ."
°° The two King brothers, unrelated to the Martin Luther Kings, were members of the influential Clennon W. King family.

to create public disorder, they were released on bail with their trial set for December 12. To gain national publicity, the Albany Movement officers agreed to a suggestion from SNCC. So, on Sunday, December 10, an integrated group of eight young people took the train from Atlanta to Albany, sitting in the "whites only" car. Several hundred Albany blacks were on hand to greet the Freedom Train on its arrival at 3:30 in the afternoon. The Freedom Riders entered the white waiting room, and were ordered out by Chief Pritchett.° Accompanied by Charles Jones of SNCC and Bertha Gober, an Albany State student, the group left and made their way to some nearby cars. So far, as A. C. Searles later reported, "There was no traffic, no disturbance, no one moving." Chief Pritchett made what Mayor Kelley later termed a "mistake" and arrested all but one of the demonstrators and Willie Mae Jones, an Albany student bystander. "Things had gone so smoothly," Searles said, "I think it infuriated the Chief."

By losing his cool, Chief Pritchett "organized," as a bad employer does his workers, the protest that followed. Mass meetings and marches, singing and praying, reached a fever pitch over the next two weeks. On Tuesday, December 12, over four hundred black high-school and college students marched past the courthouse, protesting the arrest and trial of the Freedom Riders. The youngsters were herded into a fifteen-foot-wide alley alongside City Hall where they patiently waited for two hours in the rain as the police booked them, one by one. Slater King led a prayer on the steps of City Hall, and was arrested and sentenced to five days for contempt of court. Another group of three hundred circled City Hall, and was arrested for unlawful assembly and parading without a permit. Dr. Anderson, who had known Ralph Abernathy since they were students at Alabama State College, telephoned Abernathy and Martin Luther King, Jr., and asked them to come to Albany. He did so over strong objections from SNCC, jealous of possible publicity benefits going to SCLC and King. While others were less than enthusiastic about the invitation, Albany's ministers were receptive, believing that King's presence would bolster their attack on segregation in Albany. King, Abernathy, and Ruby Hurley, the southeastern regional director of the NAACP, were among the speakers at a packed meeting of over one thousand people on Friday night, December 15, 1961, at the Shiloh Baptist Church. "Don't stop now," King cried out to a chorus of amens. "Keep moving, don't get weary. We will wear them down with our capacity to suffer." There was the inevitable invitation to march, to go to jail. King, according to one

° They were: James Forman, SNCC's executive secretary; Norma Collins, SNCC office manager; Lenore Tait, a volunteer worker; and Bernard Lee, SCLC's Youth Director, black; and Robert Zellner of SNCC, Per Laursen, a Danish writer, Tom Hayden, "Casey," his wife, and Joan Browning from Georgia, white.

biographer, was "a little startled" when asked to lead the march, having no plans for action in mind at the time. Dr. Anderson issued the call: "Be here at 7 o'clock in the morning. Eat a good breakfast. Wear warm clothes and wear your walking shoes."

The expected masses, however, did not show at the appointed time and place. The ordinary citizen does not like jail much, and the enthusiasm of an emotionally-charged mass meeting has a way of fading as livelihoods and other realities are considered. Despite the exemplary willingness of Albany's black leadership to undergo the risk of jailing, even death, the great majority of Albany's blacks were not moved to follow, certainly not to jail. The movement organizers spent a decidedly nervous day rounding up a great crowd, and at 4:30 Saturday afternoon, December 16, some 250 people, with Martin Luther King, Jr., at their head, bravely marched downtown where a long line of yellow raincoated policemen waited. Paddy wagons blocked the intersections, ready, and Chief Pritchett, red-faced, halted the marchers two blocks from City Hall. "Does anyone here have a permit for this parade? If not, I will have to place you under arrest if you continue." King replied, "We are simply going to pray at City Hall." Then, in an orderly column on the sidewalk, the marchers dropped to their knees and prayed. They rose, and stepped off, singing, "We shall overcome . . . ."

The entire group was arrested for parading without a permit. The Albany arrest total rose to 737, and over 400 remained in jail. The conduct of Chief Pritchett and his men was correct. As Coretta King rather wryly put it, "He tried to be decent, and as a person he displayed kindness . . . . Our people were given fair warning. Often they would refuse to disperse, and would drop on their knees and pray. Chief Pritchett would bow his head with them while they prayed. Then, of course, he would arrest them and the people would go to jail singing." Pritchett once remarked, "We met 'non-violence' with 'non-violence,' and we are, indeed, proud of the outcome." The police, as Watters and Cleghorn observed in *Climbing Jacob's Ladder,* conducted "arrests with such skill and efficiency that white violence was prevented and Negro goals denied." Indeed, white flare-ups were remarkably minimized in Albany. As *The New York Times* reported: "There were no indications that the 30,000 white residents of Albany were greatly aroused over the dispute." Many prisoners, however, had to be farmed out to jails in neighboring counties where their treatment left much to be desired. In the Lee County stockade, as an instance, fifty-one women were forced to sleep, if they could, on wet and dirty mattresses tossed on the concrete cell floor. From Saturday night to Monday night, one woman recalled, "we were 88 in one room . . . with 20 steel bunks and no mattresses." A man told Howard Zinn, on hand to report events to the

Southern Regional Council, "We were put in a bull pen, 60 men, 16 beds, all standin' up on one another. The food? Oh, bad, man!"

King refused bail, and announced: "If convicted, I will refuse to pay the fine. I expect to spend Christmas in jail. I hope thousands will join me." His arrest secured the desired publicity, but that, in turn, aroused the jealousies of some within the Albany Movement. Abernathy bugled a call for a pilgrimage of black Americans to descend on Albany. Washington exhibited concern lest matters get out of hand and require federal intervention. Mayor Kelley of Albany and Governor Ernest Vandiver of Georgia called Attorney General Kennedy to plead that Justice head off outside "subversives" and "agitators." The city fathers opened negotiations, and surprisingly secured an advantageous compromise. A city official declared, "We killed them with kindness," the New York *Herald Tribune* termed the Albany compromise "one of the most stunning defeats of [Martin Luther King's] career." C. B. King, attorney Donald L. Hollowell of Atlanta, a leading civil rights lawyer, and Marion Page, acting as head of the Albany Movement as Dr. Anderson languished in jail, met with Chief Pritchett, Mayor Kelley, and the city attorney. They worked out a verbal truce: The city would accept desegregation of bus and train facilities, free demonstrators on bail, and hear black grievances in return for a moratorium on demonstrations pending the hearing scheduled before the newly elected City Commission on January 23. Fearing that King's lieutenants would exploit national pressures on Albany to secure an agreement behind their backs, the movement leaders bought a truce that would expire after King—and SCLC—returned to Atlanta, leaving the local leadership free to resume their campaign against discrimination as they saw fit. SNCC pressed for the move, as well for fear that King, whom they had begun to mock as "de Lawd," would prove to be less militant than they would like. And there was, too, in view of funds to be raised, support won and credit gained, the question as to which group was to be scored with a victory in Albany. Hence, the compromise. Having no choice, Martin Luther King, Jr., accepted release and returned to Atlanta.

The second act in Albany was a reprise with variations. The movement undertook an ill-thought-out boycott of white merchants only to discover that the black community lacked, in this instance, the clout to compel concessions. A bus boycott secured a desegregation agreement from the private bus line, but the movement carried on the boycott, insisting that the city give written assurance that it would not interfere, and so drove the bus company out of business. A wiser strategy, that of accepting the company offer and contesting the city in the courts should the need arise, might have had happier results. The city fathers heard the black petition requesting desegregation of various city facilities as agreed, but, with Mayor Kelley and Buford Collins dissenting, issued a rejection a few days later. With typical arrogance, the commissioners advised that the movement "earn acceptance for their people by encouraging the improvement of their moral standards."

Martin Luther King, Jr., and Ralph Abernathy returned to Albany, first on February 26, 1962, to stand trial for their December arrest, and again on July 10 for sentencing. Before the by-now usual television cameras and assembled newsmen, King announced that he and Abernathy would serve forty-five days in jail rather than pay the $178 fine imposed. Wyatt Tee Walker and Andrew Young of SCLC opposed the resumption of the direct action campaign in Albany. As Young told Pat Watters many years later, "We couldn't see any handles to anything." At the May SCLC board meeting, Reverend Fred Shuttlesworth had proposed that SCLC join his Alabama Christian Movement for Human Rights in a campaign against segregation in Birmingham. And there were those within SCLC who believed that Birmingham offered more "handles" for fruitful SCLC activity.

King, however, was bent on making a moral protest. As Abernathy told Walker and Young in arguing for a new offensive in Albany, "when you are called on to witness, you can't always analyze what might happen. You just have to go." The day after the sentencing, Reverend Charles K. Steele of SCLC arrived from Tallahassee and led twelve men, nine women, and eleven teenagers, all black, downtown where they were promptly marched off to jail, singing "We Shall Overcome." Ominously, bricks and bottles were thrown by black rowdies at the police present at several mass rallies in the black community. On the Senate floor, Senator Joseph Clark, Democrat from Pennsylvania, declared that events in Albany demonstrated "that there are still, unfortunately, areas of our country in which the Constitution of the United States, as represented by the Fourteenth Amendment, is not in effect." The Kennedy Administration was alarmed at King's arrest and possible intensification of civil disobedience in Albany. A Democratic primary was underway in Georgia, the winning candidate for the gubernatorial nomination was assured of a fall victory, and there were fears that renewed demonstrations in Albany would benefit racist Marvin Griffin—he promised to brain demonstrators with a sapling pole—and defeat moderate Carl Sanders. (Sanders won by a comfortable margin.) Burke Marshall was busy on the telephone, and among other calls made one to Mrs. King, assuring her that the Justice Department "would use whatever influence it could to obtain his release." The next day, July 2, an unidentified, "well-dressed Negro man," as Chief Pritchett described him, appeared at City Hall and paid the fines levied against King and Abernathy, who reluctantly left jail. As

Abernathy told a mass rally that night, "I've been thrown out of lots of places in my day, but never before have I been thrown out of jail."

No one has publicly admitted to putting up the money. Some assume that the Kennedy Administration somehow was involved. Pat Watters, a knowledgeable journalist, writes in *Down to Now*, "It was a justifiable suspicion—they wanted King out." Perhaps Mayor Kelley and Chief Pritchett had read of the incident in which Montgomery Police Commissioner Clyde Sellers paid King's fine "to save the taxpayers . . . the expense of housing him." Whoever acted and for whatever reasons, the release did not defuse the Albany protests. Over the next week, small groups of blacks, with some non-resident whites, nonviolently attacked segregation at lunch counters, the public library, parks, and other public places. There were few arrests; seven young people were jailed for a lunch-counter sit-in. But for the most part, the police simply turned people away or facilities were closed. With a major demonstration scheduled for Saturday, the city fathers secured at midnight Friday an omnibus injunction from Federal District Judge J. Robert E. Elliott, a known segregationist just appointed by President Kennedy. The injunction barred "unlawful picketing, congregating or marching in the streets . . . participating in any boycott in restraint of trade . . . any act designed to provoke breaches of the peace." King, Abernathy, Marion Page, Walker, Charles Jones, and Ruby Hurley were specifically enjoined from further activity. The temporary injunction was effective until July 30 when a hearing would be held on a city petition for a permanent restraining order.°

At the Shiloh Baptist Church, the Reverend Benjamin Welles exhorted his Saturday audience of about seven hundred, "I've heard about an injunction but I haven't seen one. I've heard a few names but my name hasn't been called. But I do know where my name is being called. My name is being called on the road to freedom. I can hear the blood of Emmett Till as it calls from the ground . . . . When shall we go? Not tomorrow! Not at high noon! Now!"

It speaks to the efficacy of the injunction that only 160, more than a hundred under eighteen years of age, followed Welles.°° Singing "I Ain't Gonna Let Nobody Turn Me 'Round," the group walked from the church toward City Hall. They were intercepted by the police and

° The temporary injunction was set aside the following Tuesday by the Circuit Court of Appeals.
°° The issuance of a federal injunction posed a problem for King. He was perfectly aware that once successful it would be used again and again to stymie the civil rights movement much as injunctions had forestalled labor organization earlier. As Coretta King put it in her autobiography, "Yet since the federal government had always supported us on constitutional questions, it was difficult for Martin to go against it. It had been the only friend we had in the South."

arrested. Sixty-four were put in a cell designed to hold twelve children, fifty-two in one for eight.

The next evening, Mrs. Slater King, then six months pregnant, drove with friends to the Camilla jail, where the youngsters were being held, to bring food to the prisoners. Told to leave, the women did so. As Mrs. King slowly made her way to her car, a deputy sheriff cursed her and threatened to arrest her if she did not hurry. "If you want to arrest, go ahead," she retorted. Mrs. King was knocked to the ground, kicked, hit twice on the side of the head, and knocked unconscious. Reviving, she managed to drive back to Albany. Later, she suffered a miscarriage as a consequence of the brutal beating.

That night Vincent Harding, a black Mennonite minister, led a prayer vigil on the City Hall steps. Ordered to move on, the group of seven remained in place and were arrested. The next day, forty participants in a peaceful march protesting the brutality to Mrs. King were arrested. An estimated two thousand black youths gathered, and when the police moved to disperse the crowd, rocks and pop bottles flew. A state trooper was hit, bloodied. It was a minor affair, but nonetheless profoundly disturbing to the advocates of nonviolent civil disobedience. Pat Watters reports that Andrew Young, voice almost breaking, told three husky black youngsters, "You're too yellow to march. But you stand over here and throw things and give us a bad name. Those folks who marched could hold their heads high. Not y'all." Martin Luther King declared July 25 a "Day of Penitence," and toured Albany's poolrooms, taverns, and hang-outs, speaking out against violence and preaching nonviolence: "What happened last night hurt our movement. They know how to deal with violence. But when they are up against non-violence, they don't know what to do . . . . You have to be non-violent in spirit and militant in action."

King insisted that direct action be confined to small prayer vigils, at least for a time. SNCC was displeased, and the Albany Movement was not happy. SCLC, it was felt, had preempted leadership and shaping events to its advantage. The "SNCC kids" thought penitence demeaning. According to King biographer David L. Lewis, at least one "fretful" meeting was held between King, SNCC, and others in Slater King's backyard to discuss these matters. As a result of the pressures for a more militant posture, King apparently decided to have himself arrested again in an effort to galvanize Albany's black community. On Friday, June 27, King, Abernathy, and Dr. Anderson were arrested along with ten others as they knelt to pray on City Hall steps.

Albany was a test of a theory then gaining currency within the civil rights movement, particularly in SNCC and among its followers and partisans. Writing in *New America* in the fall before Albany, Tom Hayden articulated this view:

During the two-year span of the movement-revolution in the South, the thought has crossed many minds that one center, one place should be used as a scene of dramatic protest, which could expose to those in power, and to their constituency, the gaping inadequacies of the policy of repression in the face of an indigenous and national morality. And perhaps too, it would stimulate effective federal action so that the national government would for once exert its force as a moral leader rather than waiting for the public to pull it along . . . . The jail and the police power of the state will be abandoned as weapons and the mentality that relies on these will be reached only when the sustained force of the people in motion makes them inadequate as the bulwarks of the *status quo*. Filling the jails and swamping the courts are not mere slogans. They are the non-violent techniques necessary to immobilize the jails and the courts as instruments of repression.

For a time, Albany must have seemed the place for such an apocalyptic moment of truth.° King was in jail, and surely others would follow. Before the movement ran its course, over 1,200 would spend some time in jail between 1961 and 1962, trying, as Howard Zinn phrased it, "with the sheer weight of their numbers to act as a substitute for the federal government in enforcing the Constitution of the United States." The number of those arrested, as well as their courage, was impressive. However, as it turned out, their weight was not sufficient to break the centuries-old grip of racism.

By mid-August 1962, the Albany Movement had lost much of its momentum. Demonstrations and arrests continued, but not in large numbers. Groups of eighteen, twenty-eight, and thirty, praying on the City Hall steps, were arrested during the first week following King's arrest. A white SNCC field worker, William Hansen, was badly beaten, his jaw and several ribs broken, in the Dougherty County jail. When attorney C. B. King went to check on Hansen's condition, he was slugged by Sheriff Cull Campbell and thrown out into the street, bleeding profusely from a head wound. Martin Luther King, Jr., was tried and given a suspended sentence on August 10. A white couple and six blacks were arrested when they attempted to integrate a bowling alley. Blacks were admitted to an Episcopal Church and a Catholic Church but turned away at a Baptist and Methodist Church. And so it went, a demonstration here and an arrest there. The public park was closed and the swimming pool sold to a private party. A black

---

° Hayden, writing at the time of McComb, Mississippi, estimated that "if 3,000 or half that number" were willing to go to jail, "the entire character of the movement would be altered."

delegation finally met face to face with the City Commission to no avail. Seventy-five Protestant ministers, Catholic and Protestant laymen, and Jewish rabbis arrived from the North to demonstrate and be arrested. Twenty fasted for two days in jail before accepting bail; the rest remained incarcerated for a week. The Ku Klux Klan rallied, some three thousand strong, in a cow pasture. The city government wisely refused permission for a parade through Albany.

SNCC continued its voter registration forays into the surrounding black belt counties, withdrawing, ironically, to Albany from time to time for sanctuary. The first suit under the 1957 Civil Rights Act secured an injunction barring discrimination by the Board of Registrars of "Terrible" Terrell County. Blacks were a majority, but out of a total black population of 8,209 in 1960, only 51 dared register. Of 4,533 whites, 2,894 were registered. SNCC workers were harassed constantly. Ralph Allen, a white student at Trinity College from Melrose, Massachusetts, was nearly run down by a truck and then beat up by the driver and several bystanders. Joseph Pitts, an Albany student working with Allen, was struck with a cane. When Allen and Charles Sherrod accompanied some blacks to the voter registration office—voter registration in Georgia is an all-year-round affair—they were arrested for "investigation, vagrancy, and all that crap." When a group of about forty blacks met at the Mount Olive Baptist Church in Sasser, a Terrell County hamlet, to discuss voter registration, Sheriff Z. T. Mathews appeared with a group of threatening whites. The sheriff took names, questioned members of the audience, and otherwise sought to intimidate the gathering. "We want our colored people to go on living like they have for the last hundred years," he told *Times* reporter Claude Sitton. Dire warnings were issued as to what "disturbed white citizens" might do, and Sitton and other reporters present left after the rally convinced that, had there been no newsmen present, something dreadful might well have happened that night in Sasser.

Sherrod, Allen, and others complained to the Justice Department, and on August 18 the Department asked the United States District Court to prohibit law enforcement officials from intimidating prospective voters in Terrell County. Two nights later, in retaliation, Shady Grove Baptist Church in neighboring Lee County, used as a voter registration center, was dynamited and burned to the ground. The homes of four black families active in voter registration drives were riddled with bullets in a night-riding attack. A SNCC registration worker was wounded by a shotgun blast in Dawson. On September 9, night riders burned the Mount Olive Church in Sasser and the Mount Mary Church in Chickasawhatchee, five miles away. Eight days later, the I. Hope Baptist Church near Dawson was burned.

"Albany was successful only if the goal was to go to jail." Ruby

Hurley's wry conclusion was widely shared among observers and participants of the civil rights movement. Civil rights agitation and activity continued in Albany—arrests would rise to two thousand by July 1963—but attracted little attention elsewhere. Other places and events were catching the headlines and preempting television coverage. The movement struggled along, holding weekly meetings until 1968, but attendance dwindled considerably as time went on. The majority of blacks in Albany were not galvanized into activity as a large part of the Montgomery community had been by the bus boycott. In part, this was because Chief Pritchett had so deftly handled the demonstrators as to minimize their martyrdom, and, in part, because the Albany Movement appeared unable to concentrate on one particular goal, which, conceivably, might have rallied a majority of the black community as well as created possibilities for negotiations and for winning specific concrete gains. As Howard Zinn perceptively noted in his report to the Southern Regional Council: "There has been no consistent, clear-cut plan of action for the Albany Movement. . . . Like so many other developments in the Deep South in recent years, certain specific streams of action were deliberate, but the confluence of those streams was a matter of chance . . . . While there are advantages to such fluidity, there are also drawbacks. Sometimes there has been a tendency simply to repeat old actions under new circumstances. The movement delayed legal action, for instance, . . . and continued to depend mainly on demonstrations, instead of linking the two. There has been a failure to create and handle skillfully a set of differentiated tactics for different situations."

The weaknesses of the Albany Movement, no doubt, accurately reflected those of various black communities in the South at the time. There was a new middle class emerging as well as a new working class, no longer willing to cooperate with, or to tolerate segregation. While there were untapped reservoirs of leadership abilities and talents, and more experience to build on than commonly supposed, there was nonetheless a lack of certain kinds of experience and expertise that could only come with greater political participation than then allowed in much of the South. The ways and uses of power were as yet unfamiliar as were the complexities of a multiracial society where segregation no longer provided acceptable guidelines of behavior or rules for playing the game. (This was also true for southern whites but they did have the advantages that come with possessing power.) Short of an impossible instant revolution, one must learn how to accept, achieve, and build future progress on present compromises. By the same token, however, one does not learn what must be done unless one tries to do what ought to be done. Albany, in a sense, was a learning tree for the civil rights movement in the South. As Andrew Young told Pat

Watters in 1970, "There wasn't any real strategy in Albany. I remember being around and not knowing what to do . . . . We didn't know then how to mobilize people in masses. We learned in Albany. We put together the team of SCLC staff people there that later won the victories. They hadn't even known each other then."

This is not to say, however, that Albany was without its consequences for others than the SCLC. The burned churches were rebuilt, three of them with donations from organized labor, readers of the *Atlanta Constitution*, Governor Nelson Rockefeller of New York, the United Church of Christ, the Protestant Episcopal Church, the National Council of Churches and the Albany Movement. Jackie Robinson headed the SCLC drive which raised over $80,000 in eight months from these and similar sources. Ironically, the last church burned was rebuilt first by local whites who contributed money and labor out of Christian charity, southern paternalism, and affection. The Federal Bureau of Investigation responded with commendable alacrity, arresting three men and a sixteen-year-old boy for the September arson. They pleaded guilty and were sentenced to seven years in prison. Two other white men were arrested in October and charged with the burning of the Shady Baptist Grove Church. The first black to run for office in Albany since Reconstruction, Thomas C. Chatman, ran second in a three-man race for city commissioner. A federal injunction in 1964 secured the right to conduct protest marches, and public facilities were desegregated by the Civil Rights Act of that year. And Albany hired six black policemen, something no one truly believed possible in 1961.

Albany put the South on notice that a change was in the offing. As Wyatt Tee Walker put it, the Albany Movement represented "a big beginning in the Deep South." The events of 1961 and 1962 in Albany also pointed up the weaknesses of the Civil Rights Acts of 1957 and 1960 and cast light on the civil rights strategies of the Kennedy Administration. During the 1961 troubles, Robert Kennedy sent a telegram to Chief Pritchett congratulating him on keeping the peace. Coretta King reports that her husband was "quite annoyed" by Kennedy's and Burke Marshall's failure to understand "our plight." They suggested that it might be wise to "close up" in Albany, a suggestion in keeping with the Kennedy "keep-the-lid-on" approach to civil rights disturbances. One reason for this posture was pragmatic: The administration honestly believed it was powerless when it came to protecting individual constitutional rights. As Deputy Attorney General Nicholas de B. Katzenbach once said, the Department of Justice "is ill-equipped to assume responsibility for the performance of ordinary police functions." What authority that did exist, empowering the President to intervene when local and state authorities failed to protect constitutional rights (Sections 332-334 of Title 10, United States Code), was considered a remedy for major breakdowns of civil order, and not for routine police harassment. At the outset of the Kennedy Administration, the Attorney General, in an address at the University of Georgia, declared: "I say to you today that if the orders of the court are circumvented, the Department of Justice will act. We will not stand by or be aloof. We will move . . . We will not make or interpret the laws. We shall enforce them—vigorously, without regional bias or political slant." The operative phrase was "if the orders of the court . . .," for as Burke Marshall argued in the Speranza lectures of 1964, cases "clearly beyond the very large limits of permissibility set by federal constitutional standards" are "almost outside the reach of federal action," except where the government must enforce a federal court order.

Actually, the administration's position was somewhat more complicated than Marshall's defense would allow. It intervened to protect Freedom Riders in Montgomery, but not in Albany where court orders ought to have been easily obtainable since the local officials were clearly in violation of the ICC ruling barring segregation. However, in Montgomery, there was a major breakdown of civil order while in Albany, relatively speaking, there was no such breakdown. As long as the local police maintained order, no matter how many went to jail in violation of their constitutional rights to freedom of assembly, petition, and speech, there would be no federal intervention. The Kennedy Administration bought a short-run civil peace at a long-run cost—the escalation of civil disobedience to confrontation, the deliberate courting of violence in order to provoke federal action.

The difficulties inherent in the Kennedy position were amply illustrated when ex-Air Force Staff Sergeant James Howard Meredith applied for admission to his home state university, "Ole Miss," at Oxford, Mississippi. After going through the necessary preliminaries, Meredith, on May 31, 1961, filed suit in the United States District Court for southern Mississippi, contending that he had been denied admission on racial grounds. On September 20, 1962, Governor Ross Barnett, an avowed segregationist, personally blocked Meredith's first attempt to register as a student at Ole Miss. Governor Barnett was in clear violation of court orders, but instead of acting, the Kennedy Administration temporized while state officials repeatedly barred Meredith from his rightful place. On September 27, the federal government backed down, abandoning a fourth attempt to register Meredith, recalling the federal marshals who accompanied him for fear of "major violence and bloodshed."

Behind the scenes, the Attorney General, and later, the President, engaged in an incredible series of telephone calls with Governor Barnett and an intermediary, Tom Watkins, a Mississippian attorney and friend of the governor. The Kennedys sought assurances that the

governor would cooperate "in maintaining law and order and prevent-
ing violence in connection with federal enforcement of the court
orders." The governor's assurances were, to say the least, equivocal. At
one point, President Kennedy and Governor Barnett agreed that
Barnett and Lieutenant Governor Paul B. Johnson would go to Oxford,
while Meredith slipped into Jackson to register. They had not considered Meredith's wishes in the matter: All along, he insisted in going in
the front way and not through the back door—that, after all, being the
point of integration. However, Governor Barnett called off the agreement, pledging white Mississippians, "We will not surrender to the
forces of tyranny." The governor also proposed to the Kennedys that he
would withdraw—that is, retreat—if the federal authorities would stage
a show of force. Later, he suggested a staged capitulation of Mississippi
to the Army, which Robert Kennedy properly and coldly dismissed as
"a foolish and dangerous show."

Governor Barnett was found guilty of civil contempt, and given the
weekend to Tuesday, October 2, to purge himself or face arrest and a
fine of $10,000 a day. On Sunday, September 30, 1962, Tom Watkins
assured Attorney General Kennedy that the governor would recognize
federal authority and that Mississippi highway patrolmen would assist
federal marshals to maintain peace and order. Unbeknownst to
Washington, however, the governor also gave the head of the state
highway patrol sealed orders authorizing him to withdraw his men at his
own discretion.

At midnight, September 29, President Kennedy called the Mississippi
National Guard to active duty and dispatched federal troops to
Memphis to stand in reserve. He called on the government and the
people of Mississippi to "cease and desist" all their obstruction to
Meredith's entry and to "disperse and retire peaceably forthwith."
Meredith was flown from Memphis to Oxford in a federal plane,
escorted on campus by federal marshals and taken to his quarters on
Dormitory Row. A force of 320 United States Marshals took over the
Lyceum, the university's administration center. Students gathered at
"The Grove," a tree-shaded, grassy mall in front of the Lyceum,
heckling "2-4-1-3, we hate Kennedy," then with increasing violence,
shouting, "Kill the nigger-loving bastards." At dusk, bottles and bricks
began to fly. The mob grew to over 2,500, mostly vigilantes from off the
campus and from out of town.* The state troopers, supposedly on hand
to support the marshals in keeping the peace, drove off. As the rioters
repeatedly charged the stoical marshals, President Kennedy addressed
the nation over television and radio. He appealed to reason and for
patriotism. For the students at Ole Miss, he had these words, "The eyes

---

* Of two hundred rioters arrested, only twenty-four were students.

of the nation and the world are upon you and upon all of us, and the honor of your university and the state are in balance."

The balance was precarious indeed. Guns were fired, and the marshals were nearly overwhelmed before being given the order to use tear gas. A Telenews cameraman from Dallas, Gordon Yoder, and his wife, were set upon by the mob; Paul Guihard, a correspondent from Agence France Presse, was murdered; Roy Gunter, a young juke-box repairman was killed by a stray .38 bullet; a marshal was shot in the throat. Of 166 marshals injured that night, 29 suffered gunshot wounds. Hundreds were injured before federal troops joined the marshals around five o'clock in the morning and drove off the last of the rioters. Chief United States Marshal James P. McShane escorted Meredith to the office of the university registrar and he was enrolled at 8:30 A.M. By Monday evening, over 5,000 soldiers and guardsmen patrolled Oxford, a town of 6,500 population, and their number was doubled the following day. Withdrawal, however, began almost immediately. By the end of the month, only five hundred remained to ensure Meredith's safety. The troops were withdrawn on June 5, 1963, and Meredith graduated on August 18, 1963, with a bachelor of arts degree in political science.

Though Governor Barnett clearly did not purge himself of contempt of court charges, the case against him was allowed to lapse. (It was dismissed as moot in 1965.) Significantly, when Deputy Attorney General Burke Marshall was about to file an affidavit in the Barnett case, he was asked not to do so by the Attorney General—"and I guess by the President." The Cuban missile crisis was in full flood, and the administration did not want to rile the waters of national unity.

Had the Kennedys acted against Barnett, much subsequent travail might have been averted. As Judge Minor Wisdom argued in his dissent over the dropping of the contempt procedures against the Mississippi governor: "What cannot be overestimated . . . is the importance of federal courts standing fast in protecting federally guaranteed rights of individuals. To avoid further violence and bloodshed, all state officials, including the Governor, must know that they cannot with impunity flout federal law." But with the Kennedys, political considerations outweighed all other ones. As pollster Samuel Lubell discovered, President Kennedy had not been hurt politically by sending United States marshals to Montgomery—perhaps because of the contrast to President Eisenhower's calling up troops for Little Rock—but was damaged by the troop order to Ole Miss, and in 1963 to the University of Alabama.

With a presidential year in the offing, and the spring outbreak of protests and civil disorder in Birmingham, the administration was anxious to demonstrate impartiality in civil rights matters and to offset what it perceived as a white backlash. Albany, appropriately, provided the occasion in a rather astounding case, a large-scale criminal prosecution of civil rights activists. It was, clearly, one of those cases that had best not been prosecuted. In 1961, a handcuffed black prisoner, Charlie Ware, was shot while in custody by Sheriff Warren L. Johnson of Baker County. Luckily, Ware lived and he sued the sheriff for $125,000, charging a violation of his constitutional rights. An all-white jury dismissed the claim when it finally came up for trial in April 1963. One of the jurors, Carl Smith, owned a grocery in the all-black section of Albany. His store was picketed shortly after the trial as part of a general boycott of white merchants sponsored by the Albany Movement. Signs demanded that Smith hire blacks; no mention was made of the Ware trial and the boycott had been on for over a year. After one day's picketing, Smith folded up his $200,000-a-year gross business.

Nine civil rights activists, including Dr. Anderson and Slater King, were indicted for obstructing justice or for perjury. FBI agents, not noticeably present during Albany's time of troubles, swarmed into Albany, "thick as hogs," said C. B. King.° "At least 38" agents worked on the case, according to a prosecution admission during the trials. The indictments were announced by the Attorney General himself. A Justice Department representative flew down from Washington to sit with the United States Attorney throughout the trials of the Albany Nine. Blacks drawn for possible jury duty were peremptorily challenged by the federal government. The defendants were all found guilty, except Dr. Anderson whose trial ended in a hung jury. Slater King and the Reverend Samuel Welles were sentenced to a year and a day in prison. Joni Rabinowitz, who did not picket, was sentenced from three months to four years on a three-count perjury charge. It was a strange case in a troubling time.

° The FBI was singularly unsuccessful in finding enough evidence to prosecute the deputy sheriff who kicked Mrs. Slater King or the sheriff who caned attorney C. B. King despite the presence of witnesses at both events.

X

Blacks in Motion

BLACKS CONTINUED TO BE IN motion throughout the 1960s, and civil rights activities increased in number and passion. The recessions of 1958 and 1960–62 which, as we shall see, hit black workers hard, slowed the black migration considerably. From 1960 to 1963, the annual average out-migration of blacks from the South dropped to 78,000 as against the 1950s annual average of 145,000 but the migration soon recovered, rising to over 125,000 from 1963 on. Washington, D.C., became majority black in 1960, and by 1965 six of the country's ten largest cities—Philadelphia, Detroit, Baltimore, Cleveland, Washington, and St. Louis—were over 30 percent black. The black population of the United States grew faster than the white, and was markedly younger.°

Rising expectations coupled with youthful impatience quickened the number and pace of civil rights demonstrations. Civil disobedience became less civil, and the constraints of nonviolence visibly chafed an ever large number of black militants. When Adlai Stevenson, appointed United States Ambassador to the United Nations by President Kennedy, rose to make his maiden speech to the world assembly, some fifty demonstrators, mostly black, rose in the gallery to hoot and jeer, crying out "Vive Lumumba!" As author James Baldwin later noted in a *New York Times Sunday Magazine* article, the demonstration over the murder of outsted Congo Premier Patrice Lumumba, "shocked and baffled most Americans." Though "a very small echo of the black discontent now abroad in the world," the United Nations affair

---

° The white population grew 7.4 percent from 1960 to 1966; the black, 14.4 percent—almost twice as fast. The median age of whites in 1966 was 29.1; of blacks, 21.1. About 35 percent of the white population was under eighteen years of age as compared with 45 percent for blacks.

presaged a new mood. As Baldwin wrote, "the time is forever behind us when Negroes could be expected to 'wait.' "

There were gains, rarely enough for the impatient. Theaters, restaurants, hotels, and lunch counters were desegregated in about fifty more southern and border cities each month during the period from mid-May to September 1963, according to figures compiled by the Department of Justice. Modest successes encouraged even more far-ranging forays against discrimination and racial prejudice. During the five years from June 1963 to May 1968, some 1,117,600 Americans participated in 369 civil rights demonstrations; 15,379 were arrested, and 389 injured. White terrorism against blacks and civil rights workers accounted for an estimated twenty-three deaths. When asked, "Why now?," Roy Wilkins ventured this explanation: "It's cumulative. It's the emergence of Africa. It's being hungry. It's the G.I. Bill. It's major league baseball with Negroes. It's the eight thousand to ten thousand Negroes graduating from college each year. It's kids being impatient."

"Social dislocation," in Bayard Rustin's felicitous phrase, became a most effective weapon in the struggle for civil rights. But as Rustin repeatedly emphasized, social dislocation is a *technique* of struggle, not a program. In important respects, it was a limited one. Admirably suited for the assertion of dignity in the face of degradation, nonviolent tactics succeeded in integrating public accommodations, contributed, by dramatizing its effects, to the toppling of *de jure* segregation, and helped expand voting rights. But social dislocation was not productive of jobs, housing, schools—the pressing needs of newly urbanized blacks. As James Farmer ruefully confided during the height of the lunch-counter sit-ins, how do you sit in for non-existent jobs? Where is the leverage?

"As the century following emancipation draws to a close," the Commission on Civil Rights observed in its 1963 report, *Freedom to the Free,* "more forces are working for the realization of civil rights for all Americans than ever before in history. Government is active in every branch and at every level, if not in every region. Voluntary associations in the field have multiplied at such a rate that it is difficult to catalogue them." Yet, the report concluded, "The final chapter in the struggle for equality has yet to be written." And with good reason, for the civil rights struggle acquired new dimensions in the 1960s as it, so to speak, moved out of the South into the North and West and confronted *de facto* segregation as well as broad questions of economic and social policy.

In the South, civil rights forces came up against their known enemies—white supremacists and racist laws—and fought for clearly defined integrationist goals—equality before the law and in public accommodations, school desegregation, and the vote. In the North, however, the law was, or quickly became so, against discrimination.

Public accommodations were relatively easily integrated, and there were no racist barriers to voting. But there were, as everyone soon discovered, "complications." That there was discrimination, few denied; but nearly everyone, however, believed that it could be eliminated. This belief gave impetus to legal attacks on *de facto* public-school segregation in the North. Housing patterns shaped by both discrimination and the sheer growth of black urban communities created what were in fact segregated schools in more and more central cities. Gerrymandering reinforced this unhappy development. By the early 1960s, 87 percent of the black elementary-school children of Chicago attended virtually all-black schools; 45 percent of Detroit's black pupils were in schools overwhelmingly (80 percent) black; and in Philadelphia, 38 elementary schools were *de facto* segregated schools. A 1962 survey of two hundred public-school systems spread across nineteen states and including 75 percent of the black population in the North found some 1,141 schools with nonwhite enrollments of 60 percent or more. Sociologist Robert A. Dentler pertinently summed up current research findings about such schools: "Minority segregated public schools in the North tend quite uniformly to have poorer facilities, less qualified staffs, and inferior programs of instruction than majority segregated schools."

Irked by school-board policies condemning their children to such a school, black parents in New Rochelle, New York, hired attorney Paul Zuber to challenge gerrymandering and *de facto* school segregation in the courts. There was some skepticism about this course in black circles, a belief that while one could challenge *de jure* segregation in the courts one could not succeed in doing the same for *de facto* segregation. Undaunted by the legal conservatism of his elders, the 35-year-old Zuber brought suit, demanding that the New Rochelle Board of Education provide open enrollment to allow black parents to send their children to other schools within the school system. With an assist from Thurgood Marshall, Zuber won. He was called on to fight like cases elsewhere, and open enrollment became the most widely used administrative scheme for combatting *de facto* segregation. Within limits, open enrollment was successful. Parents were naturally reluctant to send young children great distances to schools in strange neighborhoods, but the major obstacle to open enrollment and other efforts aimed at *de facto* segregation is best illustrated by a question: How do you integrate, say, the schools of Manhattan, already 75 percent black or Puerto Rican by 1960?

Angry, bitter, and frustrated by a lack of jobs and opportunities in the urban slums of the North, an increasing number of blacks, especially among the young, clamored for more militant, direct, mass action. Often, this pitted black against black; the young and feisty against the older and established leadership; the militantly angry against liberal whites. Writing in *New America*, Eleanor Holmes Norton described a scene that would be repeated many times in many places over the next few years: "The lineup was classic at New Haven's NAACP meeting . . . . From opposite ends of the long stage the advocates for each position faced one another. Waiting to speak against the sit-out [a proposed demonstration against slum conditions and bulldozer development] were five or six ministers, real estate men, and other 'solid figures' from the Negro community. Facing them were young Negro unionists and students. Seldom since the sit-ins imbued the civil rights struggle with a sense of immediacy have the lines been so distinctly drawn."

Ironically, as Mrs. Norton pointed out, the targets of militant ire were not right-wing reactionaries or exploitive landlords, but a progressive mayor and a liberal-sponsored redevelopment program that, the militants charged, "has built skyscrapers and high-rent apartments while the slum area has thrived with unusual health." Richard Lee, young and visionary, was elected mayor of New Haven with black, liberal, and labor support on a promise to rebuild the city. He was generally credited with being one of the best of a "new generation" of mayors then coming into office in the country's major cities. Yet, Lee's efforts at rejuvenating New Haven were condemned as a manifestation of a "subtle, nagging, northern brand of racial discrimination."

The New Haven militants lost their battle to win over the NAACP chapter but went ahead under the aegis of the local CORE chapter to carry out a sidewalk "sit-out" of some 250 people. Their concrete demands were modest enough—a city ordinance that would close a loophole in Connecticut's anti-discrimination law that excluded housing with three or less units from coverage and a rent-hike ban—but their presence on the sidewalk was an omen of an escalating militancy in the North. More and more blacks and civil rights activists would come to agree with Mrs. Holmes "that conditions for Negroes in northern slums are not better than the South—just different." Impatience, she added, "made direct action seem peculiarly relevant to attempts to bring segregation in the North out in the open, and to destroy it."

One of the first indications that all was not well in the North came out of the trade union movement. And, as usual, A. Philip Randolph was its spokesman. On July 18-19, 1959, seventy-five black trade unionists met in New York City, at Randolph's request, to discuss problems confronting black workers and those which faced black union leaders within the black community. Once before, with Frank Crosswaith in the 1930s, Randolph had attempted to organize a black trade unionist group, the Negro Labor Committee. It was unsuccessful, the principal difficulty being the lack of a sizable and firm base of black union members. During the 1940s and 1950s, however, black workers entered the unions in ever larger numbers, and by 1960, some 1.5 million were members of the AFL-CIO. Moreover, many blacks came to hold posts in labor organizations, large and small, and participated regularly in union conventions.

The "committee of seventy-five" decided what the existing situation required was a permanent organization patterned after the Jewish Labor Committee, a group that Randolph had worked with on various labor and civil rights projects over the years. The proposed Negro American Labor Council (NALC) would speak for organized labor in the black community just as the Jewish Labor Committee did in the Jewish community; and in carrying out its fight for equality in the labor movement, the new organization would ally itself, as its Jewish counterpart had done, with other civil rights organizations. The "committee of seventy-five" called for a founding convention in a declaration which foreshadowed the tone and style of the NALC, established some ten months after the New York City meeting:

"We resent Jim Crow locals; we deplore the freeze-out against Negroes in labor apprenticeship and training programs; we disclaim the lack of upgrading and promotional opportunities for Negroes; we repudiate the lockout against Negroes by some unions, we, above all, reject 'tokenism,' that thin veneer of acceptance masquerading as democracy. Since hundreds of thousands of Negroes are the victims of this hypocrisy, we ourselves must seek the cure, in terms of hundreds of thousands, in the dimensions of a mass organization."

Randolph's reasons for helping to establish the Negro American Labor Council were, as he presented them, clear-cut and logical. He argued that since trade unions are essentially urban organizations and since blacks were moving to cities in large numbers, it thus followed that "labor's future is tied up with the future of the Negro." Randolph emphasized that AFL-CIO President George Meany "is not a racist," yet Meany "hasn't a sense of the urgency of the question that is necessary in the 20th century." (The NALC, as it turned out, did sharpen Meany's sense of urgency.) Randolph doubted, as he did from time to time, if anyone "except a Negro" can have that sense. The NALC, was "a response to the basic need of the Negro masses to have a voice of their own." And, Randolph firmly added, "the voice of black labor is not going to be consonant with those [voices] that come from non-Negro sources or from Negroes themselves, that are non-labor."

An impetus for the founding of the Negro American Labor Council was the plight of the black worker. At the time, economists were given to treating unemployment in the United States as troublesome "pockets" of an otherwise expanding economy. But to black workers, these "pockets" were seas of quicksand sucking them down to economic oblivion. Overall unemployment rose from 3.8 million in 1959 to over

4.8 million in 1961; the overall rate of unemployment, from 5.5 percent in 1959 to an 8.1 percent peak in February 1961, and to an annual rate for that year of 6.7 percent. According to Department of Labor estimates, nonwhites comprised a full 20 percent of all the unemployed. This figure included Puerto Ricans as well as blacks, but statistics for the winter of 1960–1961 also showed that the black unemployment rate was almost twice as high as that of white unemployment—13.8 percent as against 7 percent. An Urban League survey of unemployment among blacks in fifty cities uncovered an even higher rate, "frequently twice to three times that of the total unemployment rate." Thus, in Chicago, where the total unemployment rate was 5.7 percent, the percentage of black jobless was 17.3; in Louisville, Kentucky, the total rate was 8.3 percent, while the corresponding figure for blacks was 39.8 percent; in Pittsburgh, the figures were 11.6 as against 24 percent; in New York City, 6.4 as against 10 percent. These grim statistics also suggest why unemployment was viewed with much less urgency by the white community than by the black; in St. Louis, there were 35,000 unemployed blacks out of a total of 72,700 jobless; more strikingly, in Gary, Indiana, 18,000 out of a total of 20,200 were unemployed; in Detroit, the figure was 112,000 out of a total of 185,000.

But even when he had a job, the black worker's position was far from enviable. In 1958, the median wage of the black male worker was only 59 percent as much as that of the white worker—$2,652 as against $4,569. As Randolph commented wryly: "When a Negro worker goes into the market as a consumer he cannot presume to pay only 58 percent for comparable goods and services . . . purchased by white workers. The fact is, Negroes pay relatively much higher prices." Similarly, white women averaged $2,364 a year, while black women— much more often the breadwinners of the family—earned only $1,055.

The position of the black workers deteriorated beneath the onslaught of the 1959–1963 recession. In manufacturing, blacks were confined by and large to the semiskilled and unskilled jobs. Often these were the dirty jobs that white workers no longer wanted; yet, in the early 1960s, because of the drop in the number of manufacturing jobs (due in turn to the recession and the encroachment of automation), competition for all kinds of work intensified. In that situation, the black competed at a great disadvantage.

In the building and construction trades, one of the few areas where the work force was then expanding, black workers were all but barred from the top-of-the-line mechanical crafts—electricians, plumbers, steamfitters, iron workers, and sheet metal workers. Within these apprenticeable skilled trades, fathers passed their jobs on to their sons or nephews, excluding almost all outsiders. Black workers, however, did share some of the building construction prosperity. Black workers were well-represented in the so-called trowel trades, constituting roughly 26 percent of the construction laborers, 27 percent of the cement and concrete finishers, 16 percent of the plasterers, and about 12 percent of the nation's bricklayers. The pay is good for these mostly union jobs which require a high order of skills. (Gross hourly earnings in contract construction in 1960 were $3.08 as against $2.26 in manufacturing.) But these jobs lacked status because the work was often uncertain, dirty, and hard, and did not pay as well as the top five crafts where blacks were virtually excluded. Roughly 4.5 percent of all the new workers entering these five crafts over the decade 1950 to 1960 were blacks. Yet, the percentages of all the workers within those crafts who are black changed only slightly, rising from 1.9 percent to 2.4 percent in ten years. Julian Thomas, Urban League director of industrial relations, reported that in seven out of thirty-two major cities, the league did not find a single black apprentice. There was one black apprentice electrician in each of four cities and one plumbing apprentice in five. Throughout the thirty-two cities surveyed in 1957, Urban League investigators found a total of roughly one hundred black apprentices among all fields. "It is difficult," Thomas commented, "to encourage a Negro youngster to take an interest in apprenticeship training when it takes us three years to get one Negro electrician hired in the nation's capital!" Roy Wilkins remarked that "given a continuation of present rates of advance, it will take Negroes 138 years, or until the year 2094, to secure equal participation in skilled-craft training and employment."

Despite the ample raw material for grievances on the part of black workers, the Negro American Labor Council did not win widespread support; its growth failed to match expectations, reaching a peak of some ten thousand in the early 1960s. A 1961 rundown of the various unions to which NALC vice-presidents belonged—most of them as paid functionaries—suggests that NALC membership was drawn from the United Auto Workers, the United Steelworkers, the International Union of Electrical Workers, Hotel & Restaurant Employees, the Retail Clerks, District 65—now independent but then affiliated to the Retail, Wholesale, and Department Store Union of the AFL-CIO, the Brother-hood of Sleeping Car Porters, the International Longshoremen's Association, and the Teamsters. NALC chapters were established in most of the major industrial centers of the North—Chicago, Detroit, New York, Pittsburgh, and Youngstown.

Although the NALC never attained "the dimensions of a mass organization," it did enliven the labor scene. Piqued by Randolph's biting criticism of labor's record at the 1959 AFL-CIO convention, AFL-CIO President George Meany barked, "Who the hell appointed you the guardian of all the Negroes in America?" Meany admittedly was also annoyed by Randolph's failure to observe the amenities; Randolph reserved his ammunition for the convention floor instead of raising his objections as a member at an AFL-CIO executive council meeting. Whatever the cause, the flare-up of Meany's temper gained wide publicity for Randolph's charges of discrimination within some unions. However, Benjamin McLaurin observed, dramatization of union discrimination by the nation's press was not "because the newspapers had any love for the problems of the Negro worker. The truth of the matter is, they didn't have too much faith in the federation's program, and here was an opportunity to give the trade union movement a black eye." There was more to the exchange than that, however. It revealed the considerable tension that was growing up between the black and white wings of the civil rights coalition.

Much of the civil rights progress achieved to that date—and since—can be attributed to the effective cooperation of Jewish, labor, and liberal, and black anti-discrimination groups. They were largely responsible for the passage of fair employment legislation in eighteen states by 1960; they were whatever force that existed behind the drive for open occupancy in housing; they backed attempts to implement the United States Supreme Court's school desegregation decision; and they gave of time, money and moral support to the students involved in the sit-ins. Yet, the coalition, especially on the labor side, was severely strained by even so mild a protest as that raised by Randolph and the NALC.° Later, liberals—but never unionists—would revel in the excesses of black rhetoric, especially when leveled at liberal accomplishments, but at the dawn of the 1960s many white liberals felt at one with the Jewish trade unionist who reacted to the NALC with, "They'll tell

---

° Another factor contributing to strained relationships among anti-discrimination forces was the growth of black professionalism in the field. The Jewish defense agencies—the American Jewish Committee, the Anti-Defamation League, the American Jewish Congress, and the Jewish Labor Committee—had been active in the field of civil rights for decades. They operated, as a JLC statement put it, "on the assumption that the problem of bigotry is indivisible." JLC staff, as an instance, were instrumental in organizing local labor committees to combat discrimination in key industrial cities. William Becker, JLC's man in San Francisco, was the prime mover in California's adoption of a state FEPC law in 1959. The American Jewish Committee's National Labor Service provided unions with anti-discrimination literature and advice. It was helpful in developing full-time civil rights departments in both the AFL and the CIO before the merger in 1955. Despite their protests to the contrary, the JLC and the National Labor Service came to be considered by many white trade unionists as the pro-black voice within organized labor. This was paralleled in the broader society where many felt that the Jewish defense agencies were *the* advocates of civil rights. Charles S. Zimmerman, the JLC's chief civil rights spokesman and later its chairman, was appointed in 1958 head of the AFL-CIO's civil rights committee just as black militancy was on the rise. (He resigned in 1961.) As a Jewish civil rights professional once (in 1961) summed it all up: "Among professionals in intergroup relations, the Jews are the longest in the field, the most skilled and most experienced. Negro professionals resent this. Negroes have developed their own leadership and they don't want whites—Jews or anybody else—to be in the forefront of the civil rights fight."

me about discrimination?" Well-meaning people were concerned as the winds of change stirred the surface of black life in America, setting events in motion that were taking black Americans into increasing militant and uncharted courses of action. What white liberals regarded as "progress," blacks increasingly came to reject as mere "tokenism," and correspondingly many white liberals began to regard black militancy as "racist," or more appropriately, "racial" self-seeking. The seeds for the break-up of the civil rights coalition were being sown early in the 1960s.

Prodded by Randolph and the NALC, organized labor intensified its efforts against discrimination within its own house. The federation set aside an entire day at its 1961 convention for the discussion of civil rights matters led by Martin Luther King, Jr., and Randolph. The convention adopted a resolution calling for "appropriate action" by the executive council against unions that persisted in discrimination. Randolph called the resolution, "the best ever." However, the federation's hands were tied by its lack of power over the local unions of its affiliates. The AFL-CIO is a federation of near autonomous national and international unions and of itself cannot intervene in local union affairs. The AFL-CIO was unable to do little more than encourage affiliates to undertake anti-discrimination programs. Programs were undertaken, but many existed only on paper. As a consequence, labor leaders realized that federal action was essential to eliminate discrimination in hiring—over which most unions have little or no say—and on the job. In his 1963 New Year's statement, AFL-CIO President George Meany called for a fair employment practices commission to bring the force of law behind the AFL-CIO's policy pronouncements. In characteristically blunt fashion, Meany told the House Judiciary Committee on July 17, 1963:

> The plain fact is that Negro workers as a whole, North or South, do not enjoy anything approaching equal employment opportunity.
>
> We ask you now, as we have asked the Congress for many years, for effective enforceable legislation to correct this glaring injustice, which must be corrected in order to make the other aspects of a civil rights program effective.
>
> We have a selfish reason; in fact, we have two of them.
>
> First, we need the statutory support of the federal government to carry out the unanimously adopted principles of the AFL-CIO. . . .
>
> Why is this so? Primarily because the labor movement is not what its enemies say it is—a monolithic, dictatorial, centralized body that imposes its will on the helpless dues

payers. We operate in a democratic way, and we cannot dictate even in a good cause. . . .

Second, we want federal legislation because we are tired of being the whipping boy in this area.

We have never at any time tried to gloss over the shortcomings of unions on the subject of equal opportunity. Yes, some of our members take a wrong headed view; I have just said so, I have said so before, and I repeat it again.

But we in the labor movement publicly deplore these few holdouts against justice. We do our utmost to bring them around to the right side. And at the same time, the employers—who actually do the hiring—escape in many instances with no criticism whatever.

If there has been any widespread outcry from employers who want to hire Negroes but have been prevented from doing so by a union, it has not reached my ears.

Despite intensive lobbying by the AFL-CIO, with a powerful assist from the Leadership Conference on Civil Rights, the Kennedy Administration refused to incorporate an anti-discrimination in employment ban in its civil rights measure. According to Theodore Sorensen, the President wanted "the best bill possible at the earliest time possible" and feared that FEPC would drive away moderate support. The administration proposed a measure that would place a ban on discrimination in public accommodations that had substantial effect on interstate travel; the proposed act would also empower the Attorney General to file suits for desegregation of public education on his own initiative. The President endorsed fair employment practices in principle in the message accompanying the June 19 civil rights package. But demonstrations would escalate in number and intensity and over 250,000 Americans would have to march on Washington before the administration would reluctantly swing around to public support of fair employment practices legislation.

While baleful omens of future insurgency simmered beneath the surface of northern slums, there was a resurgence of civil rights activity in the South, most notably in Birmingham, Alabama. One of the world's youngest major cities, Birmingham was laid out in a Jones Valley cornfield at the anticipated junction of two railroads. Incorporated in 1871, the city flourished, thriving on the exploitation of vast iron ore and coal deposits found in the north central portion of Alabama. Whites and blacks were drawn to the new city by the promise of jobs in the expanding iron and steel industry. Birmingham's population jumped from 3,800 in 1880 to over 130,000 by 1910, reaching 340,887 in 1960 and becoming roughly 35 to 40 percent black. Though industrially a forerunner of the new South, Birmingham, unlike urbane Atlanta, was retrogressive in race relations.° "Birmingham's whites and blacks share a community of fear," wrote Harrison Salisbury after a visit in the spring of 1960. The streets, the water supply and the sewer system, Salisbury noted in his *Times* account of race relations in Birmingham, were about the only public facilities whites and blacks shared. "Ball parks and taxicabs are segregated. So are libraries. A book featuring black and white rabbits was banned." Since the founding of the Alabama Christian Movement for Human Rights (ACMHR), the SCLC's largest affiliate, by the Reverend Fred Shuttlesworth in 1956, there had been a dozen bombings of black homes and churches and fifty cross-burning incidents. Dynamite attempts had been made against the two principal synagogues. Klansmen castrated a black man, Judge Aaron, and in 1959, abducted and beat with tire chains the Reverend Charles Billups, a young Baptist minister and a charter member of the ACMHR. When the manager of the local bus terminal endeavored to obey the ICC's 1961 ruling banning segregation in interstate travel facilities, Birmingham's commissioner of public safety, Theophilus Eugene "Bull" Connor arrested him four times in two weeks. "Every channel of communication," Salisbury reported, "every medium of mutual interest, every reasoned approach, every inch of middle ground has been fragmented by the emotional dynamite of racism, reinforced by the whip, the razor, the gun, the bomb, the torch, the club, the knife, the mob, the police, and many branches of the state's apparatus.

SCLC chose this rather formidable and forbidding place for its "Project C"—"C for Confrontation"—at the behest of Rev. Fred Shuttlesworth. A slight, intense, cocoa-complexioned figure, Shuttlesworth, then forty-one, sensed that segregation in Birmingham was not quite as invulnerable as many Alabamans and outsiders believed. SCLC decided to hold its September 1962 convention in Birmingham as a gesture of support for a boycott initiated by students at Miles College with Shuttlesworth's guidance and backing. White merchants, in

---

° When Richard L. Davis, a black member of the United Mine Workers' executive board, arrived in Birmingham in the winter of 1897–1898 to encourage unionization of black and white miners, he reported: "The one great drawback is the division between white and colored . . . . While white and colored miners work in the same mines and maybe even in adjoining rooms, they will not ride even a work-train with their dirty mining clothes on together." Yet, Davis enjoyed some success. Birmingham's *Labor Advocate* urged, "Obliterate the Color Line," declaring, "the common cause of labor is more important than racial differences." When a state convention disenfranchised black voters in 1901, the Alabama State Federation of Labor pointedly elected Silas Brooks, a black vice president of the Alabama United Mine Workers, as first vice-president and J. H. Bean, a black carpenter from Selma, second vice-president. A series of lost strikes in Birmingham, however, doomed this auspicious beginning; UMW membership plummeted from eighteen thousand (roughly half black) to seven hundred in 1908.

August, agreed to negotiate and as earnest of their good faith removed "white" and "colored" signs from water fountains and rest rooms. The signs were promptly restored as soon as SCLC ended its deliberations, leading Shuttlesworth to the not unfounded suspicion that the merchants had reacted to fend off the national publicity that would have followed any demonstrations by SCLC delegates. This minor spurt of Machiavellianism, nonetheless, indicated that an important sector of white power was sensitive to pressure. The question, of course, was, How much? As Wyatt Tee Walker put it, "We've got to have a crisis to bargain with. To take a moderate approach, hoping to get help from whites doesn't work. They nail you to the cross."

Unlike in Albany, SCLC was better prepared and enjoyed a greater strength in Birmingham. Shuttlesworth had pulled together a powerful leadership group in the Alabama Christian Movement for Human Rights—A. G. Gaston, owner of the A. G. Gaston Motel and a millionaire; John Drew, a prosperous insurance broker; Arthur Shores, a young lawyer; Lucius Pitts, president of privately endowed Miles College; the Reverend Edward Gardner, ACMHR's vice-president; and the Reverend Charles Billups. It was a broad-based group, making possible the strategy cogently outlined by King: "With a strong base in the Shuttlesworth-led forces in the Negro community, the vulnerability of Birmingham at the cash register would provide the leverage to gain a breakthrough in the toughest city in the South."

King's biographers agree that King, still smarting after events in Albany, wanted a victory to restore SCLC's prestige. And, too, he wanted, as did other black leaders, civil rights restored to its rightful priority on the national agenda, especially in 1963, the centennial year of the Emancipation Proclamation. King had described 1962 as "the year that civil rights was displaced as the dominant issue in domestic politics . . . . The issue no longer commanded the conscience of the nation." At a January 1963 White House meeting with the President and Attorney General Robert Kennedy, King had been told that the Kennedys had no plans for proposing any civil rights legislation in 1963. (An attempt to amend Senate Rule 22—the rule which facilitated filibustering—had failed and this, in the Kennedy view, presaged the worst for civil rights legislation.) Camelot's concerns remained centered on global matters.° In 1962, the trade expansion fight and the Cuban missile crisis engaged Washington as did President Kennedy's dispute with General de Gaulle over the future character of Europe and the

---

° This concern, however, gave the civil rights movement leverage. In his June 11, 1963, civil rights speech, President Kennedy used it as a rhetorical device: "Are we to say to the world—and much importantly to each other—that this is the land of the free, except for the Negroes; that we have no second-class citizens, except Negroes; that we have no class system or caste system, no ghettos, no master race, except to Negroes?"

limited nuclear test ban treaty in 1963, the following year. While King readily conceded that the Kennedy Administration "outstripped all previous ones in the breadth of its civil rights activities," he faulted Americans for their willingness to accept token victories as evidence of progress. "If tokenism were our goal," he excoriated, "this Administration has adroitly moved us toward its accomplishment. But tokenism can now be seen not only as a useless goal, but as a genuine menace. It is a palliative which relieves emotional distress, but leaves the disease and its ravages unaffected. It tends to demobilize and relax the militant spirit which alone drives us forward to real change."

The revival of militancy, howsoever necessary, was not to be left to happenstance, as in Albany. SCLC held a three-day strategy session at its Dorchester Center near Savannah, Georgia. Provisions were made for every contingency, including bail money, great chunks of which was raised through the efforts of singer Harry Belafonte. Seventy-five prominent friends of the civil rights movement were invited to the singer's New York City apartment for a briefing on "Project C" from King and Shuttlesworth. The latter grimly informed his awed listeners, "You have to die before you can begin to live." King, Abernathy, Walker, and Andrew Young met repeatedly with Shuttlesworth and Birmingham's black leadership to avoid wounding local sensibilities. Walker reconnoitered downtown Birmingham, noting means of access to each store, the number of seats at each lunch counter, and the like. With commendable caution, SCLC held demonstrations in abeyance throughout early 1963 pending the outcome of a mayorality election.

On April 2, 1963, citizens of Birmingham chose moderate Albert Boutwell as mayor over arch segregationist T. Eugene "Bull" Connor in a run-off election. The old administration of Mayor Arthur G. Hanes challenged the results on a technicality and continued in office while the question went to court. Black moderates, including the influential A. G. Gaston and Dr. J. L. Ware, head of the powerful Baptist Ministers Conference, counseled caution and urged the postponement of the direct action campaign until the moderate whites took office. But King pressed for an immediate start; as the ACMHR Manifesto stated: "This is Birmingham's moment of truth in which every citizen can play his part in her larger destiny."

Chief among those citizens, paradoxically, was the Commissioner of Public Safety. SCLC knew a good enemy when they saw one. The irascible "Bull" Connor could reasonably be expected to react so as to mobilize the black community and perhaps in turn to compel federal intervention. Success against Connor would heighten a victory sure to have widespread repercussions throughout the South if not the nation. At the start, however, Connor reacted mildly enough, perhaps attempting to emulate Albany's Police Chief Laurie Pritchett. Lunch counters were quickly closed on the first day, April 3, to avoid confrontation, and the day ended with the arrest of twenty or thirty blacks seeking integrated service at downtown lunch counters. Protest marches followed the aborted sit-ins. On Saturday, April 6, Shuttlesworth led a group to City Hall where forty-five were arrested. On the next day, Palm Sunday, the Reverend A. D. King, Martin's brother and a Birmingham minister, let twenty-five nonviolent pilgrims off to jail. As harbingers of intimidation and terror, police dogs snarled, tugging at their leashes as the police moved to disperse a crowd of onlookers. SCLC quickly evolved a tactic for maximizing the impact of small group arrests. As Wyatt Tee Walker explained to author Robert Penn Warren, "And here we are at the mercy of—they don't do it with malice—of the white press corps . . . . They can't distinguish between Negro demonstrators and Negro spectators. All they know is Negroes, and most of the spectacular pictures printed in *Life* and in television clips had the commentary 'Negro demonstrators' when they were not that at all." According to Walker, demonstrations were delayed for an hour or so until the crowd collected, swelling in one instance to fifteen hundred people. "They followed us twenty-three [demonstrators] down the street, and when the UPI took pictures they said: fifteen hundred demonstrators—twenty-two arrested. Well, that was all we had."

"Bull" Connor went easy on the demonstrators, counting on an injunction, secured by the city on April 10, to quell King and his followers as had a federal injunction in Albany. But the Birmingham injunction was obtained in a state court, and King did not feel similarly constrained. "The injunction method," he later wrote, "has now become the leading instrument of the South to block the direct-action civil rights drive and to prevent Negro citizens and their white allies from engaging in peaceful assembly, a right guaranteed by the First Amendment." King saw it as his "duty" to violate the injunction, and prepared to do so on Good Friday, April 12, 1963.

Dressed in denim trousers and a workshirt, a stylistic gesture toward the new militancy, King joined Abernathy, Shuttlesworth, and the blind singer Al Hibbler in leading fifty hymn-singing volunteers on a march from the Zion Hill Church to City Hall. "It seemed that every Birmingham police officer had been sent into the area," King wrote of the experience. "We started down the forbidden streets [lined by nearly a thousand spectators] that led to the downtown sector. It was a beautiful march. We were allowed to walk further than the police had ever permitted before." Such were the small victories of those now distant days.

The marchers were soon jailed, however. King and Abernathy were first placed in solitary confinement, but after a series of telephone calls by the anxious Mrs. King—including one to the President who assured Mrs. King of the government's interest in the safety of her husband and informed her that FBI agents were enroute to Birmingham—King was allowed to call his wife and jail conditions were improved for the arrested civil rights spokesmen. While in jail, King wrote his famous "Letter from a Birmingham Jail," a reply to eight Birmingham clergymen who had characterized King as an "outside agitator" and condemned the demonstrations as "unwise and untimely." King wryly retorted that, for blacks, "wait" had come to mean "never." As for the charge of extremism, he asked, "Was not Jesus an extremist for love?" Drawing on Christian ethics, he argued that as one ought to obey just laws one has the moral responsibility to disobey unjust laws, especially so if the minority bound by the unjust law had no part in its making. The Apostles, King said, were "outside agitators," and he deplored the white clergymen's silence about the conditions that brought the demonstrations into being. Firm in his faith in redemptive love and polite to the end, King closed on the prediction: "One day the South will know that when these disinherited children of God sat down at lunch counters they were in reality standing up for what is best in the American dream and for the most sacred values in our Judeo-Christian heritage."

While King's arrest aroused national concern—Washington cocked a worried eye at Birmingham and a collation of celebrities dispatched telegrams to the White House deploring the "brutal use of police dogs" against peaceful demonstrators—protests in Birmingham failed to materialize in the desired "massive nonviolent assault on segregation." On Easter Sunday, small groups of blacks sought admittance at six white churches, were admitted at two, the First Baptist and the First Presbyterian, and turned away at four. Rev. A. D. King led another prayer pilgrimage to the city jail. By the time of their arrest, a crowd of about two thousand had gathered and when the police attempted to arrest one of the shouting bystanders, rocks were thrown from the rear of the crowd. The police moved into the throng, clubs swinging. Patrol cars arrived bringing six large police dogs and the crowd rapidly melted away.

Unpublicized discussions between SCLC, the Alabama Council on Human Relations, local merchants, and the mayor-elect took place, but the white participants were reluctant to act without broader support from among Birmingham's industrial and business elite. King and Abernathy decided to accept bail on April 20, feeling a need to bolster faltering support and hoping for a way out of the impasse. King and his fellow defendants were tried on April 26 and fined $50 and sentenced to five days imprisonment. They were permitted twenty days in which to file an appeal. As *The New York Times* correspondent observed, "the mild sentences . . . obviously came as a surprise to Dr. King and the other defendants."

Birmingham, apparently, sought to emulate Albany in killing off demonstrations by "kindness," delays, legalities, and even negotiations. Officials favorably disposed toward the Albany way, however, reckoned not on "Bull" Connor or the segregationist fevers rampant in Birmingham and Albany. On April 24, William L. Moore, a 35-year-old eccentric white Baltimore mail carrier, was found murdered on a lonely Alabama road. He had been on a one-man freedom walk; his bullet-pierced body still held signs, one reading: "Equal Rights for All—Mississippi or Bust." When ten black and white members of CORE and SNCC crossed into Alabama on May 3, in an attempt to complete Moore's trek, they were arrested and poked with electric cattleprods by highway patrolmen as they lay limp, a nonviolent, noncooperative gesture, to the accompaniment of approving shouts from onlookers—"Kill them!" "Stick them again!" and "Throw them niggers in the river!"

Unable to mobilize the black masses of Birmingham, for there was considerable opposition to the timing and character of the demonstrations, SCLC resorted to a daring, if desperate tact—a children's crusade. (Criticized later by blacks and whites for using children, King retorted: "Where had [the critics] been with their protective words when down through the years Negro infants were born into ghettos, taking their first breath of life in a social atmosphere where the fresh air of freedom was crowded out by the stench of discrimination?") SCLC staff—James Bevel, Andrew Young, Bernard Lee, and Dorothy Cotton —went to the schools and recruited some six thousand youngsters willing to "walk to freedom." On May 2, shortly after noon, the first contingent of three hundred youngsters gathered at the Sixteenth Street Baptist Church. After exhortation from King and other SCLC leaders, they marched off in groups of ten to fifty, singing "We Shall Overcome." Cheered on by some four hundred spectators, they were intercepted by the police a scant two blocks away. Over a period of four hours, ten waves of children, aged six to sixteen, surged downtown. A few fled when arrest threatened, but most maintained discipline, dropping to their knees to pray as the police approached. On that day, 959 children were jailed along with ten adults.

"Bull" Connor was determined that there be no repetition. When a thousand volunteers jammed the Sixteenth Street Church the following day, the police appeared and barred the exits and succeeded in imprisoning about half the would-be demonstrators. Police dogs were released, and several young people were severely bitten as the police charged into the crowd escaping from the church. Firemen hosed down blacks, water at fifty to a hundred pounds of pressure tore a T-shirt off one youth's back, caused a cut around the eye of a young girl, and gave a woman a nosebleed. Rocks and bottles were thrown; a photographer and two firemen were hurt.

SCLC had its confrontation, and it succeeded. Burke Marshall flew in from Washington to talk and talk and talk, until, tentatively at first and then with greater assurance, negotiations began. In Washington, the indefatigable Attorney General used the telephone to head off the kind of crisis that would make federal intervention mandatory. Secretary of the Treasury C. Douglas Dillon and Defense Secretary Robert S. McNamara called influential Birmingham businessmen and industrialists, urging them to give full backing to Chamber of Commerce peace-making efforts headed by Sydney W. Smyer, a prominent real estate figure and president of the Chamber. Eugene V. Rostow, Dean of the Yale Law School and a presidential adviser, called a graduate, Roger Blough, board chairman of United States Steel, and asked that he intercede with his Birmingham associates, notably the president of the United States Steel subsidiary, the Tennessee Coal and Iron Company, in the interest of achieving a settlement.

Demonstrators thronged the streets daily. James Bevel quieted an unruly crowd on Saturday, May 4, fearing an outbreak of violence. Dick Gregory arrived from Chicago, and was arrested on Monday afternoon, and by Tuesday, over two thousand protestors were shoehorned into Birmingham jails. As the police repeatedly attempted to drive blacks back into the black section of the city, using hoses, dogs and clubs, blacks retaliated, jeering and taunting and by throwing rocks. Fred Shuttlesworth was knocked against the side of a building by a high pressure jet of water, and was taken to the hospital badly bruised. He had been trying to restore discipline, pacifying the unruly. There were few arrests, less than fifty, though at least a dozen were injured, including three police officers.

Negotiating whites requested a truce; "Bull" Connor requested state troopers from Governor George Wallace. Virtually the whole state highway patrol encamped on the outskirts of Birmingham, over 500, and 250 under Alabama's director of public safety, Albert J. Lingo, who had ordered the use of electric prods on the CORE/SNCC group not five days before, entered the city, itching for a bloody showdown.

Burke Marshall redoubled his efforts, reminding the whites of the minimal nature of black demands—a cup of coffee, token jobs, amnesty for demonstrators—while warning King against provoking the call for outside troops, saying that no outside force could impose a solution that ultimately had to come from within. King and his associates accepted a brief truce on condition that the details of a settlement be worked out during its term. King and Abernathy were then jailed, ostensibly to serve the sentence imposed for their Good Friday offense but in all likelihood as an act of provocation by bitter-end whites. Shuttlesworth prepared a march of thousands against the forces of Connor and Lingo but Joe Dolan, Marshall's assistant, managed to get the irate civil rights leader on the telephone to Robert Kennedy, who calmed him down with promises of unofficial intervention to get King and Abernathy released. Kennedy managed this, thereby averting a sure bloodbath.

Negotiations nearly broke up over the question of amnesty for the arrested demonstrators. The whites boggled at simply dismissing the charges while the blacks wanted their people out of jail no matter what. According to Ronald Goldfarb, a former Justice Department Criminal Division attorney, the negotiators called the Attorney General and asked what he could do to resolve the impasse. "Kennedy called Walter Reuther, who in turn sought the advice of Joseph Rauh . . . and the following plan was proposed: The AFL-CIO, the United Steelworkers Union, the Auto Workers Union, and the Industrial Union Department of the AFL-CIO each raised $40,000 . . . ." The $160,000 was wired to Birmingham, and 790 demonstrators still imprisoned were released on bonds totaling over a quarter million dollars.

"The city of Birmingham has reached an accord with its conscience," King, Shuttlesworth, and Abernathy informed the nation on Friday, May 10, 1963. The four-point settlement provided: 1) desegregation of lunch counters, rest rooms, fitting rooms, and drinking fountains in all downtown stores within ninety days; 2) placement of blacks in previously all-white clerical and sales positions in the stores, through up-grading or hiring, within sixty days; 3) release of prisoners; and 4) establishment of permanent communication between white and black leaders. King termed the agreement, "the most magnificent victory for justice we've ever seen in the Deep South." He cautioned, "We must move now from protest to reconciliation," urging his followers to "evince calm, dignity and wise restraint."

Predictably, lame-duck Mayor Arthur G. Hanes called the white negotiators "a bunch of quisling, gutless traitors." (A voice of militant black intellectuals, the monthly *Liberator,* condemned the "so-called agreement" as "a sell out.") The Ku Klux Klan held a rally on Saturday, May 11, just outside of Birmingham and at 11:15 that night two dynamite blasts demolished the front half of the home of Rev. A. D. King. Luckily, King, his wife, and five children escaped injury. Another explosion, roughly a half hour later, rocked the A. G. Gaston Motel, injuring four, fortunately only slightly. The younger King quickly defused the angry crowd that gathered outside his damaged home, and then hurried to join Wyatt Tee Walker at the motel in seeking to pacify the growing number of angry young men who had spilled out of nearby bars at the sound of the blast. "Throwing rocks won't help," Walker urged. "This is no good. Please go home." Back came the cry, "Tell it to 'Bull' Connor. This is what nonviolence gets you." Grocery stores were looted, burned. "Let the whole fucking city burn," a rioter shouted, a cry later echoed in the "Burn, baby, burn" of northern slums. "I don't give a goddamn—this'll show those white motherfuckers." Crowds rampaged through a nine-block area, smashing store windows, disabling police cars. Black civilian defense workers, white police and firemen, and SCLC leaders worked to bring the riot to an early end. State troopers poured in, and by seven in the morning an uneasy peace carpeted the area. Some fifty persons were injured, none seriously, and the *Birmingham News* estimated property damage at $41,775.

Exhausted, the city quieted down. Federal troops ordered to nearby bases were not needed, nor did the President need to federalize the Alabama National Guard. Martin Luther King, Jr., who had been in Atlanta visiting his family for the weekend, returned to counsel nonviolence and observance of the desegregation agreement. President Kennedy hailed the settlement as a "fair and just accord" and pointedly added, "the Federal Government will not permit it to be sabotaged."

On May 20, a United States Supreme Court decision involving sit-ins, in effect, nullified the convictions of Birmingham demonstrators arrested for defying local and state segregation laws. Three days later, the Alabama Supreme Court unanimously upheld the election of Mayor Albert Boutwell, and the reign of "Bull" Connor ended. It echoed again, tragically, on September 14, when white terrorists tossed a bomb through a window of the Sixteenth Street Baptist Church into the midst of a Sunday School class. Four young girls, ages eleven to fourteen, were killed, and twenty other children were injured by the blast. The bombing was a grim reminder of the persistence of white hatreds of blacks; it was also a desperate retaliatory burst from the defeated. The old order in Birmingham—and in much of the South—was cracked forever. Bombings, acts of terror, murder could not restore the old segregated ways or halt the changes set in motion by the Shuttlesworths, those whites willing to negotiate despite fear, and, above all, by the unknown people of great courage and quiet determination willing to go to jail for freedom.

Birmingham, Bayard Rustin passionately declared, "taught white America many lessons—not the least of them that Negroes were serious when they said they would fill the jails until southern cities were impoverished and that social dislocation is a reality that confronts all segregated institutions. . . . The Negro masses are no longer prepared to wait for anybody; not for elections, not to count votes, not wait on the Kennedys or for legislation, nor, in fact, for Negro leaders themselves. They are going to move. Nothing can stop them from moving. And if that Negro leadership does not move rapidly enough and effectively enough they will take it into their own hands and move anyhow."

Birmingham proved to be something of a catalyst. According to a Justice Department count, there were at least 758 demonstrations in 186 cities across the South in the ten weeks following the Birmingham confrontation. Press reports tallied by the Southern Regional Council indicate that some 14,733 persons were arrested in the eleven southern states for demonstrations, an impressive figure when compared to the 3,600 arrested at the height of the 1961 sit-ins. A Justice Department report of demonstrations for the period June 7 through June 13, 1963, gives some idea of the variety and flavor of direct action at the time:

June 14, 1963
Demonstrations for period June 7 through 13

ALABAMA Gadsden	300 demonstrators marched here on 6/12/63 protesting arrest of woman demonstrator.
CALIFORNIA Los Angeles	On 6/7/63 CORE picketed the Beverly Hilton Hotel.
WASHINGTON, D.C.	On 6/14/63 demonstrations at White House, District Building and Justice Department.
FLORIDA Bradenton	Beach closed 6/8/63 after demonstrations and whites milling around.
FLORIDA Sarasota	Negroes picketed downtown theaters on 6/7/63.
FLORIDA Tallahassee	Negroes picketed theaters. Demonstrating for the last two weeks, 6/12/63. Demonstration at State Office Building cafeteria on 6/7/63.
GEORGIA Atlanta	Demonstrations at cafeteria Saturday, 6/8/63. Fights started; 100 persons gathered to watch.
GEORGIA Savannah	About 300 Negroes on 6/13/63 marched with placards into downtown area demanding immediate desegregation. Shots fired at Negro home, no one was hit. Arrests in last 10 days passed the 500 mark. 3,000 demonstrated on 6/12/63.
MARYLAND Cambridge	More than 300 shouting white persons demonstrated. Both Negroes and whites marched, 6/13/63. Mayor has asked Governor Tawes to declare martial law, 6/14/63.
MARYLAND Ocean City	On 6/9/63 members of CORE conducted sit-in here. Re: restaurants.
MISSISSIPPI Jackson	Demonstrations continue after shooting of Medgar Evers. Police arrested 90 persons on 6/13/63.

MISSOURI	30 Negro parents blocked transportation,
St. Louis	demonstrations re: schools, 6/7/63.
NEW JERSEY	Some 700 prisoners at the Rahway, N.J., prison
Rahway	farm reported on sick call in what officials
	declared was a demonstration stemming from
	racial tensions, 6/10/63.
NEW YORK	Biracial demonstrators protesting alleged job
New York	discrimination fought with police 6/13/63 at
	the construction of Harlem Hospital.
NORTH CAROLINA	More than 1,000 Negroes demonstrated Friday
Greensboro	night 6/7/63, conducted a street "sit-in."
	Demanded desegregation.
NORTH CAROLINA	Mayor declared state of emergency Friday,
Lexington	6/7/63 as 500 whites battled about 50 Negroes
	who have been demonstrating.
OHIO	Demonstrations at State Legislature for fair
Columbus	housing bill on 6/13/63.
RHODE ISLAND	250 Negroes and whites jammed House
Providence	galleries 6/13/63, demonstrating for fair
	housing bill.
SOUTH CAROLINA	100 Negro demonstrators were arrested while
Beaufort	attempting to get service at restaurant. More
	than 300 have been arrested in week-long drive,
	6/10/63.
SOUTH CAROLINA	Thirty-three Negroes were arrested on 6/13/63
Charleston	for trespassing after seeking services at a hotel
	and drugstore lunch counter.
TENNESSEE	Police arrested 12 demonstrators at grocery
Nashville	store, demonstrating for jobs, 6/7/63.
TEXAS	200 demonstrated against desegregation of
Texarkana	Texarkana Junior College, paraded into
	downtown district. No arrests.
VIRGINIA	More than 250 Negro demonstrators jammed
Danville	into the Municipal Building steps 6/13/63 and
	requested some to hear desegregation demands.
	Demonstrations occurred for past two weeks.

Events—and a people in motion—conspired to force the Kennedy Administration to take a stand on civil rights, though reluctantly.[*]

---

[*] In *Kennedy Justice*, Victor Navasky quotes Burke Marshall as recalling: "When President Kennedy sent up that [1963 civil rights] bill every single person who spoke about it in the White House—everyone of them—was against President Kennedy sending up that bill; against his speech in June; against making it a moral issue; against the March on Washington. The conclusive voice within the government at that time, there's no question about it at all, that Robert Kennedy was the one. He urged it, he felt it, he understood it. And he prevailed. I don't think there was anybody in the Cabinet—except the President himself—who felt that way on these issues, and the President got it from his brother." Vice President Lyndon Baines Johnson also deserves some credit.

When Federal District Court Justice Hobart H. Grooms ordered the University of Alabama to admit two black applicants, Vivian Malone and James A. Hood, to its summer session beginning on June 10, Governor George C. Wallace, newly elected on a segregationist platform, indicated that he would carry out his campaign pledge to "stand in the schoolhouse door" to halt integration. Working out a hastily improvised script, the Alabaman did indeed stand in a university doorway with an upraised hand to turn away a federal party escorting the two students to register. The President federalized the Alabama Guard—three thousand army troops were on stand-by orders at military installations within the state—and on the arrival of troops, the governor walked off stage and the two black students were registered on June 11 without incident.

That evening, the President of the United States went on television to discuss civil rights. After reviewing in moving terms the plight of America's downtrodden black minority, he asked, "Who among us would then be content with the counsels of patience and delay?" Events in Birmingham and elsewhere, the President said, "have so increased the cries for equality that no city or state or legislative body can prudently choose to ignore them. The fires of frustration and discord are burning in every city, north and south. Where legal remedies are not at hand, redress is sought in the streets in demonstrations, parades and protests, which create tensions and threaten violence—and threaten lives." Seeking to channel these politically explosive emotions, President Kennedy urged: "We face, therefore, a moral crisis as a country and a people. It cannot be met by repressive police action. It cannot be left to increased demonstrations in the streets. It cannot be quieted by token moves or talks. It is a time to act in the Congress, in your state and local legislative body, and, above all, in all our daily lives."

It was, as Arthur M. Schlesinger, Jr., later remarked, "a magnificent speech in a week of magnificent speeches." Even so great a talk before so large an audience no longer sufficed. Good intentions were "blown with restless violence round about the pendant world." And, as the summer of 1963 ran out its fateful course, it seemed likely that even a far superior civil rights measure than ever before proposed could not halt the beast of confrontation slouching toward an American Armageddon. Shortly after midnight, the day of the President's civil rights speech, Medgar Wiley Evers, the 37-year-old, husky, courageous Mississippi field secretary of the NAACP, was gunned down by a sniper as he returned home from a mass meeting. His funeral touched off a bitter, though brief riot on June 15. Luckily, John Doar of the Justice Department was on hand to assist black leaders in calming the angry black youth of Jackson, Mississippi. Claude S. Sutton of *The New York*

Times encapsulated the new mood in a telling quote from a black youth: "The only way to stop evil here is to have a revolution. Somebody have got to die."

XI

March On Washington: 1963

LIKE UNTOLD NUMBERS OF his fellow Americans on August 28, 1963, the President of the United States watched on television portions of the March on Washington for Jobs and Freedom. John F. Kennedy had every reason to be pleased, or so he believed. He marveled, as nearly everyone did, at the spirit and self-discipline of the marchers, some 210,000 strong, as they moved from the Washington Monument to assemble before the Lincoln Memorial. "One cannot help but be impressed," he declared in a statement on the march, "with the deep fervor and the quiet dignity that characterizes the thousands who have gathered in the nation's capital from across the country to demonstrate their faith and confidence in our democratic forms of government." While that was not precisely the reason the marchers had gathered in so large a number, the march had gone well. The country heaved a sigh of relief that there was no violence and gave itself over to paeons of praise of the marchers' orderliness and demeanor. The March for Jobs and Freedom became a celebration, which, of course, was only part of its truth.

Though he now welcomed the march as advancing "the cause of 20,000,000 Negroes," President Kennedy originally opposed it—and with cause. His fear of disruption and violence was real and rooted not only in the growing white backlash but also in the uncertain temper of the country's black communities. The Kennedy name was an anathema in the South, and white retaliatory violence had escalated. Fifty civil rights marchers were cornered in a Danville, Virginia, alley one evening in early June by white police, firemen, and deputies, and beat unmercifully. Whites and blacks clashed in Cambridge, Maryland, and elsewhere. Black and white moderates were under pressure to act more militantly. Roy Wilkins, the epitome of black moderation, was arrested while picketing a Woolworth store along with the late Medgar Evers. The Reverend Dr. Eugene Carson Blake, a dignified churchman and the chief executive officer of the United Presbyterian Church in the United States, was arrested while marching with an interracial CORE group cracking the color line at Baltimore's Gwyn Oak Park. Some 125,000 blacks and whites marked the anniversary of the 1943 Detroit race riot, which took thirty-four lives and injured a thousand or more, with a Freedom Walk on June 23. Martin Luther King, Jr., marched arm-in-arm with Walter P. Reuther in a show of black and white solidarity. A week later, black extremists threw eggs at King during a Harlem visit.

New voices were being raised—and heard. Charismatic Malcolm X, thirty-seven, ruggedly handsome, tall, light-skinned, with coldly appraising eyes behind horn-and-steel rimmed glasses, preached "God's wrathful judgment [on] this white man stumbling and groping blindly in wickedness and evil and spiritual darkness." With contempt for the middle-class black, "one installment away from disaster," Malcolm X had nothing but scorn for "integration," a word, he said, "invented by a northern liberal." It is, he added, writing in his *Autobiography of Malcolm X*, "a foxy northern liberal's smokescreen that confuses the true wants of the American black man." He appealed to black pride in the hopes of building black power and self-reliance. "As other ethnic groups have done," he wrote, "let the black people, wherever possible, however possible, patronize their own kind, hire their own kind, and start in those ways to build up the black race's ability to do for itself. That's the only way the American black man is ever going to get respect . . . . The black man in the ghettos, for instance, has to start self-correcting his own material, moral, and spiritual defects and evils. The black man needs to start his own program to get rid of drunkenness, drug addiction, prostitution. The black man in America has to lift up his own sense of values." Malcolm X also dared strike a very American note on behalf of blacks—the right to bear arms in self-defense.

Evil suffered patiently as inevitable, De Tocqueville observed in *L'Ancien Regime*, "seems unendurable as soon as the idea of escaping from it is conceived." Malcolm X articulated that anguish in a cascading anger. "Four hundred years the white man has had his foot-long knife in the black man's back—and now the white man starts to *wiggle* the knife out, maybe six inches! The black man's supposed to be *grateful?* Why, if the white man jerked the knife *out*, it's still going to leave a scar!"

In his *Autobiography*, Malcolm evidences mixed feelings toward violence, shading from violence as necessary defense to violence as a catharsis. "Negroes have the right to fight against [white] racists by any means that are necessary." And "I *believe* in anger. The Bible says there is a *time* for anger." The black condition, as it were, sanctioned violence: "It takes no one to strike up the sociological dynamite that stems from the unemployment, bad housing, and inferior education already in the ghettos. This explosively criminal condition has existed for so long, it needs no fuses; it fuses itself, it spontaneously combusts from within tiself . . . ." Such were the times, however, that all of white America—and much of black America—could hear only the incitement to violence that emanated from Malcolm X.

The civil rights revolution opened a sociological Pandora's box. Bayard Rustin and other black spokesmen and theoreticians began talking and writing about "the street Negro." CORE and SNCC courted his favor; the NAACP and SCLC, too, competed for his allegiance. "America's most dangerous and threatening black man is the one who has been kept sealed up by the Northerner in the black ghettos," Malcolm declaimed. And many agreed with him. Black rhetoric ballooned. The inner-city slums reached a condition described by sociologist Lewis A. Coser, "Since the lower class tends to rely more exclusively on external restraints, their removal through the revolution furnishes a socially sanctioned outlet for aggression." *Time* magazine quoted Cecil Moore, the 48-year-old head of the Philadelphia branch of the NAACP, as boasting, "My basic strength is those 300,000 lower class guys who are ready to mob, rob, steal and kill." The Reverend Gardner Taylor of Brooklyn's black Concord Baptist Church, predicted, "Miscalculation of the moment of truth which is upon us could plunge New York, Brooklyn, Philadelphia, Chicago, Detroit and Los Angeles into a crimson carnage and a blood bath unparalleled in the history of the nation."

When President Kennedy first heard of the proposed March on Washington, there was talk of a mass sit-in in the legislative galleries, of street stall-ins, of lie-ins on airport runways, and of an encampment on the White House lawn. The specter of thousands of milling, angry blacks threw Washington into a tizzy. That this is not what blacks or their spokesmen had in mind was beside the point. President Kennedy was understandably worried about the possibility of civil disruption and the probable congressional backlash. "We want success in Congress," he told civil rights leaders at a White House meeting, "not just a big show at the Capitol. Some of these people are looking for an excuse to be against us. I don't want to give any of them a chance to say, 'Yes, I'm for the [civil rights] bill, but I'm damned if I will vote for it at the point of a gun.' It seemed to me a great mistake to announce a march on Washington before the bill was even in committee. The only effect is to create an atmosphere of intimidation—and this may give some members of Congress an out."

The President met with the civil rights leaders on June 22, the day before he left for Europe on a triumphal tour.° Since plans for the march were already well underway, the President could not, reasonably, expect the demonstration to be called off. He acknowledged, in a backhanded way, that direct action demonstrations had brought results, saying at one point in the discussion, "I don't think you should be totally harsh on 'Bull' Connor. He has done more for civil rights than almost anybody else." Still, there was such a thing as a "wrong demonstration at the wrong time." In the present phase, "the legislative phase," as he put it, "To get the votes we need, we have, first, to oppose demonstrations which will lead to violence, and second, give Congress a fair chance to work its will." Ever political, the President cited a recent poll showing that national approval of the administration had fallen from 60 to 47 percent. Vice President Lyndon Johnson made the congressional calculation for the benefit of the visitors: "We have about 50 votes in the Senate and about 22 against us. What counts is the 26 or so votes which remain. To get those votes we have to be careful not to do anything which would give those who are privately opposed a public excuse to appear as martyrs. We have to sell the program in twelve crucial states—and we have less than twelve weeks."

The black spokesmen present readily acknowledged the political realities, but also made it clear that they, too, had their constituencies to worry about.°° "The Negroes are already in the streets," A. Philip Randolph gravely informed the President and his advisers. "It is very likely impossible to get them off. If they are bound to be in the streets in any case, is it not better that they be led by organizations dedicated to civil rights and disciplined by struggle rather than to leave them to other leaders who care neither about civil rights nor about nonviolence? If the civil rights leadership were to call the Negroes off the streets, it is

---

° President Kennedy, according to Theodore C. Sorenson, "valued the trip partly because it did interrupt the nation's attention to this problem [of civil rights]. Too much attention, he believed, would accelerate demands and expectations more rapidly than they could be fulfilled, and thereby increase tensions during a long, hot summer." The President was sharply criticized by black leaders for taking off for Europe at a time of domestic turmoil over civil rights. Yet, as Sorenson points out, the President had other problems, a fact civil rights activists were prone to overlook. There was a tax bill, the Test Ban Treaty, a threatened railroad strike and a *coup d'état* in the works in Vietnam. Yet, there is an ordering of priorities and it is clear that civil rights was only moved up the ladder after demonstrations had increased in number and intensity.

°° And their constituents did not live in the twelve states that worried Kennedy and Johnson. Excepting the South, blacks lived and voted in congressional districts whose representatives and senators were strongly pro-civil rights. One could predict that continued demonstrations in the South would only reinforce southern opposition in Congress to civil rights measures while strengthening northern support. Up to a point—one not reached at the time of the March on Washington—demonstrations in the North would increase the zeal of northern congressmen for civil rights legislation while the reaction of those from states with few black residents remained, as Vice President Johnson pointed out, problematical.

problematic whether they would come." James Farmer reinforced Randolph's argument: "We would be in a difficult if not untenable position if we called the street demonstrations off and then were defeated in the legislative battle. The result would be that frustration would grow into violence and would demand new leadership." Martin Luther King, Jr., said that it was "not a matter of either/or but of both/and." The March on Washington, he added, could serve as a nonviolent channel of "legitimate discontents" as well as a dramatization of the issues. "It may seem ill-timed," he said. "Frankly, I have never engaged in any direct action movement which did not seem ill-timed. Some people thought Birmingham ill-timed." The President's wry interjection, "Including the Attorney General," was, in Kennedy fashion, an acceptance of the inevitability of the march.

At a mid-July press conference, after his return from Europe, the President noted that the march was not "a march on Washington" but rather "in the great tradition" of peaceful assembly "for a redress of grievances." He "looked forward to being here. I am sure members of Congress will be here. We want citizens to come to Washington if they feel that they're not having their rights expressed." Shortly before the march, he expressed a fear that the sponsors might not be able to muster the one hundred thousand people promised. If it fell short of that goal, he remarked, it might persuade some members of Congress that the demand for action on civil rights was greatly exaggerated—and perhaps he sensed that the larger the turnout the more propitious the moment. As columnist Murray Kempton perceptively observed, "The White House knew that the ordinary Negro cherished the Kennedy brothers and that the larger the assemblage the better disposed it would be not to embarrass them."

A. Philip Randolph had nurtured the idea of a mass march on Washington ever since his "magnificent bluff" of 1941. Bayard Rustin raised the question of a Washington mass demonstration with Randolph following the modest youth marches of 1958 and 1959. The sit-ins and Freedom Rides and the broader civil rights struggles in the South preempted the stage, however. The idea was broached again during the winter of 1962–1963. Randolph asked Bayard Rustin, then executive secretary of the War Resisters' League, to draft a memorandum outlining the proposed march in detail. Working with Norman Hill, then an assistant program director of CORE, and Tom Kahn, a leader of the Young People's Socialist League, Rustin drafted a detailed blueprint for a Washington protest. Convinced that second-class citizenship could only be eliminated through changes in the economy and social structure, the three stressed economic demands. What began as a "revolt for dignity," they argued, had acquired new dimensions. As

Kahn put it in a brilliant League for Industrial Democracy pamphlet on "The Economics of Equality," "Did the *right* to use public accommodation amount to much without the *means* to exercise that right? What difference did the integration of hotels and restaurants make to the unemployed black worker?" Such questions were not academic. While overall unemployment rates hovered around 5 percent from 1960 to 1964, the rate for black workers rose above 12 percent. In many cities, the rate was well above that figure, as high as 30 percent in such places as Birmingham, Alabama, and Cambridge, Maryland. At the bottom of the skills ladder, newly urbanized blacks were particularly vulnerable to the inroads of automation. The median income of blacks (then $3,191 a year) had slipped from 57 to 53 percent of that of whites in less than a decade. Hence, there was a need to concentrate on what Kahn termed "the entangled problems of jobs, housing, and education."

As the march took shape, it changed character. Civil rights demands were given precedence over economic demands. As late as July 2, a memo outlining the six "purposes" of the march led off "to arouse the conscience of America to the plight of the Negro 100 years after emancipation." The demand for "an effective and meaningful civil rights bill" and a "protest against any filibuster" were listed last. These demands were placed first in Organizing Manuals, numbers one and two, issued in July and August respectively.° What had been thought of

---

° The final demands, as spelled out in *Organizing Manual No. 2* issued shortly before the march, were:

"1. Comprehensive and effective *civil rights legislation* from the present Congress—without compromise or filibuster—to guarantee all Americans

    access to all public accommodations
    decent housing
    adequate and integrated education
    the right to vote

"2. Withholding of federal funds from all programs in which discrimination exists.

"3. *Desegregation of all school districts in 1963.*

"4. Enforcement of the *Fourteenth Amendment*—reducing congressional representation of states where citizens are disenfranchised.

"5. A new *Executive Order* banning discrimination in all housing supported by federal funds.

"6. Authority for the Attorney General to institute *injunctive suits* when any constitutional right is violated.

"7. A massive federal program to train and place all unemployed workers—Negro and white—on meaningful and dignified jobs at decent wages.

"8. A national *minimum wage* act that will give all Americans a decent standard of living. (Government surveys show that anything less than $2.00 an hour fails to do this.)

"9. A broadened *Fair Labor Standards Act* to include all areas of employment which are presently excluded.

"10. A federal *Fair Employment Practices Act* barring discrimination by federal, state, and municipal governments, and by employers, contractors, employment agencies, and trade unions."

Then there is appended this footnote:

as a march of the unemployed became a march of the middle class for "jobs and freedom now!" The organizers, however, persisted to the very last in their efforts to mobilize the unemployed. Organizations were urged, in the Organizing Manuals, "to make it a *main task* to get the news of the march to the unemployed," to establish unemployed march committees, and to make it a goal "to send *one* unemployed to Washington for every *three* who can pay their way." Plans to feature the unemployed at the march, however, were hastily dropped, presumably because of the paucity of the out-of-work present.° And, finally, a proposed "massive demonstration" at the White House was dropped.

Malcolm X credited President Kennedy with the orchestration of the march, and there is some truth to the observation. Kennedy's submission of a civil rights bill to Congress on June 19 precipitated the march, while the possibility of a filibuster gave it political focus. The presidential caution against "demonstrations which can lead to violence" and strictures about "undue pressures and unruly tactics" were heeded. Yet, the ultimate character of the march was shaped by pressures within the civil rights movement and determined by the overwhelming need for unity of effort in the push for congressional action on civil rights legislation.

Writing in *New Politics*, historian August Meier makes the point that the competitive rivalry among civil rights organizations, "a power struggle for hegemony," had been "an essential ingredient of the dynamics of the Negro protest movement." In the attempt to outdo one another, Meier wrote, "each organization puts forth a greater effort and is constantly searching for new avenues along which to develop programs." While there was, in Meier's phrase, "cooperation in rivalry," there was, too, considerable sniping at one another within the civil rights movement. The NAACP, it was said, was not militant enough, and when Martin Luther King's SCLC took the initiative in the South, the NAACP lost members. Wilkins countered, with considerable justification, that CORE, SCLC, and SNCC grabbed "the publicity while the NAACP furnishes the manpower and pays the bills." In Louisville, Kentucky, for example, the NAACP, CORE, and a voter registration group mounted a boycott of downtown stores and along with parades and mass arrests won desegregation. Most of the demonstrators were NAACP members, and the campaign cost the local chapter some $6,000 while CORE copped the credit. When King accepted bail in Albany, SNCC quickly pointed the finger, and King,

---

"Support of the march does not necessarily indicate endorsement of every demand listed. Some organizations have not had an opportunity to take an official position on all of the demands advocated here."

° Data from a survey conducted by the Bureau of Social Science Research, Inc., at the march show "less than 3 percent of Negro marchers to have been unemployed."

most observers agreed, lost prestige. Yet, King's success at raising money was phenomenal, a fact that raised no little jealousy within the movement.

Credit for struggles embarked and victories won was essential to the attraction of membership and funds. Competition consequently tended to increase militance, which, no doubt, was a good thing, upsetting apathy and involving more and more blacks in the struggle for civil rights. Yet, competition could be erosive and divisive. A striving for militancy for militancy's sake posed problems of discipline; a runaway rash of demonstrations could jeopardize a major goal of the civil rights movement—an effective civil rights law. It was one of Randolph's strengths that as the grand old man he was considered above the rivalries that plagued the movement, and it was the need to demonstrate to Congress—and the country at large—that the movement was united on the question of a strong civil rights bill that made the March on Washington desirable and possible.

Initially, Roy Wilkins was skeptical. He was not a marcher by temperament, nor did he believe in mass demonstrations without a specific objective. As he told waiting reporters after the civil rights leadership meeting with the President, "I have never proposed sit-ins at the Capitol. I have said that any demonstrations, in Washington or elsewhere, should have specific, not general objectives." While the NAACP was not, as of June 23, committed to the march (announced publicly earlier in the week), Wilkins did say he might be sympathetic if a filibuster developed in the Senate against the President's proposed civil rights act. CORE was already committed, and King declared: "If there is a filibuster in Congress, we will have a nonviolent, peaceful demonstration in Washington."

Jockeying over the character of the proposed march continued behind the scenes during the last weeks of June and early July. Cleveland Robinson, secretary-treasurer of District 65 of the Retail, Wholesale, and Department Store Union and chairman of the Negro-American Labor Committee,° announced on June 21 that one hundred thousand blacks would march on Capitol Hill. He and the Reverend George Lawrence of the SCLC were named "coordinators" of the march. The Emergency Commission on Religion and Race of the National Council of Churches, formed earlier in June, met the same day and announced that it would participate in the march if southern Senators filibustered against President Kennedy's civil rights message. On the twenty-fifth, Lawrence announced at a church rally in New York City that a date had been set for the march—August 28—at a

---

° Cleveland Robinson replaced Randolph, who "retired" as active head of the NALC in November 1962.

meeting of SCLC, SNCC, CORE, and NALC representatives the day before. Groups from twenty-eight cities, he said, were committed to take part.

Southern delegates to the CORE convention, held during the last week in June, reported a rising fear of violence, saying that blacks were coming armed to many demonstrations. Reporters at the convention noted a mood of uncertainty, but also a consensus that demonstrations must continue regardless of risks. CORE endorsed the march, rejecting the administration's admonitions about continuing demonstrations. Responding to a militant and buoyant mood at the NAACP convention in Chicago the first week in July, Roy Wilkins declared the convention theme to be "accelerate, accelerate, accelerate" the civil rights attack. He predicted that the convention would stimulate demonstrations throughout the country and that the March on Washington would be carried out.

In part, Wilkins had come around to the support of the march in response to the increase in militancy within the NAACP. This, in turn, had been stimulated by the competition with the new and more direct-action oriented civil rights organizations on the scene—CORE, SCLC, and SNCC. Wilkins, too, hoped that a mass demonstration might cause the administration to beef up what he considered to be an "inadequate for the times" civil rights measure. (It lacked a fair employment practices provision.) And, finally, the march sponsors had agreed to focus on civil rights—in effect, it was to be a march against filibuster—and to drop plans for acts of civil disobedience. While Randolph had chosen Bayard Rustin to direct the march, Wilkins opposed the choice, fearing that Rustin's radical background as a pacifist with a decided direct-action bent might color the march not to his liking and leave it open to unnecessary attacks. In courtly fashion, Randolph and Wilkins sparred over the leadership question until they found a mutually acceptable formula. Randolph would be the director of the march, fully empowered to choose his own deputy. Randolph, as both men knew he would, chose Rustin.

Elegant, urbane, with a large, high-cheekboned face, expressive beneath a bushy shock of hair, Rustin, at fifty-three, was an articulate strategist of the democratic left. He had served as an adviser to Martin Luther King, was well versed in the tactics of nonviolence, and as executive secretary of the War Resisters' League was something of a free-lance agitator. Born on March 17, 1910, in West Chester, Pennsylvania, a community of some fifteen thousand roughly twenty miles west of Philadelphia where the Quakers had relocated many black freedmen before the Civil War, Rustin was raised by his grandparents. His great-grandfather had been a slave in nearby Maryland. His grandmother was two-thirds Delaware Indian and had been raised by

Quakers. Rustin's grandfather worked for the Elks and catered on the side. Rustin learned something of pacifism from his Quaker grandmother; the family, however, was brought up within the African Methodist Church.

Young Bayard attended a segregated grade school and an integrated high school, where he played left guard on the football team. He was a track star, a champion in tennis, and class valedictorian. After graduation, he attended Wilberforce in Ohio, and then left for Cheyney State Teachers' College in Pennsylvania where he got a better scholarship. Later he came to New York City, where a "sister/aunt" taught in the public schools, and he attended City College at night. Somewhere along the line, he picked up an elegant diction, with a clipped quasi-British cadence, which became so much a part of him that he is often taken for a West Indian. If one listens carefully, however, one can detect the Philadelphian, or Eastern Pennsylvanian in his pronunciation of "ou" words like "about."

To earn money, Rustin sang with Leadbelly and Josh White at Café Society Downtown. Friends treasure two rare recordings made for the Fellowship of Reconciliation fifteen years ago. One features Bayard, a countertenor, singing Elizabethan and folk songs; the other includes a narration by James Farmer while Rustin sings spirituals and protest songs. Rustin plays the piano, harpsichord, lute, lyre, and guitar and sometimes entertains friends with a talk on the history of Negro music and how sorrow songs led to jazz.

Rustin joined the Young Communist League in 1938. "They appeared genuinely interested in peace and in racial justice," Rustin has explained. During the Stalin-Hitler Pact, Rustin was asked to form a committee against discrimination in the armed forces. The day after Hitler turned East, Rustin was called in and told to dismantle the committee. He refused, and decided to quit the party and managed to do so just before it expelled him.

When A. Philip Randolph organized his first march on Washington, threatening to bring hundreds of thousands of Negroes to Washington unless fair-employment practices were instituted in the nation's defense industries, Rustin volunteered to work with Randolph and became youth organizer for the march. As a conscientious objector, Rustin might have chosen to go to a work camp during the war, but since only religious objectors enjoyed that privilege, Rustin chose protest and went to jail in 1942, where he served twenty-eight months. While in prison, Rustin's adherence to the tenets of nonviolence was severely tested on numerous occasions. He is, after all, a large man, and it isn't easy for the physically strong to restrain themselves when attacked. Yet, Rustin stopped a giant bloodthirsty Southerner dead in his tracks by offering the man a chance to clobber him.

After the war, Rustin gravitated toward civil rights activity while keeping up his peace work. Between his participation in the first Freedom Ride in 1947, helping Randolph organize against discrimination in the armed forces, and logging up a record of twenty-four arrests for civil rights activities, he served as chairman of the Free India Committee, put in time in Ghana, Nigeria, and Tanganyika, where he worked with Kwame Nkrumah, Dr. Nnamdi Azikiwe, and Julius Nyere. He also helped organize the 1957 Aldermaston peace march in England. If such a phrase can be used about Rustin, for a time following his resignation as adviser to Martin Luther King, Rustin had been rather at loose ends. Rumors were circulated in the black community that he was a draft-dodging communist and of loose moral habits. Just about the only respected black leader who kept up his friendship with Rustin was Randolph, who simply said, "I will not hear that discussed in my presence." Rustin had won Randolph's trust; his abilities and talents were put to a new test by the formidable task of organizing the March on Washington in something less than eight weeks.

Operating out of a ramshackle office on West 130th Street in Harlem, a lithe bundle of energy, smoking far too many cigarettes, Rustin pulled together diverse groups into what Walter Reuther called "a coalition of conscience." The march struck a responsive chord. Church groups, like the Presbytery of New York, looking for some way to express support of civil rights, decided to join. As George Dugan reported in the July 7 *New York Times*, "almost overnight America's religious forces have switched from mere verbal condemnation of racial discrimination to active, personal participation in the fight against it." The formal announcement, so to speak, of march plans was made at a meeting of the Leadership Conference on Civil Rights on July 3. Seven black organizations gave their backing—the NAACP, SCLC, the Urban League, the National Committee of Negro Women, the NAACP Legal Defense and Education Fund and SNCC (CORE was already involved). Altogether some one hundred civil, labor, and religious organizations announced their support that day of Kennedy's civil rights bill and their agreement to support the march. Wilkins said that participants would march down Pennsylvania Avenue and rally at the Lincoln Memorial. The original "big six"—Randolph, Wilkins, Young, King, Farmer, and Lewis—were joined as sponsors of the march by Mathew Ahmann, executive director of the National Catholic Conference for Interracial Justice, the Reverend Dr. Eugene Carson Blake, of the United Presbyterian Church and vice-chairman of the Commission on Religion and Race of the National Council of Churches of Christ in America, Rabbi Joachim Prinz, President of the American Jewish Congress, and Walter P. Reuther, president of the United Auto Workers and chairman of the Industrial Union Department of the AFL-CIO.

Some plans went awry. The hoped for endorsement of the march by the AFL-CIO did not materialize. Randolph, who can be cavalier on occasions, did not always follow the detailed instructions meticulously set out in Rustin's memoranda. As Walter Reuther pointed out in his argument at the AFL-CIO Executive Council meeting on August 12, while the AFL-CIO "was not consulted prior to the announcing and setting of the date . . . , everyone was in somewhat the same position." (Rustin quotes a black leader as saying, when approached, "Damn that Phil Randolph! If only he'd talk with us first before putting us in the position where we can't say we aren't going along with these damn things he wants." Brusquely, Meany said, "We'll do our work on the Hill. Let them do what they want." The AFL-CIO's executive council's statement endorsed civil rights, recognized "the right of these organizations to go to Washington," the right of affiliated unions to participate, and expressed "the hope that the march will be helpful and peaceful." As Meany explained the AFL-CIO's stand to Jervis Anderson, author of Randolph's biography, "While we did not object to any of our affiliates participating, we were worried that the march might touch off a situation which might set us back legislatively. I was fearful that there would be disorder, that people would get hurt, and that it would build up resentment in Congress."

There was opposition to the march, and not only the muted opposition of the Kennedys. Arthur B. Spingarn, serving his twenty-fourth year as president of the NAACP, expressed doubts about the wisdom of the march, fearing an adverse reaction from senators wavering on the President's civil rights measure. James Meredith, recently hailed as the hero of the integration of "Ole Miss," considered the march "inadvisable." A Gallup Poll, taken in early August, found 63 percent of the public "unfavorable" to the march, although many were sympathetic to civil rights goals. Under Secretary of Commerce Franklin D. Roosevelt, Jr., appearing on the television show, *Youth Wants to Know*, doubted that the march would have a positive effect. Echoing the Kennedy line, he said Congress should be allowed to work without pressure. Senator George Aiken of Vermont said, "I guarantee that there will be no legislation this year if any effort is made to intimidate Congress by bringing 300,000 people up there to sit on the Capitol lawn." *The New York Times* warned that the march might be "a highly volatile affair." Liberal Congressman Emanuel Cellar, Democrat of New York, expressed fear that the proposed march might cause uncommitted legislators to oppose the President's civil rights bill. Several southern senators expressed hopes that there would be a riot at the march, which, they admitted, would hurt the civil rights cause. And the New York *Herald-Tribune* trumpeted, "The March Should Be Stopped."

Once the civil rights leadership determined that the march should go on, support mounted rapidly. Fourteen major Jewish, civic, religious, labor, and fraternal organizations endorsed the march and urged members to participate. Mayor Robert F. Wagner of New York City announced that he would attend and proclaimed August 28 "Jobs and Freedom Day." Some one thousand employees of the City's Welfare Department pledged their participation as did ten thousand Pennsylvanian NAACP members. Robert S. Pike of the National Council of Churches predicted that 30,000 to 45,000 Protestants, including clergy, would be in Washington on August 28. Cardinal Cushing named eleven priests from the Boston area as marchers. The leaders of the major Protestant denominations declared that they would be on hand on the great day. New York locals of the International Ladies' Garment Workers' Union, AFL-CIO, offered to pay the fare of all members wishing to go on the march. Rachelle Horowitz reported to Rustin on August 22 that twenty-one trains were scheduled to bring 20,500 people from points West—Chicago, Cincinnati, Detroit, and Pittsburgh—points Northeast—Boston, New York, and Philadelphia—and points South—Savannah and Jacksonville; 4 planes would carry 1,400 from Los Angeles, Seattle, Denver, Chicago, Cleveland, Buffalo, Grand Rapids, and seven other cities; and 812 buses would sweep in from all over the country to carry in 45,810 more people. March leaders began talking of 100,000 to 200,000 in attendance. And when New York City parishioners went to mass on the Sunday before the march, they heard their priests recommend that they take part. As the *Catholic News* put it, "The moral issue impels us now."

The march exceeded all expectations. People poured in from the far corners of the country and from the meanest city block within the nation's capital. Some 210,000 to 250,000, possibly more, black and white Americans came on August 28, 1963, to present their living petition for jobs and freedom. Most were black, roughly 70 to 80 percent. They assembled at the Washington Monument and marched with admirable dignity to the Lincoln Memorial for a long afternoon of speech making. In a courtly baritone, A. Philip Randolph began, "Let the nation and the world know the meaning of our numbers. We are not a pressure group, we are not an organization for a group of organizations, we are not a mob. We are the advance guard of a massive moral revolution for jobs and freedom." Roy Wilkins picked up the theme, and pressed home the need for a fair employment practices provision in the proposed civil rights bill before Congress. "The President," he said, "should join us in fighting for something more than pap." Whitney Young reminded the audience that there still was work to be done "back home" for civil rights. James Farmer scored points on militancy by his absence—at the time of the march, he was in jail in Palquemine,

Louisiana, for leading a demonstration against segregation. John Lewis of SNCC came prepared to deliver an angry denunciation, a mild foretaste of the ricocheting rhetoric of the later 1960s. "We will not wait," Lewis originally planned to say, "for the President, the Justice Department, nor the Congress, but we will take matters into our own hands and create a source of power, outside of any national structure, that could and would assure us a victory . . . . We will march through the South, through the heart of Dixie, the way Sherman did. We shall pursue our own 'scorched earth' policy and burn Jim Crow to the ground—nonviolently." Archbishop O'Boyle got wind of these fiery imprecations, and said he would not give the invocation if Lewis went on as phrased. Lewis was persuaded, in the interest of harmony and the lobbying needs of the moment, to tone down his remarks. He remained angry, but restrained. While condemning the "immoral compromising" of politicians, he cushioned his threat of a march through the South, "if we do not get meaningful legislation," saying, "But we will march with the spirit of love and the spirit of dignity that we have shown here today." Martin Luther King capped the day with his magnificent, memorable, and soaring speech, "I have a dream . . . . This is our hope."

The march placed before the nation with a dramatic intensity the unresolved issues of human rights. "The day was important in itself," author James Baldwin said, "what we do with this day is even more important." Some notion of what might be done was embodied in a pledge taken by the assembled demonstrators with Bayard Rustin leading at the close of the day:

"I affirm my complete personal commitment to the struggle for jobs and freedom for all Americans.

"To fulfill that commitment, I pledge that I will not relax until victory is won.

"I pledge that I will join and support all actions undertaken in good faith in accord with time-honored democratic traditions of nonviolent protest, or peaceful assembly and petition, and of redress through the courts and the legislative process.

"I pledge to carry the message of the march to my friends and neighbors back home and to arouse them to an equal effort. I will march and I will write letters. I will demonstrate and I will vote. I will work and make sure that my voice and those of my brothers ring clear and determined from every corner of our land.

"I will pledge my heart and my mind and my body, unequivocally and without regard to personal sacrifice, to the achievement of social peace through social justice."

Randolph hoped, as he told a Socialist party conference on civil rights the following day, that the pledgees would "return to their communities to build fires under their Congressmen." Referring to the civil rights bill, Randolph reminded his audience, "You cannot move Senators and Congressmen just because a measure is right. There has to be pressure." If there was a filibuster, he said, "we will have a counterfilibuster through town meeting discussions at churches here in Washington and perhaps all around the country." There was talk of bringing five hundred to one thousand demonstrators a day to Washington for such meetings each day of any filibuster in Congress against civil rights measures. King announced that civil rights leaders were "advocating a mass write-in campaign so that people in the tens of thousands will urge doubtful Congressmen to pass this legislation." The demonstration, King said in a post-march interview "has already done a great deal to create a coalition of concern about the status of civil rights in this country. It has aroused the conscience of millions of people to work for this legislation.

Yet, there is some question about the effect of the march on Congress. The Southerners, who had hoped for violence, were disappointed and deprived of whatever aid or comfort violence at the march might have given them in the legislative battle coming up in Congress. Only the convinced, however, bothered to respond to the march organizers' invitation to attend. Waverers, apparently, continued to waver and fence-sitters, to sit. When Senator Mike Mansfield, the Democratic leader, was asked if he thought the march would help or hinder legislation, he replied, "I couldn't say." Senator Jacob K. Javits, Republican of New York and a sympathizer, called the march "unforgettable," adding, however, "It may or may not change the votes of any member of Congress, but it will certainly establish a mood for the coming civil rights Congressional battle." Senator Kenneth B. Keating, Republican of New York, was cautiously optimistic, "It may have its effect on the waverers." The ever-ebullient Senator Hubert H. Humphrey, standing on the steps of Lincoln Memorial looking over the vast crowd, said, "All this probably hasn't changed any votes on the civil rights bill, but it is a good thing for Washington and the nation and the world."

President Kennedy certainly agreed that the march had turned out well, but he was sanguine about its legislative consequences. As he reminded the "big ten" as they drank coffee or sipped tea and munched on sandwiches around the long table in the Cabinet Room shortly after the march, "very strong bipartisan support" would be needed to get a bill through Congress. The votes, as yet, were not there, nor was there any sign that the march had changed the situation. However pleased by the march, the President did not exactly embrace its demands, especially that for a fair employment practices provision in his bill. According to Theodore C. Sorensen, the President brought the exhausted but exhilarated civil rights leaders "back to the harsh world of legislative committees, compromises and constituent pressures. He doubted that any votes in the Congress had been changed. He doubted that any segregationists had been converted. But he felt that the march had helped to unite the adherents of civil rights more closely; and merely the absence of violence in such a huge and restless crowd had awakened new interest and won new adherents in white America."

While prospects of passage for the civil rights bill were uncertain in fall 1963, close observers of the congressional mood sensed the beginnings of a favorable ground swell. The turn-around reaction of Senator Philip A. Hart, Democrat of Michigan, was a good omen. Senator Hart had expressed doubts that the march could have any effect on the legislative chances for civil rights. The day after the march, he reversed himself. "If the spirit captured by news stories and television is correct," he told reporters, "it could produce increased public awareness and public support. This in turn could produce support in Congress."

This, broadly speaking, is what happened. Viewed as a part of a process, a cumulation of events that led to the passage of the 1964 Civil Rights Act, the March on Washington stands out, not as a beacon of light in the surrounding darkness, but as the most visible expression of a massive thrust for civil rights. A living petition in this number could not long be denied. Gunnar Myrdal, writing twenty years earlier in his monumental study of race relations, *An American Dilemma*, made the point that civil rights forces in American society, whether organized or not and irrespective of differing strategy and tactics, "all work on the national conscience" seeking "to fix everybody's attention on the suppressed moral conflict." The conflict was no longer suppressed and the March on Washington worked on the national conscience superbly. Participants left the march standing taller, a feeling they communicated to millions more over television. Floyd McKissick, a Durham, North Carolina, attorney and the national chairman of CORE, hailed the march as signaling "the end of the Negro protest and the beginning of the American protest." While it did not quite turn out that way as the 1960s unfolded, it sufficed for the day. Black Americans had not been given their elemental civil and political rights but America had been put on notice that what Myrdal termed "a century-long lag of public morals" was at an end.

Paradoxically, however, although the march was a grand coming together of civil rights forces, it also marked a divergence between militants and moderates, a parting of ways. Lobbying for the civil rights bill became the provenance of the Leadership Conference, agitation increasingly that of the so-called "street Negro" and those who courted his favor. The tragic death by bombing of four young girls at a

Birmingham Bible class on September 15 intensified passions already smoldering within the nation's black communities. Rustin joined author James Baldwin in demanding that President Kennedy send federal troops to Alabama to "break the hold" of Governor George C. Wallace. Their prediction of rioting "unless this is done" carried a scarcely veiled threat. At a rally on September 22 in New York City's Foley Square, Rustin, a Quaker and pacifist for thirty years, struck a new note. "If the Federal government does not give black men and women and tiny children protection," he said, "they would not be men with red blood in their bodies if they did not take whatever weapons were at hand." Rustin, *The New York Times* reported the next day, called for a "nonviolent uprising" in one hundred cities. "Only the power of black bodies and some white bodies in the streets creating social confusion and disrupting the ability of the government to operate can bring victory."

Randolph sought to keep the "big ten" leaders of the march together. A memorandum drafted by Rustin proposed that "this coalition brought together to effectuate the March on Washington, continue, wherever practicable, their joint efforts in behalf of the national Freedom movement." This movement, argued Rustin, "awaits guidance and direction . . . . A great fire was lighted on August 28. But as with all conflagrations, it must be carefully tended. Otherwise, it can go out or become a runaway brush fire carrying with it many dangers to the cause to which all are dedicated." A hiatus between August 28 and a filibuster, Rustin added, would be a setback. The "big ten," he wrote "have obligations—to themselves and to the hundreds of thousands now enrolled in the Freedom movement." Rustin proposed nonviolent demonstrations in one hundred cities "with national spotlight publicity" and demands for jobs, the integration of schools and public accommodations, for voting rights and against police brutality. The deadline would be Thanksgiving Day and the goal, "one significant step to freedom in each city." Such a program of action, Rustin concluded, would help to develop in one hundred cities "strong movements ready and able to swing into action when a filibuster developed."

The "one hundred steps," however, were never taken—at least not as outlined by Rustin. There was, instead, a six month lull, mistaken by many as a truce. The march movement petered out in an abortive "Christmas selective buying and giving campaign" aimed at upgrading and hiring blacks in department stores; the march office was disbanded; and the "big ten" discontinued their meetings. The Kennedy civil rights bill began its tortuous journey through Congress. The Senate approved the Limited Test Ban Treaty; the Diem regime in South Vietnam was overthrown in early November; and President John F. Kennedy was murdered in Dallas, Texas, on November 22, 1963.

Within the civil rights movement there was a growing debate and division over strategy, tactics, and even goals. Black consciousness veering on black nationalism became a force within CORE and SNCC. It became more difficult for whites, even in CORE, the most interracial of all the civil rights organizations, to achieve leadership posts.° Integrationists won out over blacks who wanted to go their own way at a SNCC conference, in fall 1963, arguing that whites were needed for the success of a projected "Freedom Summer" voter registration drive in the Deep South. Bayard Rustin urged white students to concentrate more of their energies on the organization of unemployed whites. The Students for a Democratic Society, then the student arm of the League for Industrial Democracy, later undertook such a project, without lasting success, however.

Before the march, on August 1, President Kennedy had expressed the hope that "if there is a period of quiet . . . we should use it to redress grievances." The white liberal establishment tended to view the legislative struggle for the President's civil rights bill as such an attempt. Within the civil rights movement, however, there were other pressures boiling up behind the slogan "Freedom Now!" Some of them, as we have noted, were competitive contests for leadership or ascendancy in the struggle for funds. Other pressures reflected the need for jobs, housing, and education. Still others reflected the black leadership's fear that the lull following the march was a dropping back into apathy on the part of the black masses. For some, nonviolent direct action had become a way of life. "One of the beauties of nonviolent direct action," Marvin Rich, then community relations director of CORE, wrote in *New Politics*, "is that it permits the uneducated and the unskilled to join with the more highly trained and make a personal contribution. You don't have to be a doctor, or a lawyer or minister to walk a picket line or to sit-in. For far too long civil rights activity has been the near monopoly of the educated and the skilled. Now, significant numbers of working-class Negroes are participating in demonstrations and some are taking leadership positions." Thus, "the civil rights movement [for many] is a struggle to achieve recognition of the intrinsic value of the individual as a human being . . . . The individual member who pickets, serves on a negotiating team, and makes strategy decisions, is also asserting his own self-respect. He is acting to achieve his own freedom within him. In this sense, the nonviolent demonstrations are

---

° Black women, too, were being relegated to secondary positions. During this period, I had occasion to observe the East River Chapter of CORE in action. The young women, as is often the case among teen-agers, were more sophisticated and possessed more skills than the young men. It took considerable effort, therefore, to name a young black male to head every committee. In almost every instance, women were named as secretary of this or that committee.

more than means of achieving specific demands. They are also ends in being. . . . [This] has great importance in a complex society where there seems to be so little the individual can do about the great issues that affect him. For the Negro, who has been deprived for generations of all opportunity to master his fate and to assert his manliness and humanity, the demonstrations are especially important."

This was—and is—an attractive idea. It skirts, however, demonstrations for demonstrations' sake, militancy for militancy's. It also ignores the frustration that can build up when nothing follows undirected sound and fury or the negative reactions to demonstrations that appear to be without point or obtainable goals. When a CORE group on March 6, 1964, blocked traffic and dumped garbage on New York City's Triborough Bridge, ostensibly to call attention "to the need for better schools, housing and jobs for Negroes," motorists were rather irritated, becoming angry at the demonstrators, and not noticeably developing any sympathy over the sad plight of blacks in nearby slums.

In truth, the demonstration had more to do with the need of one faction of CORE to prove itself more militant than another than it did with a true concern over the sorry state of the black condition. The same consideration lay behind the sit-in at the opening of the 1964 World's Fair, although resulting in less unfavorable publicity and consequences in terms of public reaction. Just before the fair opened, a new civil rights group, ACT, had been formed by Jesse Gray, who had won notoriety as the leader of a successful Harlem rent strike and who, in 1972, became a New York State assemblyman; the Reverend Milton A. Galamison, leader of the 1964 New York City school boycotts; and Gloria Richardson, chairwoman of the Cambridge, Maryland, Nonviolent Coordinating Committee. Congressman Powell and Malcolm X were "consultants"; and though ACT did not, in fact, survive long, many feared at the time it would attract members, thunder and cash from CORE and the NAACP. In addition, a group of CORE dissidents threatened to tie-up all approaches—roads and subways—to the fair.

The opening day, April 22, 1964, was a dispiriting occasion, what with overcast skies and intermittent rain, enlivened only by the verve of parading and performing professionals and chanting civil rights demonstrators. These were on hand, in the words of James Farmer, to "contrast the *real world* of discrimination and brutality experienced by Negroes, North and South, with the *fantasy world* of progress and abundance shown in the official pavilions." To underscore the point, Farmer smuggled onto the fairgrounds under his raincoat an electric cattleprod used in Louisiana against blacks seeking their constitutional rights. It was displayed to the press as Farmer, Rustin, Michael Harrington, and various others sat patiently for hours in the entryway to the New York City Pavilion. Fair officials wisely chose to allow peaceful picketing and the distribution of leaflets. There was not much of a turnout that day and for a while it appeared, to the dismay and discomfort of the sitting demonstrators, that there would be no arrests. Finally, however, the police arrived and Farmer and his backers were carried bodily to waiting paddy wagons. Altogether, some three hundred were arrested, proving that national CORE could mount a militant protest and more than match the militants who had promised a universal tie-up. Some 2,800 cars supposedly were to "stall" on the highways approaching the fair, and emergency cords were to be pulled on all subway lines. But only twelve cars showed up for stall-in duty and only one created enough fuss to cause an arrest. A dedicated band managed to hold up an IRT subway train for a short time, which resulted in twelve more arrests among the militants. The "insurrection" fizzled to the greater glory of CORE's legitimate leadership.

The day was not without its humor. The sit-ins, in reality, blocked but a few first-day visitors. The Ford Pavilion simply shut down when sit-ins occurred. One suspects that somewhere officials debated the wisdom of making arrests with friends of CORE in high places urging that they be made with dispatch. There was an aura of unreality about the whole affair, a television staginess. Inside militants versus outside militants; hysteria in the mass media; and a soupçon of the white backlash all making up the televised potpourri of the 1960s. One heavily-shod, steel-helmeted worker ground his heel into the bare leg of a young girl sitting in at the New York Pavilion. A young matron instructed her child as they stepped over inert sitters, "When I tell you to step on 'em, I mean step hard."

The unity generated by the march barely survived the lull. The last minute get-together behind the February 1964 New York City school boycott ended when Milton Galamison insisted on yet another. Rustin was not available to direct the second; the NAACP parted company with Galamison; and CORE called for a new coordinating council that would exclude the Brooklyn pastor. While schools in the heart of New York City's black neighborhoods were successfully shut down, the second boycott on March 16 drew only some 168,000 pupils above the normal 100,000 or so absentees. In September, a boycott called by whites protesting pupil transfer plans—early forms of what has become known as "busing"—pulled out more pupils from school than Galamison's march effort.

Yet, while demonstrations appeared to some to be self-defeating, or becoming so, there were gains scored. The mere threat of a boycott sometimes brought success as in Philadelphia where the NAACP secured jobs for blacks as Trailways bus drivers or in Atlanta where "Operation Breadbasket," backed by the churches, secured white-collar employment in department stores. CORE negotiated agreements with leading chain supermarkets which opened up nearly one thousand sales positions. Nonviolent direct action took the form of a mock election in Mississippi where eighty-two thousand disenfranchised blacks cast ballots in a gubernatorial election. Several hundred blacks were able to register to vote in Selma, Alabama, in the face of police harassment and brutality, and, most encouraging, voter registration, a nonviolent tactic in the struggle for civil rights, rose in South Carolina from six hundred a month at the end of the summer of 1963 to two thousand six months later.

While direct action erupted here and there, the burden of securing passage of the civil rights bill rested with the Civil Rights Leadership Conference. It carried the burden of a sustained effort that stretched out over some eight months. Thousands of representatives of the principal civil rights organizations, a dozen trade unions, including the AFL-CIO, Americans for Democratic Action, the Americans' Veterans Committee, the American Civil Liberties Union, various churches, the entire spectrum of the labor-liberal coalition, came to Washington during the House and Senate debates over the bill at the behest of the Leadership Conference. Clarence Mitchell of the NAACP, Andrew Biemiller of the AFL-CIO, Jack Conway of the Industrial Union Department of the AFL-CIO, and the Reverend James Hamilton of the National Council of Churches lobbied indefatigably. The testimony of 269 witnesses before six congressional committees filled eight volumes, totaling 5,751 pages. While much of the South remained adamant in opposition, Gallup polls showed a decline—from 82 percent in June 1963 to 72 percent in February 1964—in Southern opposition to proposed bans against discrimination in public facilities. Mayor Ivan Allen of Atlanta, Georgia, backed the Kennedy bill, and newspapers in Atlanta, Miami, Norfolk, Charlotte, Winston-Salem, Raleigh, Greensboro, Memphis, Nashville, and Little Rock endorsed it.

The House Judiciary Committee reported out the bill, including an FEP provision, on November 20, 1963, the day President Kennedy prepared for a speech-making trip to Texas. The death of the President two days later rendered the fate of the bill uncertain. President Lyndon B. Johnson, however, quickly responded to the challenge. "First," he said in his message to Congress on November 27, "no memorial or eulogy could more eloquently honor President Kennedy's memory than the earliest possible passage of the civil rights bill for which he fought so long."

Considering that the bill was then in the hands of the House Rules Committee, chaired by hostile eighty-year-old Howard W. Smith, Democrat of Virginia, it was moved with relative dispatch. President Johnson encouraged a petition of discharge, which by threatening to circumvent Judge Smith altogether, speeded up committee consideration. The House acted in eleven days, passing the bill in February 1964. The Senate began consideration on March 9. Proponents of the bill maintained constant contact with the Leadership Conference, which applied pressure at sensitive points at the appropriate time. Over six thousand of the clergy and laity gathered in a National Interreligious Convocation on Civil Rights at Georgetown University on April 28 to demonstrate support of the bill. Denominational delegations fanned out to visit congressmen, and one Republican senator from the West was overheard grumbling, "Oh, I will have to vote for it in the end because you've got those damned pastors on my neck!"

Senator Richard Russell of Georgia headed the southern bloc in opposition. Devoted to President Johnson, he could not attack him personally though he fought the bill with a strategy someone called, "punt and pray." On one hand, Russell was hamstrung by his loyalty, and on the other as a Southerner, he could not afford to compromise, even with the Senate Minority Leader Senator Everett Dirksen, Republican of Illinois. Senator Humphrey cultivated Senator Dirksen with "moderation." Dirksen literally rewrote the bill, modifying it with respect to defining the limits of federal enforcement. Some liberals were unhappy over this "compromise," but most agreed with Senator Jacob Javits that "no title has been emasculated . . . the fundamental bill remains." The act prohibited discrimination in most places of public accommodation and in programs receiving public assistance, authorizing termination or the withdrawal of federal funds upon failure to comply; banned discrimination by employers and unions; created an Equal Employment Opportunity Commission; established a federal Community Relations Service; authorized the United States Office of Education to provide technical and financial aid to assist communities in school desegregation efforts. After Victor Hugo, Senator Dirksen allowed that "Stronger than all the armies is an idea whose time is come."

On June 19, 1964, after eighty-three days of debate, the Senate passed the bill by a vote of 73 to 27. The House approved the final version on July 2 by 289 votes to 126. That evening, President Lyndon B. Johnson signed the act.

XII

Defenders of the
American Dream

THE PASSAGE OF THE CIVIL
Rights Act of 1964 created a crisis for the civil rights forces. Activity in
the North became somewhat frenetic as protestors lay down before
construction-site bulldozers, closed down schools, ran rent strikes, and
conducted shop-ins, where demonstrators filled supermarket shopping
carts with groceries only to discard them after purchases were rung up
on cash registers, threatened stall-ins, even a water-wasting campaign in
which Brooklyn CORE supporters were to be asked to let water run out
of faucets until demands for "an immediate working plan on housing,
schools, employment and police brutality" were met. The situation was
exacerbated by television's hunger for the sensational.° Competing
leaders outbid each other in threats and in raising demands, knowing
that they could catch attention by doing so. The carefully worked out
programs of the established civil rights organizations went unreported.

The 1964 school boycotts, an all-night siege of San Francisco's
Sheraton-Palace Hotel on March 6 by over a thousand chanting,
marching, sitting, and door-blocking civil rights demonstrators, and the
World's Fair opening made the administration in Washington understandably nervous. It was an election year, and Governor George C.
Wallace of Alabama scored surprising successes in the Democratic
primaries of Wisconsin (34 percent), Indiana (30 percent), and Maryland (43 percent). Political pundits talked knowingly of a "backlash"
among white working-class Americans and predicted a flight from the
Democratic party on the race issue to Republican ranks. Civil rights

---

° In *The Making of the President 1964*, Theodore H. White observes, "At no time, to
this writer's knowledge, has television ever shown to the nation the spectacle of a Negro
community of decency."

leaders in the spring discussed bringing over fifty thousand protestors to the Atlantic City convention of the Democratic party in August. The White House responded by wheeling and dealing, citing the likely Republican candidacy of Senator Barry Goldwater, a conservative from Arizona, as a reason for a slowdown of demonstrations. According to Theodore H. White, the indefatigable chronicler of presidential races, white liberal money men were persuaded to threaten a cut-off in funds for civil rights activity as a means of containing the wilder enthusiasms of civil rights activists. The Democratic National Committee held back releasing funds allocated for voter registration drives among blacks to assure their use for registration and not hell-raising. The message was "cool it," and Roy Wilkins called civil rights leaders together to work out a "moratorium" on demonstrations. Wilkins, King, Young, and Randolph signed a call, after three hours of debate on July 29, "to observe a broad curtailment, if not total moratorium, of all mass marches, mass picketing, and mass demonstrations until after election day." James Farmer of CORE and John Lewis of SNCC, after consulting with their people, rejected the moratorium. But, in point of fact, the militants were unable to mount any demonstrations of any significance during the quietus imposed by the political necessities of the 1964 election.

Between the time Roy Wilkins issued his invitation to civil rights spokesmen to discuss a cooling-off of demonstration fevers and the July 29 civil rights summit, however, Harlem did erupt in what sociologist Kenneth B. Clark termed an "unplanned revolt." As a consequence, the moratorium was mistakenly viewed as a defensive reaction to the white backlash, or even a recoil from the violence of the street outbreaks. However, as Tom Kahn, a member of Bayard Rustin's "kitchen cabinet," analyzed the issue it "was not whether the movement should retreat in the face of the backlash, but whether the movement's energies and resources would be concentrated on political action—as a practical consequence of which (and not as a principle), conventional demonstrations would be curtailed in the interim period." In any event, neither the co-signers of the moratorium nor the militants influenced Harlem's "weird social defiance." The July 18 outbreak certainly was not, as all observers quickly agreed, a race riot in the classic sense of white mobs assaulting black mobs or vice versa. It began on a steamy Saturday evening at a rally on the corner of 125th Street and Seventh Avenue sponsored by three New York City CORE chapters. Speakers assailed the police and "the man"—by extension, all whites—for the death of fifteen-year-old James Powell, shot by an off-duty police officer, Lieutenant Thomas Gilligan, in an altercation on East Sixty-seventh Street the previous Thursday. The youth, who was taking a remedial reading course at a nearby junior high school, allegedly pulled a knife on an apartment house superintendent who had turned a hose on a group of horse-playing black youngsters.

The CORE speakers warmed up the crowd—"It is time to let 'the man' know that if he does something to us we are going to do something back"—nonetheless the meeting might have ended with a mere burst of rhetoric but for the Reverend Nelson C. Dukes of the Fountain Springs Baptist Church. He called on the crowd to march on the Twenty-eighth precinct station house. As the crowd taunted the police, Dukes, Ernest Russell of East River CORE, and several members of the rally audience presented "demands"—Police Commissioner Michael Murphy should come to Harlem and announce the suspension of Lieutenant Gilligan— to the inspector in charge. When the police sought to erect gray saw-horse barriers to contain the crowd, a scuffle broke out. Some sixteen demonstrators were arrested and the bottles, garbage can covers and debris began to fly. As the police shoved the milling crowd back toward Seventh and Eighth Avenues, Nelson Dukes, according to *Times* reporter Paul Montgomery, shook his head, saying, "If I knew this was going to happen, I wouldn't have said anything." Then, continues Montgomery's account, "he walked away."

He left an escalating civil disorder. Mobs soon began surging up and down a seven block area encompassing Harlem's chief commercial center, breaking windows, looting stores, smashing cars, and harassing any whites in sight. The police panicked, firing so many rounds that spent shells crunched under foot on the pavement and more ammunition had to be rushed from the police firing range in the Bronx. The Progressive Labor party, a Maoist sect, proclaimed the revolution, won a dot of publicity and a court order restraining them from "inciting" a riot. Jesse Gray, the rent-strike leader, called for a "hundred revolutionaries willing to die." Roy Wilkins cut short a Wyoming vacation, saying "I don't care how angry Negroes are . . . we can't leave [our cause] to bottle throwers and rock throwers." James Farmer and Bayard Rustin roamed the streets of Harlem, seeking to calm the hot-tempered.° The rioting jumped the East River to Brooklyn's Harlem, Bedford-Stuyvesant, and finally fizzled out after four days and nights. In the wake of smashed glass, over-turned cars, and scattered trash, one missile-tosser lay dead, while forty-eight policemen and ninety-two civilians suffered assorted injuries.

Other black slum residents proved to be edgy, though less so than in the riots of succeeding long hot summers. When two policemen stepped into a dispute between two blacks at a street dance in Rochester, New York, it took a curfew, tear gas, and 400 state troopers reinforced by

---

° Rachelle Horowitz in *New America* reported that Rustin did get volunteers for positive nonviolent action where Jesse Gray found none "willing to die."

1,300 National Guardsmen to restore peace in the hometown of Eastman Kodak, an industrial city of some 319,000 souls, roughly 10 percent black. In three days of tumult, some 350 were injured, nearly 1,000 arrested and one white man was killed by some black youth.

The 1964 riots, a slum rash that also broke out in three New Jersey communities—Jersey City, Paterson, and Elizabeth—in the Chicago suburb of Dixmoor, and in Philadelphia, were spontaneous. Some snuffed for "conspiracy," reading a reality into hastily drawn leaflets that the authors only wished did exist. The Federal Bureau of Investigation summed up the events that cost five lives and an estimated $6 million in property damages as follows:

"A common characteristic of the riots was a senseless attack on all constituted authority without purpose or objective. While in the cities racial tensions were a contributing factor, none of the nine occurrences was a 'race riot' in the accepted meaning of the phrase. They were not riots of Negroes against whites or whites against Negroes. And they were not a direct outgrowth of conventional civil rights protest. Victims of the rioting were often Negro storeowners as well as whites. The assaults were aimed at Negro as well as white police officers struggling to restore order. While adult troublemakers often incited the riots, the mob violence was dominated by the acts of youths ranging in age to the middle twenties. They were variously characterized by responsible people as 'school dropouts,' 'young punks,' 'common hoodlums,' and 'drunken kids.' "

The riots as such played little or no role in the 1964 Presidential race. Theodore H. White reports that Senator Goldwater, much to his credit, approached President Johnson at the height of the summer's outbreaks and volunteered to eliminate appeals to the passions of race in the campaign ahead. President Johnson agreed to this proposal, and both adhered to what was essentially a private compact between the two men.° The riots involved only a tiny fraction of a handful of black communities and were widely condemned by the responsible black leadership. Even so, many came to feel that the rioters had acted out the hostility toward "whitey" felt by most, if not all black Americans. Overtly or covertly stated, this became a community stamp of approval for the wildest of excesses in the succeeding years. What was as alarming was the gap revealed by the riots between black spokesmen and the rapidly expanding underclass in the black slums of the nation.

While the new voices from that underclass were as yet to be heard, they were in the wings waiting. Indeed, if anything characterizes this

---

° When the Goldwater campaign organization produced a documentary film stressing the riots and the looting in picturing "immorality," Goldwater ordered its showings canceled, saying "It's nothing but a racist film."

period of the mid-1960s, it is the emergence of new black spokesmen. Organizations, many on paper, or in the leadership's heads, proliferated. "Almost every week," reported *The New York Times*, "a new civil rights organization with a new philosophy is born in the metropolitan area and another man or woman is acclaimed as a civil rights leader . . . . Experience, education, and social standing are not necessary for this kind of leadership. What is necessary is the ability to articulate the desperate feelings of the impatient members of the community." The old constraints, however, continued with perhaps lesser force, though. That is, white America simply because of its overwhelming presence and power, influenced the choices of leadership made. One perhaps ought to keep in mind Anna Arnold Hedgeman's observation, "Negroes are seldom supported [by whites] when they select their own leadership." Nonetheless, black Americans, even the most fervid of nationalists or revolutionaries, still chose leaders who not only spoke *for* them but *to* white America. By the same token, white Americans still assumed, as black spokesmen frequently wished, that any given black leader spoke for all blacks, failing, as ever before to recognize gradations of color, caste, class, local interests, or points of view among blacks. While this helped, at least on one level, to create a black identity, it also made for some confusion about who spoke for whom. When A. Philip Randolph gently corrected Rev. Dr. Eugene Carson Blake, who had referred to Martin Luther King, Jr., as "clearly the religious leader of this [March on Washington] demonstration," by introducing Roy Wilkins at the White House meeting following the march as "the acknowledged leader of the civil rights movement in America" and King as "the moral leader of the nation," he was making a distinction that many whites simply did not recognize.

This confusion about leadership roles among black Americans was not limited to Washington. On the intellectual stock market, as an instance, highs in James Baldwin, Le Roi Jones, Eldridge Cleaver, and George Jackson followed one another with bewildering rapidity. In New York City, after the 1964 riot, Mayor Robert F. Wagner met with Martin Luther King, Jr., and Bayard Rustin. King made some sensible suggestions, recommending the creation of a civilian review board to hear complaints within the police department and "a massive program to free the Negro from the long night of economic deprivation and social isolation." For his pains, King got small thanks and boos when he toured riot-torn Harlem with the mayor. "No leader outside Harlem should come into this town and tell us what to do," Adam Clayton Powell thundered from his pulpit. By failing to consult key black spokesmen in Harlem, Mayor Wagner had needlessly offended not only Powell but a host of others. White America was being put on notice that the day had passed when those in power need only speak to a Booker T. Washington or a Walter White or a Martin Luther King.

The difficulties of choosing among spokesmen was, however, compounded in the North by the derangements of slum life. While most blacks in the North continued their traditional affiliation with the Baptist and Methodist churches, indeed individual congregations were often larger in number in the North than in the South, the hold of the church was loosened considerably, in E. Franklin Frazier's phrase, by "the shock of the disintegrating forces in urban life." The established black political machines thrived on low voter registration and participation; the young, "new Negro," discouraged or blocked, turned from civil rights protest, not to politics but to creating alternate agencies for achievement and action.° This trend, incidentally, was encouraged by the "maximum feasible participation" bias of the Johnsonian war against poverty. In the second edition of *Beyond the Melting Pot*, Nathan Glazer and Daniel P. Moynihan cite a study that shows blacks and Puerto Ricans abstained *more* from politics in the mid-1960s than in the mid-1940s. Instead of a movement from protest to politics, as urged by Bayard Rustin, there was a by-passing of politics mid-decade by substantial segments of northern black communities.

This was less the case in the South where civil rights forces increasingly focused on voter registration and get-out-the-vote drives. Despite white harassment and repression, the move toward greater political involvement among blacks, in some respects, was easier in the South than in the North. Civil rights activists in the South were building brand new political institutions. The heady wine of protest need not be forced into partially filled old bottles, but could flow, relatively speaking, unhindered into new ones. The Voter Registration Project (VEP) of the Southern Regional Council, after 1970 an independent agency, funded successful drives in many parts of the South. VEP began a two-and-one-half year $870,371 program in March 1962, reaching into the eleven southern states of the old confederacy. Local NAACP chapters, CORE groups, SCLS and SNCC field staffs drew funds from VEP for voter registration drives in their respective locales. While not all of the increase in black voters throughout the South can be attributed to VEP sponsored efforts, a majority can. Of the more than five million blacks of voting age in the South's eleven states, only

---

° In Adam Clayton Powell's congressional district only 25 percent of the eligible voters were registered in 1964. In New York City, less than 30 percent of those blacks who could vote were registered. The Dawson machine in Chicago was not noticeably enthusiastic about voter registration, either. In 1950, the five key black wards on Chicago's South Side contained 420,687 people. Of these, over half were registered to vote. But ten years later, the number of registered voters had dropped to 185,368.

1,386,654 were registered at the start of VEP. Over one-half million were added to the rolls by April 1964, or 38.6 percent of those eligible; an additional two hundred thousand were added over the summer of 1964, raising the total to 2,174,200 or 43.8 percent of those eligible.

All things considered, it was a major achievement. Breakthroughs were scored in every state but one, Mississippi. Valiant efforts by SNCC field workers and NAACP activists yielded little in the face of fear induced apathy and outright intimidation. Louisiana and Virginia did not do so well either, moving up 3.9 and 5.1 percentage points from 1962 to 1964; but 27.8 and 24 percent, respectively, of voting age blacks in those states were already registered as compared with Mississippi's 5.3 percent in 1962 and 6.7 percent in 1964. Alabama, with the second lowest percentage of black voters registered in 1962, at 13.4 percent, registered 42,000 black voters, a gain of 9.4 percent points, bringing the percent of eligible black voters to 22.8 percent. Black registration had been moved off dead center throughout the former confederacy, except in the Magnolia State. When Sam Black, a 23-year-old black native son and SNCC field worker, opened a voter registration drive in Green-wood, Mississippi, in June 1962, he had to commute because he could find no one among the town's fearful black populace to put him up. Black was beaten and later arrested when he charged that the burning of four black businesses near the VEP office was arson. Tried, he refused a suspended sentence on agreement that he would refrain from civil rights activities. His example encouraged some 150 black citizens to go and register but they were successfully rebuffed. The following night, February 28, 1963, James Travis, Robert Moses of SNCC, and Randolph Blackwell, VEP field director, were fired on from a passing car as they were driving out of Greenwood. "Bullets rained all through the car," Moses later recalled. Travis was hit in the neck, slumped over on to Moses' lap, and the car went off the road. Travis was operated on and survived but there were no arrests. The shooting stands for a whole series of incidents that inhibited black voter registration in the state, aptly described in the title of historian James W. Silver's excellent book, *Mississippi: The Closed Society*.

Mississippi was two societies; the white majority of 1.2 million (58 percent) and the black minority of 916,000 (42 percent) locked in a deathlike embrace of hatred and fear. Blacks had been a majority in the state until the 1930s and Mississippi still contained a larger proportion of blacks within its boundaries than any other state but fewer, all told, than in New York City alone. (Of Mississippi's eighty-two counties, twenty-nine still had a black majority in 1960.) In the early 1960s, Mississippi remained one of the two most rural states in the union, with 62 percent of its population living on farms or in tiny villages. While wealthy Mississippians might be found living in Jackson, one of the new cities of the South with a burgeoning population that bounced from 62,000 in 1940 to 144,000 by 1960, the state was one of the poorest in the nation—the median family income of whites, $4,209 a year; that of blacks, $1,444. Mississippi was the state where the supremacist White Citizens' Councils must, perforce, be described as "moderate." The Southern Regional Council report of July 14, 1964, was damnably accurate: "Here every datum of economics and every fact and twist of history have conspired to keep its white people deeply and ofttimes harshly resistant to change and its Negro people ill-equipped for it."

The early voter registration drives were so discouraging—3,871 new black names had been added to voter rolls after two years of effort—that VEP decided to throw in the towel, "reluctantly," in November 1963. More money had been spent with fewer results than in any other state, Wiley Branton, then VEP director, said. Further spending in Mississippi would take funds from more fruitful endeavors. In a 1962 report to VEP, Robert Moses spelled out the situation with admirable clarity: "We are powerless to register people in significant numbers anywhere in the state and will remain so until the power of the Citizens' Councils over state politics is broken, the Department of Justice secures for Negroes across the board the right to register, or Negroes rise up en masse with an unsophisticated blatant demand for immediate registration to vote. Very likely, all three will be necessary before a breakthrough can be obtained."

Mississippi blacks and SNCC field workers, however, persisted. As Robert Penn Warren so brilliantly perceived in *Who Speaks for the Negro*, "the work for voter registration is, in itself, an elaborate educational process, a process involving, as I saw it that morning [at a Jackson meeting], the rudiments of English syntax, of the syllogism, of American history, of political organization, and of the simple business of planning and working with other people . . . . All these things are basic for the long-range growth of political power, but they are equally important for the growth of other kinds of power—and for the fulfillment of a person." To keep up, in Warren's phrase, "the development of the will to stand up and act," the civil rights groups in Mississippi—NAACP, CORE, SCLC, and local organizations—banded together in the Council of Federated Organizations (COFO). Aaron Henry, the courageous Clarksville druggist and head of Mississippi's NAACP, was named president. Robert Parris Moses, the thirty-year-old Harlem-born, Harvard-educated mathematician and philosopher and SNCC field worker, became COFO's director.

COFO operated on nerve, an imaginative daring. Some Yale Law School volunteers discovered an obscure provision in the Mississippi electoral law, which provided that a citizen might vote even if not on the rolls if he submitted on election day an affidavit that he was qualified to vote. In a brilliant application of nonviolent direct-action techniques, COFO decided to crash the August 1963 Mississippi primary. No great number was involved—500 to 700 in Greenwood, 26 in Ruleville, 14 at Thorton, and 10 at Tchula voted (none were deemed valid), and 30 in Canton and 430 in Jackson tried but were refused. Nonetheless, it was a morale boosting triumph. As Stokely Carmichael reported, "Two years ago we would have been shot for a stunt like this." Of such change, progress was then measured in Mississippi. "As it was," Carmichael's report continued, "reception from whites was polite at first. But hostile crowds gathered as Negroes continued going into the polls. There was no violence."

Next, COFO ran a mock election parallel to the 1963 statewide gubernatorial race. Aaron Henry ran for governor with Ed King, a white chaplain at Tougaloo College as his running mate for lieutenant governor. Allard Lowenstein, a white New Yorker and later a prominent liberal, Dave Dennis, CORE director in Mississippi, Moses, and Annelle Ponder of SCLC worked out the original idea. Nearly a quarter of the eligible black voters and roughly three times the actual number on the voting rolls (27,791), turned out to cast 90,000 ballots. It was an impressive demonstration of political interest.

Out of these political try-outs came the Mississippi Freedom Democratic party (MFDP) and the famed Freedom Summer of 1964. Planning for the summer began in the fall of 1963 when the hard logic of the advantages to be accrued from the presence of white volunteers —the nation and the FBI, it was assumed, would be more concerned over the fate of white, middle-class college students than they were over that of black youngsters—overcame the objections of the black consciousness faction in SNCC. The seriousness of political intent is underscored by another decision; after the 1964 Civil Rights Act passed, SNCC staff in Mississippi decided not to "test" the public accommodations provision. Demonstrations would detract, it was felt, from the Freedom Summer and the building of the MFDP. The call went out for volunteers, and the National Council of Churches set up spring training at Western College for Women at Oxford, Ohio. College students—some seven hundred in all—came from Swarthmore, Cornell, Yale, Harvard, Mount Holyoke, Bryn Mawr, Smith, Colorado, Stamford, University of California, and a host of others.* Volunteers had to be at least eighteen years of age, able to pay their own way, willing to live with black families and share the obvious dangers.

---

* The students were backed up by one hundred paid field workers with SNCC, another forty with CORE, a network of NAACP chapters, some one hundred clergymen and a hundred lawyers, mostly volunteers, from the NAACP Legal Defense Fund, the Lawyers Constitutional Defense Committee, the National Lawyers Guild and the Lawyers Committee for Civil Rights under Law.

Mississippi prepared as if for an invasion. Crosses were burned on the night of April 24 in sixty-four of the state's eighty-two counties. In June, when the first contingent of volunteers had arrived, a half-dozen black churches were burned. Ten more would burn in July, six in August, and five in September. From January 1964 to August 1964, thirty blacks were murdered around the state. The state highway patrol was increased from 275 to 475 men, but availing naught. Mystery still surrounds the death of a fourteen-year-old youth, wearing a CORE T-shirt, found floating in the Big Black River and that of two adults whose bodies were recovered from a Mississippi bayou. On Sunday, June 21, three civil rights workers, Michael Schwerner, twenty-four, a former New York social worker on the staff of CORE, Andrew Goodman, twenty-one, son of a New York building contractor and a junior at Queens College, and James Chaney, twenty-one, a black Mississippian and a CORE field worker, were returning to their base in Meridan after inspecting a burned-out church fifty-five miles to the northwest in Neshoba County. Passing through the county seat, Philadelphia (population, 5,500), they were arrested for "speeding." Released late at night, about 10:30, after Chaney paid a $20 fine, they drove off, and were never seen alive again—except by their murderers. Within a week, President Johnson had ordered an FBI investigation, and the use of military helicopters and 210 sailors in the hunt for the missing three. Six weeks after the search began, FBI agents, acting on information uncovered by CORE and other informants, uncovered the bodies buried in an earthen dam under construction on a farm five miles south of Philadelphia. Chaney had been savaged, shot once in the head and twice in the body; Schwerner and Goodman were each killed by a single shot in the head.°

At Freedom Summer's end, COFO reported 450 "incidents," occurring between June 15 and September 15, including three persons killed, eighty beaten, three wounded by gunfire in thirty-five shootings,

---

° Despite a national outcry, little justice was done. As FBI Chief J. Edgar Hoover's investigations of civil rights cases in Mississippi were hampered by "water moccasins, rattlesnakes, and red-necked sheriffs, and they are all in the same category as far as I am concerned." Law enforcement in Neshoba County, he added, "is practically nil, and many sheriffs and their deputy sheriffs participate in crime." In this, Hoover was right. On December 4, 1964, acting under two Reconstruction-era statutes against depriving individuals of their civil rights, FBI agents arrested twenty-one white men, including Sheriff Lawrence Rainey of Neshoba County, Deputy Sheriff Cecil Price, and several Ku Klux Klan leaders. The killings were plotted by the KKK, according to the FBI. Price had arrested the three youths on fictitious charges, delaying their release so that they might be captured and murdered in the darkness of night. Indicted by a federal grand jury, seventeen of the defendants were brought to trial before Judge William H. Cox, a Kennedy appointee, who threw out the indictment. "The indictment," he declared, "surely states a heinous crime against the state of Mississippi, but not a crime against the United States."

thirty-five churches burned, thirty homes and other buildings bombed.

For all the energy expended, little had been achieved—that is, if one only counts the some 1,200 new black registrants added to the voting rolls within the state. Nonetheless, the fortress of white supremacy, once believed impregnable, had been breached. The volunteers had planted the seeds for a long-delayed harvest. COFO established forty-seven "Freedom schools," scattered around the state, where illiterates and near-illiterates learned to read and write as well as how to go about registering to vote. Community centers were established, a base was created for future political power. The Freedom Summer clinched the case for a federal enforcement of voting rights, and Mississippi would never be the same. When federal examiners arrived in Mississippi, following the 1965 Voting Rights Act, black registration rose from 28,500 or 6.7 percent of those eligible, to 139,099, or 32.9 percent. In Neshoba County, where no blacks were registered to vote at the time of the Chaney-Schwerner-Goodman murders, 953 were registered by 1966. Three years later, Charles Evers of Fayette became the first black mayor of an integrated community in the South. By 1972, over 300,000 black Mississippians, roughly 59.37 percent of the eligibles, would be registered to vote and the Magnolia State would, in 1973, lead the South with 145 elected black officeholders.°

Mississippi loomed large in the national conscience as Democratic party delegates gathered in Atlantic City for the 1964 convention. The fears aroused by the Harlem, Rochester, and Paterson-Elizabeth, New Jersey, riots were offset by the shock of the Chaney-Schwerner-Goodman murders. Perhaps no convention in Democratic party history was as broadly sympathetic to civil rights as the one that opened on August 24. Morality and practicality, however, did clash as the Credentials Committee of the Democratic National Committee considered the conflicting claims of the regular Mississippi delegation and of the biracial delegation of the Freedom Democrats. The latter had a moral claim; the former, a legal claim to seats at the convention. There was a problem of precedent in recognizing an unofficial group pressuring aside delegates duly chosen by law and in accord with party rules. As Murray Kempton phrased it in *The New Republic*, "No party manager can accept the notion that any stranger can come to the national convention and claim his right to sit and vote on no higher credentials than his courage and suffering."

The MFDP had been created in the spring of 1964 to give political body to the registration efforts of the Freedom Summer. It was also the political organization of the disenfranchised. County, state, and district

---

° Local officeholders, alas. There is only one black representative in the Mississippi legislature.

conventions were held; a slate of sixty-eight delegates and alternates, all but four black, was chosen and sent off to Atlantic City. Blacks, as usual, had no part in the choosing of the Mississippi regular delegation, which, in fact, was predisposed to support the Republican nominee, Senator Barry M. Goldwater. As an MFDP statement put it, "the convention must choose between a loyal delegation with no power and few votes and one of doubtful loyalty representing the state administration and a majority of voters." Worried lest angry blacks from the nearby slums of Philadelphia, northern New Jersey, and New York City descend, despite the moratorium on civil rights demonstrations, upon Atlantic City in support of the MFDP's demands for recognition, President Johnson, indirectly, proffered a compromise. Though, in reality, and one supposes that the President, who was firmly in command of the convention proceedings, knew this, there was no real danger of a mass invasion of blacks, the President, and his managers, wanted to avoid television eyecatching demonstrations outside the convention hall as well as a televised bruising floor battle. David L. Lawrence, former governor of Pennsylvania and head of the Credentials Committee, and Senator Hubert H. Humphrey, the leading vice-presidential hopeful, were assigned the task of working out a solution. In its first version, the compromise would seat both delegations and split the vote among them. *The New York Times*, which supported this proposition in an August 16 editorial, said that the choice the convention faced was between "Political tradition and political morality."

State Senator E. K. Collins of Laurel, Mississippi, spokesman for the regulars before the Credentials Committee, pledged his loyalty to the national ticket and defended his delegation's right to the contested seats on legal and traditional grounds, citing the overwhelming support normally given the Democratic party by Mississippians. (In the election, Mississippi would break that tradition by 356,447 votes for Goldwater to 52,591 for Johnson.) The Reverend Edwin King, the white chaplain at Tougaloo College and an MFDP committee member, passionately informed the Credentials Committee, "The Freedom party is an open party. They [the regulars] are a closed party of a closed society." Joseph L. Rauh, Jr., a Washington attorney and counsel to the MFDP, stressed the regulars' disloyalty. "Are you going to throw out of here the people who want to work for Lyndon Johnson, who are willing to be beaten and shot and thrown in jail to work for Lyndon Johnson? Are we for the oppressor or the oppressed?"

Rauh called up a stream of witnesses to Mississippi barbarity, including Aaron Henry, Rita Schwerner, wife of one of the three murdered civil rights workers, and Martin Luther King, Jr. But the day belonged to Fannie Lou Hamer, wife of a sharecropper whose family was thrown off the plantation where they had labored for eighteen years after she led a group of twenty-six blacks to register in Ruleville, the hometown of Senator James O. Eastland. A robust woman of great dignity, she testified in a voice timbered by the blues, electrifying her listeners with an account of what it is to be black in Mississippi and want to vote.

> I was carried to the county jail and put in the booking room. They left some of the people in the booking room and began to place us in cells . . . .
> And it wasn't too long before three white men came to my cell . . . . I was carried out of the cell into another cell where they had two Negro prisoners. The state highway patrolman ordered the first Negro to take the blackjack.
> The first Negro prisoner ordered me, by orders from the state highway patrolman, for me to lay down on a bunk bed on my face, and I laid on my face.
> The first Negro began to beat, and I was beat until he was exhausted . . . . After the first Negro . . . was exhausted, the state highway patrolman ordered the second Negro to take the blackjack. The second Negro began to beat and I began to work my feet, and the state highway patrolman ordered the first Negro who had beat to set on my feet and keep me from working my feet. I began to scream, and one white man got up and began to beat me on my head and tell me to "hush."
> One white man—my dress had worked up high—he walked over and pulled my dress down and he pulled my dress back, back up. I was in jail when Medgar Evers was murdered. All of this is on account we want to register, to become first-class citizens, and if the Freedom Democratic party is not seated now, I question America . . . .

There was not much question, as Theodore H. White reports, but that President Johnson had the muscle to impose whatever solution he thought fit on the convention. The widespread sympathy won by the MFDP delegation, however, did change the character of the compromise. For three days, delegates, informally and formally, wrestled with the problem. Robert Moses and other leaders in the MFDP delegation sent for Martin Luther King, Jr., and Bayard Rustin to help line up delegates for the group's appeal to the convention. Failing a full-fledged floor fight over the contested seats, the MFDP hoped for a credentials minority report favoring a plan advanced by Congresswoman Edith Green of Oregon. She proposed that all members of both delegations willing to take an oath of allegiance to the national ticket be seated. The prospect, of course, was that all the MFDP delegates would so swear and that most of the regulars would not. But the requisite eleven votes for a minority report evaporated under pressure from the President's camp and in the face of fears of an untoward demonstration on the convention floor. Mrs. Green withdrew her proposal. On the third day, Senator Humphrey, backed by Walter Reuther, brought the beleaguered MFDP another compromise. It offered more than what President Johnson had been prepared to give and was, as Theodore H. White described it, "In all historic aspects, a true triumph for Robert Moses of the summer project."

On Tuesday evening, temporary Chairman John O. Pastore read the compromise ruling adopted by the Credentials Committee, and the motion to accept was passed in thirty seconds. The convention had ruled that no Mississippi regular delegate could sit unless he pledged support to the national ticket; that two Freedom party delegates would be seated and "honored guest" status would be accorded to the rest; and, most significant of all, that at the next convention, and thereafter, no delegations would be seated from states where the party process deprived citizens of the right to vote by reason of their race or color. The convention accepted the compromise gladly, but would the MFDP delegates accept it at all? That question was hotly debated all night long, with SNCC and CORE staff members bitterly opposed to accepting the compromise. When Stokely Carmichael heard its terms, he snapped, "This proves that the liberal Democrats are just as racist as Goldwater." There was resentment over the choice of Aaron Henry and Rev. Edwin King, who were "named" by the Credentials Committee as recognized delegates rather than elected by the delegation itself. Fannie Lou Hamer was against acceptance, but others in the delegation, notably Henry and King, urged that the compromise be accepted.

National black spokesmen expressed hope that the MFDP would agree to the compromise. Roy Wilkins favored it from the start and Martin Luther King, Jr., at first predisposed to back the rejection on moral grounds, was convinced by Bayard Rustin to lobby for the compromise among the Mississippians. James Farmer posed the issue: he thought rejection "morally right but politically wrong." SNCC managed to minimize the effect of suasion from King and the others by blocking moves to invited civil rights leaders to speak to the delegation in caucus before it made its decision. According to newspaper accounts, the vote went sixty to forty against the compromise. (SNCC denied the accuracy of the report, claiming that rejection was near unanimous.)

The moral stance of the MFDP delegation, however, was vitiated when the militants forced the delegation into a demonstration. As millions watched on television, the Mississippi and Alabama regulars stalked out of the convention, an impressive triumph for the civil rights forces. Briefly, as the cameras switched outside the convention hall to a civil rights rally, it appeared as if the Mississippi Freedom party delegates had changed their minds and were about to march into the hall and take their assigned places. Instead, using walkie talkies, purloined passes and badges, the Freedom delegates erupted onto the floor of the convention, seized the vacated Mississippi seats, and locked arms to resist evacuation efforts. When the convention resumed its deliberations three turbulent hours later, the broad sympathy won by the upright stance of the MFDP in rejecting the compromise had been all but wiped away by the intransigence of a handful of militants.

The debate over the Mississippi challenge reverberated throughout the civil rights movement and had a decided impact on the emerging black movement. The hairline crack visible at the time of the March on Washington so easily got over by a blue penciling of John Lewis's militant speech became a deepening chasm between moderates and integrationists on one side and militants and radicalists on the other. Fundamentally, the division lay between those who still believed that the American dilemma might be resolved by the achievement of the American Dream and those who viewed the dream as a deception and the dilemma as unreconcilable. The character of the gulf that yawned before the civil rights movement, however, was not immediately apparent. It was obscured by the politics of 1964, which posed a consensus Lyndon B. Johnson against extremist (of the right) Barry Goldwater.

Rustin's belief that it was time to move from protest to politics gained credence from the 1964 black performance at the polls.° Fewer than 4

° Rustin's formal argument was advanced in a brilliant February 1965, *Commentary* article, "From Protest to Politics, The Future of the Civil Rights Movement." But he had worked out his position, in part, through arguments with Martin Luther King, Jr., and MFDP delegates over the compromise. Unlike some, Rustin understood why the Mississippians could not accept the compromise. As he noted, in a discussion carried out in *New America*, shortly after the Democratic party convention, "They had nothing but death and destruction and fear all around them and to come up to Atlantic City and take any other position I think was psychologically impossible." Still, he urged the compromise. "Often compromises are necessary," he said, "in order to maintain a position for effective struggle." In Atlantic City, he added, "we were confronted by a major decision because all the potential allies of the Negro struggle urged us to accept the compromise. I'm not arguing now whether the compromise should have been accepted, I'm making quite another point—that no abstract principles provide answers to tactical questions. Every ally within the party said: 'That's good, it's not what any of us wanted, but it's the best we could get.' On the other hand you had the SNCC people predominantly saying: 'This is not enough.'

"This was, it seems to me, the loss of an opportunity at the Democratic convention for one of the Freedom party delegates might have used his speaking right as an occasion for setting that convention on fire with a real program for social change in this country, to which there would have had to be some response from other segments of this convention . . . .

"I think we've gone as far as we can go politically with protest as usual. The main thrust of our activity must be directed into the political arena and protest must be given its most million blacks voted in 1960, and nearly one-quarter of that number voted Republican; nearly 6 million voted in 1964, and 94 percent voted for Lyndon B. Johnson. President Johnson got 61 percent of the popular vote and carried all but six states. Author James Baldwin vehemently insisted that the black vote was "anti-Goldwater, not pro-Johnson." But the very size of the vote belies the negativism. It certainly would not have been so large had not President Johnson pushed the Civil Rights Act of 1964 through Congress. Significantly, despite the landslide for Johnson, the black vote retained its importance. Without it, the Democrats would have lost four *more* southern states (they lost five)—Tennessee, Virginia, Florida, and Arkansas.° Liberal congressmen were aided by the black vote—Weltner and Mackay of Georgia and Grider of Tennessee, for example. Of greater importance was the election of two blacks to the Georgia senate and another to the Tennessee legislature. CORE boasted of the election of Archibald Hill, chairman of its Oklahoma City chapter, to the state legislature. In Macon County, home of Tuskegee Institute, blacks elected two justices of the peace, a member of the school board, and a member of the board of revenue.

When the moratorium on demonstrations ended on election day, there was no great rush into the streets by the black masses. Super militants blamed "apathy," but most black Americans, like the rest of the country, appeared to be "waitin' on Lyndon," to see what he would make of the promised "Great Society." As the President prepared for the legislative push that would extend the welfare state, civil rights groups turned to politics. For a time, it appeared as if the grit of protest would become a political pearl, as predicted by those who saw the movement as a potential catalyst for broad social change. Roy Wilkins declared, "What we [the NAACP] are looking for now is political activity, flexibility." A. Philip Randolph urged again his "coalition of conscience" of civil rights, church, and labor organizations. "The Negro," he declared, "has developed a new sense of political power. He must use that power as does labor—to defeat his enemies and elect the friends of justice." CORE set up a political action department. Martin Luther King, Jr., announced plans for demonstrations in Alabama and Mississippi "based around the right to vote."

Despite voter registration successes in the South over 1963 and 1964, it was apparent that registration still proceeded at a hopelessly slow pace, especially in the rural black belt counties. In Texas, Tennessee, and Florida, the percentages of eligible blacks registered to vote were

_____

effective political form so that we can make real gains and not only bear witness to injustice."
°   Alabama, Georgia, Louisiana, Mississippi, and South Carolina—where less than 45 percent of the eligible blacks were registered to vote.

well above 50 percent—57.7 percent, 69.4 percent, and 63.8 percent respectively. But of the region's total black eligibles, only 40.8 percent were on the rolls. Mississippi, as noted before, was low man on the voting totem poll. Alabama was second with only 22.8 percent of the black voting-age population (about 481,320), or 110,000 registered at the end of 1964. Justice Department suits under the federal civil rights acts had scored some impressive breakthroughs in such black belt counties as Macon, Bullock, and Jefferson in Alabama and Washington, Beinville, and Jackson parishes in Louisiana. The Civil Rights Act of 1964 had expedited voting suits brought by the federal government, nonetheless suits take time and do not, in and of themselves, overcome intimidation, fear or outright violence. In Dallas County, Alabama, where blacks comprise 57 percent of the total population and 15,115 were of voting age, at the end of 1964 only 320 blacks registered to vote; 9,543 whites were on the voting lists. In neighboring Lowndes County, where blacks outnumbered whites approximately four to one, not one black had succeeded in registering to vote. The Mississippi Freedom Summer pointed up the need for stronger federal intervention on behalf of the right to vote. Even where southern officials ostensibly observed the law, obstructions were cast up and delay became a fine art. As Martin Luther King, Jr., wrote in *The New York Times Sunday Magazine* of March 14, "Selma has succeeded in limiting Negro registration to the snail's pace of about 145 persons a year. At this rate, it would take 103 years to register the 15,000 eligible Negro voters of Dallas County."

In fall 1964, Bayard Rustin had urged "a *national* campaign for federal registrars." But the coalition that had mounted the March on Washington with such conspicuous success had lost much of its momentum. In part, this was because it had achieved its major goal, the Civil Rights Act of 1964, and, in part, because what had been a civil rights movement was, in transition, becoming a black movement. Realizing that the 1964 act was inadequate when it came to assuring the right to vote, President Johnson contemplated introducing appropriate legislation. He was in a fever to get the Great Society under way. "Hurry, boys, hurry," he implored his staff. "Get that legislation up to the Hill and out. Eighteen months from now, Ol' Landslide Lyndon will be Lame-Duck Lyndon." On February 6, President Johnson announced his intention to strengthen voting rights but evoked little response either from Congress or the coalition. Within a month, however, events in the hitherto little-known Alabama city of Selma (population, 28,385) would revive the coalition and set the movement marching together once again.

Selma, a black belt city struggling to emerge out of the old King Cotton South by industrialization, was a shrewd choice as a field of civil rights action. Located on the west bank of the Alabama River, some fifty miles due west of Montgomery and roughly a hundred miles south of Birmingham, Selma was a potential base for operational forays into eight counties where the population, overwhelmingly rural, was 50 percent or more black. (In five of those counties, the population was 60 percent or more black.°) The city was governed by the moderate administration of Mayor Joseph T. Smith, representing a coalition of businessmen and enlightened old families. Wilson Baker, Selma's commissioner of public safety, was a professional police officer. So Selma promised to be something of an oasis for hard-pressed civil rights activists. When Martin Luther King, Jr., arrived to stay for a time he registered with eleven black companions at Selma's leading hotel, the first blacks ever to do so. Voter registration, however, was in county hands and in Dallas County Sheriff James G. Clark, a burly 42-year-old, the movement had what it needed in an enemy, another "Bull" Connor.

Fresh from his triumphal acceptance of the Nobel Peace Prize and an exhilarating banquet in Atlanta, honoring its native son, Martin Luther King, Jr., came to Selma to announce the purpose of a new SCLC drive: "We will seek to arouse the federal government by marching by the thousands to the place of registration . . . . We must be willing to go to jail by the thousands. We are not asking, we are demanding the ballot." King's participation was a guarantee of federal involvement in what had been a local effort sparked, in large part, by SNCC and a handful of local militants, including Amelia Boynton, who had run for Congress in 1964. (She got three hundred votes.) Twelve Democratic and three Republican congressmen, headed by Michigan's Charles Diggs, came to Selma to investigate. King conferred with Vice President Humphrey and Attorney General designate Nicholas de B. Katzenbach and was assured that a strong voting rights bill would be sent to Congress "in the near future."

SNCC came to Selma early in 1963 when the newly married Reverend Bernard Lafayette and his wife, Colia, arrived armed with a VEP grant to carry on voter education work. Along with Frank Holloway and Worth Long, they labored unsung and unceasingly. Voter classes began with one student, a Mr. Major Washington, sixty-seven, who brought another and then several more until the movement was able to mount "Freedom Day" demonstrations when blacks lined up outside the county courthouse, over two hundred strong, with the sheriff snapping pictures of each and every one. SCLC sent in field workers to organize, but Selma's 1964 efforts were overshadowed by the Mississippi Freedom Summer. An injunction secured in the state courts against all civil rights activists hampered further work until set aside in

---

° Sumter, Greene, Hale, Wilcox, and Lowndes counties.

late 1964. The SNCC office was raided in January 1964, records and leaflets seized and nine workers arrested.

Once SCLC decided upon Selma as a starting point for 1965, the tempo of civil rights activity picked up sharply. John Lewis, Hosea Williams, and others led waves of protesting blacks, who were carted off to jail by an obliging Sheriff Clark. "You're an agitator," the sheriff stormed at Lewis, "and that is the lowest form of humanity." On January 22, black teachers lined up to register only to be driven off by nightstick-wielding deputies. King and Abernathy led a mass march toward the county courthouse on February 1; that day, 770, including the two leaders, were arrested. Another group of 550 were imprisoned the following day. King spent five days in jail and on the day of his release a court order was secured instructing Dallas County registrars to meet "more often" than twice monthly. On February 10, some 165 demonstrating high-school and younger children were force marched, kept at a fast walk and a run, for over two miles of country road on the way to jail. The sheriff and his men rode in cars, taking turns at prodding the youngsters along with cattleprods and billy clubs. The Reverend James Bevel, suffering from a cranial concussion, was chained to a hospital bed. Not twenty-five miles away in Marion, the seat of Perry County, Jimmie Lee Jackson, a black laborer, was fatally beaten in a melee created by state troopers breaking up an evening demonstration. Nine people were hospitalized, including three newsmen. Three white clergymen were set upon by white hoodlums on leaving a Selma black restaurant; one, the Reverend James J. Reeb, a Unitarian minister from Boston, died two days later, on March 11, of a fractured skull. After the climactic march to Montgomery, Viola Gregg Liuzzo, who had spent the day shuttling marchers in her car, was shot dead as she was driving back to Selma.

Terror there was aplenty, but there were moments of wry, insightful humor: Commissioner of Public Safety Wilson Baker, ruefully overlooking a busload of singing northern whites arrested for picketing the home of the mayor, and saying, "This has ceased to be a Negro movement . . . at least we had good music when the Negroes were demonstrating." Sixteen-year-old Bernard Sims telling Pat Watters how he felt about testing a movie theater for compliance with the 1964 Civil Rights Act, "It was *fun!* Because we made Sheriff Clark mad. The man who hit me said, 'Move on, nigger.' Sheriff Clark threw his billy at someone. One of us picked it up and said, 'Here it is, Sheriff,' and handed it to him." The two hundred young people marching in a hard rain to the courthouse to pray for Sheriff Clark, who had suffered a mild coronary. Demonstrating, one youngster told a *New York Times* reporter, "just wasn't the same without Jim Clark fussing and fuming. We honestly miss him."

Sheriff Clark, of course, predictably came back with more of the same. There were, however, developments that did mark Selma as different from the Albany or Birmingham protests. For the first time, southern whites actively participated. Some seventy white Alabamans—professors, businessmen, schoolteachers, housewives, and others—led by the Reverend Joseph Ellwanger of St. Paul's Lutheran Church in Birmingham, gathered on March 6 from all over the state to march to the Dallas County courthouse in support of black Alabamans' right to vote. Behind the scenes, SNCC and SCLC quarreled over tactics with the former, at first, opposed to mass demonstrations; SNCC, so they argued, wanted to get about the business of registering voters. King and SCLC wanted to bring the Selma protest to a head, precipitate federal intervention, and accelerate the passage of the promised voting rights act.* Popular support among Selma's blacks was faltering for lack of dramatic achievement or concrete results. King proposed a mass march from Selma to Montgomery through fifty miles of black belt countryside infested with white hostiles. Protests over the denial of the right to vote would be lodged with Governor Wallace. On Sunday, March 7, over five hundred blacks, with knapsacks, satchels, and bedrolls, stepped off from the Brown A. M. E. Chapel for Montgomery. With John Lewis and Hosea Williams leading (King and Abernathy were in Atlanta ministering to their congregations), the marchers, two by two, crossed the Pettus Bridge, leading out of town. (Lewis participated as an individual; SNCC did not "endorse" the march.) The highway was barred by fifty state troopers equipped with gas masks, one hundred of Sheriff Clark's deputized vigilantes, fifteen of them mounted on horses. Hosea Williams asked twice for a word with the troopers' commander, Major John Cloud. "There is no word to be had," Cloud snapped. "You have two minutes to turn around and go back to your church." As television cameras whirred, there was an awesome silence, no one stirred until Cloud barked the command, "Troopers forward!"

The marchers were driven back into Selma by tear gas and nightsticks and the charging horsemen. John Lewis had his skull fractured, and sixteen marchers ended up in the hospital while another fifty received emergency treatment. To avert further bloodshed, Wilson Baker intervened, convincing the harassed blacks to seek refuge in the Brown Chapel and arguing Sheriff Clark into withdrawing his men from Selma's jurisdiction.

Selma was back in the news, the brutality on television screens and in newspaper and magazine photographs for all who had eyes to see.

---

* After two murders, numerous injuries, and 3,800 arrests, some 50 blacks were added to the Dallas County voting list. Federal registrars added 8,906 in the year following the adoption of the Voting Rights Act of 1965.

Sympathizers from the North began arriving on every flight. King announced the resumption of the march for Tuesday, March 9, despite a temporary federal restraining order and President Johnson's urgings that it be observed. The injunction was, in fact, a byproduct of an SCLC move to secure an order enjoining Alabama to guarantee the safety of would-be marchers. Leroy Collins, former governor of Florida and head of the newly established federal Community Relations Service, flew in to confer with both sides. He persuaded the Alabama authorities not to molest Tuesday's marchers if they would turn back at an agreed upon point. Worried about future federal cooperation and fearful of the possibilities of violence, King agreed to limit the march—but out on the highway where a symbolic victory might be claimed.

On Tuesday, March 10, King led some 1,000 blacks and 450 white sympathizers over the Pettus Bridge and a quarter of a mile or so down the highway toward Montgomery. Halted by the state troopers, the marchers were granted permission to pray. As they rose back on their feet, Major Cloud ordered his men to break ranks and move to the shoulders of the highway. The road to Montgomery was open, but King declined the gambit and the marchers returned to Brown Chapel, the starting point of so many Selma endeavors, singing "Ain't Gonna Let Nobody Turn Me 'Round."

Events in Selma stirred in President Johnson a mighty and purposeful anger. He did what he could to minimize further violence and to respond to the mounting demands upon him that black Alabamans be guaranteed the right to march unmolested and black Southerners the right to vote. Selma sympathy marches were staged in Detroit, Harlem, Chicago, Los Angeles, and elsewhere with thousands expressing their solidarity with the beleaguered Alabamans. Twelve students managed to sit-in at the White House. Over four thousand religious leaders assembled in Washington to press for voting rights legislation. The President conferred three hours with Alabama Governor Wallace, and at a news conference announced that seven hundred federal troops were on a stand-by alert to intervene in Selma if necessary. "I told the governor," the President said, "that the brutality in Selma last Sunday just must not be repeated."

In an unusual departure, the President went before Congress on Monday evening, March 15, to announce that a voting rights measure would be submitted two days later. In an impressive, moving speech, possibly his greatest, Lyndon B. Johnson told the nation:

"At times history and fate meet at a single time in a single place to shape a turning point in man's unending search for freedom. So it was at Lexington and Concord.

So it was a century ago at Appomattox. So it was last week in Selma, Alabama.

There, long-suffering men and women peacefully protested the denial of their rights as Americans. Many were brutally assaulted. One good man—a man of God—was killed.

Many of the issues of civil rights are complex and difficult. But about this there can be no argument. Every American citizen must have an equal right to vote. There is no reason which can excuse the denial of that right. There is no duty which weighs more heavily on us than the duty to ensure that right.

Even if we pass this bill, the battle will not be over. What happened in Selma is part of a far larger movement which reaches into every section and state of America. It is the effort of American Negroes to secure for themselves the full blessings of American life.

Their cause must be our cause too. It is not just Negroes, but all of us, who must overcome the crippling legacy of bigotry and injustice. And [slowly but firmly] we *shall* overcome.

The bill would not pass and be signed into law until August 6 but the civil rights movement marched once again—and for the last time on such a scale—from Selma to Montgomery six days later. "Walk together, children," Martin Luther King told the three thousand gathered in Selma on Sunday morning, March 21, "don't you get weary, and it will lead us to the Promised Land. And Alabama will be a new Alabama, and America will be a new America." Under the watchful eye of the federalized Alabama National Guard, three hundred marchers— the number allowed by the federal court order—tramped through the freshening Alabama countryside.

Five days later the marchers, augmented by some twenty-five thousand, swung onto the broad street that leads downtown through the center of Montgomery and then up toward the Capitol. The roster rivaled that of the March on Washington: A. Philip Randolph, Roy Wilkins, Whitney Young, Ralph Bunche, Bayard Rustin, John Lewis, Walter Reuther, the Right Reverend Richard Millard, suffragan bishop of California's Episcopal diocese, Rabbi Abraham Heschel of the American Jewish Theological Seminary, an expanded gallery of celebrities, James Baldwin—in from Europe—and other dignitaries too numerous to name.

On the steps of the Capitol—where Jefferson Davis took the oath of office as President of the Confederate States of America—Martin Luther King, Jr., turned to address an enchanted crowd. (Governor Wallace, who refused to meet his petitioners, peeked at them through parted venetian blinds.) As millions watched over television, King began:

> Last Sunday more than eight thousand of us started on a mighty walk from Selma, Alabama. We have walked on meandering highways and rested our bodies on rocky byways.

He called for more marches on segregated schools, on poverty and on ballot boxes "until race baiters disappear from the political arena." Then working up to a grand climax evoking the Bible and the American past:

> My people, my people, listen! The battle is in our hands . . . . I know some of you are asking today, "How long will it take?" I come to say to you this afternoon however difficult the moment, however frustrating the hour, it will not be long, because truth pressed to the earth will rise again.
>
> How long? Not long, because no lie can live forever.
>
> How long? Not long, because you will reap what you sow.
>
> How long? Not long, because the arm of the moral universe is long but it bends toward justice.
>
> How long? Not long. Because mine eyes have seen the glory of the coming of the Lord, trampling out the vintage where the grapes of wrath are stored. He has loosed the fateful lightening of his terrible swift sword. His truth is marching on. Glory hallelujah! Glory hallelujah!

XIII

Black Power

SELMA WAS A REGROUPING ON THE near side of the March on Washington summit; from then on, it was downhill all the way for the civil rights coalition. Rifts that had appeared as hairline cracks in the early days of the struggle for civil rights broke wide open; unbridgeable gulfs yawned between integrationists and intransient black power advocates. Blacks, as we shall see, made progress based on the victories won by the civil rights movement but "Things fell apart; the coalition cannot hold," to paraphrase the much quoted W. B. Yeats. White liberals spun off into anti-war activity—the United States bombed North Vietnam on February 7, 1965—while the black center fell into bickering pieces. The harsh truth was that the coalition could not survive, let alone surpass, its stunning success—the passage of the Civil Rights Act of 1964 and, after Selma, the Voting Rights Act of 1965.

What held the coalition together was an overriding national need: The resolution of an American dilemma expressed in a stated creed of equality coexisting with a *de jure* denial of equal justice. Within this parameter, the civil rights movement accomplished much in a very short time. Blacks began, as we have seen, to move in earnest with the sit-ins and Freedom Rides of 1960 and 1961. As the need for federal legislation became more apparent, the movement broadened, gathering in the forces of the coalition—blacks and whites, churches and civic groups, liberals, radicals, and trade unionists. The climax came when over 210,000 marched on Washington on August 28, 1963. Within a year, Congress passed more legislation with enforcement teeth than it had in the whole period since 1875, the height of Reconstruction. As Yale historian Professor C. Vann Woodward summed up this achievement: "Insofar as federal laws are capable of coping with these knotty problems [racial discrimination in public schools, public accommodations, and voting rights], Congress has just about fulfilled its role." The Civil Rights Act of 1966, in effect, completed the job. As Senator Sam J. Ervin, Democrat of North Carolina, observed, "For the first time, we have a bill which proposes that other than southern oxen are to be gored." The act prohibited threat of injury to persons engaged in the exercise of their constitutional rights; assured the selection of state and federal juries without regard to race; and banned racial and religious discrimination in the sale, rental and financing of roughly 80 percent of all housing in the United States. Thereafter, federal legislation might refine or reinforce civil rights but the fundamental guarantees were assured by law. The legal foundations of racism in America had been destroyed.

Once, however, the coalition achieved its goals of national legislation aimed at equal opportunity and at securing social justice under the Constitution, it was bound to disintegrate. Class interests reasserted themselves. Each member of the coalition, naturally, returned to its own central concerns.

It is one of the paradoxes of all social movements that those who make up the movement invariably feel the breath of some catastrophe blowing down their necks; their demands are, therefore, urgent, immediate, for "Freedom Now!" As the movement reached out to touch, if not fully embrace the black masses, the *lumpenproletariat* of the cities, recruiting to its ranks upwardly mobile youth from this lower-class segment of black America, "Now" became fraught with inherent improbabilities, even impossibilities. Television aggravated what Bayard Rustin has characterized as the "instant gratification" syndrome of the slum-bred, who want *that* now! An understandable impatience became an angry insistence on instant success, not only in terms of acquiring the goods of an affluent society, but also in becoming instant plumbers or instant physicists.

However, all that was boiled down into that existential essence, "Freedom Now," could not be obtained "now." A great many things had to happen, be made to happen before change, or rather, progress could occur. Battle-scarred militants were disappointed because the results to them seemed disproportionate to the energy and devotion expended. When the Columbia, South Carolina, *State* reported on July 4, 1964, *"Southern Segregation Falls Silently, Without Violence,"* many were disappointed for while the banner headline marked a historical moment, it did not announce Armageddon nor, for that matter, a new world a-borning. Things were just better. In 1960, only three job recruiters turned up at Lincoln University, a prestigious black college in Pennsylvania; in 1965, the year the law required equal opportunity compliance by business firms, there were more recruiters, one hundred, than there were graduating members of the senior class, seventy-two.

A people on the move, those who make change, must rest; energies spent taking an objective must be recouped and regrouped for the next assault. When troops are winded, even great battles pause. Like most social movements that gain some measure of success, the civil rights movement expended much in hopes and spirit during the first half of the 1960s to win what it did, and as a result, for a time, it was exhausted and suffered a good case of battle fatigue. It is not, incidentally, the best condition for thinking out new answers to old problems, nor for the consideration of problems brought on by one's own success. Being both tired and without immediate central purpose, the movement bickered, leaders feuded, and organizations quarreled among themselves. Cities erupted with the cry, "Burn, baby, burn," and a succession of "long hot summers" fueled visions of the apocalypse.

Writing in a powerfully prophetic work, *The Fire Next Time*, Harlem-born James Baldwin, in 1963, declared: "The Negroes of this country may never be able to rise to power, but they are very well placed indeed to precipitate chaos and ring down the curtain on the American dream." Redemption, of course, is always possible: the price being "the unconditional freedom of the Negro; it is not too much to say that he, who has been so long neglected, is the key figure in his country, and the American future is precisely as bright or as dark as his." And, so Baldwin concluded, "if we do not dare everything, the fulfillment of that prophecy, recreated from the Bible in song by a slave, is upon us: 'God gave Noah the rainbow sign, no more water, the fire next time.'"

Baldwin was not alone in predicting a holocaust. It was, after all, a part of civil rights rhetoric, but none did so with such verve and before such a wide audience. Portions of *The Fire Next Time* appeared in *The New Yorker,* and the book was a best-seller. Despite Baldwin's warning, if his prophecy can be called that, nearly everyone was shocked when the fire flashed in an obscure section of Los Angeles on August 11, 1965. True, Howard H. Jewel, an assistant to the California attorney general, had warned in a memorandum to his chief that the Los Angeles police and the city's blacks were "embarked upon a course of conflict . . . ," but the report was filed. Prophets of catastrophe were apt to cite Harlem, Detroit, or Chicago as potentially combustible. The National Urban League ranked Los Angeles as first among sixty-eight cities rated in terms of housing, employment and other desirables for blacks. *Ebony,* in March 1965, listed Los Angeles among the "10 best cities for Negro employment." Unemployment among the city's half-million blacks was at 7.9 percent, but not double the city overall figure of 5.2 percent, as was the case in far too many other cities. Watts, however, was the poorest of Los Angeles' nine nearly all-black communities, with an unemployment rate of 30 percent among adult males. It had no hospital

and in a city dependant on cars only 14 percent of the families in Watts
were car owners as compared with 79 percent for all American families.
Those with jobs were condemned to ride a shoddy but expensive public
transportation system, spending, say, $1.50 to ride an hour or two to get
a job paying $6 or $7 a day. With tree-lined avenues, many attractive
California-style bungalows, nine swimming pools, over twenty-three
social agencies, Watts was, nonetheless, a far-cry from the congested
slums of, say, Chicago.

The poverty of Watts, perhaps, was more sharply felt because of the
surrounding affluence. Watts—and the subsequent summer riots of
1966 and 1967—occurred during a period of rising employment and
falling unemployment. (The overall rate fell from 4.5 percent in 1965 to
3.8 percent in 1967 and to 3.5 in 1969; the black rate was higher, but
falling, from 8.1 percent to 7.4 percent to 6.4 percent over the same
years.) The Watts riot bears out Lewis Coser's theory of relative
deprivation, denoting "the deprivation that arises not so much from the
absolute amount of frustration as from the experienced discrepancy
between one's lot and that of other persons or groups which serve as
standards of reference." It was a very modern riot. "Burn, baby, burn,"
the widely touted slogan of the rioters, inadvertently originated with a
disc jockey. Young people learned where the action was over their
transistor radios. The black middle class was not much of a moderating
influence; the Los Angeles Riot Study found that support for the riot
was "as great among the relatively well-educated and economically
advantaged as among poorly educated and economically disadvantaged
in the curfew area." Most of the rioters turned out to have been in the
area for at least ten years and most were employed. Two UCLA
sociologists Raymond J. Murphy and James M. Watson found that
people from the best (18 percent) and from the worst (25.6 percent)
sections were almost equally involved in the rioting. The riot had its
consumption effect; the looters were also consumers. The McCone
Report, named after John A. McCone who headed a commission of
prominent local citizens appointed by Governor Edward P. Brown to
look into the causes of the riot, observed, "The rioters concentrated on
food markets, liquor stores, clothing stores, department stores, and
pawnshops." Rioters were more likely to destroy the stock of the liquor
stores than to steal or drink it, and the McCone Commission found "no
evidence" of attempts to steal narcotics from ransacked pharmacies. No
residences were deliberately burned, damage to schools, libraries,
public buildings was "minimal," and certain businesses, notably service
stations and automobile dealers, were "for the most part unharmed." A
couple carrying off a couch set it down and rested whenever its weight
became too much for them. Other looters calmly observed traffic lights
as they carried booty homeward.

One could paraphrase Albert D. Biderman's observation that "it is altogether possible that year-to-year increases in crime rates may be more indicative of social progress than of social decay," and say that the Watts and following riots of 1966 and 1967 may have been more indicative of social progress than of social decay. The Watts outbreak began, as did many of the subsequent ones, in a contretemps with the police. The arrest of a drunken driver—and the police insistence on hauling away the car though the driver's brother and mother were on hand to claim it—precipitated the six-day civil disorder. Police brutality, an ill-defined accusation ranging from insulting language to excessive and unjustified use of force, looms large in all explanations of the causes of the riots. A 1965 Gallup Poll found that 35 percent of black men believed that there was police brutality in their areas (only 7 percent of white men thought so). Well above a majority of Watts residents believed that such brutality occurred in their community. Paradoxically, as James Q. Wilson has pointed out, this reflects an increase, perhaps even an improvement, in law enforcement service. At one time, the police tended to "overlook" crimes committed by blacks against blacks, and this was no longer the case by the mid-1960s. And, in Watts, although a battle, between city hall and the local community over who was to contribute what, limited the effectiveness of the new Johnsonian poverty programs, social services were being extended.

The expansion of various services to the poor surely contributed to rising expectations among the poor. Sociologist James C. Davis suggests that neither the destitute nor the well satisfied are makers of revolutions. Revolutions occur when the actual situation is improving less rapidly than expected, which seems to have been so with Watts. Revolutions, or in this case, riots, may be expected "when a long-term phase of growth is followed by a short-term phase of stagnation or decline." In the case of Watts, as Bayard Rustin so perceptively noted, the check in the natural rise in expectations came from a political act, the 1964 repeal by California voters of the state's fair housing law. The McCone Report noted that the blacks of Los Angeles were "affronted" by the repeal of the Rumford Act. But Rustin comes closer to the mark: "Affronted, indeed! The largest state in the union, by a three-to-one majority, abolishes one of its own laws against discrimination and Negroes are described as regarding this as they might the failure of a friend to keep an engagement. What they did feel . . . was that while the rest of the North was passing civil rights laws, and improving opportunities for Negroes, their own state and city were rushing to reinforce the barriers against them. Small wonder, then, that blacks of Los Angeles grabbed what they could when they could." While the Watts riot had no single cause, except that which is contained in the word "slum," no doubt the feelings described by Rustin did contribute to the ultimate explosion and help explain why middle-class blacks, who otherwise disapproved of the violence and destruction, expressed empathy with the motives of the participants.

The Los Angeles Riot Study found that 38 percent of the population of the curfew area felt that the riot would help the black cause. Only 20 percent felt that it would hurt while 74 percent of Los Angeles whites felt that it would hurt. Fifty-one percent of the riot area population saw the whites as being more sympathetic because of the riot (only 33 percent of the whites felt this way). This is in keeping with Rustin's telling anecdote. When a black youth of about twenty told him, "We won," Rustin asked, "How have you won? Homes have been destroyed. Negroes are lying dead in the streets, the stores from which you buy food and clothes are destroyed, and people are bringing you relief." The youth replied, "We won because we made the whole world pay attention to us. The police chief never came here before; the mayor always stayed uptown. We made them come."

Watts did indeed bring benefits, at least to a degree. President Johnson ordered the release of $1.7 million in federal anti-poverty funds for rehabilitation; another $29 million worth of school, job training, small business, and health programs were expedited. Budd Schulberg established a writers' workshop; businessmen raised capital to start a baseball bat factory manufacturing the "Watts Walloper." The local people even organized an annual festival to commemorate the uprising. But these undeniable gains were exacted at a high cost—34 dead, 1,032 injured, and 3,438 arrested with the great majority of the victims black. It took a full contingent of the national guard, some 13,900 to restore order. Damage estimates ranged from $20 million to $35 million. Of more lasting consequence was white resentment. Conservative Ronald Reagan defeated liberal Governor Pat Brown in the following year; and lingering echoes of the riot helped Mayor Samuel Yorty, in 1969 defeat the first viable black candidate for mayor, Thomas Bradley.°

The Watts riot and its successors also contributed to the growing cult of violence among militants of both races. Some whites armed themselves; a number joined white terrorist organizations like the Minutemen. Among some blacks, it became fashionable to speak of the riots as "rebellions." Fearful whites and the more militant blacks, especially among the young, tended to see Watts and the succeeding riots as continuations or a part of the civil rights revolution. In the case of the whites, things had gone too far; in the case of the militant blacks, not far enough. Never mind that the NAACP, CORE, or any of the other civil rights organizations had no following to speak of in Watts. Dick Gregory courageously broke off a night-club engagement twenty-

---

° Bradley, however, did win in 1973.

five miles away to come to Watts in a vain effort to stem looting and violence. He was shot, fortunately only slightly wounded. Martin Luther King, Jr. flew in (not many in Watts had ever heard of him) and talked of nonviolence to a crowd of three hundred on the last day of the rioting. He called the riots "absolutely wrong, socially detestable and self-defeating." Roy Wilkins, in the New York *Amsterdam News*, declared, "God help black Americans if this is their revolution and these their revolutionaries." But the established black leadership acted and talked to no effect. There were five major riots in 1965; twenty-one in 1966; and seventy-five in 1967. Fantasists saw in this a revolution. Looting punks were the urban guerrillas of a new war against America.

Revolutionary fantasies, however, were in the air before Watts. The "SNCC kids" had given up Camus for headier readings of Franz Fanon, Malcolm X, and Mao. Working among rural blacks in the South, SNCC and CORE activists donned denim coveralls and fashioned a political appeal aimed at rural and lower-class blacks. Working in Bogalusa, Louisiana, in 1965, on various civil rights projects in the face of Ku Klux Klan persecution, CORE accepted the protection of a newly organized, armed self-defense group called the "Deacons for Defense and Justice." SNCC had long since come to an unofficial understanding that while field workers, in their own judgment, might eschew arms, they could no longer in the face of murder and terror reasonably expect local people to do so. This, in itself, is not an unreasonable proposition and was, as yet, a far cry from the glorification of violence—"as American as cherry pie"—soon to develop within SNCC and among other, predominantly young, black militant groups. With Malcolm X and Che Guevera as new cult heroes, some began to see in their activities in the rural black belt of the South the beginnings of an American "long march," of an aroused peasantry against the urban center, patterned after Chairman Mao's China success. Within the city, as the riots ostensibly demonstrated, urban guerrillas would rise and join the encroaching rural masses in tearing down the edifice of a corrupt society. Third-world cultists saw revolutionary African and Asian armies coming to their rescue in a besieged America. (The Kennedys, too, in exalting the Green Berets and guerrilla tactics in South East Asia, must bear some responsibility for this new enthusiasm.) Stokely Carmichael, a charismatic, lanky and telegenic youth, born in Trinidad, educated at New York City's prestigious Bronx High School of Science and a graduate of Howard University, gave this inchoate infantile leftism philosophic paint—and a slogan—in the cry "Black Power."

When Carmichael went to Lowndes County, Alabama, during the summer of 1965 to participate in a voter registration drive, he had already, at twenty-four, some five years' experience in the movement. He had started working on voter registration with James Forman in

Fayette County, Tennessee, in 1960; participated in the Freedom Rides; joined a Howard University's Young Peoples' Socialist League chapter where he came, for a time, under the influence of Bayard Rustin; joined SNCC and served in various campaigns throughout the South, including the Mississippi Freedom Summer. Carmichael was profoundly affected by the murder of Jonathan Daniels, a theological student shot down by an angry white outside a Haynesville grocery store. Daniels had been working on voter registration in and around Selma the summer of 1965. At a protest meeting in Haynesville, Carmichael cried out, "We're going to tear this county up: Then we're going to build it back brick by brick until it's a fit place for human beings!" In Lowndes County, which shares with Wilcox County the dubious honor of having absolutely no blacks registered as voters before federal examiners arrived in 1965, what Carmichael had to say about black power made indisputable sense. (The examiners would register, with SNCC aid, 2,688 black voters out of 5,122 eligibles in the first year.) Black power in Lowndes County, where blacks were 80 percent of the population with an average annual income of $943, Carmichael explained, "will mean that if a Negro is elected sheriff, he can end police brutality. If a black man is elected tax assessor, he can collect and channel funds for the building of better roads and schools serving black people—thus advancing the move from political power into the economic arena."

SNCC promoted an all-black political party in Lowndes with a black panther as a symbol. It was abortive; black voters would elect a black coroner in 1970, long after SNCC left. Carmichael, however, also worked at building a base within SNCC, activity that would pay off in his election as SNCC Chairman the following spring. In an all-night secret meeting held outside Nashville, Tennessee, on May 14–15, 1966, Carmichael took over SNCC. At first, John Lewis, a committed integrationist, was reelected, 66 to 11. Discussion continued on into the night, people left, and in the weary hours of the morning, Lewis's election was challenged by a nonmember. Another vote was taken, and Stokely Carmichael became chairman. "What happened that night," John Lewis sadly recalled years later, "was the beginning of the end of SNCC. Breaks were created, wounds were opened that never were healed. I didn't consider it a repudiation of me. It was a very sad thing, a tragic thing for SNCC."

James Forman, the executive director of SNCC and its fortyish mentor, was forced out even though he apparently had a hand in the changeover in leadership. Some weeks later, he severed his connection: "I'm not prepared to give up my personal commitment to nonviolence." Others left, too. Julian Bond, SNCC's publicity director who was elected to the Georgia House of Representatives in 1965,° resigned. SNCC became a handful of fanatics. Carmichael enjoyed a momentary success in stirring up a riot in Atlanta—"We have to build a revolution"—and his successor as chairman, the colorful H. Rap Brown, helped to start another in Cambridge, Maryland. Under court indictment, Brown went underground or simply disappeared, and SNCC faded into the Black Panthers, organizationally in the persons of Carmichael and his followers and in the public eye.

Black power reverberated through CORE, transforming the integrationist organization into an all-black one. James Farmer resigned as executive director on December 27, 1965.°° Others left, including George Wiley, who later founded a welfare rights group. Floyd McKissick, a 43-year-old Durham, North Carolina, lawyer, succeeded Farmer. McKissick pledged that he would intensify CORE's economic and political programs, North and South, to free blacks living under what he termed "feudalism in 1966." CORE helped to supplement its direct action programs with the building of consumer cooperatives and credit unions to liberate blacks from "economic bondage." Roy Innis took over what was left of CORE in 1970 and carried it further into black separatism. Innis promulgated self-help entrepreneurism, schemes for separate but equal schools and a form of neo-Garveyism. Not only did the integrationist spirit go out of CORE, but so did the membership.

The NAACP, however, survived as the only civil rights membership organization. Its membership fell from a post-March on Washington peak of 510,000 to 465,000 in 1964 and 440,000 in 1965 and down to 390,235 in 1971. The decline reflected the turmoil of the late 1960s and the fall off in broad public support for civil rights activity during that

---

° Bond was refused his seat because of his anti-Vietnam War stand. The Supreme Court, however, ruled that he was entitled to his seat. As of 1973, he was still a member of the legislature from an Atlanta district. Lewis joined the Field Foundation and now heads the Voters' Education Project. Forman joined the Black Panthers as foreign minister; left in 1968 to head the Black Economic Development Conference, which solicited "reparations" from the churches. He succeeded in getting $200,000 from the Episcopal Church. As Roy Wilkins wryly noted, no denomination ever gave the NAACP that much money, obviously because the NAACP asked for justice instead of demanding revolution and black domination; exploiting white guilt was rewarding.

Carmichael, too, joined the Black Panthers, but broke away as a consequence of an obscure ideological dispute. He left for Africa, married singer Miriam Makeba, and returned to the United States in 1972 to preach Pan-Africanism. H. Rap Brown, who disappeared for several years, surfaced during a police shoot-out over the holdup of a Harlem bar. He was wounded and tried for robbery.

°° Farmer resigned to launch a new undertaking, a federally financed National Center for Community Action Education, but the financial rug of $860,000 was yanked from under him by Congressman Adam Clayton Powell, then head of the House Labor and Education Committee. Farmer taught for a while at Lincoln University, became a subcabinet member of the first Nixon Administration, only to resign to take up teaching and lecturing once again.

period. Nonetheless, along with the labor movement, various liberal organizations, Catholic and Protestant church groups, the Jewish social agencies and membership organizations, the NAACP sustained the Leadership Conference on Civil Rights and backed whatever civil rights accomplishments can be tallied for the balance of the decade. Significantly, the Leadership Conference broadened its scope during this time from narrow civil rights concerns—the establishment and enforcement of rights in law—to embrace a wider scope, "The realization of social and economic conditions in which alone the fulfillment of these rights is possible."

The media, however, hared after the wilder excesses of black power and ignored the programmatic concerns of the NAACP and its allies as well as the substantial achievements of black Americans. There were, between June 1967 and May 1968, 236 riots and disturbances resulting in 8,133 casualties and 49,607 arrests, but involving less than one percent of the total black population, approximately 200,000, according to the National Commission on Causes and Prevention of Violence. This tiny minority as well as the infinitesimally small number of super-black militants received newspaper and television coverage far in excess of that given the overwhelming majority of law abiding, hard-working black citizens. Throughout the 1960s and down to the present, this majority has been overwhelmingly in favor of participating fully in the mainstream of American life.

The civil rights revolution, as of the mid-1960s, succeeded in eliminating de jure segregation. It also secured, in large measure, equal opportunity, certainly in law though less so in practice. There were changes, improvements, and progress. The Economic Opportunity Act of 1964 declared that it is "the policy of the United States to eliminate the paradox in the midst of plenty in this Nation by opening to everyone the opportunity to live in decency and dignity." Over 1965–1970, some $2.3 billions were committed to a variety of anti-poverty programs—the ever popular Head-Start pre-kindergarten education program, Job Corps, the Neighborhood Youth Corps and other work training efforts, and other programs aimed at rehabilitating the poor. Overall federal expenditures for all welfare services—social insurance, public aid, health programs, education, housing, veterans, and other social welfare operations—rose from 24.9 billions in 1960 to 76.7 billions at the end of the decade. It was the largest rise in such expenditures over a decade since the beginnings of the welfare state in the New Deal of President Franklin D. Roosevelt.

Yet, in the midst of unprecedented prosperity, a tight job market, and greatly extended social services, most Americans, so far as one can judge, were in agreement with their President when, at Howard University, between Selma and Watts, on June 4, 1965, he declared:

"But the harsh fact of the matter is that in the battle of true equality too many are losing ground every day." The President detailed current consequences of "the devastating heritage" of slavery and of "a century of oppression, hatred and injustice," terming them "facts of this American failure." These included the doubling of the unemployment rate for blacks; the slip in the median income of black families from 57 percent to 53 of the white family median income between 1952 to 1963; a black infant mortality rate that was 90 percent greater than that of whites; the lack of training and skills; the crowded slums. He associated himself with those who saw black poverty as different from white poverty, at least in part. The differences were not racial, but "the consequence of ancient brutality, past injustice, and present prejudice." He did not view the black experience as comparable, in its entirety, with that of other minorities. "They made a valiant and a largely successful effort to emerge from poverty and prejudice. The Negro, like these others, will have to rely mostly on his own efforts. But he just cannot do it alone. For they did not have the heritage of centuries to overcome. They did not have a cultural tradition which had been twisted and battered by endless years of hatred and hopelessness. Nor were they excluded because of race or color—a feeling whose dark intensity is matched by no other prejudice in our society." °

President Johnson did not propose leaving black Americans to go it alone. To help decide what needed to be done so that the American Negro might "fulfill the rights which, after the long time of injustice, he is finally about to secure . . . to move beyond opportunity to achievement," the President called a White House Conference on Civil Rights of scholars, experts, and outstanding black leaders.

The conference, held on June 1 and 2, produced little that was new, except discussions and some unease. A handful of black militants, about twenty by *The New York Times* account, postured outside the

---

° The consensus on the need to do something about racial injustice and poverty was extraordinary. Republicans and other fiscal conservatives might cavil at the expenditures proposed but few refused to recognize the necessity of doing something about poverty, and in particular black poverty. It was a conservative economist Milton Friedman who, in proposing a "negative income tax" as a substitute for the growing variety of welfare programs, helped publicize the idea of a guaranteed annual income. In 1967, the Urban Coalition, a convocation of some one thousand representatives of business, labor, religion, civil rights, and local government reiterated the substantive points of President Johnson's Howard speech and endorsed a program embodying much of what was proposed by the 1966 White House Conference on Civil Rights. Participants not only included the expected labor leaders, George Meany and Walter Reuther, civil rights spokesmen, A. Philip Randolph, Roy Wilkins, Whitney Young, and Martin Luther King, Jr., and other notable liberals, but such captains of industry as Henry Ford II and of finance as David Rockefeller and the presidents or board chairmen of many of the country's greatest corporations—the Aluminum Company of America, Metropolitan Life Insurance Company, General Electric, Standard Oil, du Pont, Sears Roebuck, Morgan Guaranty Trust, American Airlines, to name a few.

conference, shouting "Uncle Tom" at the blacks who entered. Floyd McKissick charged that the conference had been "rigged by the Administration" and proposed some resolutions, including one stating that the Vietnam War was using resources needed to eradicate poverty at home and another, advocating home rule for the District of Columbia. The 2,400 conferees approved a 100-page report, containing what conference Chairman Ben W. Heineman, a railroad executive, termed "attainable goals" and "not pie-in-the-sky." The report called for stern enforcement of civil rights statutes, "guaranteed employment" for all able to work, affirmative action to break down school segregation, large-scale construction of low-cost, integrated housing, equalization of educational efforts by raising per pupil expenditure to $1,000 a year, the "acceptance of the government's responsibility for guaranteeing minimum income to all Americans," and a wrap-up of various civil rights proposals then before Congress (and subsequently embodied in the 1966 Civil Rights Act).

The conference, however, broke up on a querulous note, a far cry from President Johnson's summons "to fill these rights." The Reverend Hartford Brooklings expressed the feelings of many present, saying: "All this seems to be tomorrow when we face a problem that is like yesterday." Vice President Hubert Humphrey, in a stirring speech, termed "Freedom Now" not a catchword but "a moral imperative for all Americans." He condemned black separatism and the white backlash, but warned that the struggle for civil rights had shifted from Congress and federal courtrooms to state capitals and city halls. "It is in our states and local communities where we must wage the war against America's shame—slumism." Speaking in his usual careful and measured tones, A. Philip Randolph declared that the old solutions for achieving better race relations were no longer adequate. "Most Negroes," he said, "are not asking white people to love them or like them or understand them. They want their neighbors to accept them. They insist that they be granted their rights as citizens and human beings." Randolph gravely continued, "Let me warn this conference that the Negro ghettos in every city are now centers of tension and socio-racial dynamite, near the brink of similar [to Watts] racial explosions of violence."

"This eruptive potential," he wrote in the spring 1966 issue of *Dissent*, "is seething just under the surface in portions of every large city within the United States, awaiting only some slight additional pressure or some unpredictable incitement to propel the explosion." To prevent that catastrophe, Randolph proposed a $185 billion "Freedom Budget" to finance a ten year "*total* war" against poverty. Whitney Young had proposed a $145 billion "domestic Marshall Plan" in 1963, indicating that America's black leadership—and rank and file—were receptive to such far-ranging ideas. Johnson's war against poverty, as invaluable as it was, especially as a precedent for national concern, nonetheless was limited to job training, self-improvement, education, and community action. As economist Leon Keyserling testified before a House Labor Committee hearing, the OEO program, given congressional funding, could accomplish no more than a fraction, possibly 7 percent, of its goal. Roughly 34-million Americans, in the mid-1960s, were living in poverty and an equal number lived above the poverty ceiling of $3,000 a year but well below minimum decencies. One-fifth of the nation still lived in slums and some 40 percent of the American people lacked adequate medical care at costs within their means. Randolph viewed the black role in American society "not as a beneficiary, but as a galvanizing force" awakening "the American conscience with respect to unemployment and poverty." White poor, outnumbering black poor, would also gain from a total commitment to a Freedom Budget. Though Randolph, as usual, was persuasive, the politics of a booming economy worked against economic and social undertakings of so vast a scope. With a falling rate of unemployment, a tight labor market, and a growing involvement in Southeast Asia, the country was not in a New Dealing mood. Most people agreed with the basic OEO perspective that training would suffice.

Let the economy do it—that expressed public opinion and public policy. And despite such disquieting notes as the continuing high unemployment rate among black youth (25 percent over 1965), there was evidence of progress sustained by the economy. The unemployment rate for married black men was less than 2 percent—roughly identical with that of married white men; per capita income of blacks rose faster than white income in 1963 and 1964; and the number of black families moving out of poverty in 1964 was almost equal to the number of white families crossing the line. As the President's Council of Economic Advisors put it in their 1964 report: "The progress of the last two years confirms a crucial lesson. A prosperous economy and the labor demand that it generates are potent forces for eliminating discrimination and income differentials even though they cannot create equality. Improved Negro purchasing power will not fully overcome the effects of discrimination, but it will have a beneficial influence."

The prosperity of the mid-1960s was an incubator for black power, which may be defined as a range of demands from that of a hitherto deprived minority for a fair share to outright separatism. Black power was a cry for "more" which was fed, in part, by the rapid rise in per capita income and aggravated by the remaining discrepancies. The median income of black families, for example, outside the South, was 80 percent of that of white families; better than in the past but not, as yet, parity. Black power, at one level, is a doctrine of self-reliance. As

Stokely Carmichael put it: "We are just going to work, in the way *we* see fit, and on goals *we* define, not for civil rights but for all our human rights." Since, however, black power as an ideological concept rested on, or envisioned, a community of race rather than one of class, it was inherently racialist or even racist in character. Carmichael, at least in his earlier phases, denied that this was so. He expressed hope for a coalition between poor blacks and poor whites as "the only coalition which seems acceptable to us" and as "the major internal instrument of change in American society." Political power, he argued, is "the key to self-determination." With power, "the masses could *make or participate* in making the decisions which govern their destinies, and thus create basic changes in their day-to-day lives." However, black power was no mere electing of black public officials. "A man or woman who is black and from the slums cannot be automatically expected to speak to the needs of black people." So, black people must not only elect representatives, but *"force those representatives to speak to their needs."* How this force is to be manifested is not clear. "The power," Carmichael said, "must be that of a community and emanate from there."

Black power, as it worked out in the latter half of the 1960s, illustrates Hitchcock's law°: the transformation of the movement, not from "moderate" to "extremist," but "from a leadership which, however angry, is essentially pragmatic and concerned with specific problems and demands to a leadership intoxicated with mystical visions of group identity, ineffable perceptions of selfhood, inchoate anger, and fathomless frustration." The final stage, adds Professor Hitchcock, has been "the ritual assertion of a truism—that the oppressed group experiences a sense of selfhood not ultimately accessible to any outsider, no matter how sympathetic, and that the group's liberation involves the bursting of bands which the oppressor does not even dream exist but which are in some sense more real than the obvious chains." Black power moved along a trajectory from Carmichael's "We can build a community of hope only where we have the ability and power to do so: among blacks," to Imamu Amiri Baraka's (Le Roi Jones) "Our brothers/ are moving all over smashing at jelly white forces. We/ must make our own/ World, man, our own world, and we cannot do this/ unless the white man/ is dead . . . ."

Roy Wilkins once said that he was "disturbed" by the careless use of the phrase "civil rights movement," because it is "an umbrella that takes in everybody." He then gave a very quick but accurate thumbnail sketch of the movement at the time, January 1966. The umbrella

---

° After James Hitchcock, professor of history at St. Louis University, who first noted in the March 1973 issue of *Commentary* that events of the 1960s appeared to have contrived to stand Charles Peguy's dictum on its head—"everything which has begun in *politique* has ended in *mystique*."

covered "local groups that are headed by people you never heard of until last week. But it also takes in very small groups like Snick (SNCC) which, I think, would not claim more than 200 so-called members or staff members in the United States, but which is very singular and devoted and dedicated in its purposes. It takes in Martin Luther King's organization, which is a group of affiliates, largely clerical, and behind that a loyal army of people who believe in Dr. King personally as a symbol, but do not constitute an organized body. It takes in CORE, which is a very active group, but medium in size. It takes in the Urban League, which is a specialized professional social work organization of highly trained people in a limited number of cities—70 or 75 at the most—embarked on a program that envisages partnership and understanding and education and mutual help. And it takes in the NAACP, which runs the spectrum [chapters in 1,600 cities in all 50 states]. It takes in, for example, our friend Dick Gregory, who is a one-man army by himself, you know."

When James Meredith was shot by a Memphis eccentric on the second day of his pilgrimage from Memphis to Jackson, Mississippi, the hurried response of the various civil rights spokesmen indicates the relief felt at once again confronting a familiar enemy. Meredith set out on his walk with a handful of friends on Sunday afternoon, June 5, 1966, to dramatize the "all-pervasive and overriding fear that dominates the day-to-day life of the Negro in the United States, especially in the South and particularly in Mississippi." The first black graduate of "Ole Miss," the state university at Oxford, hoped to encourage black Mississippians to register to vote and "to get rid of this fear." He was ambushed, barely ten miles inside Mississippi. Seventy-five shotgun pellets struck his head, neck, back, and legs—fortunately only superficially. The shooting made Meredith—something of a loner and an iconoclast of the black movement—a symbol. King, McKissick, and Carmichael flew to Memphis to resume the march, and Wilkins, Farmer, Lewis, and Young were not far behind. An anxious attempt was made to keep Meredith in the hospital, but he was discharged and returned to New York to recuperate in full. (He returned to participate in the last leg of the march three weeks later, but by then he no longer figured prominently in its purpose.) Momentarily, there were hopes that the march could be capitalized on—as was the Selma march—to secure passage of the 1966 Civil Rights Act, which would strengthen federal protection for civil rights activists among other things, but instead the leaders fell out over the march "manifesto." Wilkins and Young refused to go along with a wholesale condemnation of American society and a demand for sweeping revisions of the pending legislation, believing that the manifesto would hamper efforts to secure passage of the pending bill. King, unhappily, signed the manifesto in the interest of unity and because he wanted to maintain his connection with the young militants of CORE and SNCC. The latter actually lobbied against the bill, charging that any civil rights group or congressmen for passage shared "the hypocrisy of President Johnson and his Administration."

Charles Evers, NAACP field secretary in Mississippi, disassociated himself from the manifesto, saying, "I don't want this to turn into another Selma, where everyone goes home with the cameramen and leaves us holding the bag." The so-called Meredith march had its high moments of courage—among them Martin Luther King's prayer pilgrimage to Philadelphia where Chaney, Goodman, and Schwerner had been murdered in 1964—as well as some foolhardy moments—for example, the taunting of white onlookers and the intermittently protective highway patrol. There was an ugly moment of confrontation at Canton, Mississippi, when state troopers refused to allow the marchers to pitch their tents in the yard of a black school. (The local all-white school board denied them use of the property.) Tear gas was used to disperse the marchers; those who fell in the melee, or failed to move fast enough, were butted with rifles and kicked by booted troopers.

When marchers broke out in the old songs or cries of "Freedom Now," Carmichael and his followers yelled, "Black Power" or "White blood will flow!" Whenever King spoke of nonviolence and Christian love, the young militants mocked him as "de Lawd," or otherwise snickered at his preachings. Perhaps whites did get the message when Carmichael declared, "Tell the white folks most all the scared Negroes in Mississippi are dead." P. L. Elian, an elderly black man whose father had been a slave "right here in Tate County," talking with New York *Post* reporter Pete Hamill about Martin Luther King, was right about the times, if not the march itself, when he said, "I think the daylight's breakin'." The march, however, ended in Jackson, Mississippi, with Meredith in the vanguard, on June 26, but not happily. Roy Wilkins reported to the NAACP convention in July, that though the NAACP had supplied much of the money, food, housing, and transportation for the march, its field secretary had been barred from participation in its final rally.

Black power, as a slogan, preempted the stage. The shouting obscured a decline in membership and financial support of the civil rights organizations. CORE had a deficit of $200,000 in 1966 as did the NAACP, while SNCC had a deficit of $100,000. SNCC became an embattled group of fifty fanatics. Uneasy over the black power philosophy of the militants, the anti-Semitism voiced by poet Imamu Amiri Baraka (Le Roi Jones) and other black militants, and uncertain about answers to the civil rights complexities of the urban North, white liberals cut back their support. Contributions to the Commission on

Religion and Race of the National Council of Churches plunged 25 to 50 percent in 1966; those to the Commission on Religion and Race of the predominantly white United Presbyterian Church failed to reach $100,000 as compared with $131,000 in 1965 and $196,000 in 1964. As Gayroud S. Wilmore, Jr., the black executive director of the commission put it: "What I have seen is a kind of sadness on the part of the white liberals—a sadness that their contribution was not highly regarded by the civil rights organizations." Many were disenchanted; an administration spokesman was quoted in *The New York Times* as saying that the Congress and the President would have accepted a civil rights bill "twice as sweeping" as the one considered in 1966 had civil rights leaders put aside their differences and given the legislation all-out support. (SNCC, as we have noted, actually opposed the 1966 bill.) "People like Stokely Carmichael and Floyd McKissick blew it by taking the attitude that they had enough of the white man's laws—that the laws didn't do any good. Even Martin Luther King sounds like that at times."

As the pastor of the national civil rights congregation, King, at the time, appeared to be floundering, rushing off in far too many directions at once. Some white liberals hoped that he would lead the anti-war movement, and King did speak out against American involvement in Vietnam. "The promises of the Great Society," he declared, "have been shot down on the battlefield of Vietnam. . . . the poor, white and black, bear the heaviest burdens both at the front and at home." King was one of the leaders of the 1967 Spring Mobilization Against the War in Vietnam, leading a column of 125,000 in a march from Central Park to the United Nations Plaza. His stand was certainly consistent with his life-long pacifism. King, however, was criticized by Roy Wilkins, Whitney Young, Jackie Robinson, and Ralph Bunche, who argued that his stand was a disservice to the civil rights movement. Unlike the children of America's white middle class, black youth were fighting in Vietnam and many blacks felt it disloyal to stand against the war. Certainly, not many followed King in his anti-war activities, and the anti-Vietnam War movement remained largely white.

King went north, renting an apartment in Chicago's North Lawndale, a west-side slum predominantly black in population. "There are more Negroes in Chicago," he said, "than in the whole state of Mississippi, and if we don't get nonviolent groups, the alternative is Watts." King shared the apartment he was to occupy three days a week with Andrew Young, SCLC's executive director, and Bernard Lee, a King assistant. King hoped to develop a northern-based movement around his "End-the-Slums" campaign. The Reverend James Bevel, a 29-year-old veteran of SCLC's southern campaigns, was on hand to head SCLC's northern invasion. With a black population of over a million, concentrated in 23 percent of the city's total area, Chicago appeared to be a promising place to start a northern "freedom movement." But tactics that had proved successful in the South did not work in the North. In the first instance, King's followers were unable to provoke by confrontation the kind of response on the part of city officials that would prompt federal intervention. Instead of denouncing King or his allies, Al Rany's Coordinating Council of Community Organizations and the United Auto Workers, Mayor Richard J. Daley greeted King's arrival in the city by asserting that the city's slum eradication program was well under way. City "fact sheets" cited 29,000 apartments sealed and sprayed for rats and insects within the year; 6,000 suits and $154,000 fines levied against slum landlords; 31,000 public housing units constructed over the last twenty years and 3,000 more to be available over the next four years; 23,000 children in Head-Start kindergartens; and 11,000 youths in the Neighborhood Youth Corps in the summer of 1965, and 7,000 that winter. The Chicago black community was divided over King's efforts and many local leaders resented his intervention. The Chicago NAACP, after a year or so of correspondence, withdrew from the Chicago Freedom Movement, but it was not the only sign of disaffection among the forty-four organizations involved. Many took umbrage at the involvement of the youth gangs, such as the famed Blackstone Rangers.

"Massive civil disobedience can use rage as a constructive and creative force," King argued before SCLC's tenth annual conference in 1968. "To dislocate the functioning of a city without destroying it can be longer lasting, costly to society but not wantonly destructive. Moreover it is more difficult for government to quell by superior forces. . . . Our real problem is that there is no disposition by the Administration or Congress to seek fundamental remedies beyond police measures." Nor was there any disposition on the part of the urban masses to follow King, who had announced a massive, detailed program for social justice in Chicago. He called for integration of the *de facto* segregated public schools, expansion of rapid transit facilities, removal of public funds from banks refusing mortgage loans to blacks, the allocation of public services according to population density, and the construction of "new towns," including 10,000 low-rent public housing units. King announced the program at an impressive rally at Soldiers' Field on Sunday, July 10, 1966. Chicago park officials estimated a turnout of 23,000, and SCLC, 65,000. On that hot humid day, some 5,000 left the Soldiers' Field rally to follow King to City Hall where King posted the movement's demands on the door.

But the number of blacks willing to follow King into the streets dwindled as he led a series of forays into neighboring white communities. The invading blacks and their white supporters, ministers, priests and nuns, were heckled, cursed, and stoned by hostile whites. At times, there were more policemen on guard than marchers in the streets. King threatened a march on all-white Cicero, where a bloody riot had occurred fifteen years earlier when a black family attempted to move in. The prospect of a bloodbath—Cicero was outside Chicago's police jurisdiction—intensified negotiations between civil rights leaders and Chicago's civic leaders. On August 26, 1966, King and Al Rany concluded a formal agreement worked out with Mayor Daley and seventy-nine of Chicago's outstanding political, economic, and religious figures. Various public agencies pledged themselves to extending open housing; banks agreed to lend mortgage money to home buyers regardless of race; the Real Estate Board withdrew its opposition to the "philosophy of open housing"; labor unions and church groups undertook anti-discrimination programs. The prestigious weekly, *The Christian Century*, declared that King's movement had taken "the first successful step in a thousand-mile march." It had exposed "intransigent social hatred in the city's lily-white neighborhoods," and "certainly no other approach to Chicago's complex explosive racial problem" would have brought "the full range of relevant agencies and establishment figures to the conference table."

King called off his march on Cicero, but he could not restrain some 205 angry young black-power exponents. Led by Robert Lucas of CORE, they marched into Cicero under the protection of some two thousand National Guardsmen, and when a mob attacked, marched back again beneath a hail of bottles, cans, and rocks. But neither the bravado of the militants nor the conscience prickings of Martin Luther King sufficed to seriously affect the constellation of power in Chicago. Several of SCLC's Chicago programs did score minor successes. A six-month rent strike by Bevel's Union to End Slums won a victory for tenants in Lawndale. More than a dozen community unions were organized with the invaluable help of the AFL-CIO. And the Reverend Jesse Jackson's Operation Breadbasket by the selective use of consumer boycotts secured several thousand jobs for black workers. Agreements with four major grocery chains opened markets for black produced products and services as well. Yet, months of voter registration and voter participation work under the guidance of a dozen SCLC stalwarts came to nothing.

King's march into the urban North was frustrating—for the man and for the movement. His works were both sung and sniped at. The Chicago agreement was termed a "sell-out," and militants carped at King's achievements. Local black leaders resented the publicity and public veneration he received. And for King, who so deeply believed in the redemptive power of nonviolent direct action, the riots of the period were profoundly disturbing. Even though most black spokesmen had warned of the social explosiveness of the slums, the riots of the summer of 1967 came as a shock. On July 12, Newark's four days of rage resulted in the death of twenty-one blacks and two whites; scarcely ten days later, on July 23, another four-day outbreak, this time in Detroit, exacted its grim toll—thirty-three blacks and ten whites killed. Before the 164 civil disorders of 1967 ran their course, eighty-three persons, most of them black, would lay dead. (Eighty-two percent of the deaths and more than half the injuries occurred in Newark and Detroit.) King, visibly shaken, endorsed the emergency use of armed force, and with Wilkins and Young joined A. Philip Randolph in an appeal to the rioters: "No one benefits under mob law. Let's end it now."

The mob, however, paid little attention to such exhortations; time and the presence of troops were much more effective. Neither the civil rights movement nor the established black leadership enjoyed any significant influence over the *lumpenproletariat* of the center city. (Nor did the super militants, but they made noises that sounded as if they did.) "We have not devised the tactics for urban slum reform," King told his SCLC conferees in the wake of the summer's riots. "We spent ten years in the South using new tactics of nonviolence that were successful. But in the northern cities, with time running out, we failed to achieve creative methods of work. As a result, a desperate, essentially leaderless mass of people acted with violence and without a program." Casting about for a fruitful way to channel black rage into a movement for social change, King called for a Poor People's March on Washingtor in spring 1968. "Not to act," he said, "represents moral irresponsibility." The Poor People's march was a "last desperate demand" aimed at staving off "the worst chaos, hatred and violence any nation has ever encountered."

Unlike the 1963 March on Washington, the Poor People's March did not elicit a broad-based response. King's talk of "disruptive dimensions" alarmed potential supporters, and his assurance that he would call off the demonstration in the event of violence contributed to the confusion (and really was not very reassuring) about the proposed march's character and goals. Bayard Rustin warned King: "Given the mood in Congress, given the increasing backlash across the nation, given the fact that this is an election year, and given the high visibility of a protest movement in the nation's capital, I feel that in this atmosphere any effort to disrupt transportation, government buildings, etc., can only lead to further backlash and repression." Rustin, and not only he, was clearly worried. "There is in my mind," he wrote King, "a very real question as to whether SCLC can maintain control and discipline over the April demonstration, even if the methods used are limited to constitutional and nonviolent tactics." Demonstrations, of all kinds, were increasing in nastiness as the student outbreaks, notably at Columbia University that spring, amply attest.

Actually, King himself appeared uncertain. Preparations for the Poor People's March got under way slowly and engendered little momentum. When a strike of Memphis sanitation workers, mostly black, erupted into a racial crisis, King, with evident relief, turned to efforts aimed at rallying support for the strikers. The strike, once again, brought together the two most important elements of the civil rights coalition—the black community and the labor movement. As a special report of the Southern Regional Council pointed out, the Memphis sanitation men's walkout was "More Than a Garbage Strike." It began as a simple workers' grievance and a race issue. On January 31, 1968, twenty-two employees in the sewer department were sent home when it began to rain. White employees, however, were not, and when the rain stopped, they were put to work and paid the full day's wages. When the black workers complained, they were paid two hours "call-up" pay. They called a meeting of AFSCME Local 1733, and went on strike the following Monday, February 12.

Memphis had no formal agreement with any of several organizations representing its twenty thousand public employees. Mayor Henry Loeb termed the strike illegal and refused to discuss matters with union officers. The strike over a limited grievance soon became a strike for union recognition as well as a host of related issues. As Jesse Epps, a black Mississippian and AFSCME organizer assigned to Memphis, put it: "The basic issue is not pay, but recognition of the union. There has never been the unity in the Negro community of Memphis that there is now, and the reason is that recognition of the union involves recognition of the workers *as men*. The mayor wants to say, 'Go on back to work and then we'll do right about your complaints; you know our word is as good as our bond.' Just as if Memphis were a Delta plantation."

The police broke up a sit-in at City Hall with billy clubs and mace. King was drawn to the struggle, which was so reminiscent of Montgomery, Birmingham, and Selma. The black community, approximately 38 to 40 percent of Memphis's 527,492 total population, rallied behind the striking sanitation men, over 90 percent black. King flew in to address a mass rally of fifteen thousand on March 18, promising to return to lead a march on City Hall. He did so on the twenty-eighth, but the march aborted in an outbreak of drunken disorder and police violence. Stores were looted and there was some arson. The police shot one sixteen-year-old boy to death, clubbed 60 others, and indiscriminately arrested some 280 demonstrators, looters, and bystanders. King was upset and dismayed by the outbreak. Still, he held firm in his belief that it was possible "to hold a nonviolent march."

Plans were made for such a march the following week. Time was allowed to enable Bayard Rustin to bring in civil rights and labor leaders from around the country. The city enjoined the march—now set for Monday, April 8. King spent most of Thursday, April 4, in Room 306 of the Lorraine Hotel, planning Monday's defiance of the injunction. That evening, he was to dine out with his aides at the home of a local minister, the Reverend Samuel B. Kyles. As he and his colleagues jested on the motel balcony, waiting for Ralph Abernathy to finish his last-minute ablutions, a shot rang out and Martin Luther King fell back, murdered by a lone assassin.

King's death was a stunning reminder that the first phase of the civil rights revolution was indeed over. At Bayard Rustin's behest, the movement would reassemble in Memphis to march on behalf of the striking black workers and honor King. Ralph Abernathy would mobilize eight thousand, mostly young and black, to carry out the Poor People's March, an encampment in the nation's capital, that ran from early May to July. There were sporadic demonstrations, including a five-day vigil at the Department of Agriculture that effectively underscored the existence of malnutrition and hunger among the poor, and several hundred arrests. Attempts to mobilize the resident black community, by and large, failed. On June 19, Solidarity Day, about fifty thousand people gathered to reenact the 1963 March on Washington, booed Vice President Humphrey and cheered Senator Eugene McCarthy. Most, then, went home while a handful of the defiant remained in Resurrection City. Abernathy and a number of his followers were arrested when they refused to leave after their camping permit expired.

A wave of violence ripped through a hundred towns and cities following King's murder, evoking the calling out of 21,000 federal troops and 34,000 National Guardsmen. When it was worked out, forty-six persons were dead, all but five black. The year 1968 was a bad one. Contenders for the presidential nominations engaged in acrimonious debate over the law-and-order issue and the war. President Johnson decided not to run; presidential-hopeful Robert Kennedy was murdered. The Soviet Union invaded Czechoslovakia, and Americans brawled over our conduct in Southeast Asia. Demonstrations were staged and violence fomented outside the Democratic convention in Chicago. Blacks and working people voted overwhelmingly for Humphrey; the white middle-class liberals refrained enough to assure the election of the Republican candidate, Richard M. Nixon.

Racial outbreaks marred the opening of the school year. In New York City, a strike by teachers, seeking to protect their rights as unionists, under so-called "community control," polarized the city. The separatist children of integrationist black parents insisted on all-black "segregated" dormitories at colleges. The Black Panthers, an intrepid band of black buccaneers, became the folk heroes of the radical-chic, Tom Wolfe's brilliant phrase describing the affluent donors to fashionable radical causes. Founded by Huey Newton and Bobby Seale, the Panthers established a reputation for militancy by bursting in on the startled California legislature waving unloaded rifles. Never larger than a thousand or so in number, they enlivened Marxist rhetoric by rhythmically shouting in unison, "Off the Pig," and won over liberals with a "Breakfast for Children" program. Armed, they were shot at, allegedly shot back, and certainly murdered some of their own.

Largely ignored was the real progress being made by most black Americans. Keeping this in mind, then super militancy, the anger of the slum proletariat, even the violence of the riots and the guerrilla-like sniping of the police can be seen for what they are—the birth pangs of a second reconstruction.

XIV

Second
Reconstruction

THE CIVIL RIGHTS REVOLUTION
was made possible by the Great Migration, the flight of American blacks
from rural poverty, and the crippling impotence of the segregated South
to the industrial urban North. Without a black presence in Harlem and
such cities as Detroit, Philadelphia, and Chicago, A. Philip Randolph's
1941 March on Washington would have been an empty gesture rather
than a calculated magnificent bluff. Without growing black political
power in certain key northern industrial states, civil rights legislation
would have been a chimera and blacks would not have been set in
motion in Montgomery, Birmingham, Selma . . . nor would the 1963
March on Washington have been possible. Within two decades, a
pattern of segregated life was broken in law and in fact. That has been
one of the great social and moral achievements of our time, perhaps the
greatest. It was the signal accomplishment of the civil rights coalition
that came into being over the two decades following Randolph's
successful ruse. Acknowledging this, however, still leaves unanswered a
most crucial question: Has the revolution been a success?

As an opening for a new beginning in America, we can answer, I
believe, with an unqualified yes. But its full accomplishment awaits a
second reconstruction, the full integration of black Americans into the
mainstream of American life. If we accomplish this, other minorities,
now partially excluded, will find their rightful place for, as observers
from De Tocqueville to James Baldwin have noted, reconciliation of the
races is central to the future of American democracy. We must look to
blacks in motion—not only to those involved in the civil rights
movement directly, but also to those who fled the rural poverty of the
South, for the success or failure of that economic and geographic
migration is the crux of the second reconstruction. It is that movement

of a people that has made integration an imperative for our democracy. Segregation successfully had contained blacks to the rural South, reinforcing the agricultural kingdom of cotton with the bonds of sharecropping, tenant farming, and near-serfdom. World War II marked a major change in our economic life from an old constrained, depressed, pre-Keynesian economy to one of abundance, expansion, and opportunity. While sheer economic expansion in the North and West offered new openings, the press of economic change also transformed the South. Within the context of this vast unfolding expansion, the shackles of segregation, as intolerable as they were in the past, became excruciating and had to be struck off.

The first victories, as we have noted, occurred in the northern, western, and border states and within those industries that may be characterized as truly national. Although there were setbacks, the openings afforded under the wartime presidential ban on discrimination in employment were never fully shut off, and in time even widened. As a consequence, the flight of black Americans from the ill-favored South to greater opportunity in the North became a flood. The grand shift in America's black population that began anew with World War II accelerated in the 1950s and continued strong throughout the 1960s. Before World War II, three-quarters of all black Americans lived in the South, mostly in rural areas. They left at about a rate of 1.5 million a decade until the 1960s, when there was a slight drop to 1.4 million migrating blacks. Today, while roughly 53 percent of the United States total of 22,672,570 blacks still live in the South, only a million or so remain down on the farm and more than seven out of every ten black Americans live in the city. The black population, according to census figures, has declined from 24 percent of the South's total to 19 percent in 1970.

While the Census Bureau experts have concluded that "the destination of southern Negroes did not change drastically during 1960–70," there were significant and revealing shifts in the migratory pattern. First, as we can see from the following table, there have been significant shifts in the distribution of black Americans, especially the rise in the West. New York and California continued as attractive destinations drawing 396,000 and 272,000 black Americans, respectively over the 1960s, as were New Jersey, Michigan, and Illinois, attracting 120,000, 124,000, and 127,000 respectively. However, while east north central states continued to attract large numbers of black immigrants, their proportional share declined. The southern New England states, New Jersey, and Maryland, by contrast, increased their net migration to 272,000 blacks during 1960–70 as compared with about 200,000 in the 1950s and about 125,000 in the 1940s. This dispersal reflects a broadening of opportunities as well as a willingness to seek new

DISTRIBUTION OF THE NEGRO
POPULATION BY REGION
1940 TO 1970

U.S. and REGION	1970	1960	1950	1940
United States	22,672,570	18,871,831	15,042,286	12,865,518
Northeast	4,342,137	3,028,499	2,018,182	1,369,875
North Central	4,571,550	3,446,037	2,227,876	1,420,318
South	12,064,258	11,311,607	10,225,407	9,904,619
West	1,694,625	1,085,688	570,821	170,706

PERCENT DISTRIBUTION

United States	100.0	100.0	100.0	100.0
Northeast	19.2	16.0	13.4	10.6
North Central	20.2	18.3	14.8	11.0
South	53.2	59.9	68.0	77.0
West	7.5	5.8	3.8	1.3

(U.S. Department of Commerce, release CB 71-34, March 3, 1971.)

prospects. It is a continuation of the Great Migration out of the South that began shortly before America entered World War I and evidently continues to this day.

It is now fashionable to decry the move from rural shack to slum tenement as little better than no move at all. And so it might be if that were all. Migration only contributes to reconstruction to the degree that it improves the lot of those involved, and broadly speaking, it certainly has. The median annual income of rural black families in 1969 was $3,197, approximately one-half of that of those living in central cities, $6,578. Our concern here, however, is with movement and direction. Newcomers often must accept hand-me-down quarters that the older residents no longer desire. If all goes well, then comes the move to a better neighborhood and ultimately to the suburbs. That has been the pattern, and surely its continuity for black newcomers to the urban scene is one of the indices of the success or failure of the second reconstruction. The importance of the suburbs lies not only in quiet, safe streets, but also in new opportunities. Industries and corporate headquarters are relocating into suburban areas. Some employment experts estimate that, as of the early 1970s, roughly 80 percent of all *new* employment opportunities in metropolitan areas are being created in the suburbs. Over the last two decades, for example, St. Louis lost 9 percent of its jobs while its suburbs registered a 144 percent gain. Jobs rose in Baltimore by 6 percent, but by 161 percent in the surrounding suburbs. Jobs increased by 10 percent in New York City over the same period, but jumped 51 percent in the metropolitan region outside the city. Discrimination in housing and real estate policies has worked against black buyers and would-be black suburban residents. Costs, too, rose sharply as the demand for suburban housing outpaced supply. According to the prestigious New York Regional Planning Association, few houses in the New York suburban area cost less than $30,000. Therefore, the association's experts say, a full 80 percent of the area's population, as of 1971, could not afford to buy a suburban home.

Despite economic and discriminatory obstacles, however, some blacks already have begun the trek from the city to the suburbs.° As of 1970, it was barely a trickle. Blacks make up only 4.5 percent of the total suburban population in the country's key metropolitan areas. This is but a slight percentage gain from the 4.1 percent that blacks represented in 1960—but, in numbers, the new suburban dwellers are now 2.5 million strong. Though little integration has occurred, the trend appears to be upwardly mobile. More blacks moved to the suburbs in the 1960s than in the 1950s, and according to a study by Reynolds Farley of the University of Michigan, "the migrants are probably of higher status than during the previous decade." In 1959, the median family income among blacks in the suburban areas was far below that of blacks in central cities, but by 1967 it was higher. Nonwhite families with annual incomes of $3,000 or less constitute 27 percent of nonwhite families in Newark, but only 13 percent in suburban East Orange. Significantly, among young black couples with children under eighteen, 27 percent in 1970 lived in suburbs as against 17 percent of young black families without children.

While the movement of blacks to the suburbs may seem pitifully small, one must keep in mind that there has been movement—and improvement—within the cities for mobile black Americans. Newark's slum-ridden Central Ward has been losing black families steadily over the last decade to better neighborhoods within the city. A crowded Central Harlem has lost members of its middle class to residential St. Albans, a suburban enclave within New York City limits. As soon as they better themselves, black families flee Cleveland's notorious Hough section for better neighborhoods out around Western Reserve University. Simply focusing on the increasing black population of many of our central cities, as so many commentators do, obscures the constant movement of blacks seeking better housing and better neighborhoods within the city. No one, so far as I know, has calculated the number of

---

° Some black suburbs, incidentally, are older than this statement would allow. Turners Station, outside Baltimore, was settled by recently freed slaves just after the Civil War. Originally, of course, it was a village, and became a suburb, as did its neighbors, simply because of the metropolitan spread. Kinlock, outside St. Louis, was founded in 1900 and incorporated in 1939. Robbins, outside Chicago, was incorporated in 1916. Lincoln Heights, near Cincinnati, Ohio, was developed in the 1920s. All of these suburbs have grown over the years but most rapidly in the most recent decades.

such moves, but when one considers that the percentage of black families earning, in constant 1969 dollars, over $7,000 a year rose from 23.5 percent in 1960 to 43.3 percent in 1969, one suspects that number must be impressive.

The most remarkable achievement of the civil rights revolution, however, may be the opening of opportunity in the new South for black Southerners. Again the indices are as yet imperceptible—a decline in the net outward migration of blacks, an increase in the black population of key cities in the South, and a return to the South among some who had fled North in the 1940s and 1950s. We simply do not know how much of the slight fall in the outward migration of 100,000 over the 1960s can be attributed to improvements in the economic and social conditions of blacks in the South. Yet, when black high-school graduates decide to leave home in the rural black belt counties of Alabama and Mississippi, they do not today invariably go north or west. Some go south to the Gulf area where economic expansion over the last few years has created jobs; others head for Atlanta, Birmingham, or even any one of a number of fast-growing smaller cities where jobs may be found. Head counts are hard to come by, but the growth in the black population of such urban centers as Atlanta, as can be seen in the following table, is impressive.

Blacks as Percentage of Total Population		
City	1960	1970
Atlanta	38	51.3
Baltimore	35	46.4
Dallas	19	24.9
New Orleans	37	45
St. Louis	29	40.9

(*Statistical Abstract of the United States—1971*. U.S. Department of Commerce, Bureau of the Census, Table No. 2.

Interestingly, a number of civil rights activists, graduates of the movement, have remained in the South to work on voter registration, economic development, and other projects involving a growing black participation in southern life. Mary E. Mebane [Liza], writing in the July 4, 1972, Op Ed page of *The New York Times*, records her surprise when a cousin told her that she and her husband were moving to Birmingham, Alabama. "Birmingham! Alabama?" She recalled that, not so long ago, it was a standard comment of North Carolina blacks that "I'm as far south as I plan to go," and when "nobody would casually think of casually traveling into South Carolina or Georgia and the very name Alabama and Mississippi aroused something akin to terror." Then came a day when she became aware that "a vague drift" of blacks returning South had become something stronger. Disenchantment with the North and increased job opportunities in the South, Ms. Mebane says, certainly account for some returning, but cannot be the main cause because jobs still pay better in the North and disorder always existed. "I think the primary reason for the influx of blacks into the South is the Civil Rights Act of 1964–65," she concludes. "Once the overt signs of racial discrimination were removed—'White Only' and 'Colored Only'—and some of the most vicious racist practices discontinued, either because of Government action or black political muscle, the North lost much of its allure." And this must be accounted as reinforcing the second reconstruction.

The traditional American quest for opportunity characterized the Great Migration and provided the impetus behind the civil rights movement. Economic progress then ought to be evident if we are indeed experiencing a second reconstruction. The indices are encouraging, especially if we take note of the *rate* of change in climbing the job ladder, in economic levels, educational attainment, and the like. Incidentally, in considering the economic progress scored by blacks over the 1960s, it is important to keep in mind that the black population of this country is proportionately younger—on the low side of the income producing years—than the white. The median age for white Americans is 28 years and for black Americans, 21.2 years. Between 1960 and 1970, the total nonwhite work force rose from 6.9 million to 8.5 million; while the number of black non-farm laborers dipped from 951,000 to 866,000, the number of black craftsmen and foremen rose from 415,000 to 691,000, and that of black operatives, or semiskilled workers, from 1.4 million to over 2 million. As these figures show, black workers moved upward out of the ranks of the unskilled into those of the semiskilled and skilled. While 60 percent of employed nonwhite Americans were in the white-collar, craftsmen, and operative occupations—the better-paying jobs—as compared to 81 percent of white Americans, nonetheless the rate of change over the decade was higher for nonwhites (72 percent) than whites (24 percent). Other job ladder changes were as equally notable. The number of nonwhite farmers and farm workers fell by 513,000 over the decade to 328,000 and that of private nonwhite household workers by 329,000 to 653,000. The employment of nonwhites as service workers rose by 333,000 to 1.5 million, as clerical workers by 610,000 to 1.1 million, and as sales personnel by 78,000 to 179,000. The latter category was the smallest gain numerically by nonwhites, yet it represents a jump of 77 percent as against one of 13 percent for whites. Nonwhite managers, officials, and proprietors rose in number over the decade by 120,000 to 298,000, a 67 percent rise against a white rate of 16 percent. The nonwhite increase among professional and technical workers was the most impressive gain of all—a rise of 435,000 to a 1970 total of 766,000, or a 131 percent gain as against a white increase of 45 percent.

These changes in the nonwhite occupational mix helped sustain a rise in income for black Americans. Black family median income as a percentage of white family median income was 61 percent in 1970 as compared with 53 percent in 1960. The median income for all black families was $6,279 as compared with $10,236 for all white families. Still a considerable lag; the dollar gap between the black and white medians actually increased by $706 between 1960 and 1970. But the percent of change, which has more to do with direction, was higher for black families (57 percent) than for white families (41 percent). And perhaps of even greater significance are the gains scored by young black families, with the head under age thirty-five, who live outside the South. Their income as a percentage of comparable white incomes rose from 78 percent in 1959 to 96 percent in 1970. Where husbands and wives worked, the comparable figures are 85 percent to 104 percent.°

There has been a broad transformation. In 1959, over one-half—55 percent—of *all* black Americans were below what the federal government defines as the poverty level. (For a non-farm family of four, the threshold of poverty, in 1970, was $3,968. Adjustments are made to take into account various factors, such as family size and residence, as well as changes in the Consumer Price Index.) By 1970, only a third—34 percent—were under the poverty line and the percentage dropped further to 29 percent as of 1971. Nearly everyone has commented unfavorably on the increase in black welfare recipients, a rise from 7 percent to 21 percent of all black Americans over the 1960 decade. This is normally cited as evidence of things getting worse but, in truth, it shows an improvement for the black poor. Daniel P. Moynihan, in his controversial report, *The Negro Family: The Case for National Action*, prepared for the 1966 White House Conference on Civil Rights, made much of this, arguing that the black poor "confront the nation with a new kind of problem . . . , the establishment of a stable Negro family structure." His case depends on a graphic presentation of the rise in the number of Aid for Dependent Children (ADC) cases even as the unemployment rate continued to drop after 1963. (Before 1961, ADC cases and unemployment rose or fell *together*.) Presumably, the change after 1963 suggests that giving a black male a job will no longer insure family stability. But as Laura Carper pointed out in *Dissent*, there is a remarkable correlation between the increase in ADC cases and the date

---

° In the South, the rises were almost as sharp but not as high. For black couples, with the head under thirty-five, the percentages were: 62 percent in 1959 and 80 percent in 1969; for those with both partners working, 64 percent and 85 percent respectively.

of changes in the social security law authorizing greater social and case work for the poor. "Prior to 1962," Ms. Carper writes, "if an applicant was a poor housekeeper, mentally disturbed, or evidence of a male friend could be found, her application for ADC was denied; after 1962, she was accepted if she showed need, regardless of her housekeeping practices, her mental health or her social life." Moynihan, in short, had grouped the wrong things; the facts show not the deterioration of the Negro family, but an extension of social services to those poor denied such services in the past. Most poor blacks once got nothing; today, more are getting something.

Other indices of change show improvement for America's major minority group. (Figures are from the Bureau of Labor Statistics study, "The Social and Economic Status of Negroes in the United States, 1970.") Illiteracy is disappearing; the percentage of black Americans unable to read and write decreased by almost a half—7.5 percent to 3.6 percent—over the decade. There is little significant difference in the illiteracy rate between black and white Americans under age forty-four; the bulk of those black citizens unable to read or write are over sixty-five. The percentages of blacks aged twenty to twenty-nine who have completed at least a high-school education was 61 percent in 1970 as compared to 40 percent in 1960. The median year of school completed by black Americans between the ages of twenty and thirty-four is 12.0, not significantly below that for the same white age group, 12.5. The total of black students enrolled in college rose sharply from 234,000 in 1964 to 727,000 in 1972, and the bulk of the enrollment is in integrated institutions of higher learning. By 1970, about 6 percent of all blacks twenty-five to thirty-four had completed college compared with about 16.5 percent of all whites in the same age group. The home ownership rate for blacks rose from 38 percent in 1960 to 42 percent in 1970 as compared with an unchanging rate of 64–65 percent for whites. There has been an improvement in the quality of housing, at least as measured by plumbing facilities. The percentage of black-occupied housing with all plumbing facilities rose from 59 percent to 83 (12 percent short of the white percentage), while the number lacking such facilities dropped markedly from 41 percent in 1960 to 17 percent by 1970. Since 1965, the maternal mortality rate for black and white mothers has been very low—below 1.0 per one thousand live births. Infant mortality rates° are higher among blacks than whites, but there has been a steady decline since 1960, the decline slightly greater for blacks than for whites.

Economic progress does not necessarily entail participation in America's economic and political institutions, while reconstruction

---

° See footnote at bottom of next page.

certainly must. There has been an increase of black activity of all sorts. Professor Charles L. Sanders of Atlanta University reports that black economists, journalists, ministers, teachers, accountants, lawyers, political scientists, psychiatrists, nuns, and other professionals have organized at least twenty-two national all-black groups. But how much weight one should give to these groups is by no means certain since most apparently are black nationalist in orientation and so are not likely to embrace all the black members of their respective professions. Black entrepreneurs and managers are as yet a tiny minority of the overall black community. As Martin Luther King, Jr., observed in his speech before the 1960 convention of the AFL-CIO, "Negroes are almost entirely a working people. There are pitifully few Negro millionaires and few Negro employers. Our needs are identical with labor's needs—decent wages, fair working conditions, livable housing, old age security, health and welfare measures, conditions in which families can grow, have education for their children and respect in the community."

We are, as many have observed, a middle-class country. And it is through the trade unions that American workers have become a part of the American mainstream. As Brendan Sexton reminds us, "unions are *inherently* powerful." Aside from their collective bargaining power, they can influence the investment of vast pension and insurance reserve funds. They can affect legislators and play an important role in the formation of public opinion. Moreover, one ought not discount the work place as an education. As Michael Harrington has pointed out, "Workers . . . are concentrated in very large numbers, subjected to a common discipline in the work process, and forced—in the defense of their most immediate interests—to build collective institutions. They therefore have a cohesion, a social weight, in excess of their members." Unions, therefore, may well be *the* crucial institution within our society for blacks. If they cannot participate fully in the life of the labor movement then it is unlikely that they will be able to participate fully in the life of the country.

First, an observation: More black people belong to unions than any other nonreligious organization. According to a Department of Labor study, black workers, in 1970, accounted for over 12 percent of all union members, "a somewhat higher proportion than their representa-

---

° Source: U.S. Department of Health and Welfare

| | Infant Mortality per 1,000 Live Births | | | |
| | Under 28 Days | | 28 Days to 11 Months | |
Year	Black	White	Black	White
1960	26.9	17.2	16.4	5.7
1968	23.0	14.7	11.6	4.5
Gain	3.9	2.5	4.8	1.2

tion in the total wage and salary work force [of about 11 percent]."
AFL-CIO spokesmen estimate that roughly 2 million out of a total
membership of some 15.6 million members are black. There are another
500,000 or more affiliated with independent unions with a total
membership of 4.6 million.° As is the case with the nation, blacks enjoy
a concentrated strength within certain unions and are tiny minorities
within others. Two small unions, the 6,000-member Brotherhood of
Sleeping Car Porters and the 3,000-member United Transport Service
Employees, both affiliated with the AFL-CIO, are virtually all-black.
The powerful 600,000-member Laborers' International Union and the
50,000-member International Longshoremen's Association are about 40
percent black. Some 45 of the 126 AFL-CIO unions have "substantial"
black memberships—that is, a larger percentage of black members than
the 11 to 12 percent black participation rate in the overall labor force.
To give a few important examples: The State, County, and Municipal
Employees, 600,000 total membership; the merged Meat Cutters-Packinghouse Union, 500,000; Letter Carriers, 210,000; Postal Clerks,
166,000; International Ladies' Garment Workers' Union, 455,000;
Building Service Employees, 389,000; the Laundry Workers, 25,000;
the American Federation of Teachers, 400,000; and possibly the
Steelworkers, 1.1 million, are among the unions with 20 percent or more
black memberships. Of the independent 1.7 million United Auto
Workers, about 25 percent—or 40,000—are black.

While blacks are pitiful in number within key "father-and-son" craft
unions, 9 percent nonetheless are union members as compared with a
10 percent employment participation rate in the industry as a whole.
Minority youth are entering the so-called critical crafts; 18 percent of
all new apprentices are nonwhite as against 1.9 percent of all
journeymen electricians, iron workers, plumbers, pipe fitters, and sheet
metal workers. One of the many offsprings of the civil rights movement
is the Recruitment Training Program—headed by the first black
graduate of Little Rock's Central High School, Ernest Green—which
has been largely responsible for the apprenticeship breakthrough.

There has been, as one observer has noted, a black upsurge within the
unions. *Business Week* reported in 1968 that one out of three new union
members is black. One must keep in mind, however, that, despite
discrimination, black workers have belonged to unions since the
inception of the labor movement in this country. Spurgeon Gandy, a
vice-president of the Detroit local of the Building Service Employees
International Union, is the grandson of an Alabaman black mine
worker. His father, too, started in the mines, but left to seek work in
Detroit's auto plants. He belonged to the United Auto Workers, and his

° 1968 figures.

son now organizes hospital workers. There are many such stories. Still, the current black upsurge within the unions, is in part, a product of the civil rights movement. Blacks are organizing new local unions among hospital workers, municipal employees, and in the retail and service industries. Black caucuses form at union conventions, and black pride provides the thrust for black representation within the labor movement.

Within the unions, as within society at large, the representation is as yet inadequate. Just as one now finds that elected officials from all black, or predominantly black, geographic political units are likely to be black, so one finds ample elected black leadership from among local unions with large black memberships. There is less representation at the national union level, though this is changing. (Most unions with any minority membership of any consequence have appointed minority staffs as organizers, service representatives, and in other professional capacities.) As we have noted, two black trade unionists, A. Philip Randolph and Frederick O'Neal, president of integrated Associated Actors and Artists, sit on the AFL-CIO's Executive Council. Three blacks sit on the executive board of the merged Meat Cutters-Packinghouse Union and there are two on the United Auto Worker's 27-man top governing council. (The auto union employs eighty black international representatives on a staff of 1,050 and there are black elected officers in a growing number of the union's most powerful local unions.) The Longshoremen, the Laborers' and the Municipal Employees, each have a black vice-president as do a number of other unions. A study conducted for the Urban League in Chicago in 1968 by Harold M. Baron found that among black "policy-makers" in private organizations, "unions had a larger percentage—13 percent—than any other institutions." And, with the possible exception of the South, there is not much doubt that blacks have won more power and status in the unions than in any other significant social institution.

From its inception, the civil rights movement has viewed the vote as central to its concerns. The NAACP fought long and valiantly to abolish the poll tax as a means of assuring the franchise to black Americans, particularly in the South. Appropriately, the final march of the united movement from Selma to Montgomery in March 1965 was over the right to vote. Selma, at the time, had no black elected officials, even though the city, with a population of 28,385, was nearly 50 percent black. Seven years later, in 1972, half of the city council seats were won by blacks. Black registration had increased from 2.3 percent of those eligible in 1965 to 67 percent. Selma, long regarded as the historic symbol of "massive resistance" to black voting rights, had become, as John Lewis of the Voters' Education Project put it, "a new symbol."

Black power is an ill-defined term; far too many of its exponents treat it as Humpty Dumpty, not Lewis Carroll, was wont to treat words: "When I use a word, it means just what I choose it to mean—neither more nor less." At its most simple and innocent guise, as Bayard Rustin notes, "black power merely means the effort to elect Negroes to office in proportion to Negro strength within the population." There is nothing wrong or inherently radical about such an objective. By extension, however, politics gets us to the heart of our society and to its reconstruction. As Rustin has repeatedly argued, "It is clear that Negro needs cannot be satisfied unless we go beyond what has so far been placed on the agenda. How are these radical objectives [democratic social change] to be achieved? The answer is simple, deceptively so: *through political power.*" Now in politics, at least at the start and on the surface, gains are measured by offices won. On the national scoreboard, black Americans are racking up points for the second reconstruction with new victories in each election. In 1967, just two years after the Voting Rights Act of 1965 was passed, there were only 475 black elected officials in the entire United States. Five years later, after the 1972 elections, there were an estimated 2,240.°

"We see this as evidence that blacks are gaining more and more clout in the nation's electoral system," said Dr. Frank D. Reeves, law professor at Howard University and executive director of the Joint Center for Political Studies. "It's a dramatic demonstration of progress toward realization for black Americans of the ideals of representative democracy." While Dr. Reeves found the continued increase in blacks elected to office heartening, he also noted that in 1971, black office holders represented only three-tenths of one percent of the total elected officials in the nation. "Blacks still have a long way to go before they realize their full representation in government," Dr. Reeves concluded. Nonetheless, the steady growth in black grass-roots political strength is impressive, especially in the South. Whereas, in 1940, Ralph J. Bunche estimated that there were fewer than 250,000 black voters in the South, this vote, as of 1971, is nearly 3.5 million. The percentage of black eligible voters registered in the eleven southern states, at 58.61 percent, is almost at parity with that of whites, 64.97 percent. In Arkansas and Texas, the proportion of black voters registered (80.89 and 68.16) is greater than that of white eligibles registered (61.39 and 56.76). In number, however, white voters in the South—17.3 million in all—vastly outnumber blacks, even if all black eligibles (5.9 million) were to register.

The second reconstruction involves a certain "catching-up," evident in the election of Andrew Young of Atlanta, Georgia, and Barbara Jordan of Houston, Texas, to Congress, the first southern blacks sent as representatives to Washington in over seventy years, and in the election

° According to the *National Roster of Black Elected Officials,* published in March 1971 by the Joint Center for Political Studies, there were 1,860. The Voters' Education Project reported in January 1973 that there were 381 additional black officials elected in the southern states in 1972.

of numerous local officials and state legislators in the South. Black congressmen now number fourteen (fifteen if one adds the voice-but-no-vote delegate from the District of Columbia), and there is one black senator. As of 1971, there were only two key statewide elected officials—California's superintendent of schools, Wilson Riles, and Michigan's Secretary of State, Richard Austin. In 1972, one hundred and seventeen blacks, were elected in Alabama, all to local offices. These included mayors in the interracial towns of Pritchard, Union-town, and Brighton, as well as in nearly all-black Tuskegee. Blacks were elected for the first time to the Arkansas General Assembly, the last southern state house to have been without black representation. Blacks were elected for the first time to the city councils of Brunswick, Georgia; Natchez, Mississippi; and Sequin, Texas, and to the Orange County, North Carolina, board of supervisors.

What is perhaps even more remarkable, considering the political history of the South since Reconstruction, is the wooing of the black voter by white politicians. During the summer of 1971, John Lewis returned to Mississippi where he had first fought for civil rights not ten years before. He and Georgia State Representative Julian Bond were drumming up interest in voter registration. They visited Belzoni where the Reverend George Washington Lee had been murdered in 1954 for voter registration activity, and where courageous Gus Courts had been driven by violence several years later. "Do you know," Lewis says, with a note of surprise in his voice, "the mayor of that city, a middle-aged white man, came to our mass meeting, shook our hands, welcomed us to Belzoni *and* said we were doing a wonderful job." The "closed society" has begun to open its doors, although violence still erupts. Yet, as John Lewis reports of the 1971 tour, "Across the delta and throughout the state, VEP workers were given official receptions and police escorts in towns where, as civil rights workers and organizers in the 1960s, they had been arrested as outside agitators and troublemakers."

Politics is the arena from which new black leaders are emerging. One can no longer speak of a Booker T. Washington or a Walter White or a Martin Luther King, Jr., as *the* spokesman for his people. Nor is it so easy to bring together a tiny group as representative of all black Americans as it was when "the big six"—Farmer, King, Lewis, Randolph, Wilkins, and Young—were regularly summoned to the White House. There always has been, certainly since the end of slavery, a broad-based black leadership in America. Its views have encompassed the extremes of black nationalism as well as a variety of approaches to integration. But, the broader society only became aware of this complexity as the civil rights movement became a black movement with various tendencies contending for power and recognition. Down to and including the civil rights movement, black power was largely a moral power—that is, black leaders sought to move America by speaking to our dilemma: the contradiction between segregation and our commitment to equality. Having broken through the barriers, blacks, as Bayard Rustin predicted, have had to move from protest to politics.

That transformation is far from complete in the mid-1970s. Blacks, as we have noted, are as yet underrepresented in our representative institutions, particularly in our political ones. And there are natural confusions as to purpose; the shift from exerting a moral power to exercising political power is not an easy one. Slogans of black solidarity cannot paper over real differences within the black community any more than patriotic slogans can paper over differences within the country. As an instance, in 1972, the organizers of the National Black Political Conventions pushed through a host of resolutions by appealing to black unity and by taking advantage of the lateness of the hour in the conference deliberations. Mayors Richard Hatcher of Gary, Indiana, and Kenneth A. Gibson of Newark, New Jersey, headed the conference, but the stands taken were colored by the black nationalist ideology of its *eminence gris*, poet Imamu Amiri Baraka (Le Roi Jones), including an attack on Israel and on busing to achieve integrated schools. Once back home, the delegates in great number disowned these more controversial stands. Despite the rhetoric of black power, most black voters are not separatists. Moreover, many black politicians still must appeal, in part, to white voters, and once elected, most—if not all—must deal with white elected officials.

This, of course, is the reality of any minority within America. The civil rights movement was born of the black American's wish to fully participate in America as an equal to all other Americans. His effort to do so encompassed broader economic and social concerns because so many blacks were a part of our country's underclass, the rural and urban poor. But the depth and scope of the economic and social programs needed to bring the underclass into the working and middle classes are beyond that which a minority can achieve by itself. So, the civil rights movement became a coalition as well as a catalyst for a broader movement of social change. That much remains to be done is self-evident; that much has been accomplished, less so. Nonetheless, as black Americans perceive their situation, there has been change, much of it for the better, and most of it due to the civil rights struggle. A Gallup Poll taken in 1972 shows that while whites, by and large, believed that life in America had gotten worse in recent years, the majority of blacks said things were getting better. And so they were.

"Societies, like individuals," R. H. Tawney once observed, "have their moral crises and their spiritual revolutions." The civil rights struggle was over such crises and how well America fared may be summed up in the burden of this brief history: When blacks marched, the walls came tumbling down.

Acknowledgments

The civil rights movement at its peak in the 1960s encompassed countless concerned Americans eager to right an ancient wrong. Without slighting the importance of the varied actions that took place during that most exciting period of our country's history, I have tried in this account to follow a single strand, a line of march that flows from A. Philip Randolph's great gesture of defiance in 1941 down to the magnificent March on Washington on August 28, 1963. I have explored some of its ramifications and its disconcerting aftermath.

In tracing out this history, I have acquired an intellectual debt only partly discharged by the selected bibliography that follows. Specifically, I would like to thank: Eugenia and Jervis Anderson, who planted the seed of an idea and encouraged its growth; Arnold Aronson, who provided necessary background to an understanding of the role of the Leadership Conference on Civil Rights; David Bensman and Carol Steinsapir, who uncovered useful material about the 1963 March; Charles Bloomstein, who helped nudge the book to completion; George Houser, who generously shared his knowledge of the formative early days of CORE; Tom Kahn, who shared his insights and helped shape my thinking about the civil rights movement; Warren Picower, who gave me assignments for *Tuesday Magazine* that deepened my understanding of a people in motion; Arch Puddington, who graciously backstopped some statistics; and Bayard Rustin, who, over the years, has been for me—and others—a mentor of civil rights and democratic social change. I am deeply grateful, moreover, to Robert and Joyce Gilmore and the A. Philip Randolph Educational Fund for financial assistance enabling me to devote full time to the writing of this book; to the People's Educational Camp Society, Inc., for a research grant; to Knox Burger, my agent, for his wise advice; to Bram Cavin, my editor, for his helpful guidance; and to Barbara Palumbo for her editorial skill at catching my errors and improving my writing.

Bibliography

Much has been written about the civil rights movement and its participants. I have not attempted anything like a complete bibliography, but merely content myself—and hopefully, the reader—with a listing of those books I found of particular interest.

Anderson, Jervis, *A. Philip Randolph: A Biographical Portrait*. New York: Harcourt Brace Jovanovich, Inc., 1973.

Ashmore, Harry S., *The Negro and the Schools*. Chapel Hill: The University of North Carolina Press, 1954.

Baldwin, James, *Notes of a Native Son*. Boston: Beacon Press, 1955.

——— *Nobody Knows My Name*. New York: The Dial Press, Inc., 1961.

Farmer, James, *Freedom—When?* New York: Random House, Inc., 1965.

Franklin, John Hope, *From Slavery to Freedom*. New York: Alfred A. Knopf, 1967.

Frazier, E. Franklin, *Black Bourgeoisie*. New York: The Free Press, 1957.

——— *The Negro Church in America*. New York: Schocken Books, 1964.

Garfinkel, Herbert, *When Negroes March*. New York: Atheneum, 1969.

King, Coretta Scott, *My Life With Martin Luther King, Jr.* New York: Holt, Rinehart & Winston, Inc., 1969.

King, Martin Luther, Jr., *Stride Toward Freedom*. New York: Harper & Row, Publishers, 1958.

Lewis, Anthony and *The New York Times*, *Portrait of a Decade*. New York: Random House, Inc., 1964.

Lewis, David L., *King, A Critical Biography*. New York: Praeger Publishers, 1970.

Lincoln, Charles E., *The Black Muslims in America*. Boston: Beacon Press, 1961.

Lomax, Louis E., *The Negro Revolt*. New York: Harper & Row, Publishers, Inc., 1962.

Lubell, Samuel, *White and Black: Test of a Nation*. New York: Harper & Row, Publishers, Inc., 1964.

Malcolm X, *The Autobiography of Malcolm X*. With the assistance of Alex Haley. New York: Grove Press, 1965.

McMillen, Neil R., *The Citizens' Council: Organized Resistance to the Second Reconstruction, 1954–1964*. Urbana: University of Illinois Press, 1971.

Miller, William Robert, *Martin Luther King, Jr.: His Life, Martyrdom & Meaning for the World*. New York: Weybright and Talley, Inc., 1968.

Muse, Benjamin, *Ten Years of Prelude: The Story of Integration Since the Supreme Court's 1954 Decision*. New York: Viking Press, 1964.

—— *The American Negro Revolution*. New York: The Citadel Press, 1970.

Myrdal, Gunnar, *An American Dilemma*. New York: Harper & Brothers, 1944.

Peck, James, *Freedom Ride*. New York: Simon and Schuster, Inc., 1962.

Reddick, L. D., *Crusader Without Violence: Martin Luther King, Jr.* New York: Harper & Brothers, 1959.

Rustin, Bayard, *Down the Line*. Chicago: Quadrangle Books, 1971.

Warren, Robert Penn, *Who Speaks for the Negro?* New York: Random House, Inc., 1966.

Watters, Pat, and Cleghorn, Reese, *Climbing Jacob's Ladder: The Arrival of Negroes in Southern Politics*. New York: Harcourt, Brace & World, Inc., 1967.

Watters, Pat, *Down to Now: Reflections on the Southern Civil Rights Movement*. New York: Pantheon Books, 1972.

White, Walter, *A Man Called White: The Autobiography of Walter White*. Bloomington: Indiana University Press, 1970.

Zinn, Howard, *The Southern Mystique*. New York: Alfred A. Knopf, 1964.

Index